Congressional Theatre

Congressional Theatre is the first book to identify and examine the significant body of plays, films, and teleplays that responded to the actions of the House Committee on Un-American Activities during the "Show Business hearings" that it held between 1947 and 1960. Brenda Murphy discusses the dramatization in the works of HUAC's effects on American life and the political, social, and moral issues that its actions raised for American citizens. Among the writers discussed are Arthur Miller, Bertolt Brecht, Lillian Hellman, Maxwell Anderson, Elia Kazan, Barrie Stavis, Herman Wouk, Eric Bentley, Saul Levitt, Budd Schulberg, Carl Foreman, Abraham Polonsky, and Walter Bernstein.

Brenda Murphy is Professor of English at the University of Connecticut. Her books include *Tennessee Williams and Elia Kazan: A Collaboration in the Theatre* (Cambridge, 1992) and *American Realism and American Drama, 1880–1940* (Cambridge, 1987). She is also the editor of *The Cambridge Companion to American Women Playwrights.*

The American theatre and its literature are attracting, after long neglect, the crucial attention of historians, theoreticians, and critics of the arts. Long a field for isolated research yet too frequently marginalized in the academy, the American theatre has always been a senstive gauge of social pressures and public issues. Investigations into its myriad shapes and manifestations are relevant to students of drama, theatre, literature, cultural experience, and political development.

The primary intent of this series is to set up a forum of important and original scholarship in and criticism of American theatre and drama in a cultural and social context. Inclusive by design, the series accommodates leading work in areas ranging from the study of drama as literature to theatre histories, theoretical explorations, production histories, and readings of more popular or paratheatrical forms. While maintaining a specific emphasis on theatre in the United States, the series welcomes work grounded broadly in cultural studies and narratives with interdisciplinary reach. *Cambridge Studies in American Theatre and Drama* thus provides a crossroads where historical, theoretical, literary, and biographical approaches meet and combine, promoting imaginative research in theatre and drama from a variety of new perspectives.

Congressional Theatre

Dramatizing McCarthyism
on Stage, Film, and Television

BRENDA MURPHY

CAMBRIDGE
UNIVERSITY PRESS

PUBLISHED BY THE PRESS SYNDICATE OF THE UNIVERSITY OF CAMBRIDGE
The Pitt Building, Trumpington Street, Cambridge, United Kingdom

CAMBRIDGE UNIVERSITY PRESS
The Edinburgh Building, Cambridge CB2 2RU, UK http://www.cup.cam.ac.uk
40 West 20th Street, New York, NY 10011-4211, USA http://www.cup.org
10 Stamford Road, Oakleigh, Melbourne 3166, Australia

First published 1999

Printed in the United States of America

Typeface New Baskerville 10.25/13 pt.   *System* QuarkXPress [BA]

A catalog record for this book is available from
the British Library.

Library of Congress Cataloging–in–Publication Data is available.

ISBN 0 521 640881 hardback

For George

Contents

Contents

List of Illustrations

Acknowledgments

Primary thanks are due to my husband, George Monteiro, for his invaluable criticism, advice, and encouragement throughout the writing of this book. I have also profited by the sagacious editorial advice of Don B. Wilmeth and Anne Sanow.

I am greatly indebted to the gifted researchers who assisted me in the work on this project, all three of whom went far beyond the call of duty: Michael Menard, Susan Abbotson, and Heather Masciandaro. For providing the funds that made their help possible, and for the funds that allowed me to travel to the libraries and museums whose collections were indispensible to my study, I am indebted to the University of Connecticut Research Foundation. For the sabbatical leave that gave me the time to write this book, I am equally indebted to the University of Connecticut.

The research collections and staffs of a number of libraries have been indispensible to this project: the Billy Rose Theatre Collection, New York Public Library for the Performing Arts; the Museum of Television and Radio, New York; the Harry Ransom Humanities Research Center, University of Texas at Austin; the Lilly Library, Indiana University; the John D. Rockefeller, Jr., Library, Brown University; the Library of Congress; and, above all, the libraries of my home institution, the University of Connecticut, particularly the Homer Babbidge Library and its Inter-Library Loan Division, and Special Collections at the Thomas R. Dodd Research Center. I am particularly grateful to the many librarians and curators who have made me the beneficiary of their experience and expertise in the course of this project.

My friend and colleague Regina Barreca provided me with some invaluable documents. Helen Coxe Cheney kindly made available to me the text of Louis O. Coxe's *The Witchfinders*.

For permission to reprint photographs from the Billy Rose Theatre Collection, I am grateful to the New York Public Library, Astor, Lenox, and Tilden Foundations.

Introduction

The historian, essentially, wants more documents than he can really use;
the dramatist only wants more liberties than he can really take.

Henry James, Preface to *The Aspern Papers*

History was dangerous in those days. History is always dangerous.

Abraham Polonsky, Interview, *The Box*

In 1976, as *Scoundrel Time*, her memoir of the 1950s, was about to
appear, Lillian Hellman was questioned about Senator Joseph
McCarthy in an interview with *Rolling Stone* magazine. She responded
that "McCarthyism came from powerful places. . . . McCarthy is a very
inaccurate name for a shameless period. McCarthy only summed up
the angers and fears of a great many people."[1] In fact, Senator
McCarthy was only the most visible embodiment of the worst excesses
of Congressional investigating committees, excesses that were associated in the public's mind during the early fifties with the term
"McCarthyism."[2] I have found that many well-informed Americans are
surprised to hear that Joseph McCarthy never served on the House
Committee on Un-American Activities (HUAC), the Congressional
body that is most closely associated with "McCarthyism." McCarthy's
own bases of operation, the Senate Subcommittee on Internal Security
and the Senate Committee on Government Operations, are not exactly
household words, perhaps because they were essentially one-man
shows, better known as "McCarthy Committees" than as anything else.
HUAC, on the other hand, is well-known as Congress's anti-Communist
investigating arm, and, although it had several chairmen who were
almost as desirous of press coverage as Senator McCarthy – Martin
Dies, John Rankin, and J. Parnell Thomas, for example – no single
individual ever usurped the Committee's image in the public mind. It
was HUAC, which conducted the Hollywood Ten hearings and the sub-

sequent Show Business investigations, that captured the public's attention, rather than any individual congressman.

The Hollywood Ten hearings of October 1947 were HUAC's major media event. The Committee managed to stay in the limelight for a decade, however, by means of its much more extensive Show Business hearings of 1951 and 1952 and its perennial "Investigations into Communist Activities in the Los Angeles Area" and "Investigations into Communist Activities in the New York Area." This was in spite of the short-lived but determined headline-grabbing of its rival in the Senate, during the period between McCarthy's speech at Wheeling, West Virginia, on 19 February 1950, when he claimed to have the names of 205 Communists in the State Department, and his censure by the Senate on 2 December 1954. The impact of the Committee's investigations, and the industry blacklist that proceeded from them, on the movie industry and Hollywood community has been well-documented by historians, although the extensiveness of this effect is still being realized, as each year brings more documents to light, and more memoirs and biographies record their effects on individual lives.[3]

Never a direct target of the Committee in the way that the mass media were, the Broadway theatre never resorted to official blacklisting. Nevertheless, the show business investigations had a tremendous effect on American drama and theatre between 1947 and 1960. In the thirties and forties, actors, directors, and writers were accustomed to moving freely between Broadway and Hollywood, sometimes working on several different films and plays in the same year. During the HUAC hearings, an artist who was blacklisted in Hollywood could often find work in New York, particularly in the nascent Off-Broadway theatre, but being branded a Red generally had a negative effect at the box office. Not surprisingly, the New York theatre retreated from dramatizing overt political and social questions between 1945 and 1960, creating instead what Arthur Miller has called "an era of gauze" in the intensely personal and psychological plays of Tennessee Williams, William Inge, Carson McCullers, Robert Anderson, and others. In this most pervasively and oppressively ideological of times, the American theatre has seemed to critics and historians to have ignored the fundamental political issues that were dividing the country.[4] The one exception has been assumed to be Miller himself, who, as a target of the Committee, showed courage in adapting Ibsen's *An Enemy of the People* in 1950 and in writing his own *Crucible* in 1953, two treatments of political demagoguery and the manipulation of mass hysteria against a scapegoat.

This view ignores the persistent subtext beneath the apparent self-absorption of the theatre of the fifties, however – a subtext in which political, social, and moral issues were engaged and debated with intensity and passion.[5] Miller was not the only American playwright who found the use of historical analogy useful in attacking McCarthyism. Playwrights like Lillian Hellman, Bertolt Brecht (temporarily exiled to Santa Monica, California), Barrie Stavis, and Saul Levitt developed an aesthetic strategy that was firmly grounded on the representation of recognizable historical events – events that drew an immediate emotional response from the spectator. In their plays, the Spanish Inquisition and the Salem witch hunt become powerful historical analogies for HUAC. In the context of the Inquisition, the coercion of Galileo into recanting his belief that the earth moves around the sun was analogized with the situation of the friendly witness who repudiated his leftist beliefs and his leftist friends in order to appear cooperative with the Committee. The most sympathetic of Christian scapegoats, Joan of Arc, was a natural historical analogy for witnesses like Miller and Hellman, who were viewed as having been pilloried by the Committee for following the dictates of their consciences and refusing to bring harm to others by naming names.

The representational field in these plays was by no means limited to the distant past. Saul Levitt evoked the American Civil War in *The Andersonville Trial* and Arthur Miller the recent war against the Nazis in *Incident at Vichy*. Herman Wouk argued in favor of the state and against the dictates of the individual conscience in *The Caine Mutiny Court-Martial*. Miller engaged in an analogical debate over the morality of naming names with Elia Kazan and Budd Shulberg through the medium of the tightly knit community of Brooklyn longshoremen in Schulberg and Kazan's *On the Waterfront* and Miller's *A View from the Bridge*. Film and television writers followed a similar strategy, particularly when films were adapted from plays, although the political implications were often considerably weakened during the studio production process. Occasionally, however, the discussion of the issues was allowed to go out directly to a mass audience right before the vigilant eyes of self-appointed censors, under the cover of historical drama. This was the case with Abraham Polonsky, Walter Bernstein, and Arnold Manoff, the three blacklisted writers who wrote the *You Are There* series for CBS television, with the help of producer Charles Russell and a number of "fronts," about Galileo, Joan of Arc, Socrates, the Salem witch trials and the Boston Tea Party. Common to many of these plays is a fundamentally forensic structure. All of them involve cultural institutions of interrogation, and many use the trial as a structural principle for the play's action. Reflected at the center of these theatrical representations, in other words, was HUAC's major weapon, the committee hearing, which was in reality a trial without a defense, a jury, or even, in many cases, evidence against the accused.

In this book, I have examined the dramatic representations of the Un-American Activities Committee. I have done so in the context of the Committee's own self-created drama, drawing on the anthropological model developed by Victor Turner to analyze the "social drama" of the HUAC hearings, in which American society tried through the redressive procedure of formal Congressional proceedings to heal itself of a deep ideological breach between Left and Right that had been widening since the first World War. I have also found the theory of scapegoating by comparatist René Girard illuminating in my examination of HUAC's social and cultural effects, and in developing my own model for the five-part ritual framework of the Hearings themselves. It is not theory but practice that is in the foreground of this book, however. Always keeping in mind the limitations of my own cultural perspective, I have tried to bring to light the significant body of dramatic works that quite consciously dramatized the effects of the Committee on American life and debated the political, social, and moral issues that its actions raised for American citizens.

If there is a larger contention in this book, it is that plays, screenplays and teleplays are written by individuals, and realized on stage or film in collaboration with other artists and craftsmen, in the inescapable context of events, both public and personal, that occur in those individuals' lifetimes. For cultural and literary critics and historians to ignore the unique personal histories of authors, and the impact of their experiences, both public and private, on the work they produce, is to offer at best a partial and limited analysis of that work. While a study with the fairly broad scope of this one cannot pretend to do the job thoroughly for any single writer, it can suggest some ways in which a single phenomenon in the United States's recent past, the Show Business investigations of HUAC, affected the complex weave of relationships – public and private, personal and political, aesthetic and ideological – that characterize the participation in the cultural moment of the years between 1947 and 1960 by writers who felt its effects keenly and personally.

As I show in the third chapter, there have been several direct dramatizations of individual experiences with the Committee in various performance media, of varying quality and sophistication. The great majority of writers, however, have made use of the aesthetic strategy of historical analogy. Employed most straightforwardly, the strategy is to construct a dramatization of a historical event so as to highlight its similarity to the events of the present, but to leave it to the spectator to make the connection. The writer thus compels the spectator or reader to participate in the process, taking on some of the responsibility for seeing the resemblance between contemporary events and the event in the past, and the implications of that resemblance. For these writers, the practical value of the use of analogy lies in this collaborative process. In a political climate in which, under the Smith Act, one could be prosecuted for conspiring to advocate subversive ideas, the ability to deny authorial responsibility for the political implications of a play and to secure the audience's complicity in developing them was an important consideration.

Despite the deliberate aesthetic camouflage, any serious critic who was even minimally aware of the Committee's activities noticed the analogies that were being made in these works, and the courageous ones did not hesitate to discuss their agreement or disagreement with their political implications. These writers were working in a culture that was attuned to their dramatic idiom and responsive to its contemporary subtext. This book is intended to make the subtext available again, to allow for a reconsideration of this passionate and compelling commentary on one of the nation's most divisive cultural crises.

PART ONE

THE COMMITTEE AND
THE CULTURE

1

The Stage Is Set

Critical comment on the performance of the Dies committee indicates that most reviewers would not recommend further government subsidies of $25,000 to stage such a dull and witless circus, a show certainly too poor in entertainment value (though it is summer) to justify the expense of production.

Champion Labor Monthly, September 1938

[The Hollywood Ten hearing] has been launched with that ineffable touch of showmanship which the naive Easterner associates with a Hollywood premiere, lacking only in orchids, evening dress and searchlights crisscrossing the evening sky.

Cabell Phillips, *New York Times*, 26 October 1947

In a speech to the American Association for the Advancement of Science on 13 September 1948, President Harry Truman warned that crucial scientific work might "be made impossible by the creation of an atmosphere in which no man feels safe against the public airing of unfounded rumors, gossip and vilification." This atmosphere, he said, "is un-American, the most un-American thing we have to contend with today. It is the climate of a totalitarian country in which scientists are expected to change their theories to match changes in the police state's propaganda line."[1] Even for the blunt-speaking Truman, these were strong words, and their meaning was emphasized by the story that appeared next to the report of his speech on page one of the *New York Times*: a report on the pursuit of one Arthur Adams by the House Committee on Un-American Activities (HUAC), which quoted chairman J. Parnell Thomas as saying that the Committee had "a great amount of testimony" on Adams, and that he hoped that Adams "could be found, be brought to Washington, and be questioned."[2] Regardless of the guilt or innocence of Mr. Adams, his fate was sealed. He had been named by HUAC, and he faced the recriminations of a populace, a large por-

9

tion of which believed he was a Communist conspirator simply because he was called before the Committee and questioned about his affiliations without benefit of trial, judge, jury, or the right to cross-examine his accusers or present his side of the case. If he was a teacher, an employee of the government or the film industry, a member of an AF of L union, or an employee of a business that followed the directives of the U. S. Chamber of Commerce or the American Legion, he would almost certainly lose his job. He might also be harassed by his neighbors, his children attacked at school, his family hounded out of the neighborhood. Such was the atmosphere Truman was talking about, the atmosphere surrounding the House Committee on Un-American Activities at its most powerful, in the years from 1947 to 1956.

The House Committee on Un-American Activities was established on a temporary basis in 1938 "for the purpose of conducting an investigation of (1) the extent, character, and object of un-American propaganda activities in the United States, (2) the diffusion within the United States of subversive and un-American propaganda that is instigated from foreign countries or of domestic origin and attacks the principle of the form of government as guaranteed by the constitution, and (3) all other questions in relations thereto that would aid Congress in any necessary remedial legislation."[3] The temporary Committee was chaired by Martin Dies (D-Texas) from its inception until its end in 1944. In the context of the rising global political tension that was soon to erupt in World War II, the establishment of the Committee was one of a number of measures taken to ensure the national security by guarding against subversion of the government from within the United States. In June 1940, the Congress passed by a vote of 382 to 4 an expanded version of the Alien Registration (Smith) Act, which called for the registration and fingerprinting of all aliens over the age of fourteen and the deportation of the criminals and subversives among them. In a provision that was to be fundamental to the activities of the Committee, the bill also made it a crime to conspire "to organize or help to organize any society, group, or assembly of persons who teach, advocate, or encourage the overthrow or destruction of any government in the United States by force or violence; or to be or become a member of, or affiliate with, any such society, group, or assembly of persons, knowing the purposes thereof."[4] Although a number of efforts to have the Communist Party of the United States declared illegal failed, it was argued that, since Communism advocated the overthrow of government, by violent revolution if necessary, to accomplish the "dictatorship of the proletariat," any member of the Communist Party by definition advocated "the overthrow of the United States Government by force and violence." Twelve leaders of the Communist Party were tried and convicted under the Smith Act, and the convictions were upheld by the Supreme Court in 1951.

In 1945, through a smart parliamentary maneuver, Representative John Rankin (D-Mississippi) engineered the establishment of a permanent House Committee on Un-American Activities, but was in turn maneuvered out of the Committee chairmanship. John S. Wood (D-Georgia) chaired the Committee from 1945 until 1952, with a brief but influential interruption, when it was chaired by one of its most avid members, J. Parnell Thomas (R-New Jersey). With another brief interruption when it was chaired by Harold Velde (R-Illinois), the Committee was presided over by Francis E. Walter (D-Pennsylvania) from 1955 to 1963. In 1947, President Truman had headed off attacks on his administration by demanding a loyalty oath for federal employees. In April 1951, the president stiffened the test of loyalty for employees of the U.S. government. Under the first executive order, an employee could be fired if "reasonable grounds existed for belief that the person involved is disloyal to the government of the United States." In 1951, all that was required for dismissal was "reasonable doubt as to the loyalty of the person involved."[5] In 1953, President Dwight Eisenhower authorized dismissal of any federal employee who cited the Fifth Amendment to avoid testifying at a congressional hearing.

The force behind this increasing pressure to affirm one's loyalty was an intensification of the environment that Truman had warned about in 1948. The McCarran Internal Security Act, passed over President Truman's veto in September 1950, read in part: "Whenever there shall be in existence [an Internal Security Emergency], the President, acting through the Attorney General, is hereby authorized to apprehend and by order detain, pursuant to the provisions of this title, each person as to whom there is reasonable ground to believe that such person probably will engage in, or probably will conspire with others to engage in, acts of sabotage."[6] The McCarran Act required the registration of all Communists and Communist organizations with a new Subversive Activities Control Board and provided for "internal security emergencies" and the detention of suspected subversives. James V. Bennett, director of the Federal Bureau of Prisons, announced in September 1952 that $775,000 had already been expended for the activation and rehabilitation of six "relocation camps," the facilities where Japanese Americans had been interned during World War II, which were capable, he estimated, of holding more than sixty thousand Communists.[7] In 1954, Congress passed the Communist Control Act, which virtually outlawed the Communist Party and denied certain civil rights to Communists and "Communist-front" organizations.

In taking these extraordinary measures, the government was reacting to a number of events inside and outside the United States that contributed to the country's ever-increasing anxiety about what FBI Director J. Edgar Hoover referred to as the "enemy within." In 1950 and 1951, Americans witnessed the conviction of Alger Hiss for perjury related to charges of espionage, Senator Joseph McCarthy's (unsupported) charge that 205 State Department workers were members of the Communist Party; the upholding by the Supreme Court of the conviction of U.S. Communist Party leaders under the Smith Act; the arrest of atomic spy Klaus Fuchs in England; the sentencing of Julius and Ethel Rosenberg to death for conspiracy to steal atomic secrets; the fall of China to the Communists; the outbreak of the Korean War; and the first successful atomic explosion by the Soviet Union. A good indication of the country's mood is the activity of the U.S. Chamber of Commerce, which released a series of pamphlets suggesting ways to deal with what it perceived as the menace to the American way of life posed by Communism. The 1946 pamphlet "suggested the institution of a strict federal loyalty program and an investigation of Communist influence in the cultural media, notably the motion picture industry"; the 1947 pamphlet called for the Department of Justice to publish, biannually, "a certified list of Communist-controlled front organizations and labor unions" and demanded an "anti-Communist" modification of the Wagner Act; the 1948 pamphlet demanded "federal legislation barring Communists from positions in teaching, social work, book reviewing, and libraries." The 1952 "master plan" virtually disregarded the Constitution in calling for "an untrammeled investigation and prosecution of Communists, the complete exclusion of Reds and fellow travelers from all agencies and professions affecting public opinion, from all educational or literary positions, from jobs of high visibility, prestige, and salary, particularly those in the entertainment field, and from any plant or factory large enough to have a trade union local."[8]

The country's anxiety about Communism reached a peak during the short career of Senator Joseph McCarthy (R-Wisconsin) as the chief anti-Communist spokesperson. This career ran its course between his charges against the State Department in 1950 and his defeat in the "Army-McCarthy Hearings" and censure by the Senate for "conduct that tends to bring the Senate into dishonor and disrepute, to obstruct the constitutional processes of the senate, and to impair its dignity" in 1954. The intense focus on Communism during the McCarthy years, however, was thoroughly prepared for by the steadily building intensity of the House Committee on Un-American Activities, which had focussed the country's attention on Communists and "Communist sympathizers" as early as 1938. By 1950, the Committee had firmly established two rituals. The first was a ritual of absolution for its "friendly" witnesses, which included accusation, exposure, repentance – proven by informing on others – and absolution. The second was a ritual of degradation for its "unfriendly" witnesses, consisting of accusation after accusation, followed by the continuous taking of the Fifth Amendment; despite the Supreme Court's warning that no guilt could be inferred from a witness's seeking the Fifth's protection – "I decline to answer because the answer may tend to incriminate me" – it carried an insinuation of guilt. As Representative Richard M. Nixon (R-California) spelled it out for a witness, "It is pretty clear, I think, that you are not using the defense of the Fifth Amendment because you are innocent."[9]

The Federal Theatre Project, 1938

Under the chairmanship of Martin Dies, the Special Committee was largely a tool for attacking the New Deal, and one of its first targets in 1938 was the Federal Theatre Project (FTP), which was seen as the most vulnerable of the Works Progress Administration's projects. J. Parnell Thomas launched his attack on 27 July 1938 in the *New York Times*, declaring that HUAC would make a sweeping investigation of the FTP and the Writers Project based on "testimony given before him at . . . informal and confidential hearings . . . being held by individual members of the committee." Declaring that the FTP was a "hot bed of Communists" and "infested with radicals from top to bottom," Thomas told the reporter that "practically every play presented under the auspices of the project either centered on a plot sympathetic to the cause of communism or serves as a vehicle for the propagation of New Deal theories." He also charged that Project Director Hallie Flanagan "wrote and produced a Communist play called 'Hear Their Voices' while on a trip to Soviet Russia."[10] Flanagan's unequivocal denial of the charges had no effect on Thomas. Stepping up the rhetoric, he charged on 10 August that the FTP, "a government agency, supported by public funds, has become part and parcel of the Communist party, spreading its radical theories through its stage productions. . . . practically every single play presented under the auspices of the Theatre Project is sheer propaganda for communism or the New Deal."[11] As historian Walter Goodman has noted, among the WPA projects, Federal Theatre was always considered something special,

> a somehow frivolous enterprise when so many were out of work and hungry. Moreover, the notion of singling out for subsidy several thousand writers and actors strained the generous impulses of many Congressmen. Even if Federal Theatre had been operated in a condition of absolute ideological purity, it could not have held out against the anti-New Deal forces who were regrouping in 1938 and dreamed of destroying the WPA altogether; if they could not have hung Federal Theatre on a charge of radicalism, they would have done it on a charge of using dirty words.[12]

During the public testimony of Hallie Flanagan on 6 December 1938, the Committee offered no evidence for any of the charges made by Thomas beyond the testimony of the witnesses they had interviewed in their secret hearings. While Flanagan tried continually to return the Committee members to the charges that had been made and the brief she had prepared to refute them, the questioning ranged all over the lot as the congressmen tried to find something in her background that would establish her as a Red. A great deal of questioning centered on an article that Flanagan had written about workers' theatre for *Theatre Arts Monthly*. One of the best-known moments in the Committee's history occurred as Representative Joseph Starnes (D-Alabama) questioned Flanagan about this article. Noting that she had referred to "a certain Marlowesque madness" among the workers' theatre participants, Starnes asked, "You are quoting from this Marlowe. Is he a Communist?"[13] In her account of the hearing, Flanagan remembered that "the room rocked with laughter, but I did not laugh. Eight thousand people might lose their jobs because a Congressional Committee had so pre-judged us that even the classics were 'communistic.' I said, 'I was quoting from Christopher Marlowe.'"[14] The questioning continued:

Mr. Starnes: Tell us who Marlowe is, so we can get the proper reference, because that is all that we want to do.

Mrs. Flanagan: Put in the record that he was the greatest dramatist in the period immediately preceding Shakespeare.

Mr. Starnes: Put that in the record because the charge has been made that this article of yours is entirely Communistic, and we want to help you.

Mrs. Flanagan: Thank you. That statement will go in the record.

Mr. Starnes: Of course, we had what some people call Communists back in the days of the Greek theater.

Mrs. Flanagan: Quite true.

Mr. Starnes: And I believe Mr. Euripides was guilty of teaching class consciousness also, wasn't he?

Mrs. Flanagan: I believe that was alleged against all of the Greek dramatists.

Mr. Starnes: So we cannot say when it began.[15]

Hallie Flanagan's brief was never entered in the record of the hearing. The Federal Theatre Project, a target of the House Appropriations Committee as well as HUAC, was abolished in the wake of the hearings, despite approval by the Senate Appropriations Committee, with the appropriations bill reading specifically that "none of the funds made available by this joint resolution shall be available: (a) After June 30, 1939, for the operation of any Theatre Project."[16] The theatre and entertainment community had placed its support solidly behind the FTP. As Flanagan noted,

> the variety of organizations and individuals coming out publicly for the continuance of Federal Theatre included every theatrical union, representing a combined membership of thousands; the Screen Actors' Guild, the Screen Directors' Guild, the Screen Writers' Guild, speaking for the vast Hollywood industry; entire companies of plays on Broadway, dramatic critics from coast to coast; distinguished actors, producers, directors, designers from New York and Hollywood; college and community theatres from the North, East, South, and West; the Federation of Arts Unions representing painters, sculptors, musicians, and artists of every field.[17]

In a typically theatrical show of support, Talullah Bankhead and a supporting cast had flown to Washington to testify before the Senate Appropriations Committee. The three major talent guilds in Hollywood had sponsored a national radio broadcast and mass demonstration. All of this good will and lobbying activity was to no avail, a perhaps ominous sign of the temper of the times.

The Hollywood Investigations

HUAC was established on a permanent basis in January of 1945, just five months before Germany surrendered to the Allies and eight months before Japan succumbed to atomic attack. Although Martin Dies had conducted a series of "subcommittee" hearings in which he personally "cleared" actors such as James Cagney, Fredric March, and Humphrey Bogart, who were accused by informants of Communist ties in 1940, the Committee did not turn its full attention to Hollywood until shortly after the war ended. In cooperation with motion-picture studio owners, HUAC held hearings that were aimed ostensibly at rooting out Communist infiltrators in the motion-picture industry. The Committee first targeted mainly writers, the well-known leftists of the Screen Writers Guild, in the 1947 hearings whose putative purpose was searching for Communist propaganda in Hollywood films. In 1951, when members of the Committee had discovered the power of publicity that attended their Show Business investigations, a second and far more comprehensive set of hearings was aimed at Hollywood figures who sent money into "Communist coffers" by contributing to various leftist causes.

Anti-Communist sentiment had been building in Hollywood since the early thirties, when a number of left-wing writers such as John Howard Lawson, Samuel Ornitz, and Herbert Biberman had come from the East and become active in making the Screen Writers Guild the most left-wing of Hollywood unions. *Variety* reported in 1933 that

> Communism is getting a toehold in the picture industry . . . [among] a crowd of pinks listed on studio payrolls as writers, authors, scenarists and adapters. And though most of the new red movie recruits are getting anywhere from $500 to $1,500 a week their program calls for a fantastic sovietizing of the lots. Meeting place of the pinks is Venice. There they gather at least once a week to plan for the millennium when studios will be writer-controlled and producers will be hired hands. Most of the leaders of the literary-communist movement are easterners who have hit Hollywood during the past two years.[18]

After two particularly bitter strikes during the thirties, there was no love lost between the Hollywood producers and the unions, particularly the Screen Writers Guild. HUAC had had its eye on Hollywood since its earliest days under Martin Dies. In August 1938, Dies released a report from Committee investigator Edward F. Sullivan stating that Communism was rampant in the movie industry. In July 1940, Dies, at home in Beaumont, Texas, took private testimony from former Communist Party member, and probable paid police-informer, John L. Leech.[19] Leech gave Dies the names of forty-two movie people and repeated them to a Los Angeles County grand jury a few weeks later, when a number of the names were leaked to the press. The result was that "newspaper headlines all over the country emblazoned their front pages with the news that Humphrey Bogart, James Cagney, Fredric March, Franchot Tone, Lionel Stander, and over a dozen other stars had been named as Communists. Dies, alone in 'executive session,' promised clearance to all those who would 'cooperate.' Within two weeks of the 'leak' all but one of the named, actress Jean Muir, had appeared and all except Stander had been 'cleared' by the HUAC chairman."[20] Stander was promptly fired by Republic Studios.

The next foray into Hollywood occurred in 1945, when John Rankin announced in a press conference that "one of the most dangerous plots ever instigated for the overthrow of this Government has its headquarters in Hollywood," which he called "the greatest hotbed of subversive activities in the United States." "We're on the trail of the tarantula now," said Rankin, "and we're going to follow through."[21] A more temperate "committee spokesman" put the investigation in proportion, noting that the investigation involved "propaganda both clever and childish, in movies." While nothing immediate came of this attack, it is a good indicator of the ardent fervor with which the Committee conducted its assault on Hollywood. The most even-handed of the historians of HUAC, Walter Goodman, has suggested some simple motivations for this vehemence. "To Rankin, Hollywood was Semitic territory. To Thomas, it was New Deal territory. To the entire Committee, it was a veritable sun around which the press worshipfully rotated. And it was also a place where real live Communists could readily be found."[22] We have already seen Thomas's dislike of the New Deal in his comments on the FTP. Rankin regularly gave clear evidence of his dislike of Jews and foreigners, on the floor of the House, as when he commented on a petition from the Committee for the First Amendment that opposed HUAC: "I want to read you some of these names. One of the names is June Havoc. We found . . . that her real name is June Hovick. Another one was Danny Kaye, and we found out his real name David Daniel Kaminsky. . . . Another one is Eddie Cantor, whose real name is Edward Iskowitz. There is one who calls himself Edward Robinson. His real name is Emmanuel Goldenberg. There is another here who calls himself Melvyn Douglas, whose real name is Melvyn Hesselberg."[23] But it was the double promise of Communists who were celebrities that really drew the Committee to Hollywood, and they hit pay dirt with the hearings that investigated the so-called "Hollywood Ten" – actually nineteen – in 1947.

In their study *Inquisition in Hollywood*, Larry Ceplair and Steven Englund estimate that approximately 300 "movie people" – artists, technicians, backlot and front-office workers – joined the Communist Party during the decade from the outbreak of the Spanish Civil War to the first wave of HUAC subpoenas (1936-47).[24] Although HUAC had had its eye on Hollywood, and particularly on the Screen Writers Guild, since the early days of the Dies Committee, the focus was intensified in May of 1947, when a subcommittee consisting of Thomas, John McDowell (R-Pennsylvania), and two investigators conducted a week of hearings in Los Angeles, during which they listened to fourteen actors, writers, and producers. After being "amazed at the revelations made by the witnesses and their frankness in naming names, places, dates, Communist card numbers, etc.," Thomas concluded that "90 per cent of Communist infiltration was in the screen writing field" and that many of the "names" were "prominent persons, including prominent script writers."[25] Two weeks later, the subcommittee issued an indictment based on what the witnesses had told them. It charged that the National Labor Relations Board was abetting the effort of Communist organizers to take control of the industry; that scores of highly paid screenwriters were injecting propaganda into movies; that White House pressure had resulted in the production of "some of the most flagrant Communist propaganda films"; that subtle techniques were used for glorifying the Communist Party, while the Communists prevented the production of films which glorified loyal American citizens; and that the heads of the studios had done nothing to prevent all of this.[26] Exposure was essential; public hearings were promised. As Walter Goodman has noted, "not one of the . . . charges would ever be substantiated, but the publicity which these coming attractions received bespoke high success for the feature event."[27]

This was the first stage of the Committee's grandstand production, the hearings of 20–30 October 1947, which produced the "Hollywood Ten" and became the Thomas Committee's greatest source of notoriety. After investigators had spent the summer in Los Angeles collecting "several volumes of testimony from people in all branches of the industry,"[28] on 21 September 1947 the Committee issued forty-three

Figure 1. Anti-Semitism did not stop Senator John Rankin from using
Old Testament iconography to bolster his pursuit of Communists.
In this publicity photo, he is draped with an anti-Communist petition
to assume the authority of an Old Testament prophet.

subpoenas to people in the film industry, requiring them to appear at Committee hearings in Washington the following October. These proved to be an elaborately staged set of hearings; they centered on nineteen "unfriendly" witnesses, sixteen of them writers and all suspected Communists, who were subpoenaed to appear after a number of "friendly" witnesses, including Jack Warner, Ayn Rand, Adolphe Menjou, Robert Taylor, Ronald Reagan, and Gary Cooper, had drawn a picture of the Red propaganda in Hollywood films. Calling it "the most thoroughly publicized investigation [HUAC] has ever undertaken," the *New York Times* report noted that "it has been launched with that ineffable touch of showmanship which the naive Easterner associates with a Hollywood premiere, lacking only in orchids, evening dress and searchlights crisscrossing the evening sky."[29] The staging included "the biggest auditorium at the Capitol outside the House and Senate chambers themselves," batteries of microphones and loudspeakers, press tables accommodating 120 reporters and special writers, six newsreel cameras poised above the witness table, and batteries of klieg lights, with extra photofloods dangling from the chandeliers. In a display of media almost unheard of in 1947, three major networks and two local radio stations recorded every word of testimony and spot-broadcast some of it directly from ringside.[30] It was the first of the Congressional media shows, preparing the way for the Army-McCarthy Hearings seven years later and the Watergate and Iran-Contra Hearings in the seventies and eighties.

Careful thought had been given to the presentation of the witnesses as well as the staging. The *Times* report noted that the testimony was "a careful synthesis designed for maximum impact on the public consciousness. Its substance is that Communists have elected the film industry as the principal vehicle for poisoning the American mind." Larry Ceplair and Steven Englund have shown that the structure of the hearings was as carefully crafted as a four-act play.[31] Act One consisted of the testimony of Jack Warner, who boasted of having "spotted" and fired twelve Communists from his studio. Act Two "introduced a long stream of 'friendly witnesses' . . . who matter-of-factly named three dozen 'Communists' whom they knew to be working in Hollywood"[32] Act Three, wrote Ceplair and Englund, "was strictly comic opera." This included a parade of stars, such as Robert Taylor, Robert Montgomery, Ronald Reagan, Gary Cooper, and George Murphy, whose function "was not to provide the Committee with information, but with luster. They did not name names, but lent

"Now showing."

Figure 2. As these newspaper cartoons show, the American public understood the theatrical tactics of the Show Business hearings quite well. Illustrations: top, © by *The Tennessean*, 1947; bottom, reprinted by permission of the *Akron Beacon Journal.*

(their) names" and "provided HUAC with the means of neutralizing the impact on public opinion of the hostile and equally celebrated Committee for the First Amendment, due to arrive in Washington for the start of the final act on Monday, October 27."[33] The charge that Communist writers had used the film industry for pro-Soviet propaganda was based on the analysis by witnesses like Ayn Rand and Robert Taylor of three pro-Soviet films that had been produced during the war years, one at the request of President Roosevelt, with the conscious aim of winning the support of the American public for its wartime ally, the Soviet Union. The films were *Song of Russia* (MGM, 1943), *Mission to Moscow* (Warner Brothers, 1943), and *North Star* (Samuel Goldwyn, 1942). All were sentimental films aimed at evoking the same emotional support for the U. S.'s alliance with the Soviet Union that *Mrs. Miniver* produced for its alliance with Britain. The Committee spent several days taking the testimony of "experts" on Communism, such as Ayn Rand and Adolphe Menjou, who professed to have made a "particular study of Marxism, Fabian Socialism, communism, Stalinism, and its probable effects on the American people, if they ever gain power here."[34] Besides giving a copious supply of names to the Committee, Menjou, with Richard Nixon's encouragement, offered a "test" for identifying a Communist:

Mr. Menjou: If you belong to a Communist-front organization and you take no action against the Communists, if you do not resign from the organization when you know the organization is dominated by Communists, I consider that a very, very dangerous thing.
Mr. Nixon: Have you any other tests which you would apply which would indicate to you that people acted like Communists?
Mr. Menjou: Well, I think attending any meetings at which Mr. Paul Robeson appeared, and applauding or listening to his Communist songs in America. I would be ashamed to be seen in an audience doing a thing of that kind.
Mr. Nixon: You indicated you thought a person acted like a Communist when he stated, as one person did to you, that capitalism was through.
Mr. Menjou: That is not Communistic per se, but it is very dangerous leaning, it is very close. . . .
Mr. Nixon: You indicated that belonging to a Communist-front organization, in other words, an association with Communists, attending these planned meetings, making statements in opposition to the capitalistic system are three of the tests you would apply.
Mr. Menjou: Yes, sir.[35]

Mr. Menjou's "tests" were actually quite close to those applied by the committee in subpoenaeing witnesses and demanding the names of those who attended meetings or who voiced opposition to such institutions as HUAC itself. Equally useful to the Committee's presentation was the testimony of Gary Cooper, who was not a self-proclaimed expert, but very clearly just a regular citizen when he appeared before the Committee. Asked by Thomas, "Do you believe as a prominent person in your field that it would be wise for us, the Congress, to pass legislation to outlaw the Communist Party in the United States?," Cooper replied, "I think it would be a good idea, although I have never read Karl Marx and I don't know the basis of communism, beyond what I have picked up from hearsay. From what I hear, I don't like it because it isn't on the level."[36]

Act Four consisted of the testimony of the eleven unfriendly witnesses who were actually called to testify in October 1947, the "Hollywood Ten": John Howard Lawson, Dalton Trumbo, Ring Lardner, Jr., Alvah Bessie, Herbert Biberman, Lester Cole, Edward Dmytryk, Albert Maltz, Samuel Ornitz, and Adrian Scott – plus Bertolt Brecht. The "unfriendly nineteen" had decided that their ultimate hope lay with the Supreme Court, which they thought would overturn a citation for contempt of Congress if they presented a case based on the First Amendment of the Constitution, which protects freedom of speech. They settled on a strategy of reading statements that denied the Committee's right to inquire into their political beliefs on various grounds and asserting their right to answer the Committee's questions about their Party affiliation "in their own way" – that is, by evading the questions. With the appearance of the first unfriendly witness, John Howard Lawson, it was clear that this strategy would not be effective. Thomas refused to allow Lawson to read his statement and gaveled him to silence whenever he tried to state his position. An increasingly frustrated and obstreperous Lawson was finally removed forcibly from the stand:

The Chairman: (pounding gavel) . . . The question is: Have you ever been a member of the Communist Party?

Mr. Lawson: I am framing my answer in the only way in which any American citizen can frame his answer to a question which absolutely invades his rights.

The Chairman: Then you refuse to answer that question; is that correct?

Mr. Lawson: I have told you that I will offer my beliefs, affiliations, and everything else to the American public, and they will know where I stand.

The Chairman: (pounding gavel): Excuse the witness –
Mr. Lawson: As they do from what I have written.
The Chairman (pounding gavel): Stand away from the stand –
Mr. Lawson: I have written Americanism for many years, and I shall continue to fight for the Bill of Rights, which you are trying to destroy.
The Chairman: Officers, take this man away from the stand –
(Applause and boos)[37]

Thomas saw to it that Lawson's performance was followed by the testimony of Investigator Louis J. Russell, who produced a Communist Party card, "registration number 47275," in Lawson's name and submitted a nine-page memo detailing Lawson's defense of the Party in his writings and his participation in "Communist Fronts." The memo was calmly read aloud into the record by Robert Stripling, the Committee's chief investigator. The impact of the two scenes was to represent the Committee as a calm and judicious presenter of facts and Lawson as a boorish and evasive witness. Similar tactics were used with the other nine Americans, lumping them all into a category of boorish men who were disrespectful toward the United States Congress and lacking in candor about their own beliefs and activities.[38]

Much of the support from the Hollywood community and the American public for the Hollywood Ten and much of the opposition to the Committee dissolved as a result of this carefully staged performance. The five witnesses who were currently employed by Hollywood studios were summarily fired. All ten were charged with contempt of Congress and convicted. They appealed the contempt citations on the grounds that their right of free speech included the right to remain silent and was impinged upon when they were forced under threat of punishment to disclose their political opinions and affiliations.[39] In 1949, the U.S. Court of Appeals unanimously upheld their convictions. On 10 April 1950, the Supreme Court refused to review the contempt convictions, and the Hollywood Ten went to jail. As Walter Goodman has noted, "the Hollywood hearings brought forward no heroes. The writers, puffed up with a sense of martyrdom, made a burlesque of a Jeffersonian cadre. . . . As for the Committee itself its premise in this investigation, that movies were being subverted by a Red underground in league with New Deal bureaucrats, was asinine; its methods were gross and its intentions despicable."[40]

The Blacklist

Between 1947 and the early sixties, HUAC wielded enormous power over writers, actors, and directors who worked in film, radio, and the new medium of television. The cooperation of studio executives, and the guilds and unions, with the Committee resulted in a blacklisting of anyone who was named as a Communist or Communist sympathizer by a witness, or who was called as an "unfriendly" witness before the Committee and accused of any association with Communists at any time in the past.

The official blacklist began with the Hollywood producers in the wake of the 1947 hearings. On 20 October, as the hearings began, Eric Johnston, president of the Motion Picture Association of America and the Association of Motion Picture Producers, sent a breezy reassurance to the writers: "Tell the boys not to worry. We're not going totalitarian to please this Committee."[41] And Jack Warner, a most cooperative friendly witness, told the Committee: "I can't, for the life of me, figure where men could get together and try in any form, shape or manner to deprive a man of a livelihood because of his political beliefs."[42] Shortly after the hearings concluded, the five of the Hollywood Ten who were employed by Hollywood studios were fired. In its letter to Edward Dmytryk, RKO said that

> by your conduct [before HUAC] and by your actions, attitude, association, public statements and general conduct before, at, and since that time, you have brought yourself into disrepute with a large section of the public, have offended the community, have prejudiced this corporation as your employer and the motion picture industry in general, and have lessened your capacity fully to comply with your employment agreement, and have otherwise violated the provisions of Article 16 of your employment agreement with us.[43]

After a two-day closed meeting of fifty Hollywood producers was held at the Waldorf-Astoria Hotel, the Association of Motion Picture Producers issued what has come to be known as the Waldorf Statement on 26 November 1947. Stating that the producers "deplore the action of the ten Hollywood men who have been cited for contempt," it went on to say that while "we do not desire to prejudge their legal rights," the producers would "forthwith discharge or suspend without compensation those in our employ and we will not re-employ any of the ten until such time as he is acquitted or has purged himself of contempt and declares under oath that he is not a Communist." Further, the producers pledged that they would "not knowingly employ a Communist," and that, in "pursuing this policy, we are not going to be swayed by hysteria or intimidation from any source." Acknowledging that this policy involved "the danger of hurting innocent people" and "the risk of creating an atmosphere of fear," and that "creative work at its best cannot be carried on in an atmosphere of fear," they promised to "guard against this danger, this risk, this fear. To this end we will invite the Hollywood talent guilds to work with us to eliminate any subversives, to protect the innocent, and to safeguard free speech and a free screen wherever threatened."[44] A three-man delegation was sent to bring the producers' decision to a meeting of the Screen Writers Guild. With this summary action by the producers and its overture to the guilds and unions, the entertainment industry's official blacklist began.

Looking back on his experience in an article for the *Saturday Evening Post* in 1961, Hollywood Ten member Ring Lardner, Jr. explained:

> The industry blacklist policy was extended to cover every person subpoenaed by the committee who failed to answer all the questions put to him, or who having been named by a witness, did not appear voluntarily to clear or purge himself. It didn't matter whether, as in the case of writers and directors, they might conceivably exert a subversive influence on the content of movies, although all the studio heads had sworn to the committee that even this was impossible under their vigilant control. Actors, musicians, technicians and stenographers were chopped from the payrolls with equal dispatch.
>
> It also didn't matter whether the grounds for not answering was the First Amendment, which the appellate-court decision in our case had rated as invalid protection, or the Fifth, which the Supreme Court had meanwhile upheld as a fully applicable use of a precious freedom that no man might legally construe as evidence of guilt.[45]

Of the years between 1948 and 1953, Eason Monroe, head of the Southern California chapter of the ACLU, said:

> These were the years of the slow steady purge – out of employment, out of community organizations, out of public posts of one sort or another, [and] out of political candidacies – of anyone who either had in his own personal record membership in the Communist Party or associated groups, or was a member of any family in which these

relationships were characteristic, or who had friends [who espoused such views], or who had ever attended a meeting, or who read the wrong literature, or for any reason at all.[46]

The capitulation of the film industry to the Committee's Red-baiting was complete and even enthusiastic. Spearheaded by the anti-Communist zealot, Roy Brewer, a long-time power in the AF of L International Alliance of Theatrical Stage Employees in Los Angeles, the producers, the guilds, and the craft unions formed themselves in March 1949 into the Motion Picture Industry Council, whose sole purpose was to cooperate with HUAC. The Council took upon itself the job of publicizing the "Communist problem" in Hollywood and the industry's efforts to purge itself of "subversives," clear repentant unfriendly witnesses, and make life as difficult as possible for those who refused to repent. In a rejoinder to Ring Lardner's *Saturday Evening Post* article, Brewer, good union man that he was, declared that no blacklist had ever existed in the film industry, putting the notion down to the machinations of "the communists," who "set about selling the American public the idea that they were the pitiable victims of a diabolical 'blacklist.'" No "right-thinking person believes in 'blacklists,'" Brewer declared:

> The term has evil overtones, echoes of a time when powerful employers created secret lists of employees they considered troublesome. By circulating these "blacklists" among themselves they were able to punish the unfortunate workers cruelly by depriving them of a chance to make a living. The practice has long since been outlawed and is recognized as unethical, immoral and illegal. Hollywood's communists cynically donned martyrs' robes as "victims of a blacklist," no doubt assuming that many Americans would overlook the fact that they were part of an international conspiracy aimed against the U.S.A.[47]

In a sense, Brewer was right about the official Hollywood blacklist. The producers didn't need a secret list in order to enforce the Waldorf agreement. HUAC itself provided the list when it published the names of all the men and women who had appeared before a congressional investigating committee and refused to cooperate: 60,000 names in all. Of these, 212 were screen artists, producers, and studio workers, all promptly blacklisted.[48] Brewer of course did not mention the more pernicious "graylists" that were maintained by the American Legion and so-called "smear and clear agencies." These included American Business Consultants, formed by three ex-FBI agents in 1947, which published *Counterattack* and *Red Channels,* the two major industry sources for the names of "subversives," whom producers could employ at their peril; the Wage Earners Committee, formed in October 1951; and Aware, Inc., established in December 1953 by Vincent Hartnett, who had worked for ABC, and some actors, and which published *Confidential Notebook* and supplements to the lists in *Red Channels.* Television producer Mark Goodson has also explained that "there were several private lists, and the major agencies and networks exchanged lists. . . . *Red Channels* would maybe have a couple of hundred names, but there might be on the other list at CBS several hundred more. Anybody could show up on a list, stars, technicians, cowboys."[49] The enterprising Vincent Hartnett made a good living as a compiler of dossiers on show-business personalities. Calling himself a "talent consultant," he charged $5 a head for short reports, and $20 for long reports.[50] The reports included any activity – such as an actor's signature on a petition or attendance at a rally or meeting that was also attended by Communists – that might open a producer to the charge of hiring "Communist sympathizers." Since the dossiers were secret, a graylistee often had no idea what he was charged with, becoming aware of the graylist only when he was fired, or stopped being hired. Francis J. McNamara, who was to become director of HUAC in the sixties, testified before the Committee that he liked to think of his work with the anti-Communist organ *Counterattack* as similar to that of Dun & Bradstreet – handing out credit ratings on people – and he pointed out that nobody called Dun & Bradstreet a blacklisting outfit.[51]

The submission of the producers and the New York "money men" to these right-wing influencers of popular opinion might be understandable, but the desertion of writers, actors, directors, and others by their guilds and unions is harder to fathom. The Screen Writers Guild was known as the most left-wing of Hollywood unions and had even been the target of an attempt at union-busting by the studios and conservative writers in the late thirties, with the short-lived Screen Playwrights, Inc. Shortly after the 1947 HUAC hearings, in November, the Screen Writers Guild elections completely changed the character of the guild, ousting radicals from positions of power. Ceplair and Englund report that

the Board then commenced to purge almost all left-wingers and suspected left-wingers from the SWG executive and administrative structure. The sweep of the moderates' broom was reflected in the composition of the Guild committees for 1948. Prior to November, 1947, leftist liberals, radicals, and Communists constituted fully a third of the membership of every committee; afterward, it was a rare committee which included even two left-wingers out of twelve or more members, and most committees had none at all. . . . It is fair to say that the Left ceased to exist in any organized, meaningful sense in the Screen Writers Guild.[52]

The SWG Board then authorized its president to turn over to HUAC investigators all union records, thus exposing any member who had expressed left-wing sentiments at a meeting to a subpoena and blacklisting.

As the Hollywood Ten went through their process of conviction, appeals, and imprisonment, the unions became increasingly timid. The last of the Ten went to prison in September 1950. It was a much changed United States that viewed a new round of Hollywood subpoenas in the spring of 1951. It had been a year since Senator Joseph McCarthy had made his baseless charge that there were 205 Communist Party members in the State Department. Alger Hiss had been found guilty of perjury and Judith Coplon guilty of conspiracy to commit espionage (a conviction that was later overturned). The Soviet Union had set off an atomic bomb. President Truman had sent troops into Korea. Communist Party leaders had been tried and convicted of conspiracy to preach subversion under the Smith Act. The McCarran Internal Security Act now required that members of the Communist Party register with the Justice Department. In April, Julius and Ethel Rosenberg would be sentenced to death for conspiracy to steal atomic secrets and President Truman would announce that federal employees might be fired if there was "reasonable doubt" of their loyalty. In March, eight radical screen actors and writers were served with HUAC subpoenas. Three of them – Larry Parks, Waldo Salt, and Richard Collins – were members of the 1947 "Nineteen" who had not been called to testify. When actress Gale Sondergaard appealed formally to the Screen Actors Guild (SAG) for support, she received a letter from the Board, which stated in part:

> Your letter (1) attacks as an inquisition the pending hearings by the House Committee on Un-American Activities into alleged Communist Party activities by a few individuals and (2) asks that the Guild protect you against any consequences of your own personal decisions

and actions. . . . If any actor by his own actions outside of union activities has so offended American public opinion that he has made himself unsaleable at the box office, the guild cannot and would not want to force any employer to hire him. That is the individual actor's personal responsibility and it cannot be shifted to his union.[53]

In October 1950, the SAG executives had drafted a loyalty oath similar to the one already employed by the armed forces and defense industries, which was not accepted by the rest of the industry. Only the opposition of the Screen Writers Guild scuttled a proposal for an industry-wide loyalty board that was placed before the Motion Picture Industry Council in June 1951.[54] As Goodman has put it, "even those who a few years before had protested against Communist-hunting expeditions now granted that the pursuit of Communists, wherever they might be found, was a natural right of Congress. In fact, it seemed to be a right of whoever cared to pursue them. From around the country came inspiriting reports of Communists being exposed, suspended, fired, evicted, tried, deported, boycotted, blacklisted, and physically set upon. The public temper invited, and the Committee joined in the sport."[55]

The 110 witnesses who were subpoenaed in the second set of hearings were on their own as they faced the Committee. All were approached by HUAC investigators and urged to testify, that is "to avow their Communist pasts, acknowledge that they had seen the light, and (as proof of regeneracy) provide the Committee with the names of others who had strayed."[56] Fifty-eight of them decided to follow this path in the wake of the agonizing testimony of Larry Parks, perhaps the most heartrending moment in HUAC history, as Parks agreed to "crawl through the mud," as he memorably phrased it, and become the first unfriendly witness to name names. In 1953, the Committee broadened its focus to include Broadway, radio, and the fledgling television industry, which were centered in New York. It held hearings at the United States Court House in Foley Square, New York, in May of that year, and in 1955 it held an extended "show business" hearing in New York, with little success. Only one of twenty-three witnesses "cooperated," while eighteen invoked the Fifth Amendment and four others refused to testify on other grounds.[57] A few days before the start of the hearings in 1955, the American Federation of Television and Radio Artists (AFTRA) authorized its local units to take disciplinary measures against any member who failed to answer questions before a Congressional committee. Under this provision, a member could be fined, censured, suspended, or expelled on the charge of conduct prejudicial to the welfare of the union. Although AFTRA had previously condemned the blacklisting organization AWARE for circulating lists of entertainment figures named in reports of the Un-American Activities Committee, it now supported the blacklisting of anyone who invoked the Fifth Amendment before the Committee.

The reality in the fifties was that an actor or writer who was subpoenaed by the Committee, or named by another witness as a Communist or "Communist sympathizer," or whose name appeared in one of the "smear and clear" organizations' lists of "subversives," could not work in the movies or television unless he or she admitted to former "Communist activities," expressed repentance and remorse for these activities, disavowed all loyalty to Communism, and reaffirmed loyalty to the United States under oath. After 1950, the ritual of requiring witnesses to "name names," to inform on others as well as confessing their own sins, became a standard part of HUAC interrogations. Thus anyone questioned by the Committee about his political beliefs and activities was faced with blacklisting if he (1) refused to answer or (2) invoked the First or Fifth Amendments, or (3) admitted to an interest in Communism in the past, repented for it, and affirmed his loyalty to the United States, but refused to implicate others.

Larry Parks, who spoke openly about his membership in the Communist Party in the early thirties, but who showed extreme reluctance in naming others – eventually being allowed to do so in executive session rather than a public hearing – was aware that his "uncooperative" demeanor would probably cost him his career, although he did manage to avoid a contempt citation and prison term. As he told the Committee: "I think my career has been ruined because of this. . . . There was another choice open to me. I did not choose to use it. I chose to come and tell the truth."[58] He was subsequently questioned about his statement by Counsel Frank Tavenner and Representative Donald Jackson of California:

Mr. Tavenner: I did not fully understand your reference to the possible destruction of your career by being subpoenaed here. You did not mean to infer by that that this committee was bringing you here because of any effect it might have on your career?
Mr Parks: No, I didn't infer that at all. What I meant, and what I said, was that because of this, in my opinion, I have no career left. . . . I have tried to cooperate with the committee in every way that I feel that I can, but I think the damage has been done. . . .

Mr. Jackson: Don't you think that more than the damage that possibly has been done you by this committee, which, after all, is an expression of the will of the American people and operates under the mandate of the people, don't you think the great damage occurred when you became a member of an organization which has been found to advocate the overthrow of every constitutional form of government in the world? Is this committee more to blame than your own act in affiliating with that organization?[59]

Larry Parks's career, at its peak with his recent appearance in *The Jolson Story*, was indeed destroyed. He was blacklisted until, after humbling himself to the Committee in 1953 and declaring in his letter of July 15 that if he were "to testify today I would not testify as I did in 1951 – that to give such testimony is to 'wallow in the mud' – but on the contrary I would recognize that such cooperation would help further the cause in which many of us were sincerely interested when we were duped into joining and taking part in the Communist Party,"[60] he was finally cleared. He had only three minor roles between 1953 and his death in 1976. Actor Lionel Stander, who had not been "cleared" when he testified before Martin Dies on 27 August 1940 that he was not a Communist, had requested an immediate appearance before the Committee when he was named by witness Marc Lawrence in 1951. When he was finally called to testify on 6 May 1953, he complained to the Committee that, "receiving the subpoena, with the press's announcement that I was subpoenaed, caused me to be blacklisted in radio, television, and motion pictures. So, I had an immediate economic motive for an immediate appearance."[61] Asked about his employment history, he responded:

Mr. Stander: . . . I worked for independent producers –
Mr. Tavenner: Approximately –
Mr. Stander: – Up until the time Mr. Marc Lawrence mentioned my name, or rather, up until the time Larry Parks said he didn't know me as a Communist.
Mr. Tavenner: Let me –
Mr. Stander: And that appeared in the paper, and just to have my name appear in association with this committee – it seems like something; it shouldn't; I agree – I know it isn't the committee's fault. It is like the Spanish Inquisition.
Mr. Tavenner: Let me remind you –
Mr. Stander: You may not be burned, but you can't help coming away a little singed.[62]
Mr. Stander remained on the blacklist.

In order to be restored to the status of loyal American, and to get off the blacklist, one had to become what leftists quickly labeled an "informer," which led to a kind of blacklisting of its own – an ostracism by the Left. When actors John Garfield and José Ferrer gave signs of being about to name names, they were excoriated by the *People's Daily World*:

> Make no mistake about it, Garfield and Ferrer are betraying every-thing that's decent and honorable in our land to the fat pigs of Wall Street who are wallowing in their blood-soaked profits. They are just as guilty, just as dishonorable, as the German actors Werner Krauss and Emil Jannings who joined Hitler's fight against communism in the early '30's. . . . They are contributing to the incitement of a holo-caust alongside of which World War II was child's play.[63]

No one, however, was attacked with greater vehemence than director Elia Kazan, who had testified about his own membership in the Party during the thirties and had named seven former members of the Group Theatre, all well known to the Committee, as the price for con-tinuing to work in films. In typical Kazan style, he had gone on the offensive, taking out a full-page ad in the *New York Times* in which he urged other liberals to "speak out," declaring: "Secrecy serves the Com-munists. At the other pole, it serves those who are interested in silenc-ing liberal voices. The employment of a lot of good liberals is threatened because they have allowed themselves to become associated with or silenced by the Communists."[64] It was assumed in Hollywood and New York that Kazan, one of the most successful and highly paid directors both in Hollywood and on Broadway, had caved in to the stu-dios – and thus the Committee – for the money. When Kazan's testi-mony was cited to Tony Kraber by the Committee in 1955, he replied, "Is this the Kazan that signed the contract for $500,000 the day after he gave names to this Committee? Would you sell your brothers for $500,000."[65] The *Daily Worker* was content with name-calling: "We have seen a lot of belly-crawling in this time of the toad, but nothing has quite equaled last week's command-performance by Hollywood direc-tor Elia Kazan. . . . Not even in Hitler days did renegade intellectuals sink so low. . . . Kazan is not content with being a toad. He must also be a philosopher of toadyism."[66]

In 1956 John Cogley did a *Report on Blacklisting* for the Fund for the Republic, which published it in two volumes, one on the movies and the other on radio and television. The study detailed what everyone in the industry knew – that blacklisting had caused hundreds of persons to be denied employment because of their political views and associations, and that the promoters of the blacklists, and in some cases those who made their living by them, were the same people who were allowed to judge who would or would not be employed. Cogley was subpoenaed to appear before the Committee and questioned, not about the presumably Un-American activity of blacklisting, but about himself and the Fund for the Republic, the object clearly being to cast aspersions on the objectivity and factualness of the report. Chairman Walter "did not have to read the report to know that he disagreed with it on two counts. First, he denied there was any such thing as a blacklist and second, he wanted all Communists driven out of films, theater, radio, television, and, if feasible, out of the country."[67] The Committee then called a number of "expert" witnesses to report on the question of blacklisting, including Brewer, James F. O'Neill of the American Legion, who said that blacklisting was reprehensible but that persons identified with the Communist apparatus should not be employed in the entertainment industry, and Francis J. McNamara, who compared his smear-and-clear work to that of Dun & Bradstreet. This instance of the Big Lie was one of the rhetorical triumphs of the the Committee. The hearings demonstrated to the public that the Committee and its supporters all opposed blacklisting, because they said they did. At they same time they reaffirmed their stance that Communists should not be allowed to work. And by subpoenaing Cogley and interrogating him, they cast an aura of suspicion around him and anyone else who would try to call blacklisting by its name.

2

The Social Drama

HUAC carefully dramatized the act of informing for purposes of waging political warfare: to intimidate some, to encourage others, and so on. It was theater or, if you like, ritual: a rite of purification that would also put the fear of God (HUAC's man in Heaven) into the as yet unpurified.

Eric Bentley, *Thirty Years of Treason*

Larry Parks was being called upon not to provide information that would lead to an acquittal or conviction, but rather to play a symbolic role in a surrealistic morality play.

Victor Navasky, *Naming Names*

Suddenly I realized that maybe there was a way to handle this that I could live with. And that was to do the following: if I could pretend to observe all the moves of the ritual, as they saw it, I might not have to do some of the things which I couldn't stomach.

David Raskin, Interview, *Red Scare*

The anthropologist Victor Turner wrote extensively about a concept that he usually called "social drama," but also discussed in terms of "performative genres" and "cultural performances." He defined a social drama as "an objectively isolable sequence of social interactions of a conflictive, competitive or agonistic type, [which] may provide materials for many stories depending upon the social-structural, political, psychological, philosophical, and, sometimes, theological perspectives of the narrators."[1] He also described it as "a limited area of transparency on the otherwise opaque surface of regular, uneventful social life."[2] Through the social drama, Turner suggested, we are able to observe the crucial principles of a social structure in action, and to judge their relative dominance at successive points in time.[3] The notion of social drama is fundamental to Turner's influential theory of the relation of art, and particularly the arts that involve performance, to culture. He wrote about this relationship from a number of perspectives, and in a number of contexts, but one of his most straightforward statements about the relationship between social drama and the drama of the theatre was published in 1984:

> Social dramas are the "raw stuff" out of which theatre comes to be created as societies develop in scale and complexity and out of which it is continually regenerated. For I would assert that the social drama form is, indeed, universal, though it may be culturally elaborated in different ways in different societies. . . . The degree of force employed may vary; the tempo may be fast or slow; the rhetoric passionate or restrained; the motivation to produce an unambiguous outcome highly variable. Some societies may regularly favor legal, others ritual, modes of redress. Class, gender, status, age variables, as well as cultural traditions, may affect the styles as well as the vehemence of social dramas.[4]

Turner maintained that a social drama is "processually structured," meaning that it exhibits a regular course of events which can be grouped in four successive phases of public action, which he characterized as breach, crisis, redressive or remedial procedures, and reintegration or schism. The first phase consists of a *breach* of regular norm-governed social relations, which is made publicly visible by the infraction of a community rule. The rule itself is a symbol of a significant relationship between persons or groups that is integral to the solidarity of the community.[5] The breach leads to a second phase of *crisis*, when people take sides, "or rather, are in the process of being induced, seduced, cajoled, nudged, or threatened to take sides by those who confront one another across the revealed breach as prime antagonists." This crisis is highly contagious and irrational, a time when hidden antagonisms become overt and ancient rancours, rivalries, and unresolved vendettas are revived. Crisis may involve physical violence, and it frequently involves the threat of violence. It may also manifest itself in a fear of supernatural dangers, such as threats of witchcraft and fear of retribution by ancestral spirits or deities. The crisis is also defiantly public. It takes its stance in the most public community spaces and challenges the representatives of order to grapple with it.

The response of the authorities to this challenge begins the third phase, the application of *redressive or remedial procedures*. These can be informal or formal, ranging from personal advice to judicial proceedings and public rituals. This phase is the most self-conscious of the four and often causes the community to reexamine its own laws and standards in light of what some of its members have done. This phase can be violent, involving interfactional fighting, witch-hunts, and even revolution, but the violence is presented as an instrument of the group's solidarity and continuity rather than an agent of sectional or personal ends. What Turner calls a "liminal" space – that is a "threshold," a limbo or transitional state that separates the participant in a ritual from both his original state and the transformed state that he eventually achieves through the ritual's enactment – is often created in the crisis phase, in which "a distanced replication and then critique" of the events leading up to and constituting the crisis is presented. This replication, which often involves an act of sacrifice, may be in the rational idiom of the judicial process, such as a trial or congressional hearing, or in the metaphorical or symbolic idiom of the ritual process, such as a blood sacrifice or religious rite, or in both. The fourth phase consists either of the *reintegration* of the disturbed social group, or of the *recognition and legitimation of irreparable schism* between the contending parties. Turner noted that, in many societies, social dramas may escalate from limited or local crises to a general national crisis, as the redressive machinery available at each hierarchical level or social control fails to function.

Turner's anthropological model of the social drama is a useful framework for understanding the HUAC hearings and the events surrounding them. While there is no single act of violation that might be seen as the precipitating breach between the Left and the Right that came to crisis in the fifties, an easily identifiable series of events, stretching back to the Bolshevik Revolution in 1917 and the Pullman strike of 1894, created an ever-escalating tension between the two factions throughout the twenties, thirties, and forties, leading to what surely was a national crisis after World War II. The revolution in Russia led to a dramatic series of repressive measures in the United States, which have been grouped by historians under the rubric of the "Red Scare." In February 1919, the Senate took the occasion of two pro-Soviet rallies in Washington to start an investigation of "any efforts being made to propagate in this country the principles of any party exercising or claiming to exercise authority in Russia . . . [and] any effort to incite the overthrow of the Government of this country, or all governments, by force or by the destruction of life or property or the general cessation of industry."[6] The Justice Department, under Attorney General A. Mitchell Palmer, conducted illegal raids on the left-wing Industrial Workers of the World (IWW) and other groups, resulting in wholesale deportations of the "foreign born." J. Edgar Hoover, a special assistant to the attorney general in 1919, prepared a legal brief on the newly formed Communist Party and Communist Labor Party, which concluded: "These doctrines threaten the happiness of the community, the safety of every individual, and the continuance of every home and fireside. They would destroy the peace of the country and thrust it into a condition of anarchy and lawlessness and immorality that passes imagination."[7]

The division between Left and Right was emphasized by the bitter and very public battles over the conviction and execution of Sacco and Vanzetti in 1927 and, several years later, over the Spanish Civil War, during which leftists went as far as to send volunteer troops – the Lincoln Brigade – to support the left-wing Loyalists who were fighting off the fascistic Franco. The Right, in turn, demonized the Left as desperate and amoral Communist operatives. Of the Lincoln Brigade, for example, Hoover wrote:

> American communists used glittering promises, underhanded tricks, and downright fraud to coax young men to go to Spain. An enlistee might be promised a lucrative position in Spain, cash rewards, or travel accommodations. A young girl would entice unsuspecting men; in return for her favors they would promise to enlist. If necessary, fictitious passports were obtained or enlistees were stowed away on boats. An elaborate "convoy" system was established, individuals being taken from the United States, usually through France, to Spain. Any tactic was used to gain fighting manpower for the communist cause.[8]

One of the most contentious rhetorical battlegrounds was created by the international Communist policy during the thirties of creating a "united" or "popular" front with other left-wing and liberal groups to fight fascism in Europe. From the Left's point of view, "Popular Front" was

> a loose term applied to a functioning coalition of organizations, all of which had in common four main objectives: to press the Roosevelt administration in the direction of a world anti-fascist alliance, to aid the defenders of democracy and the victims of fascist aggression, to counter the widely perceived threat of domestic fascism, and to

defeat the efforts of conservative big business to thwart the trade union movement and block the passage of social reform measures. . . . The fundamental unifying factor – fervent opposition or international and domestic fascism – was never lost from view.[9]

The Left used the metaphor of the "front" in meteorological terms: "fronts are unstable surfaces between bodies of air with different temperature and pressure. They do not mix, but a contact surface is formed which endures as long as the relative pressure stays constant. The Popular Front among American liberals and radicals would last until the Nazi-Soviet Pact suddenly and dramatically curtailed the Communist Party's anti-fascism."[10] To the Right, however, a "front" was a facade for Communist activities, a "Communist front" a collection of fellow travelers who were at best dupes of the small band of dedicated Communists who controlled the group, and at worst Communists "in their hearts,"[11] who hid their true colors by flying the milder liberal banner. As J. Edgar Hoover put it: "The value [to the Party] of fellow travelers and sympathizers lies in their alleged noncommunist affiliation. That is why, in most instances, communist leaders do not attempt to recruit them into the Party. They are more valuable outside: as financial contributors, vocal mouthpieces, or contacts between Party officials and non-communists. They constitute, in fact, fronts for, and defenders of, the Communist Party."[12] The Right was far more successful at conveying its version of the "front" metaphor to the public than the Left was. By the early fifties, to the typical American, the term "Communist Front" meant a subversive group, with the implication that its ultimate purpose was to overthrow the government and install a dictatorship of the proletariat.

Witnesses who were called before the Un-American Activities Committee were often accused of nothing more than participation in some activities that had been sponsored by organizations labeled "fronts," and therefore "subversive," by the attorney general's office, HUAC itself, or the California "baby HUAC," the Tenney Commission. José Ferrer, one of the most contrite and malleable of subpoenaed witnesses, was confronted by Staff Counsel Frank Tavenner:

Mr. Tavenner: The committee is in possession of information indicating your affiliation or connection with quite a number of organizations which have from time to time been cited by various governmental agencies as Communist-front organizations. You, of course, are aware that affiliation with or activities in Communist-front organizations, if true and unexplained, leave [sic] the implication that one is in fact a member of the Communist Party or has been, or that he is in fact a sympathizer of the Communist Party or an encourager of Communist Party concepts and objectives. You agree with that, do you not?

Mr. Ferrer: Yes, this has been made dramatically clear to me recently, Mr. Tavenner.[13]

On the other hand, Edward Dmytryk, the only one of the Hollywood Ten to change his mind and request to come before HUAC as a friendly witness, instructed the Committee on the nature of a Communist front. "When you say 'Communist front,'" he told the congressmen,

> you get the impression it is run by Communists. This isn't always true. I have seen Communist fronts where there are as few as one or two Communists. Also, there are two kinds of fronts. One kind is organized by the Communist Party itself, or by certain Communists; and another is an organization that starts out as an ordinary liberal organization and is infiltrated by Communists. The Communists are tireless workers as I think this committee realizes. Also as I think this committee realizes, one tireless worker in an organization can usually take over that organization. . . . I would say that for every Communist in a Communist-front organization in Hollywood, there were 100 non-Communists, and very few of them had any idea they were dominated by a Communist group. This was not because they were fools, but the Communists are clever enough to cover up that fact, and the work they do overtly appeals to many public-minded citizens.[14]

The thirties were confusing times for both Left and Right. The interest of leftists and liberals in the Communist Party, as well as its membership, shot up during the time when Communists were among the most dedicated opponents of fascism. According to J. Edgar Hoover, there were 7,500 members in the CPUSA in 1930, and 30,000 in 1935.[15] Interest among liberals dropped off sharply with the signing of the Nazi-Soviet Pact in August 1939 and the subsequent invasions of Poland by the Germans and Finland by the Russians. A number of prominent leftists severed their ties with the Soviet-controlled Party at this time, but the diehard Stalinist Communists simply shifted from an antifascist to a peace rhetoric, seeking to keep the United States out of World War II. When Germany invaded the Soviet Union on 22 June 1941, the rhetoric shifted again, and as the USSR became an Ameri-

CHAIRMAN
SENATOR HUGH M. BURNS
FRESNO, CALIFORNIA

SENATOR
CLYDE A. WATSON
ORANGE, CALIFORNIA

SENATOR
NATHAN F. COOMBS
NAPA, CALIFORNIA

Senate Fact-Finding Committee on Un-American Activities

(CREATED PURSUANT TO SENATE RESOLUTION NO. 137)

California Legislature

MARY E. HOPE, SECRETARY
501-502 BRIX BUILDING
FRESNO, CALIFORNIA

VICE-CHAIRMAN
SENATOR NELSON S. DILWORTH
HEMET, CALIFORNIA

SENATOR
EARL D. DESMOND
SACRAMENTO, CALIFORNIA

CHIEF COUNSEL
R. E. COMBS
VISALIA, CALIFORNIA

October 19, 1950

Mr. John J. Throlald
President, Queens College
Flushing, New York

Dear Mr. Throlald:

Your letter of August 31, addressed to Senator Tenney, has been forwarded to me.

We have no information as to the address of Der Arbeiter, or where extra copies may be obtained. The information we have on Mr. Gassner is attached.

Sincerely yours,

Chairman, Senate Fact-Finding Committee on Un-American Activities

GASSNER, John W.

Jan. 1949: Progressive Book Shop pamphlet lists subject as author of "Masters of the Drama."

Contributor to following issues of New Theatre Magazine:

Nov. 1936
April 1936
Aug. 1935
Nov. 1935
Feb. 1936
March 1936
May 1936
June 1936
July 1936
March 1937
April 1937

Made member of the New York Drama Critics Circle, 1937.

One of the sponsors of Child Play Contest conducted by International Workers Order, NYC, Feb. 1937.

Member of faculty of New Theatre School.

Figure 3. The Tenney Commission at work. As this report on the eminent drama critic and scholar John Gassner to the president of Queens College shows, its activities were not restricted to show business.

can ally, the days of the Popular Front returned temporarily as the country rallied to the support of "Uncle Joe" Stalin. According to Hoover, the CPUSA reached its membership peak in 1944, with 80,000 members, trailing off again in the wake of post-war Soviet imperialism and American McCarthyism to a mere 22,600 in 1955, as many as one-third of them FBI agents.[16]

If there was a moment when the decisive breach leading to the HUAC hearings occurred, it was the end of World War II and the beginning of the Cold War, when it became clear that the United States and the Soviet Union would square off in a battle to control international politics and Winston Churchill announced, on 5 March 1946 in Fulton, Missouri, that an "iron curtain" had descended on Europe. As Larry Ceplair and Steven Englund have put it, "the ideological debate became deafening. Under these conditions, the American Communist Party could be seen as a direct extension of the 'forces of darkness,' of the power, duplicity, cynicism, rapacity, and terrorism of Joseph Stalin."[17] It was not difficult in this atmosphere for the Right to depict the Communist Party as the willing pawn of Stalin's rapacious imperialistic designs. As Ceplair and Englund have recognized, however, the key step in the ideological division of the country was the

> linking of all expressions of liberalism and radicalism to communism. Here the right wing relied upon Americans' characteristic nationalism. Communism was "un-American" because it was atheistic, collectivistic, and international. This linking of Americanism to a highly specific set of values – organized religion, private property, and nationalism – made it un-American, hence Communistic, to be critical of, or to wish to change or challenge, those values and the institutions and policies which reflected them. Right-wing spokespeople hammered away at the theme that reformist activists and critics weakened America: they therefore had to be Communistic in identity or sympathy, and, in the national interest, had to be exposed and quarantined.[18]

As the external threat from the Soviet Union increased, the anxiety about a threat from "the enemy within" grew. The fall of China, the news that the Soviets had the atomic bomb, and the beginning of the Korean War heightened the state of anxiety. It is only in this context that one can begin to understand an attitude such as that of Judge Irving Kaufman, who said to Julius and Ethel Rosenberg, while delivering his unprecedented death sentence for conspiracy to steal atomic secrets: "I believe

your conduct . . . has already caused the Commur
with the resultant casualties exceeding 50,000 ar
millions more of innocent people may pay the
[The defendants had not been convicted of trea
betrayal you undoubtedly have altered the cours
advantage of the country."[19] In his book *Masters of*
presented the Right's view of the danger represen
party. The ambition of every Party member, he \
United States a communist nation": "He works c
dream a reality, to steal your rights, liberties, and [
he lives in the United States, he is a supporter of a
ing an alien line of thought. He is a conspirator
Although the Party was small, he warned, it was e
ful. Not only were Communists tireless workers fo
trained by means of "thought control" to be unq
and to bend others to their will. "This select grou
he wrote, "must be made superobedient, meanin
the hope of return. They must be constantly whipp
zied enthusiasm and never allowed to relax. The m
up' he is endangered; a noncommunist thought m
tion to the trained Party operatives, "the so-calle
never have attended a communist meeting and ma
Party organization. Yet, because of the spell of con
trol, they knowingly do the Party's work. Perhaps
enced by Marxist writings or the professed aims o
issues. In any case, deluded by communist propa;
render active assistance."[22] Because it came from th
eral Bureau of Investigation, an "expert" on Americ;
1919, most of the American public saw no reaso
characterization. The American Communist was cor
as a completely dedicated, unnaturally energetic to
that emanated from Moscow to take over America
unions, schools, entertainment and information s
State Department and the Army, on the way to ov
can government. Before Joseph McCarthy burst or
the House Committee on Un-American Activities w
ing angel.

The "redressive procedure" that the United Sta
address the crisis of ideological division was the co
a judicial procedure with a great deal of latitude,

who conducted it and few rights for the subpoenaed witnesses
vere subjected to it. Early witnesses before HUAC objected to the
nittee's denial of what they felt were their constitutional rights as
icans before an official inquiry, particularly the right to face and
-examine their accusers and the right to make a statement and
it entered into the official record in answer to the charges that
made against them. The Committee, on the other hand, insisted
t was within its rights as a committee conducting a congressional
ng to refuse these requests and to force witnesses to answer ques-
about their political beliefs and associations under pain of being
for contempt of Congress. These issues were gradually worked out
e courts during the height of the "un-American activities" crisis,
fundamental clarifications about the constitutional rights of Amer-
citizens who are called before congressional committees ultimately
; made. There was a dramatic difference, for example, in the way
·ss Larry Parks was treated by the Committee in 1951 and the way
l Dellinger was treated in 1968. When Parks's lawyer, Louis Man-
isked whether Parks would be cited for contempt if he refused to
le to the Committee's demand that he name names in executive
m, the dialogue continued:

/ood: The Committee makes no threats.
landel: We haven't approached it as a matter of threat. Just to clear
ninking so that he is fully informed in his own mind of the conse-
ces of following that path.
/ood: Counsel for the Committee did not discuss that phase of it. It is
ely possible, if Mr. Parks placed himself in the position here of being
ntempt of Congress, that the Committee may request a citation for
ourpose. On the other hand, it may not. I cannot speak for the Com-
e. Does that answer your question?[23]

nteen years later, the courts had determined that a congressional
nittee must clearly direct the witness to answer its questions and
tention to cite him or her for contempt if a citation was to hold
court. It must also make it clear to a witness the relevance of the
tion to the purpose of the hearing. Witness Dellinger clearly had
: rights before the Committee that witness Parks had had:

onley: Mr. Dellinger, my question is: Were the following persons pres-
t this conference with you: [long list of names] . . .

Mr Gutman [Dellinger's lawyer]: May I ask the legislative purpose of this question, Mr. Chairman?

Mr. Ichord: The chair will advise the counsel that, in view of the fact that this was a meeting with the North Vietnamese and other allies, friendly nations with the North Vietnamese, in view of the purview of these hearings and that the witness was a leader in the Chicago demonstration and he has so testified, it is a pertinent question and within the subject of inquiry.

Mr Gutman: I fail to see the pertinency, Mr. Chairman.

Mr. Ichord: These are individuals who attended the conference with the gentleman. The counsel has advised me that they have been so identified in the newspapers. The witness was there, and the Chair will have to rule that it is a proper question.

Mr Gutman: Mr. Chairman, since you have just stated –

Mr. Ichord: You have the right to advise with your witness if you desire, but you haven't been called to testify, Mr. Gutman.

Mr Gutman: I understand. We are talking on the question of relevancy. If I advise him on the question what to say, on the legal point of relevancy, he is merely going to have to parrot what I suggest to him.

Mr. Ichord: I think we will have to abide by the rules. Go ahead. You will be given time to confer with your client.

Mr. Dellinger: If that is the way you want it.[24]

In the early years, however, the Committee acted as though any question were fair game. It inquired into the most private beliefs and associations of citizens, holding over them the threat of prosecution as well as blacklisting if they refused to answer.

The function of the House Committee on Un-American Activities was clearly not a legislative one. Its function was much more fundamental to the social polity than that. In the un-American activities crisis, HUAC's function was what Frazer in *The Golden Bough* calls "the expulsion of evil" from the community. Its witnesses – Communists, left-wingers, liberals, and civil libertarians alike – became the scapegoat that served the society in this crisis, the "visible and tangible vehicle" to convey away "evils [that] are invisible and intangible."[25] The hearings provided a scapegoating ritual, the main object of which is "to effect a total clearance of all the ills that have been infesting a people."[26] As Goodman has noted,

the philosophy that flowered under the klieg lights of 1947 would be an inspiration for much of the Committee's later work: a philosophy that held not only that Communism was a subversive doctrine, not only that Communists in sensitive positions were threats to the nation, but that the presence in this land of every individual Communist and fellow traveler and former Communist who would not purge himself was intolerable; that the just fate of every such creature was to be exposed in his community, routed from his job, and driven into exile.[27]

In its construction of the scapegoat, the Committee relied on a number of techniques that René Girard has identified as characteristic of scapegoating, or as he puts it, "collective persecution." Scapegoating occurs, in Girard's view, when the persecutors, or the community collectively, "convince themselves that a small number of people, or even a single individual, despite his relative weakness, is extremely harmful to the whole of society." Their accusation of diabolical wrongdoing "bridges the gap between the insignificance of the individual and the enormity of the social body."[28]

HUAC was not subtle in its attempts to demonize Communists. One example is its series of "100 Things You Should Know About Communism" pamphlets, which included publications on Communism's putative effect on religion, education, labor unions, and government in addition to its overall effect on the nation. Cast in the familiar question-and-answer format of the religious catechism, the pamphlets offered American citizens the Committee's answers to the questions that it considered basic to a knowledge of American Communism. The general pamphlet begins:

1. What is Communism?
   A system by which one small group seeks to rule the world.
2. Has any nation ever gone Communist in a free election?
   No.
3. Then how do the Communists try to get control?
   Legally or illegally, any way they can. Communism's first big victory was through bloody revolution. Every one since has been by military conquest, or internal corruption, or the threat of these.
   CONSPIRACY is the basic method of Communism in countries it is trying to capture.
   IRON FORCE is the basic method of Communism in countries it has already captured.
4. What would happen if Communism should come into power in this country?
   Our capital would move from Washington to Moscow. Every man, woman, and child would come under Communist discipline.[29]

46

The *Communism and Education* pamphlet was even more blunt in its characterization of Communist evil:

1. What is Communism?
   A conspiracy to conquer and rule the world by any means, legal or illegal, in peace or in war.
2. Is it aimed at me?
   Right between your eyes.
3. What do the Communists want?
   To rule your mind and your body from the cradle to the grave.[30]

The Committee publications ascribed a series of negative characteristics to individual Communists that helped to stigmatize them for the public. "Why do people become Communists?" it asked itself, answering: "Basically, because they seek power and recognize the opportunities that Communism offers the unscrupulous." What is Communism's greatest strength? "Its secret appeal to the lust for power. Some people have a natural urge to dominate others in all things."[31] While an unnatural lust for power and domination was the principal theme in the Committee's characterization of Communists, other unsavory qualities were also suggested. In answer to the question, "What's biting these people, anyhow?" The education pamphlet replied:

> Here is at least one part of the answer given by John Hanna, a professor of Columbia University, who was formerly with the Farm Credit Administration and chief analyst with the United States Courts' Administration Office:
> "The girls' schools and women's colleges contain some of the most loyal disciples of Russia.
> "Teachers there are often frustrated females. They have gone through bitter struggles to attain their positions.
> "A political dogma based on hatred expresses their personal attitude."
> Politics based on hatred and self-pity has the same appeal for men, too, who feel frustrated by life.[32]

Finally, the Committee was not ashamed of just plain name-calling. "What is the difference in fact between a Communist and a Fascist?" it asked itself, answering: "None worth noticing."[33]

Girard maintains that "certain accusations are so characteristic of collective persecution that their very mention makes modern observers suspect violence in the air." Among these are "violent crimes which choose as object those people whom it is most criminal to attack"; sexual crimes that "transgress the taboos that are considered the strictest in the society in question"; "religious crimes, such as profanation of the host. Here, too, it is the strictest taboos that are transgressed."[34] The attacks on Communists generally focused on religious taboos. Representative John Rankin remarked on the floor of the House that "Communism is older than Christianity. . . . It hounded and persecuted the Savior during his earthly ministry, inspired his crucifixion, derided him in his dying agony, and then gambled for his garments at the foot of the cross."[35] J. Edgar Hoover wrote of atheism as "the first step toward communism." As an example, he evinced the young Lenin, who at sixteen, Hoover said, "ceased to believe in God. It is reported that he tore the cross from his neck, threw this sacred relic to the ground, and spat upon it."[36] "Communism is more than an economic, political, social, or philosophical doctrine," Hoover wrote. "It is a way of life; a false, materialistic 'religion.' It would strip man of his belief in God, his heritage of freedom, his trust in love, justice, and mercy. Under communism, all would become, as so many already have, twentieth-century slaves."[37] In his review of *Witness*, the memoir of star former-Communist witness Whittaker Chambers, Richard Nixon praised it for being "the first book of its kind which acknowledges the great hold of Communism on the human mind – which does not dismiss it as a cellar conspiracy which can be abolished by police methods." Nixon went on to agree with Chambers that "Communism is evil because it denies God and defies man. 'Man without God is a beast,' says Chambers. 'Never more beastly than when he is most intelligent about his beastliness.' But evil though it is, Communism has a tremendously malignant and potent appeal all over the world and right here in the United States."[38]

After establishing Communism as the enemy to the Judaeo-Christian tradition, the next step for the anti-Communist was to represent it as a rival religious faith, locked in a deadly contest for control of the American way of life. "Something utterly new has taken root in America during the past generation," warned Hoover, "a communist mentality representing a systematic, purposive, and conscious attempt to destroy Western civilization and roll history back to the age of barbaric cruelty and despotism, all in the name of 'progress.' Evil is depicted as good, terror as justice, hate as love, and obedience to a foreign master as patriotism."[39] Every communist "considered Lenin a god," he wrote, and Stalin "a virtual god on earth," but the reality was that Lenin "introduced into human relations a new dimension of evil and depravity not surpassed by Genghis Khan or Attila."[40] HUAC addressed the issue in its *Communism and Religion* pamphlet:

34. Where is the headquarters of the Communist faith?
    The Kremlin, Moscow, Russia.
35. Who is the head of that faith?
    Joseph Stalin, because he is the head of the Government of Russia and chief of the Communist Party of Russia. To a Communist in the United States or any other country, Stalin's word is final.

    For a Communist to defy Stalin is as scandalous to other Communists as for a religious-minded person to blaspheme God.[41]

For the Committee, the charge of Communism was indistinguishable from the charge of atheism. Of composer Earl Robinson, Staff Director Richard Arens demanded: "Now tell us about anything you have done in the use of art as a weapon, and your music as a weapon, in this global struggle in which the West and the East are engaged in, international communism, godless, atheistic communism; tell us what you have done to use your art to engage in that struggle against communism."[42]

While it is easy to see the Committee's participation in the general process of scapegoating the Communists, the function of the hearings as ritual needs more precise analysis. As Richard Schechner has suggested, a ritual can be seen variously as a structure with formal qualities and relationships; as a performance process; as collective or individual experience; or as a set of operations in human social and religious life.[43] Most useful here is to view ritual in Victor Turner's sense of "transformative performance . . . operating through a multiplicity of expressive genres and symbols in the full range of sensory codes, with the goal of relating chaos and cosmos, byss and abyss, flow and reflexivity, to one another in the heightened and deepened consciousness of participants."[44] Turner obviates the perennial question of where the dividing line between ritual and performance resides by suggesting that ritual *is* performance, but performance of a special kind. It is performance with designated work to do within the culture that develops it. It is also characterized by repetition and difference. It has a series of actions and dialogues that are repeated with each enactment. These constant elements provide the framework within which the cultural transformation takes place, as each individual enactment performs a function. The progenitors of the ritual – in this case, the Committee – perform an action on the subject – the witness – which makes a change within the social group. In the HUAC hearing, the anxiety and dis-ease of the early fifties is blamed on the Communists, and the witness becomes, in Frazer's terms, the vehicle through which the evil is expelled from the society. Either the witness denounces Communism and all his associates who are tainted with it, thus casting off the evil himself, or, by remaining silent, he becomes the vessel that contains the evil of Communism. Having contained it, the society can then render it harmless by imprisoning the witness or by blacklisting him, and thus purging him from the community. The ritual of the hearing is thus precisely the ritual of scapegoating. As Eric Bentley put it, "HUAC carefully dramatized the act of informing for purposes of waging political warfare: to intimidate some, to encourage others, and so on. It was theater or, if you like, ritual: a rite of purification that would also put the fear of God (HUAC's man in Heaven) into the as yet unpurified."[45]

Repetition does not diminish the theatrical impact of ritual, but, as long as the cultural need is there, may even emphasize it. As Girard writes: "All rituals tend to be transformed into the theatrical performances in which the actors play their parts with all the more exuberance for having played them *so many times before.* This does not mean that the participants do not experience real suffering. The drama would not be as effective as it obviously is if there were not moments of real suffering for the city and its surroundings, in other words for the community."[46] Nor does the reflexivity of the ritual, the consciousness of the participants that they are playing roles, affect the power and functionality of the ritual itself. As Turner has noted, the critical difference between aesthetic theatre and ritual is that "the actors on stage must always seem to be the characters they portray or they have failed; the ritualist must always seem to be nothing other than what he is, a frail human being playing with those things that kill us for their sport."[47]

The Committee not only was aware of the theatricality that was essential to its endeavor, but occasionally discussed its effectiveness with witnesses. During the Hollywood Ten hearings, Congressman Vail asked Emmet Lavery, president of the Screen Writers Guild, "Don't you think that the gentlemen who appeared before this committee have dramatized communism to some degree by the exhibition they put on?"[48] The literary critic Granville Hicks, perhaps the most widely respected friendly witness who was a former Communist, presented to Chairman Walter precisely the way in which he thought the Committee hearings had created an unhealthy "atmosphere of fear throughout the United States":

Mr. Hicks: I think the fear in this country is in part a very real and understandable fear of the Soviet Union and its agents. It is a fear that we should all share. It is a perfectly real thing. Over and above that, I think there is a mood of rather vague apprehension that is not rational and that is dangerous, and I do feel that that mood of irrational apprehension has been encouraged in part by congressional – I will say legislative investigating committees. . . .

Mr. Walter: . . . What can this committee do to make the American people believe, outside of the mistakes that are made, understand, that we are not determined to search into men's minds for ideas, but that we want to know what the extent of the menace is? Now, you say it is exaggerated. You say we are too worried, and I think it is our job to find out if that is the fact.

Mr. Hicks: Well, for some reason, the emphasis in all these investigating committees always falls on the fact of how much communism there is and never on how little there is.

Mr. Walter: That's right.

Mr. Hicks: It seems to me I have been sitting around here for 2 days in which it has been demonstrated that there were 10 or 12 Communists at Harvard 14 years ago and that perhaps there is one still there. Now, I would honestly think, if you could just say to the public, "Look, that's all," instead of saying, "Look how much that is; isn't that terrible?" you might do a good deal to allay the fear that is sweeping over this country.[49]

No one demonstrated a fuller sense of the relation between the theatrical format and the ritual function of the Committee's hearings than actor Lionel Stander, who maintained that his career had suffered since Martin Dies had refused to "clear" him in 1940, and despite repeated requests to come before the Committee in 1951 when he was named by witness Marc Lawrence, was not called to testify until 1953. Stander asked that the television cameras be shut off, noting "if this were a live television show in which my entire testimony would be seen by the American people just the way I make it, I don't think I would have as strenuous objections."[50] Stander's testimony was a carefully crafted performance that balanced the theatrical values of the ritual with an awareness of the enormity of its power over citizens. His performance strategies are evident even in a brief excerpt of his testimony:

Mr. Tavenner: Well, do you recall whether you left Hollywood in 1948 or 1949?

Mr. Stander: I – it might have been in 1948 or 1949. I'm not sure. I went to make a personal appearance tour of the night-club circuit, which was the only thing left to me after being blacklisted by the major studios –

Mr. Tavenner: Will you tell –

Mr. Stander: By merely newspaper accusation, without anybody charging me with anything. In fact, the last time I appeared here the Chairman very specifically said that this committee didn't charge me with anything, and I swore under oath – I would like, if you want, to introduce the record of my testimony here in August 27, 1940.

Mr. Velde: Well, you are not –

Mr. Tavenner: I stated in the beginning –

Mr. Velde: (Continuing). charged with anything.

Mr. Stander: I am not charged –

Mr. Velde: You do understand, as I stated before, you are not charged with anything this time.

Mr. Stander: I am not charged with anything?

Mr. Velde: You are not charged with anything, Mr. Stander. You are here –

Mr. Stander: I would like the record to show I am not charged with being a member of the Communist Party; I am not charged with lying under oath, because I have made continuous oaths to various governmental agencies. You are not charging me with being a Communist, right? . . .

Mr. Clardy: Will you subside until the chairman finishes?

Mr. Velde: You are brought here as a witness.

Mr. Stander: I am a witness –

Mr. Velde: Please don't –

Mr. Stander: Not a defendant. I haven't been accused of anything. I want that very straight, because through newspaper headlines people get peculiar attitudes. Mere appearance here is tantamount – not just appearance; the mere fact, in my case, I was subpenaed [*sic*], is tantamount – to being blacklisted because people say, "What is an actor doing in front of the Un-American Activities Committee?"

Mr. Clardy: Why did you want to appear before the committee so badly, then, if that is the case?

Mr. Stander: Because I was told by my agent if I appeared before the committee, and the Committee was a fair Committee, and allowed me to refute Lawrence's testimony that I would be able to get back in television and motion pictures. I had made 11 television shows in a row, and one of the biggest TV agencies and producers had told my agent that if I went – could get before the committee and could again swear under oath that I wasn't [a Communist], I would have my own TV program, which meant $150,000 a year to me.

Mr. Clardy: Mr. Stander –

Mr. Stander: So, I had a hundred-and-fifty-thousand-buck motive –

Mr. Clardy: Mr. Stander, will you subside?

Mr. Stander: For coming before the committee. . . .

Mr. Clardy: If you will just subside and answer the questions, fairly and directly, and truthfully, I am sure you will accomplish your purpose.

Mr. Stander: Are you inferring –
Mr. Clardy: Now, just a minute, Mr. Stander.
Mr. Stander: (Continuing). Anything I said wasn't the truth?
Mr. Clardy: Mr. Stander, may I tell you something? Unless you do that, whether you realize it or not, your performance is not going to be regarded as funny, because this is serious business – if you will subside and answer the questions as they are put to you, frankly, honestly, and without attempting to be smart of funny, you will have accomplished your purpose; otherwise you are going to defeat it.
Mr. Stander: I want to state right now that I was not –
Mr. Clardy: Will you please subside?
Mr. Stander: (continuing). Trying to be smart –
Mr. Velde: Mr. Stander –
Mr. Stander: (continuing). Or funny. . . .
Mr. Clardy: Won't you be a gentleman and listen to the questions and answer them? Unless you do, the very thing you want to refute is going to be left in the minds of the public indelibly. You are going to be stamped as something you may want to say you are not. Now, if you will just go along with this committee, you will have no trouble at all; but if you don't, if you continue with what you are doing, or going to do or have been doing, I am going to suggest to the chairman that you are putting on a show, that you are doing it for no other purpose than to make a show, and I am going to ask him to turn on the lights and cameras so that your performance may be recorded for posterity. Now, if you will subside and go along, I am not going to make that request.
Mr. Stander: Mr. Chairman, may I state that, first, to clear up this misunderstanding, I have never been more deadly serious in my life.
Mr. Clardy: All right, then –
Mr. Stander: If anything I said –
Mr. Clardy: That is the question.
Mr. Stander: (continuing). Seemed humorous or funny, I assure you it was purely coincidental and doesn't mirror what I deeply feel, because my entire career and the respect of my fellow artists and the American people is at stake, and I don't think that is very funny and I don't mean to be funny.
Mr. Clardy: And I do not think so either. I am a new member of this committee, and I want to give you all possible opportunity to say what you have to say, but I want you to do it in the proper way.[51]

Stander got the better of the congressmen in the battle over control of the theatre of the hearing, but they maintained the upper hand in the ritual. Stander remained on the blacklist.

The process of creating the scapegoat precedes any ritual cleansing such as occurred in the Committee hearings. Girard holds that the scapegoat can be the object of "collective persecutions," acts of violence committed directly by a mob of murderers such as the persecution of the Jews who were held responsible for the Black Plague in medieval Europe, or "collective resonances of persecutions," acts of violence, "such as witch-hunts, that are legal in form but stimulated by the extremes of public opinion."[52] Since the targets of the HUAC "investigations" were harassed and deprived of employment, and at the worst imprisoned, but only occasionally subjected to violence, they would certainly be classed as a more civilized "resonance" of the impulse of persecution. As Girard notes, however, the distinction is not essential.[53] The process of scapegoating was clear to leftists and liberals, and an occasional brave witness attempted to put it before the Committee. One of the most articulate of these was Arthur Garfield Hays, who spoke for the American Civil Liberties Union in 1948. Articulating the analogy between the Committee's tactics and those of Nazi Germany that was often in the minds of witnesses, Hays told the Committee:

> I was in Germany in 1933 when it came under Hitler in the days of the Reichstag fire. He had two scapegoats – the Communists and the Jews. The Communists were most important. He was saving the people from the Reds and they passed a law barring all Communists from the Reichstag and as a result the anti-Communists had the authority and they repealed the German constitution. He did exactly what you are doing here. He barred the Communists from the Reichstag, and if Congress adopts this principle, Congress must bar a minority party or their delegates or voters.[54]

Not surprisingly, the Committee was not very open to this interpretation of their project.

The Committee's attitude toward their activities was in keeping with Girard's description of the persecutors in the activity of collective persecution. "The persecutors," he wrote, "believe in the guilt of their victim; they are imprisoned in the illusion of persecution that is no simple idea but a full system of representation."[55] They "are caught up in the 'logic' of the representation of persecution from a persecutor's standpoint, and they cannot break away."[56] This is because the persecutors have what Girard calls a "naïve conviction of right" that keeps them from seeing their punishment of the victim as anything other than justice. "Naïve persecutors *are unaware of what they are doing.* Their con-

54

science is too good to deceive their readers systematically, and they present things as they see them. They do not suspect that by writing their accounts they are arming posterity against them. This is true of the infamous 'witch-hunts' of the sixteenth century. It is still true today."[57] As usual, Hoover is the most eloquent example of this frame of mind. He was very clear about the identity of America's "enemy within." The "trained" Party member is the one "on whom the Party depends to commit espionage, derail a speeding train, and organize riots. If asked, gun in hand, to assault the Capitol of the United States, he will be expected to obey. These members are today working to promote a Soviet America: some in undercover assignments, some in communist-front organizations, others as Party officials. They are the offensive shock troops – confidently expecting that the precise moment will arrive when conditions will make feasible the revolutionary overthrow of our government."[58] As for the collective danger, he wrote in 1958 that

> the Communist Party is a highly disciplined tool of the Soviet Union in the United States. In the thirty-eight years since it came into being, it has developed a trained and potentially effective leadership that overnight, should the situation become favorable, could expand into a mass organization of great potential power. . . . The present menace of the Communist Party in the United States grows in direct ratio to the rising feeling that it is a small, dissident element and need not be feared. As we relax our protection and ease up on security measures, we move closer and closer to a "fool's paradise."[59]

It needs to be emphasized in the face of statements like these that, although they were guilty of shamelessly deceitful defenses of the outrageous crimes of the government of the Soviet Union, American Communists were never proven to be the subversives that Hoover and the Committee constantly accused them of being, and that the general public assumed they were.

The victims of the Show Business hearings were particularly guiltless of any act of sabotage, or any planning of sabotage, or any conspiracy to plan sabotage of the government of the United States. As Ceplair and Englund have noted, "there is no evidence to indicate that the Hollywood Reds ever, in any way, conspired, or tried to conspire against the United States Government, spied for the Soviet Union, or even undermined any social institution in this country. . . . Nor did they ever try formally to propagandize Hollywood movies in the literal sense of 'subversion,' i.e., 'to undermine the principles of, or corrupt.'"[60] Hoover had an explanation for the lack of subversive activities, of course, demonstrating the power of what Girard calls the "system of representation" in which he was locked. Despite nearly forty years of ceaseless activity by tireless apparachiks, Hoover explained,

> the Communist Party, USA, has not reached the point where prepa-
> rations for sabotage are vital to its future plans. Its small numbers,
> fear of FBI penetration of its inner discussions, and the existence of
> federal laws against sabotage and insurrection militate against such
> plans. So far the communists have carefully refrained from any show
> of terrorism. Any such act, even random sorties, the communists real-
> ize, would cause more harm to the Party by counter prosecutive
> action than any damage achieved by violence. Moreover, basic com-
> munist revolutionary tactics dictate against any such sabotage
> attempts until the eve of hostilities, which we pray and hope will
> never come. According to communist teaching, the comrades should
> not "tip their hands" until the "time is ripe."[61]

Despite his acknowledgment of the thorough FBI infiltration among these extraordinarily law-abiding revolutionaries, Hoover created the impression, and apparently believed, that they could turn into efficient terrorists at a moment's notice, when the time was deemed to be right.

Girard notes several characteristics that are endemic to the representation of the scapegoat by the persecutors, characteristics which help to disguise the role of scapegoat by turning the victim of persecution into a criminal, a monster, or a source of contamination that will destroy the body politic. The imagery of contamination is perhaps the most common means by which the scapegoat is constructed as a dangerous threat to the community which persecutes him. "In many myths," Girard notes, "the wretched person's presence is enough to contaminate everything around him, infecting men and beasts with the plague, ruining crops, poisoning food, causing game to disappear, and sowing discord around him. Everything shrivels under his feet and the grass does not grow again. He produces disasters as easily as a fig tree produces figs. He need only be himself."[62] In an article for the *Hollywood Reporter*, Roy Brewer, Ronald Reagan, and others representing the Motion Picture Industry Council used a rather wild mixture of scatological and contamination imagery to imply the evil they saw in the Communist: "Any American who associates with the Communist Party is befouled. He is befouled, not by the person who exposes him, but by his own act in joining a traitorous conspiracy against his own country. This has been confirmed by the U.S. Supreme Court decision upholding the Smith Act. Read then a story which should interest you, a story of a person who finally realized that he had been besmirched by his association with the Communist Party and who sought our help in rising from Communist slime to cleaner ground."[63] The language of contamination often entered the Committee hearings in the form of metaphors of illness, such as cancers invading the body politic. Representative F. Edward Hébert (D-Louisiana) engaged in a bit of metaphorical sparring with ACLU President Arthur Garfield Hays in 1948:

Mr. Hébert: . . . when a disease is spreading either on the body politic or on the body human, it behooves us as intelligent human beings to do something to retard it. We ought to treasure our way of life. You must know that freedom can destroy freedom.
Mr. Hays: Congressman, you mean to say that under our form of government we should protect people from ideas that may contaminate them? Isn't it the very fundamentals of our Government that people are entitled to protection from everything but ideas. And do you think by law you can protect people from ideas we don't like?
Mr. Hébert: I propose to do something about them. That same argument, the spread of disease – all these signs around – particularly the drive against venereal disease – the more you say about it, the more you make it popular?
Mr. Hays: If you cancel the spread of books or literature that will contaminate you, the Congress interrupts us in spreading ideas. Either it is free speech or nothing.[64]

The language of contamination was linked in the Right's rhetoric with the notion of "thought control." The fear was that, like a creeping disease, the ideas of Communism would take over individual citizens without their knowing it, thus infecting a cell of the body politic. When enough cells were infected, the body politic would succumb to the disease. The power ascribed to Communist propagandizing was immense, and the fear generated by this rhetoric was commensurate.

Of the imagery of monstrosity, Girard writes, "physical and moral monstrosity are heaped together in myths that justify the persecution of the infirm. The fact that other stereotypes of persecution surround them leaves no room for doubt. If this were a rare conjunction it might be dubious, but innumerable examples can be found; it is the daily fare of mythology."[65] In the context of religious imagery that provided the rhetorical framework for the right-wing attack on Communism, the monstrous often became the demon. As Hoover wrote, "the communist is not an angel of mercy, ministering to the weak oppressed, and wounded, but a menacing demon spattered with blood and wielding a hammer and sickle of iron"[66]

As noted earlier, Girard indicates that the crimes ascribed to the scapegoat are fundamental attacks on the very foundation of cultural order, in this case, particularly religious institutions. Although the Committee routinely sent out press releases accusing people of being members of "subversive organizations" and implying that they were guilty of seeking to overthrow the government, its hearings led to only one conviction other than those for Contempt of Congress: the conviction of Alger Hiss for perjury in January of 1950. Although the only legitimate function of the hearings was investigation, they were in reality rituals of accusation and degradation. While a particularly ardent Committee member occasionally let slip his real belief about the Committee's function, as when John Rankin told Hanns Eisler, "this committee has given you more than a fair deal, more than a fair trial, more than you would have gotten in any other country in the world,"[67] it most often asserted its innocence of accusatory or punitive motives. Chairman Walter, for example, reminded Michael Blankfort:

Mr. Walter: We have not accused anybody of anything. When these witnesses have been subpenaed [sic] it is because we have every reason to believe they possess information that will aid us in letting the American people see to what extent this Communist conspiracy has gone in our society.
Mr. Blankfort: Yes, sir; I realize that. I don't say that –
Mr. Walter: We do not accuse anybody of anything.
Mr. Blankfort: I agree with you. I haven't said that you have.[68]

Despite their protestations that they were not a forensic body, the Committee required a tremendous amount of legal preparation on the part of witnesses. A 1951 article in *Variety* indicates the lengths to which witnesses had to go to defend themselves, even when they were willing to go before the Committee, admit their "guilt," and name names. John Garfield and José Ferrer, both movie stars and valuable properties to the studios, were provided with studio resources when they were called to testify. "Both are preparing to explain and defend every action of their professional and personal lives," the article reported, and both "have employed top counsel and spent a large amount of time and money in recent weeks going over their own actions and motives. Both have strongly denied any tie with Communism now or in the past, and they are preparing to prove their denials." What's more, they were "understood" to have gone so far as to hire investigators of their own to dig up anything be construed as derogatory to themselves, "so that they'll be thoroughly prepared with answers whether the point is false rumor or based on some shred of fact. It is understood that attorneys for the two actors have insisted upon such a procedure as a prelude to taking on the cases. They've questioned the actors exhaustively themselves and sought outside evidence in order to be assured that they are not putting themselves on the spot by defending clients of dubious political backgrounds."[69] Garfield's attorney was Louis Nizer, of the New York law firm that represented Paramount. Ferrer's chief representative, backed up by several others in Los Angeles and New York, was Abe Fortas, who had represented Owen Lattimore. Ferrer was "cleared" after a good deal of public repentance. Garfield died of a heart attack shortly before he was scheduled to make his second appearance before the Committee.

Girard writes that the persecutors "see themselves as completely passive, purely reactive, totally controlled by this scapegoat at the very moment when they rush to his attack. They think that all initiative comes from him. There is only room for a single cause in their field of vision, and its triumph is absolute, it absorbs all other causality: it is the scapegoat."[70] Thus, rather than perceiving their role in initiating a ritual purge, they see themselves as purely passive in the descent of evil upon the community, completely reactive in their confrontation with it. As friendly "expert" witness James Burnham put it in supporting the outlawing of the Communist Party, "it is the Communists, and they alone, that constitute a clear, present, and powerful threat."[71] The community forces that align themselves against the scapegoat are always the same in Girard's view: "They can all be found in the witch-hunts or in the great totalitarian regressions of the present day. First there are the religious leaders, then the politicians, and above all the crowd. They all participate in the action – at first separately, but gradually more and more in unison. Note that all these forces intervene in the order of their importance, beginning with the weakest and ending with the strongest. The conspiracy of religious leaders is of symbolic but little real importance."[72] This was certainly the case in the alignment against Communism. The calls for repression from the religious Right, by figures such as Father Coughlin, evangelist Billy Graham, and Cardinals Cushing and Spellman, proceeded from an awareness of the direct threat to their own religious ideology of the atheism espoused by Marx and Lenin. "My own theory about Communism," said Graham in 1957, "is that it is master-minded by Satan. . . . I think there is no other explanation for the tremendous gains of Communism in which they seem to outwit us at every turn, unless they have supernatural power and wisdom and intelligence given to them."[73] The politicians followed their lead and adopted their rhetoric, and the public accepted the anti-Communist ideology as a defining framework for the nation's policies, foreign and domestic. When it comes to collective persecution, Girard remarks, "Everyone is more or less equally responsible but no one will admit it."[74]

The Ritual of the Hearings

Because the crime against society that the hearings were set up to root out and condemn had only a metaphorical existence, the Committee had to invent a concrete one. Since Communism, let alone participation in leftist "front" groups, was not a crime, the hearings themselves generated a crime for which Communists and "Communist sympathizers" could be punished – Contempt of Congress. By establishing the ritual, the Committee trapped the scapegoat into a situation in which he would automatically be punished. Admission of Communist sympathies or evoking the Constitutional protection of the First or Fifth Amendments meant blacklisting; naming others meant being shunned by the Left, and possibly blacklisted anyway, as in the case of Larry Parks; refusing to say anything or to name names meant being cited for contempt of Congress and possibly imprisoned. Anyone the Committee chose to subpoena could become a criminal/victim just by being named. The ritual was self-sustaining and satisfying for the populace, and it could be performed at the will of the Committee whenever the need was felt.

In its early days, when the Committee was freely criticized both by individuals and by such organizations as the Committee for the First Amendment, it was somewhat defensive about its activities. In his opening statement at the 29 October 1947 hearings, Parnell Thomas found it necessary to state that "the committee's authority to conduct such an investigation, under authority of Public Law 601, is crystal clear. We have not violated and we are not violating the rights of any American citizen, not even the rights of the Communists whose first allegiance is to a foreign government." What's more, he said, "I am proud to say that this committee has not been swayed, intimidated, or influenced by either Hollywood glamor, pressure groups, threats, ridicule, or high-pressure tactics on the part of high-paid puppets and apologists for certain elements of the motion-picture industry."[75] By 1951, Committee members found that all they needed was bluster. At the Hollywood hearings that year, Congressman Doyle said that the idea that HUAC was interested in persecuting anyone was "damnably false." At the same hearing, Chairman Wood said, "If we could eliminate from the entertainment world people who decline to answer if they are members of the Communist Party, it would make me very happy."[76] In the context of the country's growing anxiety about "the enemy within" and the ever-deepening gulf between the Left and Right during the late forties and early fifties, the Committee hearings became a scapegoating ritual by which "Communists," a label which came to include everyone who had ever supported a cause that had also been supported by Popular-Front organizations, could be assigned the blame for the country's anxiety and division, then effectively purged and punished, and welcomed back only when they had undergone a ritual confession and affirmed their new loyalty to the values of the community. As Walter Goodman has remarked, despite the Committee's claim that it was not persecuting anyone, the Hollywood hearings investigated "no espionage, no promise of legislation, no exposure of propaganda, and not much information except in the way of marginal sociology. It was a punitive expedition pure and simple, a purging of the undesirables."[77]

Through trial-and-error after the ill-fated attempt by the Hollywood Ten to seek the protection of the First Amendment, the hearings developed a clear ritual framework, which had five parts. The first, meant to establish the "guilt" of the witness, was what the Committee, in reference to a popular radio quiz-show, often referred to as the "sixty-four dollar question": *"Are you now, or have you ever been, a member of the Communist Party?"* The witness's answer to, or refusal to answer, this question immediately established his or her function in the ritual of purgation. The most unfriendly witnesses seized the occasion for a direct challenge to the Committee's right to inquire into a citizen's political beliefs, while the Committee used it as an occasion to establish the "uncooperativeness" of the witness. The following exchange between John Howard Lawson and Chairman Parnell Thomas gives a good sense of the conflicting performance strategies at work within the ritual:

Mr. Stripling: Mr. Lawson, are you now or have you ever been a member of the Communist Party of the United States?

Mr. Lawson: In framing my answer to that question I must emphasize the points that I have raised before. The question of communism is in no way related to this inquiry, which is an attempt to get control of the screen and to invade the basic rights of American citizens in all fields. . . .

The Chairman [Thomas]: (pounding gavel): We are going to get the answer to that question if we have to stay here for a week. Are you a member of the Communist Party, or have you ever been a member of the Communist Party?

Mr. Lawson: It is unfortunate and tragic that I have to teach this committee the basic principles of American –

The Chairman (pounding gavel): That is not the question. That is not the question. The question is: Have you ever been a member of the Communist Party?

Mr. Lawson: I am framing my answer in the only way in which any American citizen can frame his answer to a question which absolutely invades his rights.[78]

While Thomas tries to place Lawson in the role of shifty and evasive witness, Lawson indeed tries to shift the issue from his own politics to the Committee's right to ask about them. A typical "liberal" strategy was employed by Screen Writers Guild President Emmet Lavery, who objected to the Committee and its investigation, but was more or less cooperative. In order to avoid confronting the issue of constitutionality, Lavery offered at the beginning of his testimony:

Mr. Lavery: I have a piece of information that I would like to put in the record on my own motion and on my volunteering, because I am not sure as a student of constitutional law, whether the committee does have the authority to demand it of me, but let me break the suspense immediately and tell you that I am not a Communist. I never have been. I don't intend to be. I will make open confession and admit that I am a Democrat who in my youth was a Republican. And if the Committee wants to know why I changed from Republican to Democrat –

The Chairman: No; we are not interested in why you changed.
[Laughter][79]

Most often, however, witnesses chose one of three answers, indicating the roles they were to play in the Committee's ritual performance: (1) they answered "yes," and went on to profess their guilt and prove their repentance by naming their comrades; (2) they answered "no," and went on to refute all charges of leftist activities that had been made against them, thus seeking to establish their "innocence," or they answered "no" and were grilled about their participation in Popular-Front activities and their support for liberal and leftist causes, of which the Committee had abundant evidence, creating a strong impression of guilt, whether they repented or not; or (3) they took the Fifth Amendment. Because of the "waiver doctrine" established in the 1948 case of witness Jane Rogers, witnesses were aware that answering any questions at all on the subject of Communist affiliations would preclude them from seeking the protection of the Fifth Amendment later in the Hearing. The Supreme Court confirmed in the Rogers case that the witness could not refuse to identify others after she had testified about herself.[80] A strategy that was known as the "diminished Fifth" evolved during the early fifties, in which the witnesses answered "no" to the question of whether they were Communists at the time of the hearing, but took the Fifth on questions of previous activity.[81] This proved ineffective against blacklisting.

The second part of the ritual was the *admission of guilt*, whether it be of the major "crime" of belonging to the party or of lesser ones like signing petitions, marching in parades, or going to meetings. Witnesses who were looking for absolution, like José Ferrer, bent over backwards to confess everything in their past that might have been tainted with leftism. Others answered reluctantly. In terms of the blacklist, the most difficult situation for a witness was to have nothing to confess. After being named before the Committee, Edward G. Robinson languished on the blacklist for some time before he appeared, in April 1952, at his own request, to clear his name. He told the Committee:

I would like to find some way to put at rest the ever-recurring innuendoes concerning my loyalty. Surely there must be some way for a person falsely accused of disloyalty to clear his name once and for all. It is for this purpose that I come again voluntarily before this committee to testify under oath. What more can I do? Anyone who understands the history of the political activity in Hollywood will appreciate the fact that innocent, sincere persons were used by the Communists to whom honesty and sincerity are as foreign as the Soviet Union is to America. I was duped and used. I was lied to. But, I repeat, I acted from good motives, and I have never knowingly aided Communists or any Communist cause.[82]

"I'm not calling him a Communist," one New York City politician said of Arthur Miller. "My objection is he refuses to repent."[83]

The third part of the ritual was the *expression of repentance*. For the Committee's purposes, the more self-abasing the confession, and the more groveling the confessor, the better. Director Nicholas Bela, for example, hit the desired note of ritual humiliation: "I have to humbly apologize for the grave error which I have committed, and beg of you to forgive me."[84] The questioners did their best to set up the witnesses, as, for example, the question from investigator Richard Arens: "Are you now thoroughly disgusted with the fact that you have been associated with the Communist ideology, which is atheistic, which is the very antithesis of Christian morality as we know it in this country?"[85] Witnesses usually ascribed their activities to youthful idealism and enthusiasm, and being led astray by conniving ideologues. Larry Parks, for example, explained that, in 1941, "being a member of the Communist Party fulfilled certain needs of a young man that was liberal in thought, idealistic, who was for the underprivileged, the underdog. . . . I think that being a Communist in 1951 in this particular situation is an entirely different kettle of fish."[86]

The fourth part of the ritual was the stumbling block for many an otherwise cooperative witness, and, in the words of Congressman Jackson, "the ultimate test of the credibility of a witness before the Committee."[87] This was what Victor Navasky has called the "Informer Principle," the *proof of repentance through willingness to name names*. Since the Committee had abundant sources of names in zealous former and now anti-Communists, in their own investigators, and in FBI informants, this was the most ritualistic part of the interrogation. As Navasky notes, "it was a corollary of the Informer Principle that the act of informing was more important than the information imparted."[88] Often the Committee knew exactly the names the witness was to give them; often the specific names had been the subject of bargaining between the witness and the Committee or an investigator before they were elicited in a public hearing. As John Wayne, speaking as president of the Motion Picture Alliance for the Preservation of American Ideals, put it: "Let no one say that a Communist can be tolerated in American society and particularly in our industry. . . . We do not want to associate with traitors. We want patriotism and justice. We hate no one. We hope those who have changed their view will cooperate to the fullest extent. By that I mean names and places, so that they can come back to the fellowship of loyal Americans."[89] Roy Brewer declared that repentant witnesses must name names because "this is the only way by which one can determine with certainty that the Party has actually left *them*."[90] The rhetorical value of demanding names was evident to the congressmen from the early days of the Dies Committee. In 1940, Martin Dies declared that he would "seek to have every Communist leader in the United States sent to jail for contempt unless they furnished HUAC with a complete list of Communist party members."[91] As Goodman has noted, "Names were the food of the second Hollywood investigation [1951–2] – not quite the delectable names of 1947 like Gary Cooper and the mother of Ginger Rogers – but many more of them, writers, directors, character actors, and here and there a star. The hunger for names was a practical matter; if counsel Tavenner had not been able to press witnesses for names and more names, his interrogation would have amounted to very little."[92] Of the 110 witness who were subpoenaed for these hearings, 58 named names, giving a total of 902, about 700 of which were repetitions. One witness, Martin Berkeley, named 155 names. John Howard Lawson was named 27 times; Ring Lardner, Jr., 14.[93]

While the Committee did not hesitate to publish the names of people who were mentioned, despite the harm that might come to them from unsubstantiated allegations, it was much more careful about the reputations of businesses. Reporting on suspected Communist Louise Brantsen, investigator Louis Russell mentioned that part of her fortune consisted of stock in a company, but, "in view of the fact that I have made no investigation regarding the company mentioned I would rather furnish its name in executive session because if the name of the firm is mentioned there might be an unjust reflection on its character."[94] At another point he stated that a contribution had been made by a Ruth Wilson, a name he was willing to mention despite the probability that there were many Ruth Wilsons throughout the country who might suffer from his use of the name besides the one he meant to incriminate. But he preferred to identify her more fully in executive session, "the reason being that she at the present may have a connection with a leading department store in the United States and I am certain that any mention of her name in connection with that department store would cast an unjust reflection upon the particular store, because I know its reputation."[95] The Committee acquiesced without objection.

The Committee displayed a certain disingenuousness about its motives for insisting on names, as when Chairman Wood said to the reluctant Larry Parks: "Now, you're leaving a very decided impression on my mind that in your thinking there was nothing, no attempt to influence the character of the pictures or other entertainment that emanated from the studios that your group was connected with, that there was nothing off color about the action or the conduct of any of the people that belonged to it. Then, how could it possibly reflect against the members of this group for the names to be known, any more than it would if they belonged to the Young Men's Christian Association?"[96] Occasionally, however, this kind of rhetorical ploy was subverted, as when Congressman Doyle asked friendly witness Robert Gorham Davis, a professor at Smith College, "why don't more men of your mental capacity feel the same way and come forward and testify as you have?" Davis replied: "Prejudice has been built up over the years, partly by the Communists themselves, but also for reasons that are quite understandable to anyone who has to see the operations of an honor system in colleges, a prejudice against informing. I think the American people generally dislike informers."[97] Occasionally the ritual of informing was questioned by members of the Committee themselves, as when Francis Walter asked of Chairman Wood during the long and agonizing interrogation of Larry Parks: "How can it be material to the purpose of this inquiry to have the names of people when we already know them? . . . Isn't it far more important to learn the extent of the activity, and what the purpose of the organization actually was, than to get a long list of names of bleeding hearts and fools, suckers, hard-boiled Communist politicians?"[98] Walter himself, however, was soon presiding over the Committee and demanding the same kind of "cooperation" that Wood had.

In its ritual role of grand inquisitor, meting out judgment of and punishment or absolution to those who came before it, the Committee was most thwarted by the witnesses who took the position that they were willing to testify about their own beliefs and activities, but not to name names or bring harm to others whom they considered innocent of wrongdoing. This position appealed to the American's contempt for the informer without giving the impression that the witness was trying to save his own skin. Two of the most effective rhetorical presentations of this position were those of Lillian Hellman and Arthur Miller. Hellman took the Fifth before the Committee in May 1952, but before her appearance, she had sent a letter to Chairman Wood, requesting that she be allowed to testify about her own activities, but not to be asked about others. She wrote, "my counsel tells me that if I answer questions about myself, I will have waived my rights under the fifth amendment and could be forced legally to answer questions about others. . . . I am prepared to waive the privilege against self-incrimination and to tell you everything you wish to know about my views or actions if your committee will agree to refrain from asking me to name other people. If the committee is unwilling to give me this assurance, I will be forced to plead the privilege of the Fifth Amendment at the hearing."[99] Wood replied that the Committee could not permit witnesses to set forth the terms under which they would testify, and he noted that "any persons identified by you during the course of committee hearings will be afforded the opportunity of appearing before the committee in accordance with the policy of the committee."[100] When Hellman was asked about a meeting of the Communist Party that she was alleged to have attended, she referred the questioner to her letter, whereupon Wood made the tactical mistake of putting the correspondence into the record. Hellman's lawyer, Joseph Rauh, had copies distributed to the press, so that, despite her Fifth Amendment silence, Hellman was able to articulate her reservations about naming names to the public:

> I do not like subversion or disloyalty in any form and if I had ever seen any I would have considered it my duty to have reported it to the proper authorities. But to hurt innocent people whom I knew many years ago in order to save myself is, to me inhuman and indecent and dishonorable. I cannot and will not cut my conscience to fit this year's fashions, even though I long ago came to the conclusion that I was not a political person and could have no comfortable place in any political group.
>
> I was raised in an old-fashioned American tradition and there were certain homely things that were taught to me: To try to tell the truth, not to bear false witness, not to harm my neighbor, to be loyal to my country, and so on. In general, I respected these ideals of Christian honor and did as well with them as I knew how. It is my belief that you will agree with these simple rules of human decency and will not expect me to violate the good American tradition from which they spring. I would, therefore, like to come before you and speak of myself.[101]

By taking the Fifth, Hellman was able to avoid a contempt citation, although of course she remained on the blacklist.

Arthur Miller had perhaps thought more about the ethical issues surrounding the demand to name names than anyone in America when he was called to testify before the Committee in a hearing on "the fraudulent procurement and misuse of American passports by persons in the service of the Communist conspiracy" in June 1956. In the early forties, Miller had written an agit-prop playlet, *You're Next*, warning the American public about the dangers of the Dies Committee. He had seen the careers and lives of friends destroyed by testimony and had watched as one of his closest friends, Elia Kazan, had made the decision to testify. His plays *The Crucible* (1953) and *A View from the Bridge* (1955) were in one sense investigations into the ethics of naming names. In his testimony, Miller patiently answered the Committee's questions about meetings he had attended and petitions he had signed, among them a petition to abolish the House Committee on Un-American Activities. When he admitted attending meetings with writers who were members of the Communist Party, the time for his ritual test had come:

Mr. Arens: Tell us, if you please, sir, about these meetings with the Communist Party writers which you said you attended in New York City. . . .
Mr. Arens: Can you tell us who was there when you walked into the room?
Mr. Miller: Mr. Chairman, I understand the philosophy behind this question and I want you to understand mine. When I say this, I want you to understand that I am not protecting the Communists or the Communist Party. I am trying to and I will protect my sense of myself. I could not use the name of another person and bring trouble on him. These were writers, poets, as far as I could see, and the life of a writer, despite what it sometimes seems, is pretty tough. I wouldn't make it any tougher for anybody. I ask you not to ask me that question.
(The witness confers with his counsel.)
I will tell you anything about myself, as I have. . . . I will be perfectly frank with you in anything relating to my activities. I take the responsibility for everything I have ever done, but I cannot take responsibility for another human being. . . .
Mr. Arens: Mr. Chairman, I respectfully suggest that the witness be ordered and directed to answer the question as to who it was that he saw at these meetings.
Mr. Jackson: May I say that moral scruples, however laudable, do not constitute legal reason for refusing to answer the question. I certainly endorse the request for direction. . . .
Mr. Scherer: There is a question before the witness; namely, to give the names of those individuals who were present at this Communist Party meeting of Communist Writers. There is a direction on the part of the Chairman to answer that question. Now, so that the record may be clear, I think we should say to the witness – Witness, would you listen?
Mr. Miller: Yes.
Mr. Scherer: We do not accept the reasons you gave for refusing to answer the question, and it is the opinion of the committee that, if you do not answer the question, you are placing yourself in contempt.
(The witness confers with his counsel.)

Mr. Scherer: That is an admonition that this committee must give you in compliance with the decision of the Supreme Court. Now, Mr. Chairman, I ask that you again direct the witness to answer the question.

The Chairman: He has been directed to answer the question, and he gave us an answer that we just do not accept.

Mr. Arens: Was Arnaud d'Usseau chairman of this meeting of Communist Party writers which took place in 1947 at which you were in attendance?

Mr. Miller: All I can say, sir, is that my conscience will not permit me to use the name of another person.

(The witness confers with his counsel.)

And that my counsel advises me that there is no relevance between this question and the question of whether I should have a passport or there should be passport legislation in 1956.

Mr. Arens: Mr. Chairman, I respectfully suggest that the witness be ordered and directed to answer the question as to whether or not Arnaud d'Usseau . . . was chairman of the meeting of the Communist Party writers in New York City in 1947 at which you were in attendance.

The Chairman: You are directed to answer the question.

Mr. Miller: I have given you my answer, sir.[102]

The Committee was for the most part respectful of Miller, and even praised his work. Demonstrating a much greater faith in the Marxist notion that "art is a weapon" than Miller himself has ever shown, Congressman Doyle asked toward the end of the hearing: "Why do you not direct some of that magnificent ability you have to fighting against well-known Communist subversive conspiracies in our country and in the world?" Nevertheless, Miller was cited for contempt of Congress at the Committee's request. He received a thirty-day suspended sentence and a fine of $500. The conviction was overturned by the courts in 1958.

The final phase of the ritual was an *expression of gratitude* to the Committee for pointing out the error of the witness's ways, and sometimes a query about what the witness could do to help the Committee fight the spread of Communism. Lee J. Cobb used the opportunity to give an apologia for naming names:

> I would like to thank you for the privilege of setting the record straight, not only for whatever subjective relief it affords me, but if belatedly this information can be of any value in the further strengthening of our Government and its efforts at home as well as abroad, it will serve in some small way to mitigate against whatever feeling of guilt I might have for having waited this long. I did hope that in my

delay to speak earlier others of the people I had mentioned might have availed themselves of this opportunity for themselves to do likewise. I think by this time I can reasonably assume that those who have desired to do so have taken the opportunity to make their position clear, and I can only say that I am sorry for those who haven't and that more haven't done so.[103]

One of the saddest of these was the belated attempt by Larry Parks to amend his 1951 testimony in July 1953, after two years on the blacklist. Since he was the first of the unfriendly witnesses to "cooperate," Parks's testimony, with its reluctance to name names, although cooperative enough to keep him out of jail, was not anti-Communist enough for the Hollywood studios. In his attempts to persuade the Committee not to make him name people, he had provided HUAC opponents with some of their strongest imagery: "Don't present me with the choice of either being in contempt of this committee and going to jail or forcing me to really crawl through the mud to be an informer, for what purpose? . . . I don't think this is American justice."[104] Desperately trying to salvage his film career in 1953, he wrote his letter to Chairman Velde promising that he would not testify as he did in 1951 – "that to give such testimony is to 'wallow in the mud' – but on the contrary I would recognize that such cooperation would help further the cause in which many of us were sincerely interested when we were duped into joining and taking part in the Communist Party."[105] He also expressed his full spirit of cooperation with the Committee: "If there is any way in which I can further aid in exposing the methods of entrapment and deceit through which Communist conspirators have gained the adherence of American idealists and liberals, I hope the Committee will so advise me. . . . Above all, I wish to make it clear that I support completely the objectives of the House Committee on Un-American Activities." Unfortunately for Parks, his repentance came too late. His career was over.

This five-part ritual displaced the cultural anxiety of the Cold War onto the scapegoat, the Communist or "Communist-sympathizer," and, more often than not, produced an illusion of reintegration and healing through its absolution of the errant witness, who could then be removed from the blacklist and accepted back into society. The ritual succeeded either in confirming the guilt of the scapegoat or in imputing guilt through the implication that anyone who refused to talk was guilty, and anyone who refused to name names was still loyal to the Communists and unwilling to assist the Committee in rooting out the Party.

According to Girard, the final stage of the scapegoat ritual is the reintegration or rehabilitation of the scapegoat, as occurs with the creation of martyrs like Joan of Arc or of cultural heroes like Socrates. As the occasion for collective persecution passes, the victimization of the scapegoat becomes apparent, and the institutions that enable it are weakened and discredited. So it was with the Inquisition, with the seventeenth-century witch hunts, and eventually with the House Committee on Un-American Activities. HUAC's power over the national psyche was greatly diminished by the disgrace of Joseph McCarthy in 1954. McCarthy's exposure to a large segment of the populace through the televising of the Army-McCarthy Hearings and the effective exposé by Edward R. Murrow on his *See It Now* program brought the public a little too close for comfort to the man behind the headlines and the reality of McCarthyism. As Arthur Miller wrote, "it was hardly ten minutes into the program when one knew it was the end of McCarthy, not altogether for reasons of content but more because he was so obviously handling subjects of great moment with mere quips, empty-sounding jibes, lumpy witticisms; it had not seemed quite as flat and ill-acted before."[106] CBS reported an unprecedented 12,348 calls in response to Murrow's program on McCarthy, 11,567 of which favored Murrow's comments and 781 of which disapproved. Similar responses, on a smaller scale, were reported by network affiliates throughout the country.[107] HUAC's Show Business hearings of 1955 did not spark the interest of the American public the way those of 1947 and 1951–2 had.

The most powerful force in the discrediting of HUAC, however, was the breaking down of the fear that caused witnesses to succumb to the Committee's demands for names or to take the Fifth Amendment, and that caused their employers to blacklist them for fear of boycotting or worse. In the early sixties, the circle of fear was beginning to crack, a circumstance that was displayed dramatically when the Committee decided to investigate the group Women Strike for Peace in 1962. The Committee was bewildered by the response of Dagmar Wilson to its implication that the organization might be a Communist front. Asked whether she would "knowingly permit or encourage a Communist Party member to occupy a leadership position in Women Strike for Peace, " Wilson replied, "Well, my dear sir, I have absolutely no way of controlling, do not desire to control, who wishes to join in the demonstrations and the efforts that the women strikers have made for peace. In fact I would also like to go even further. I would like to say that unless everybody in the whole world joins us in this fight, then God help us."[108] As Eric Bentley has noted, Women Strike for Peace was the fall of HUAC's Bastille. Whether or not the Committee and its unfriendly witnesses hitherto had "deserved each other," they had come to need each other as playmates in a game with by now agreed rules. It was smart to ask a question knowing that the witness would refuse to answer, and that you'd get him for contempt. How disconcerting, then, if the witness spoiled everything by answering the question and reversing the roles; playing cop to their robber, hero to their villain![109]

This public dismissal of the contamination theory, thought control, and all the arguments against "Communists fronts" was extraordinarily liberating. The public's terror of the American Communist, which had been established by forty years of demonization, was beginning to break down.

A similar breakdown of fear occurred in regard to the Committee itself. One of the activities for which witnesses were subpoenaed to appeared for interrogation by HUAC was demonstrating against the Committee, or working to abolish it. During the forties and fifties, charges of this activity were made with as much fervor as charges of Communist activity. For example, Arthur Miller was asked by investigator Richard Arens: "Did you sign statements or lend your name, prestige, and influence toward a movement to abolish the Committee on Un-American Activities?" When Miller replied that he did not remember, Arens came down like the avenging angel: "I lay before you a copy of an announcement of a mobilization, a rally, mobilized against the House Un-American Activities Committee, held under the auspices of the Civil Rights Congress, in which 1, 2, 3, 6 people are to speak at Manhattan Center in New York City, 3 of whom have been publicly identified as Communist agents, including on this list of people who are to speak at this rally to destroy the House Committee on Un-American Activities, one Arthur Miller. I ask you whether or not you are the Arthur Miller."[110]

By the mid-sixties, the aggressive stance of the New Left, and a new generation of witnesses who essentially had nothing to lose by alienating HUAC, had completely shifted the rhetorical balance of power in the dialogue of the hearing. Asked his home address, Steven Cherkross replied:

Opposition in America to the Johnson administration's war of genocide in Vietnam is enormous and still growing. . . . Johnson resorts to escalation in Vietnam. His method is kill all, burn all. In our country, it is increased political repression. The Johnson administration has called on a discredited, racist HUAC, a circus committee of coward yellow bellies, to launch the first official attack on the antiwar movement. HUAC in a blaze of red-baiting has attempted to divide and silence militants and revolutionaries. HUAC and Johnson hope this witch hunt will frighten the massive antiwar movement into pacificity or convert it into a loyal opposition.[111]

At these hearings, a startled Committee was brought to realize that the days of evasion and "crawling through the mud" were over. Witnesses now came before the Committee proudly proclaiming their membership in the Marxist Progressive Labor Party. Asked about the jobs he had held, Tom Hayden replied, "Well, I consider myself an organizer of a movement to put you and your committee out of power."[112]

Concomitant to, and partly enabling, this change in the stance of the Left was the considerable limitation of the Committee's powers through the courts. Labor leader John T. Watkins had refused to name names on the grounds that the names were not relevant to the work of the Committee and that the Committee did not have the right to engage in public exposure of the activities of citizens for its own sake. Watkins was cited for contempt, found guilty in district court, and given a 12-month suspended sentence and a fine of $500. In 1957, the Supreme Court reversed the decision of the Court of Appeals, which had upheld the contempt citation. For the majority, Earl Warren wrote that "there is no Congressional power to expose for the sake of exposure," and that "no inquiry is an end in itself; it must be related to, and in furtherance of, a legitimate task of the Congress." In a concurring opinion, Felix Frankfurter wrote that "prosecuting for Contempt of Congress presupposes an adequate opportunity for the defendant to have awareness of the pertinency of the information that he has denied to Congress. . . . Accordingly the actual scope of the inquiry that the Committee was authorized to conduct and the relevance of the questions to that inquiry must be shown to have been luminous at the time when asked and not left, at best, in cloudiness."[113] The Court's position was reversed two years later when it upheld the lower court's conviction in the Barenblatt case, which was conducted on similar grounds.[114] Nevertheless, after the Watkins decision, witnesses were aware that they had rights, and witnesses and their lawyers could insist on an expression of the relevance of any question to the Committee's stated business in the hearing.

Finally, the Committee was hoisted on its own petard when the young radicals of the sixties, perceiving the theatrical nature of the hearings and uninhibited by notions of dignity or professionalism, seized control of the performance. At the 1966 hearings on the opposition to the Vietnam War, a Stanford student gave the Nazi salute as he was being sworn. Another held up a fist, with the middle finger erect. Jerry Rubin dressed up as Santa Claus and Abbie Hoffman wore a shirt made from the American flag. One young man was carried off yelling, "The blood of the Vietnamese is on the American government!"[115] Gone were the polite liberals, the scared fellow-travelers, and the CPUSA members droning over and over the ironically incriminating language of the Fifth Amendment protection against self-incrimination. And the new cast of leftists encountered a new HUAC. The fervent hatred of everything Red that emanated from a Martin Dies, a J. Parnell Thomas, or a John Rankin had been displaced by a siege mentality. The new HUAC sought to cast itself as the victim. In 1965, Chairman Edwin E. Willis complained that enemies of the Committee were leaking the names of subpoenaed witnesses and blaming the Committee "in order to make us the scapegoat."[116] It was the beginning of the end. After an ineffectual attempt to change its image with a name change in 1968, HUAC was finally abolished in 1975.

3

Dramatizing Directly

Mr. Arens: Was it likewise just a little farce, your play *You're Next*, by Arthur Miller, attacking the House Committee on Un-American Activities?
Mr. Miller: No, that would have been quite serious.

HUAC Hearings, 21 June 1956

We, the citizens of the United States of America, owe these, our elected representatives, a great debt. Undaunted by the vicious campaign of slander launched against them as a whole and as individuals, they staunchly continue their investigation, pursuing their stated belief that anyone who continued to be a Communist after 1945 is guilty of high treason.

Voice-over, *Big Jim McLain*

Investigation

Big Jim McLain (1952)

In the wake of the 1947 Hollywood hearings, during which Representative Richard Nixon had made a point of encouraging the studio heads to make more "pro-American" films, a spate of anti-Communist movies was hastily released from Hollywood studios. The trend reached its peak in 1951 and 1952, when the second and far more wide-reaching round of Hollywood hearings was being held. Dorothy B. Jones, who had served as chief of the film reviewing and analysis section of the Office of War Information (OWI) during World War II, did an analysis of the films for John Cogley's *Report on Blacklisting*. Jones classified between thirty-five and forty anti-Communist movies, released between 1947 and 1954, into three types. "The vast majority were anti-Communist spy thrillers," she concluded. "These spy melodramas followed the familiar timeworn pattern. Except for a change in the identity of the foreign power involved, they were indistinguishable from the Nazi and Japanese spy stories of World War II or

75

from the endless stories about unspecified foreign powers whose spies and secret agents have peopled the Hollywood films of earlier years."[1] Another type dramatized the events of the Cold War that had taken place abroad. Among these films were some very effective films, such as *Man on a Tightrope* (1953) and *The Iron Curtain* (1948). A third type, the one that is most important in relation to HUAC, "attempted to depict and, in the case of a few films, to explain the growth and development of the Communist Party in the United States." Among these were *The Red Menace* (1949), *I Was a Communist for the FBI* (1951), *My Son John* (1952), and *Big Jim McLain* (1952). Jones concluded that

> these movies can have added little or nothing to American understanding of the true nature of communism – the ideology, shifting strategy and subtle tactics of the Communists. And there is a real possibility that most of these films had an unfavorable effect abroad during the Cold War, since they suggested that Americans have little understanding of the true dangers inherent in the Communist threat to the free world, and because of the unfavorable picture which many of these films gave of the effectiveness of our government's counter-measures against Communist espionage in this country.[2]

In a 1953 article on the "anti-Red" pictures, European critic Karel Reisz had expressed a similar view:

> The chief objection to films like *The Enemy Within* [*The Red Menace*] is that in passing American society through a wringer in order to squeeze out the Communist poison, they simultaneously tear the fabric of the decent, democratic values they are supposed to protect. And there is a practical objection, too: they make anti-communism a kind of game which, being played to the rules of the penny dreadful, no one can take seriously. . . . by their lack of serious contact with contemporary reality and their assertion of values which on this side of the Atlantic look more than a little ridiculous, [these films] must do great harm to their professed cause.[3]

Reisz identified a number of "contentions about the enemy" that were common to "anti-Red" pictures. (1) "The American Communist Party is run by a gang of cheap though diabolically clever crooks, distinguishable from other hoodlums only in that their boss lives in the Kremlin." (2) "Communists are hard, intellectual people, many of them cold-blooded scientists." (3) "In one way or another, all communists are neurotic." (4) "There are only three ways a normal, honest person can become a communist. He may be temporarily discontented by some social injustice. . . . He may be a Jew or a negro – if so, the film will patronise him and he will leave in the last reel. Or, most reliably, his clean animal instincts may let him down." (5) "Communists are closely allied to fascists, many having come over from the Bund. They are violently anti-semitic and anti-negro and privately joke about the dupes who join the party." (6) "Communists are rich, do their work for private gain or to satisfy a power mania." (7) "To get money, communists organise blind campaigns and keep the cash for themselves." (8) "Once you are a member of the Communist Party it is impossible to get out. . . . But if you go to the F. B. I. all will be forgiven." In execution, Reisz declared, "most of the films bear all the marks of the B-picture – blaring music, bad continuity and acting, arbitrary passages of violence."[4]

To Reisz's list of characteristics may be added at least two more: (9) The chief threat to Communism is Christianity and the chief threat to Christianity is Communism. (10) While intellectuals may easily be duped into joining the party, they can be saved by hard-headed, practical citizens who steer clear of too much "analysis." To this typology of the genre, Nora Sayre has added an entertaining and incisive iconography of its characters:

> These movies instruct us especially on how American Communists look: most are apt to be exceptionally haggard or disgracefully pudgy. Occasionally, they're effeminate: a man who wears gloves shouldn't be trusted. However, in films that feature dauntless FBI agents, it's very difficult to tell them apart from the enemy, since both often lurk on street corners in raincoats and identical snapbrims while pretending to read newspapers, and also because many B-actors lack distinguishing features.[5]

There is also a figure known as "the Bad Blonde: in the Fifties, you knew that there was something terribly wrong with a woman if her slip straps showed through her blouse; in this context, it meant treason. Bad Blondes tend to order triple bourbons or to be hooked on absinthe, and they often seduce 'impressionable' young men into joining the Party." Often, Communists "can be detected by their style of exhaling: they expel smoke very slowly from their nostrils before threatening someone's life, or suggesting that 'harm' will come to his family.

Recurrently, Hollywood employed the formula of substituting Communists for gangsters – hence the public could feel at home with the familiar image of the criminal." Communists "'never keep their promises,' and they're likely to go berserk when they're arrested. But they devote so much time to spying on each other that it's hard to see how they could have any free time for serious espionage." Above all, Sayre notes, "the fictional Communists are murderers, particularly of their own kind: they don't hesitate to hurl their associates in front of trains or out of windows, or to 'hound' them to suicide."[6]

Big Jim McLain, which fits squarely within the genre described by Jones, Reisz, and Sayre, was the only one of the anti-Communist pictures that focused on the House Committee on Un-American Activities and its endeavors to root out Communists. Although released by Warner Brothers, it was the first product of the producing team of John Wayne and Robert Fellows, Wayne-Fellows Productions. Wayne of course played Jim McLain, and the movie was put together by like-minded and practical artisans. The movie was directed by Edward Ludwig, who specialized in action films like *They Came to Blow Up America, The Fighting Seabees,* and *Wake of the Red Witch.* It was written by a team composed of James Edward Grant, a popular pulp novelist who had settled into writing screenplays for action films, several of them for Wayne; Eric Taylor; and Richard English, who had written articles for the *Saturday Evening Post* such as "What Makes a Hollywood Communist?" and the article the movie was based on, "We Almost Lost Hawaii to the Reds." According to Victor Navasky, English had the help of William Wheeler, HUAC's chief investigator in Hollywood, in writing the script.[7]

Even within the now zealously anti-Communist Warner Brothers, the script's forthright attack on the Fifth Amendment raised problems. The studio's head of research, Carl Milliken, expressed his concern that the script "showed HUAC officials breaking and entering, intimidating witnesses, conducting illegal wiretaps, and being physically violent." It also shows them as "expressing more than once the wish that the protective mantle which American law throws about all individuals on trial be cast aside in the case of 'these scum.'" Milliken feared that the film might "backfire . . . even to the possible extent of placing us in contempt of Congress."[8] Wayne was unconcerned about these issues, however, and Milliken's fears seem to have been unfounded. The members of the Committee allowed themselves to be featured conspicuously at the beginning and end of the movie. After beginning with a very dark shot of a stormy countryside and a voice-over quotation from Stephen Vincent Benét's "The Devil and Dan'l Webster," with the "Battle Hymn of the Republic" playing in the background, the scene fades into a shot of the hearing room, with a voice-over commenting: "We, the citizens of the United States of America, owe these, our elected representatives, a great debt. Undaunted by the vicious campaign of slander launched against them as a whole and as individuals, they staunchly continue their investigation, pursuing their stated belief that anyone who continued to be a Communist after 1945 is guilty of high treason." During this encomium, the congressmen are featured in a series of two-shots, looking purposeful, and then Counsel Frank Tavenner demands of a witness, "Are you a member of the Communist Party?" The witness takes the Fifth Amendment. Chairman Wood himself asks the witness whether he would "willingly bear arms" for the United States in the case of "armed hostilities with Soviet Russia." The witness answers, "same question, same answer." John Wayne is then heard in voice-over, expressing the frustration of the hard-working HUAC investigator, as after eleven months of his hard-slogging investigation, "proving to any intelligent person that these people were Communists, agents of the Kremlin," they "all walk out free." McLain has to restrain his assistant, Mal Baxter, played by Wayne's erstwhile stunt-double James Arness, from taking a punch at the witness, commenting in voice-over that Mal "hates these people. They had shot at him in Korea." In disgust, McLain and Baxter walk out, while Wayne complains in voice-over that "the good Doctor Carter would go right back to his well-paid chair as a professor of economics at the University to contaminate more kids." McLain says that Carter had delivered sixteen rolls of microfilm from "the laboratory" to a "Comintern courier," although it is never made clear what kind of a laboratory a professor of economics might have been frequenting.

McLain and Baxter take off for Hawaii as a voice-over proclaims, "next day was launched the investigation that made headlines, known as 'Operation Pineapple.'" The Communist-hunting seems to lose momentum for a while amidst tourist footage of the islands and of hula dancers. The investigators test their surveillance equipment by eavesdropping on a honeymoon couple in the next room. Then they go around serving subpoenas on some "unimportant" but clearly well-heeled Party members on the street and in swimming pools, because you never know when "one of them will talk and point a finger at someone higher up." Checking on CP member Willie Nomaka at his psychiatrist's office, McLain meets love interest Nancy Vallon (Nancy Olson).

The Communists are introduced at this point, with a shot of the villain, Party Boss Sturak, an elegant figure with an accent, who arrives at the home of a psychiatrist, Dr. Gelster, in a limousine. Gelster compliments Sturak on his accomplishments throughout the world, establishing his high rank in the worldwide conspiracy. Sturak asks Gelster if he knows what has prompted HUAC to launch this second investigation of the Party in Hawaii; of course he doesn't. Sturak asks about the former Treasurer of the cell, Willie Nomaka. Gelster says Willie is suffering from "severe nervous trauma," but is not dangerous because "I have his complete psychic dependence. I can control the man." Nonetheless, Sturak orders him to have Nomaka committed to a mental hospital. "Give him an overdose of something. . . . Get rid of him."

Meanwhile, McLain and Baxter meet with union representatives, with the help of Max Venaby, a former Communist labor leader who has seen the light, and now has a broken nose from "fighting Commies." McLain and Nancy do some sightseeing and fall for each other. McLain finds out from Nomaka's landlady Madge, a humorous version of the "Bad Blonde," that Willie has had a "complete nervous breakdown," and the doctor has packed all his things. Two party thugs come for Nomaka's trunk, and McLain ends up knocking one of them off the balcony to teach him some manners. After the thugs drive off with the trunk, McLain calls the police and has them picked up for questioning on a bogus charge while "the entire contents of Nomaka's trunk were microscopically photographed" by the police.

McLain goes sightseeing with Nancy again. When she starts to analyze Gelster's attraction to Communism psychologically, McLain tells her that the "why" of Communism is a lot of bull, and he is only interested in the "what," just as, when he was in uniform, he "shot at the guy on the other side of the perimeter because he was the enemy." Then follows one of the most curious scenes in the movie, when McLain goes to the leper colony on Molokai to talk to Willie Nomaka's former wife, who is now a nurse there. Here the metaphor of contamination is clearly if somewhat clumsily evoked. In voice-over McLain says, "frankly, leprosy scared me. It scares most people I guess." He remembers the fear he had as a child when his mother would read the Bible, and the "chill that ran up and down backs when she read the ancient word, 'leper.'" Mrs. Nomaka welcomes McLain and tells him that, after being a hard-working, dedicated Communist for eleven years, she had left the Party when she realized that it was "a vast conspiracy to enslave the common man." McLain and Mrs. Nomaka are then interrupted while Mrs. Nomaka goes to show one of the babies in the ward to its parents, explaining that the babies are taken from their mothers at birth and kept on the island for six months, then they are sent to the mainland, and the parents never see them again. When McLain says that must be tough, Mrs. Nomaka says, "it may be hard on the parents, but it's really much better for the babies." There is clearly no sympathy for the contaminated here. Mrs. Nomaka resumes her story, saying that she gave a "full account" of her "activities and associations" (including, presumably, those with her husband) to the FBI and came to the leper colony. "I thought, I suppose, that I might atone for the injury that I had done humanity by helping these unfortunates." She separated from Willie because she could not persuade him to leave the Party with her.

Mrs. Nomaka then shows McLain an "incoherent" letter she has received from Willie, in which he says he is returning to "the religion of his childhood" and accuses himself of fratricide. "He's obviously deranged," she says, since he was an only child. She says she hasn't answered the letter because, "like anyone else who has committed a crime against humanity," Willie "will have to find his own way back into the community of men." She says she would "not lift a hand to help any conspirator, any more than I would extend a helping hand to a – I was going to say leper – but that of course is ridiculous." Apparently, while Mrs. Nomaka is a self-constructed outcast, Willie is beyond even that. And Communism is far worse contamination than leprosy. Mrs. Nomaka asks McLain to remember that Willie is "suffering great torment of soul," and McLain tells her that he will tell Willie he met a "splendid lady who wishes him well."

Baxter finds Willie in a sanatorium, lying on a bed in a straitjacket, muttering incoherently. When Baxter goes to call the police, the attendant says they don't want any trouble, because the sanitarium is a business, after all. Baxter says, "You want to stay in business?" The attendant says, "Yes, sir." Baxter says, "Cooperate." The scene then shifts to the police grouped around Willie's bed, and McLain's voice-over: "We had Nomaka, but between nervous breakdown and the injections his 'comrades' had given him, Nomaka was of no use to us."

The scene shifts to the docks, where "Whitey," the new young labor boss, is shown refusing to let a Communist work, and he tells McLain that they are "getting things pretty well cleaned up" on the docks. This is followed by another curious scene. While the leprosy scene belabors the metaphor of contamination, this one, in a rather Swiftian way, equates the intellectual with the madman. Hans Conried appears as Robert Henried, an "intellectual" who wants to give McLain information on the Communist Party, which he says he joined ten years earlier merely to investigate it. After he talks about flying over to meet with Stalin in a jet plane of his own design, he offers his new "secret weapon" to end wars by making everyone look exactly alike: "how can you possibly fight with anyone if he looks exactly like you . . . it's like picking a fight with yourself. But it might destroy the human race." It is never made clear how this daft "weapon" would destroy the human race. The only effect mentioned is the titillating possibility of confusing husbands and wives. The implicit danger of this kind of thinking is that it is a mad extension of "Red" ideas. The notion of making everyone the same is an extension of the classless society as well as a denial of difference, the refusal to see the Communist as "the other," like the liberal intellectuals who insist on the humanity and the civil rights of the Communist, despite his contamination. That the film presents Henried's "insane" denial of difference as a weapon that could destroy the world and Mrs. Nomaka's stigmatizing and casting off of Willie as the action of a "splendid lady" is a good indication of its position on Communists.

Having provided an example of contamination by intellectuals, the film then shifts to a scene with the Lexiters, an elderly couple who have emigrated to the United States from Poland thirty years earlier. The father says he worked on the docks in San Francisco – "that was hard, but we were free, and we lived." They have retired to Hawaii quite comfortably: "Mama and I are just livin' out here on our Union pension, free and in the sun." Lexiter tells McLain and Baxter that they had a son who, after doing very well in high school, was given a trip to Russia as a prize. He remained there for a year "to study," and when he came home, he "was different." His father, who knew the evils of "men who have turned their backs on God" because of his youth in Poland, threw his son out of the house. The couple has not seen him since, but they show the investigators a picture of him in the paper. He turns out to be Ed White, the very same "Whitey" who is taking over the longshoreman's union in Honolulu. The investigators have him followed, and he leads them to seven out of ten of the "missing cell."

Baxter gets a phone call and goes to a house were four Asians are playing Ma Jong. He is hit on the head, and McLain gets a call from Police Chief Liu telling him Baxter is dead. After he identifies his partner at the morgue, McLain and the homicide squad go to work to solve the murder. McLain takes Nancy to a country club where he makes sure the Communists' surveillance equipment picks up the story that he is leaving the island. Sturak discusses the case with Gelster, while the Honolulu police listen in with their own surveillance equipment. Gelster says that Baxter died from an allergic reaction to his injection of sodium pentothal. Sturak scolds him for putting the Party in jeopardy and tells him to call a meeting of the seventh cell. After Gelster leaves, Sturak tells one of his underlings that he prefers to work with mercenaries. "These domestic Party members, these dedicated Communists. They make me sick." The underling replies, "We need them until we take power – Then liquidate."

The Communists gather at the club. They include, besides Ed White, Dr. Mortimer, a "bacteriologist" who is in charge of "unleashing his rodents" to start an "epidemic" in the harbor area when the time comes to take over; a "labor relations counselor," who, with White, will start a general strike to paralyze all the shipping of goods from the mainland to the East when the time comes; and the thugs who had fought with McLain over Willie's trunk. Sturak tells Gelster that he must go to HUAC and confess, naming everyone in the cell except for White, Mortimer, and the other labor boss. He assures them that no harm will come to them, all they need to do is plead their constitutional rights. And he assures them with oily duplicity, "We take care of our own." Then McLain, who has been listening in on the meeting with the Honolulu police, comes in. He says that, although it is unusual, he wanted to "make the pinch" himself because he wanted to punch Dr. Gelster in the nose for killing Mal. Once he's there, however, he finds he can't do it, telling Gelster he's just "too small." "That's the difference between you and us, I guess. We don't hit the little guy. We believe in fair play and all that sort of thing." When the trunk-stealing thug says he's had a "bellyful of this East Texas cotton chopping jerk," McLain asks him if he's ever chopped any cotton, and he replies, "No, I'm from the country club set. Chopping cotton is for white trash and niggers." McLain punches him and fights off all the Communists until reinforcements arrive. When Sturak complains to Liu that McLain had attacked them "without provocation," Liu replies, "we all have sufficient provocation to attack you." The police arrest Gelster and the thugs for manslaughter.

In the final scene, Sturak and White are shown taking the Fifth Amendment at a hearing as Tavenner asks them about their Communist affiliations. Liu and McLain walk out together, and Liu says, "I wonder how Mal would have felt about this Fifth Amendment." McLain replies: "He died for it. There are a lot of wonderful things written into our Constitution that were meant for honest, decent citizens. I resent the fact that it can be used and abused by the very people who want to destroy it." McLain then informs us in voice-over: "Well, they walked out free again. Another case that proved to any intelligent person that these people are Communists, enemy agents, and they walked out free. Sometimes I wonder why I stay on this job." The movie ends with McLain and Nancy watching the Navy band play while sailors board ship. A voice is heard in a reprise of the opening question from "The Devil and Dan'l Webster," "How stands the Union now?" and Wayne answers, "There stands our Union, Mr. Webster. There stands the Union, Sir." The last frame is an acknowledgment of HUAC's help: "The incidents in this motion picture are based on the files of the Committee on Un-American Activities, House of Representatives, Congress of the United States. Names and places have been changed. We gratefully acknowledge the cooperation of this Committee."

Big Jim McLain was a commercial success. It ranked twenty-seventh on *Variety*'s list of top-grossing films for 1952. It made a tidy profit for Wayne-Fellows and Warner Brothers, earning $2,600,000 in domestic rental fees for a film that had cost only $825,554 to make.[9] While it found a ready audience, most critics were understandably cool toward the movie, and not only on ideological grounds. *Time* called the picture "wildly fanciful movie melodrama," noting that "Investigator Arness, who wants to destroy the ring by beating up the Reds every time he sights one, gets killed. Wayne, who takes on eight Communists singlehanded in a free-for-all, has to be rescued by the Island police." It concluded: "*Big Jim McLain* has some pleasingly authentic Hawaiian background, but the action in the foreground is implausible and fumblingly filmed. Leathery John Wayne lopes though all the mayhem with the expression of a sad and friendly 'hound.'"[10] Bosley Crowther complained that it was hard to tell whether the film "is supposed to be taken seriously as a documentation of the sort of work that is done by the House Un-American Activities Committee in its investigations of the Communist peril or whether it is merely intended to arouse and entertain." He concluded that "the over-all mixing of cheap fiction with a contemporary crisis in American life is irresponsible and unforgivable. No one deserves credit for this film."[11]

The most negative reviews, of course, came from the liberal press. Otis L. Gurnsey, noting that "'Big Jim McLain' makes deep bows in the direction of the House UAC, with Wayne playing a sleuth for same, and with many allusions to the slippery evil of Communism and the inconvenience of the Fifth Amendment," called the movie "part travelogue, part documentary-type melodrama and part love story," concluding, "it is pedestrian in all of these phases and the only tension it builds is the sense that anyone who passes a rude remark about the Un-American Activities Committee in the Paramount theater will have an ex-Marine jumping out of the screen at him." Guernsey was already familiar enough with the anti-Communist genre to identify the "list of villains" as "an urbane, ruthless boss, a quivering doctor, a bacteriologist and a labor leader passing as an anti-communist."[12] Even the reviewers who applauded the movie's politics had difficulty in endorsing its aesthetics wholeheartedly. *Variety* spoke approvingly of "this topical story of the patriotic work going on to expose Communist activities endangering this country and its possessions in the not-so-cold war of ideology," and of "the natural exploitation values accruing to the timely subject," but noted that "the picture is being rushed into the market and bears evidence of that haste. Continuity is choppy, the script sketchy and lacking in clarity." What's more, "the investigation is tedious" and the "investigation and the hearing that follows are futile to some degree, in that the Commies use the protection of the Fifth Amendment to block real punishment for their treachery."[13] It seems that the Fifth Amendment got in the way of a good story as well as HUAC and its investigators. The warnings that were to be issued by Reisz and Jones about the dangers of presenting America's anti-Communism through the vehicle of simplistic movies were certainly relevant to this one. In the view of a British critic, "the seamier side of freedom will be found in *Big Jim McLain*, a thriller eulogizing the Un-American Activities Committee. It's great fun to be a witch-hunter, you get sent to Hawaii, drink under the palms, grin at the flower-decked dancers, lose a pal, smash up the underground, and marry the girl of your dreams. But these American activities don't, even with John Wayne, quite make a film."[14]

Big Jim McLain was not much different from any other action thriller of the early fifties in representing the American hero as a plain-talking strongman, quick to punch and slow to think, but devoted to the values of sportsmanship and able to recognize the evil in anything that wasn't "on the level." It also conveyed a vivid subtext that stigmatized Communists as breeders of disease and insanity, instigators of disaster, insidiously deceptive co-workers and neighbors, hypocritical rich men who manipulate and exploit the working man only until they can take over the world – "then liquidate." It appealed to America's self-satisfaction on the one hand and its deepest fears on the other. Its message was clear. Communism and Communists are evil and dangerous, and not "on the level." The Constitution was set up to protect American citizens who are honest and decent. Hence, we should not be allowing Communists to hoodwink us into allowing them the protection of the Constitution and impeding the efforts of the House Committee on Un-American Activities to root out and destroy the Communist menace.

Thirty Pieces of Silver (1951)

Howard Fast's play, *Thirty Pieces of Silver*, is the Left's equivalent of *Big Jim McLain*. According to Fast's introduction to the published script, it was originally written in 1948, in response to the suggestion of a Broadway producer to write about "something close and meaningful to me."[15] When he saw a draft of the script, the producer pronounced it "impossible" for Broadway in 1948. The play was first produced in Melbourne, Australia in 1951, and then in Sydney, in Prague and a number of other cities in Czechoslovakia, and in Vienna, Berlin, Budapest, Warsaw, Moscow, Antwerp, and Rome. It was finally produced in Canada in 1953, and published in the United States in 1954.[16] As its title suggests, Fast's play is a straightforward melodrama about an informer, David Graham, a low-level employee at the Treasury Department, who caves into pressure from an investigator named Fuller, an employee of the Department of Justice. When David's wife Jane calls him a "G-man," Fuller responds, "We don't like the term. It has melodramatic connotations which are hardly grounded in reality" (*Thirty Pieces*, 23).

In the course of the first act, Fuller persuades David to say that his friend and benefactor, Leonard Agronsky, "could very well be a Red" (45). In the second act, David is fired from his job at the Treasury Department by a pragmatically amoral bureaucrat named Carmichael, because he has been "mixed-up with" Agronsky. When David protests that he is "being fired for being a Communist without anyone asking me if I'm a Communist and without being given any chance to deny that I'm a Communist," Carmichael responds, "You're not being fired, Graham; you're being asked to resign. And you're not being asked to resign because anyone considers you to be a Communist" (56). David's immediate superior Fred Selwyn has moral compunctions about firing him, but explains to him the facts of life in Washington:

Agronsky is coming up before a Congressional committee on charges of being a Communist and of being mixed up with the Soviets or the party here or whatever it is. That means inevitably that every friend of Agronsky's will be checked and will come up before a loyalty board if he's a government worker. The choice to us – and to you – is whether you go before the board or resign. We think it will be better for everyone concerned if you resign. (57)

When David protests his innocence and says that he would have nothing to hide from a loyalty board, Selwyn explains the blacklist to him: "It would be a hell of a thing to go out of here *disloyal*, but it would be almost inevitable. The facts cannot be avoided. It's not what you are, but what your associates are" (58). When David finally accepts the inevitable and leaves, Selwyn admits to feeling somewhat conscience-stricken about what he has just done, and Carmichael sets him straight about the rules of the game: "I can't share your concern. That's not a very admirable character. When the department came to him, he helped them, didn't he? No great solicitude for Agronsky. Now it's his turn. This is not an age for heroes, Fred. This is not an age for morality. We have only one measure. . . . Power" (59–60).

In Act Three, Fuller returns to the Graham house and tells David that he will be reinstated in his job, if he will show his cooperativeness by signing a deposition about Agronsky. Here Fast pulls out all the stops, making sure that Fuller uses every sleazy argument on David that was used to get witnesses to cooperate with HUAC investigators. David objects to signing the deposition because it put him "in a funny position": "It says here that I know Leonard Agronsky is a member of the Communist Party and that I've seen his party card. It even gives the number of the card here. I haven't seen his party card, Mr. Fuller." Fuller responds that that shouldn't make any difference, after all, "if the number is there, it means the card exists" (89). When David still hesitates, he says, "Agronsky is in for it, and whatever you do won't change that one bit" (90). David still hesitates, and Fuller begins to get testy: "It doesn't look to me like you're trying to be particularly co-operative. The department isn't asking you to perform miracles. This is a very simple matter, and I can't think of any red-blooded American who wouldn't go along with it." He tells him that Agronsky has no call on his sympathies because his loyalty is not to the United States or "our way of life," and "the sooner we rid ourselves of his kind, the better off we will be." He compares the "service" David will perform by signing the deposition to his service in the armed forces, declaring, "you ought to know what service means" (90). When David asks what will happen to him if he doesn't sign, Fuller replies: "I'm not going to raise threats about your job, about a blacklist, about what it means to go out through a loyalty hearing," saying that he relies on his loyalty to the country to make him do the right thing. After all, "how many real white Americans are there?" (91). David signs and gets his job back, but loses his wife, when Jane leaves him, citing his betrayal of Agronsky as a measure of the new moral order. When he says he will take their little girl away from her, she responds: "Don't make trouble, David. I told you, I'm dangerous. Think of what you did to Agronsky. What kind of a world do you live in, David? If you did it to Agronsky – someone could do it to you, do you see? So don't make any trouble, David, and don't try to stop us" (95).

Jane's departure is also the culmination of the play's second plot, which is centered on her struggle to overcome the racism and anti-Semitism of her South Carolina background. She at first tries to achieve a pretense of equality with her African American maid Hilda by trying to get her to call her by her first name and consider her a friend. When Fuller comes to the house the first time, he implies that Jane might be a Red because she allows Hilda's friend Grace to enter by the front door. Hilda, however, maintains a polite distance from Jane until David fires her for objecting to his accusation that she has been eavesdropping: "I never could tolerate one of your kind who couldn't keep his place" (43). When Jane tells her how sorry she is, Hilda points out to her the emptiness of her liberal pretensions, as she lives a life of leisure and comfort while Hilda cooks her meals, cleans her house, and cares for her child. She calls on Jane to justify herself, "instead of being so damned righteous. . . . You want me to cry for you? Well I got no tears in me to cry for you. I watched white folks too long to want to cry for them – too long" (76–7). In the end, Fast implies, Jane and Hilda become genuine friends because they have reached a plane of equality and mutual dependence. Hilda is out of work, and Jane is out of her marriage. Hilda can see Jane as a "poor kid" (94). Jane can ask Hilda if she can take shelter for the night with "her people." They leave together with the child, ready to form a new "family" based on mutual respect and equality. David tells Jane, "wherever you want to go, you can, with or without your high yellow friend here." In the end, he is left alone with his job at the Treasury Department and his guilty conscience. Jane has the last word: "We're not afraid, David. This is the beginning of something, not the end. We are both dangerous now, David. Keep your hands off. Leave us alone. We're in our own land – ours as well as yours and Fuller's. So leave us alone" (96).

Central to Fast's melodrama is the equation of ethnic prejudice and anti-Communism, the converse of the Right's equation of Communism and ethnicity. As Fuller puts it in the play, "Reds? Jews and Reds? That's a fairly common equation" (31). Fuller also displays an openly racist attitude toward Hilda. The play implies that the moral bankruptcy of the Communist-hunters is clearly allied to, if not motivated by, ethnic prejudice. Jane is freed from the whole amoral world when she rejects David's betrayal of Agronsky and his firing of Hilda. Conversely, David is imprisoned in the world of Fuller and Carmichael when he signs the deposition. Fast's irony is unmistakable as Fuller tells David, "From here on, you have a few damn good friends in damn good places. That's something to hang on to" (92).

As *Big Jim McLain* demonized the Left, *Thirty Pieces of Silver* demonized the Right. Central to Fast's characterization of right-wing thinking was of course the titular Biblical allusion to the informer as Judas. Lest the audience miss the implications of the play's title, Fast makes it clear at the end of Act Two. When David pleads with Jane not to leave him, he says "you've always known what I am" (73). Jane replies that she didn't know "until last night – until you sold out Agronsky" (73). David, who thinks he has lost his job anyway, replies, "Now I'm Judas – only there's no thirty piece of silver" (74). Of course the payoff comes through in the end, just as Fast makes it plain that David is falsely accusing Agronsky in order to keep his job. This betrayal by David Graham of his friend and benefactor is tied into the ethnic prejudice and class elitism he displays. He tells Jane at one point that Agronsky, being a Russian-born Jew, is "not exactly our kind" (26), despite the fact that he was his superior officer in the military and got him his job at the Treasury Department. He has "no stake" in Agronsky. The world view of his boss, Carmichael, which casually subordinates all moral principles to the desire for power, epitomizes the same kind of cold-blooded self-interest that anti-Communist films attributed to the Communist. Investigator Fuller is a bigoted, hypocritical bully, devoid of principle and willing to practice any kind of deceit in order to get the "evidence" he needs against potential witnesses. Worst of all, perhaps, is the fundamental weakness that is exhibited by David and his superior, Fred Selwyn, who will violate every principle they know as right in order to survive in the amoral nightmare world that the play implies Washington to be. The play is a straightforward condemnation of the anti-Communist movement and denunciation of its moral principles. As Eric Bentley remarked in 1956, "it is only behind the Iron Curtain that audiences believe Howard Fast's play *Thirty Pieces of Silver*, with its American Judas, to be a representative picture of American life."[17] It is a morality play in the theatrical idiom of a modern melodrama.

You're Next (1946?)

Arthur Miller testified on 21 June 1956 before a subcommittee of the House Committee on Un-American Activities that was ostensibly engaged in investigating the illegal use of passports. While fairly courteous throughout the interrogation, Investigator Richard Arens was relentless in his grilling of Miller about his opposition to the Committee. When Arens first asked whether he recalled participating in "an attack" on HUAC, Miller replied, "I would say that in all probability I had supported criticism of the Un-American Activities Committee."[18] Miller maintained that he did not remember all the causes he had supported in his activist days fifteen years earlier, but calmly acknowledged any activities of which the Committee had evidence. Arens hammered away with his questions as if he were accusing Miller of some sort of blasphemy: "Did you sign statements or lend your name, prestige and influence toward a movement to abolish the Committee on Un-American Activities?" he demanded. Did Miller speak at a "rally to destroy the House Committee on Un-American Activities"? Arens spent some time discussing a play called *Listen My Children* that Miller had written in collaboration with well-known writer Norman Rosten in 1938, when both were employed by the Federal Writers' Project under the auspices of the Federal Theatre Project. After his memory of the 1938 collaboration was prodded, Miller said that he had written "a farcical sort of a play about standing and waiting in a relief office, and that was, I think, what you are referring to. It was a one-act sketch which was later amplified. Nothing ever came of it, I am glad to say." Arens then ventured into the always dangerous realm for the Committee of literary analysis. He asked Miller whether *Listen My Children* pertained to congressional investigating committees, and Miller replied, "if it did, then it is not what I am talking about. What I am talking about is another thing. This is a long time ago." Arens then proceeded to read the opening stage directions for the play:

Curtain slowly opens. The committee members are engaged in activity of an extraordinary variety, amid an equally extraordinary environment. Profuse flag bunting over the walls. There are several huge clocks ticking ominously. Also a metronone [*sic*] which is continually being adjusted for tempo change.

Secretary, at desk, pounds typewriter and, as alarm clock rings, she feeds the committeemen spoonfuls of castor oil.***

In center of room, in rocker, sits a man. He is securely tied to chair, with a gag in his mouth and a bandage tied over his mouth. Water, coming from a pipe near ceiling, trickles on his head. Nearby is a charcoal stove holding branding irons. Two bloodhounds are tied in the corner of room.

Asked whether this was indeed the play he had coauthored, Miller replied, "I would say that I find it amusing. I don't see what is so horrific about that. I think it is a farce. I don't think anybody would take it seriously that way," noting, "out of a kind of professional jealousy of his own writing," that he was not the author of the scene.

Perhaps annoyed by Miller's offhand attitude, and the comment of Committee Chairman Francis Walter that the scene "is a little corny," Arens moved on more aggressively to his next text. "Was it likewise just a little farce, your play You're Next by Arthur Miller, attacking the House Committee on Un-American Activities?" he asked. "No," replied Miller, "that would have been quite serious." Arens went on to ask whether Miller knew that the play had been produced by the Communist Party, and he exhibited a photocopy from the *Daily Worker* advertising a performance of the play for the benefit of the New York State Communist Party Building Congress in June of 1947. At this, Miller gave one of the most heated responses of his testimony. "Sir, you can't tax me with that," he said, "my plays have gone all over the world by all kinds of people, including the Spanish Government theater where *Death of a Salesman* has run longer than any modern play in history. I take no more responsibility for who plays my plays than General Motors can take for who rides in their Chevrolets." Asked whether a play that was produced by the Communist Party would have had to follow the Communist line, Miller replied, "Nothing in my life was ever written to follow a line. I will go into that if you will." Arens chose not to go into that and went on to other issues, leaving the question of *You're Next* hanging, where it has pretty much remained to this day.[19]

A mere eight pages long, the play centers on a barber, Jerry Marble, who is supporting a pro-labor reform candidate against a local anti-labor judge and has been collecting money for relief efforts on behalf of Republican Spain and Yugoslav war refugees in his shop near the courthouse. His friend Matty Henderson, a lawyer, comes in for a shave. Matty warns Jerry that the Rankin Committee (HUAC) is investigating the Spanish Relief Committee, and that everyone will think he's a Communist if he keeps the can on his counter. Jerry replies that the can belongs on his counter because the Relief Committee is anti-fascist and he's against fascism, commenting that Rankin doesn't seem to like any committee that is against fascism. Matty then lays out the ideological facts of life for the small businessman in postwar America. He tells Jerry that one of the judges who is having trouble getting reelected is about to start a Red hunt. If Jerry supports the reform candidate Kelly, he will no doubt be identified as one of the Reds behind Kelly. Matty reminds Jerry that if he is named in the newspaper as a Red, his customers will be afraid to patronize him because they too might be included in this guilt by association. If Rankin got hold of the story and gave it national circulation, Jerry could lose his store. He tells Jerry to get rid of the collection cans and take Kelly's picture out of the window. When Jerry asks whether this is Germany or America, Matty replies that it is indeed America, but in America, the smart barber talks baseball these days, because anything is possible with the Rankin Committee in Congress.

Jerry takes away the collection cans, but is not happy about it. He tells his wife Martha that he is now at the mercy of his enemy, Fletcher the black-market butcher, who can destroy his business simply by naming him to some politicians. When Jerry goes to work, he sees that all the shops on the street have taken down their pictures of Kelly. Then the paper boy comes in and he sees the headline, "Libertyville Cited as Red Center." Martha tells him that witnesses are going to Washington to testify about Communists in the town. And then Fletcher, who had refused credit to laborers during a recent strike, comes in to enlist Jerry's help in ending the boycott of his store. Jerry refuses and says he is going to put back the collection cans for Russian and Yugoslav relief, and for support of the anti-Franco forces. Jerry's speech to Fletcher is a statement of his personal enlightenment as well as an example of willed action in support of his beliefs. He says to tell the Committee that he is a personal enemy of General Franco because he doesn't like fascists. He says that he is putting the cans back on the counter because he had put himself away when he put the cans away. Jerry throws Fletcher out of his shop, and then gets the paper boy to shout "Beware, Rankin Threatens Liberty!" as the headline of the paper, instead of "Libertyville Cited as Red Center," and the play ends with the boy's warning shout, a call to action for the audience.

Miller's "political playlet" has a great deal in common with a piece by the playwright whose work he most admired during his leftist days, Clifford Odets. Miller wrote in *Timebends* that, "in the mid-thirties, with what [Harold] Clurman would call his 'poster play,' *Waiting for Lefty*, followed by *Awake and Sing!*, Odets had sprung forth, a new phenomenon, a leftist challenge to the system, but even more, the poet suddenly leaping onto the stage and disposing of middle-class gentility, screaming and yelling and cursing like somebody off the Manhattan streets."[20] For the young Miller, a college student just learning to write plays in the mid-thirties, Odets, and the Group Theatre which produced him, represented the greatest possibilities of the American theatre at the time: "Returning to New York on vacations, I had my brain branded by the beauty of the Group Theatre's productions," he wrote.[21]

Odets's work, and particularly *Waiting for Lefty*, wrought its influence on more than the young Arthur Miller. *Lefty* was a phenomenon, one of the watersheds in American theatre history, which not only established the career of Clifford Odets and the Group Theatre, but changed the face of the theatre in America. From the perspective of the Left, as Ira Levine has painstakingly demonstrated, the Marxist theatre underwent a shift during the thirties from an agit-prop "workers theatre" aesthetic to what Levine calls "revolutionary realism."[22] The greatest impetus for this change was the success of *Waiting for Lefty*, which, after an initial production sponsored by the Theatre Union in 1935, was produced by the Group Theatre, running for almost 200 performances smack in the middle of the bourgeois commercial theatre of Broadway. The play was immediately adopted as the centerpiece for the leftist theatre movement, with dozens of productions being adopted throughout the United States. From the perspective of mainstream commercial producers, the success of *Lefty* demonstrated that there was a paying public for leftist plays.

The strength of *Waiting for Lefty* was that it combined some of the exciting techniques of agit-prop, such as a destabilizing of the "fourth-wall" proscenium and direct exhortation of the audience to take action against a social problem, with a central aesthetic principle of Aristotelian mimetic realism, the creation of audience empathy with the characters. Audience identification was the central technique in the new leftist drama of the late thirties that Levine calls "revolutionary realism." Following the ideology of the Popular Front in reaching out to all classes and all who opposed fascism, revolutionary realism targeted the typical middle-class theatre-goer as well as the proletarian. The audience's identification with the characters, however, was to be achieved for a different end than that in traditional Aristotelian theatre. Instead of the katharsis that leaves the audience drained of emotion, and therefore of will to act, the leftists advocated "the dramatization of exemplary characters changing their lives and environment through their willpower and action. Through his sympathetic involvement with these characters, the spectator was supposed to apprehend that the enlightened exercise of his will, in concert with the wills of others like him, could change his society for the better."[23]

This was precisely the aesthetic of *You're Next*. Like one of the scenes in *Waiting for Lefty*, the play introduces the audience to a sympathetic character in Jerry Marble, a good person like themselves who is trying to do his part to fight fascism and help those who have suffered from war. Jerry is distinctly middle-class, a small businessman, a member of the petit-bourgeoisie. It is, interestingly, as a businessman that Miller invites the audience's sympathy for Jerry. The threat from HUAC, and from the anonymous attacks of McCarthyism generally, is that Jerry will lose his customers and be put out of business if he is branded a Red. Jerry is not a Red, just a humane and compassionate citizen with a mind of his own. He is thus a natural and safe character for a middle-class audience to identify with, and his moment of enlightenment, when he realizes he must fight the Committee, might be theirs too. His situation is in fact analogous to that of Arthur Miller, who, as a playwright for the commercial Broadway theatre, could be put out of business as an artist by attacks from Red-baiters if audiences refused to patronize his plays. This play of "revolutionary realism" in fact speaks directly to middle-class fears and anxieties, and the basis for its attack on HUAC is that the Committee does not play fair, that it violates the common decency and freedom of thought that we take for granted in a democracy. If it bespeaks Miller's own interests and anxieties in the mid-forties, it is also a deft manipulation of the techniques that Miller had learned from his early hero Odets in order to appeal to a middle-class theatre audience. The strangest thing in the play's history is in fact its use for a Communist Party fundraiser. While it is an effective appeal to middle America to resist the extremes of HUAC, it is hardly Marxist. It reveals the same bourgeois liberal values for which Miller was berated in the leftist press when his *Death of a Salesman* was produced two years later. It is effective because it is authentic. Unlike the abstract and programmatic sketches of the agit-prop theatre, *You're Next* is written directly out of its author's personal anxiety for his life and career as well as his political and moral convictions. It is a call for political action to resist HUAC, but it is a call from the middle class to the middle class.

Interrogation

Are You Now or Have You Ever Been (1972)

In his preface to *Thirty Years of Treason*, Eric Bentley makes it clear that he saw the performance of a ritual at the center of the HUAC Hearings:

> The transaction is called Investigation. The scene is the Old House Office Building in Washington, Room 1105 in the United States Court House, Foley Square, New York, or some high rectangular chamber in some other governmental building designed in the grand Greek post-office manner. In the early years, before television, HUAC hearings were often heard on the radio, which meant that the drama was played to a national audience. Later, Speaker Sam Rayburn forbade that, but, since hearings were nationally reported in the papers, the occasion was never contained within the room where it took place. As in a play, the actors were never really talking *to* each other but *for* an audience, and HUAC could always confidently feel that its audience was not limited to guests physically present. The Committee performed for the nation, present and future. If not the Judaeo-Christian God, then Clio, Muse of History, sat in the royal box.
>
> It is important not to think of the hearings as the drama of the witnesses only, be they friendly or unfriendly, famous or obscure, honest or nefarious. It was the drama of the witness *and the other fellow*, who was either a Congressman or an investigator paid by the Congress. No one had the authority (or temerity?) to ask the other fellow *his* name, address, date of birth, party allegiance, religious affiliation, and so on. . . . But, as Freud would have predicted, these chaps did give themselves away. The drama is there. All it needs in a reader."[24]

In presenting the play he shaped from the testimony, *Are You Now or Have You Ever Been*, Bentley would have his readers believe that the drama was simply embedded in the thousands of pages of testimony, waiting for a careful editor to cull it out. In his preface to the play, he asserts: "These characters wrote their own lines into the pages of history. Though I did abridge and tidy up the record, I did not write in additional dialogue. Transpositions – of words within a sentence or of sentences within a sequence – I tried to hold down to a minimum lest there be any distortion of the sense."[25] Nevertheless, he does recognize his creative role as that of "arrangement" of material. Noting that the testimony "has been abridged, edited, and arranged" to form the play, he wrote that "the question of what to choose from the 1952 record was a matter of which 1952 items would follow upon the 1951 items with most 'drama.' It is by 'arrangement' that the overall shape of the work is arrived at. It is by 'arrangement' that the principal shock effect of this work – juxtaposition, collage – is produced." Somewhat disarmingly, he adds, "all these processes – choice of witness, abridgment, editing, arrangement – bring into play the personal judgment, not to mention talent, of the writer responsible."[26] In other words, as Bentley was fully aware, the process of writing this play was a process of selecting the material that would construct the version of the hearings that he wanted the public to see out of the voluminous testimony that was available to him and arranging it into a dramatic structure that would present this version to an audience most effectively. The only difference between Bentley's task and that of the playwright who works from imagination and personal experience is the source of the material.

The first piece of "selection" that Bentley did was to merge the many congressmen who had been members of the Committee over the years into a single, anonymous body. Reasoning that "committee membership varied a good deal in the course of the nine years covered" and that "these variations are unimportant to the action here presented,"[27] he did not attempt to distinguish between fairly reasonable men like Doyle and fanatics like Rankin, Jackson, and Starnes in designating the Committee members as CM 1, CM 2, etc. Similarly, Thomas, Wood, and Walter are merged into a single "Chairman" and Stripling, Tavenner, and Arens, who had distinctly different styles of interrogation, into a single "Investigator." The effect is to constitute an anonymous antagonist for the witnesses, which functions simply as the Enemy, or more precisely, the Persecutor.

While the text indicates no act or scene breaks, the play is carefully structured as a four-act melodrama, not unlike the hearings of the Hollywood Ten as structured by Parnell Thomas. In the first "act," testi-

Figure 4. A scene from the New York production
of Eric Bentley's *Are You Now, or Have You Ever Been . . .*

mony by Sam Wood, the first president of the Motion Picture Alliance
for the Preservation of American Ideals, sets up the climate of Red-baiting and the cooperation between the motion-picture studios and the
Committee that enabled the Hollywood Ten to be offered up as the
Committee's first sacrificial victims. It is followed by testimony of Ed
Dmytryk and Ring Lardner, Jr., that demonstrates the strategies of resistance employed by the Ten, and ends with Lardner's dramatic removal
from the stand:

The Chairman: Any real American would be proud to answer the question,
"Are you, or have you ever been, a member of the Communist
Party?" – any *real* American!
Mr. Lardner: I could answer it, but if I did, I would hate myself in the
morning.
The Chairman: Leave the witness chair!
Mr. Lardner: It was a question that would –
The Chairman: Leave the witness chair!

Mr. Lardner: Because it is a question –
The Chairman, *pounding his gavel*: Leave the witness chair!
Mr. Lardner: I think I am leaving by force!
The Chairman: Sergeant, take the witness away!
      A Sergeant takes him away. (*Are You Now*, 15)

The first "act" establishes the identity of the persecutors and the nobility of the resisters. The second, consisting of a long and carefully edited excerpt from the testimony of Larry Parks, exhibits the relentless harassment by the Committee of a well-intentioned but weak man who finally bends to their will. One of the play's reviewers complained that the "testimony of Larry Parks seems structurally the scene which shapes the rest of the play – and perhaps that is why it seems the worst mini-drama of the lot. It simply plays too much like a bad play, as the Committee forces the witnesses into the most humiliating abjection."[28] That Parks's ordeal had a reality beyond its theatrical representation and that he was forced into humiliating abjection for no constructive purpose by an extraordinarily callous Committee evokes pathos from an audience, and that is the aim of the scene as Bentley constructed it. It begins with Parks's reluctant cooperation, as he tells the Committee about his past membership in the Communist Party and his various "front" activities. When he is first asked whether Karen Morley is a member of the Communist Party, he says that he would "prefer not to mention names" (20), and the questioning continues in other directions. When asked later about his "reluctance to testify," he says, "on naming names, it is my opinion that the few people I could name, these names would not be of service to the Committee: I am sure you know who they are. These people are like myself, and I have done nothing wrong. I also feel that to be asked to name names like this is not American justice. We as Americans have all been brought up to believe it's a bad thing to force a man to do this." The questioning continues throughout the morning and afternoon. Parks delivers an impassioned plea not to be forced to name others, ending:

> I think my career has been ruined because of this, and I would
> appreciate not having to – don't present me with the choice of either
> being in contempt of this Committee and going to jail or being
> forced to crawl through the mud and be an informer! For what pur
> pose? I don't think this is a choice. I don't think this is sportsman-

like. I don't think this is American justice for an innocent mistake in judgment, if it was that, with the intention of making this country a better place to live. . . . This is probably the most difficult thing I have ever done, and it seems to me it would impair the usefulness of this Committee. . . . If you do this to me, it will make it almost impossible for a person to come to you and tell the truth. I beg you not to force me to do this! (29)

Asked whether he meant "to infer [*sic*] that this Committee was bringing you here *because* of any effect on your career," Parks said: "No. What I said was that, because of this, I have no career left. . . . I think the damage has been done" (30). A Committee member replies: "Don't you think the damage occurred when you became a member of an organization which advocates the overthrow of every form of constitutional form of government in the world? Is the Committee more to blame than your own act in affiliating with that organization? This Committee is an expression of the will of the American people" (30).

The Committee takes a break and then reconvenes in the evening in "executive session," without the audience and the cameras, and the Chairman assures Parks that the testimony "will not be publicized until such time, if at all, as the Committee itself may deem expedient" (31). The tension rises to a peak as Parks's lawyer tries to get the Committee to reveal whether he will be cited for contempt if he refuses to name the names, and gets the answer, "it is possible that the Committee may request a citation. On the other hand, it may not. Does that answer your question?" (32). After Parks tells the Committee that he is "probably the most completely ruined man you have ever seen" (32), and his lawyer pleads for "a sportsmanlike attitude, so what he gives you will not be used, if it can be helped, to embarrass people in the same position he finds himself in today," the Chairman assures him that "nobody on this Committee has any desire to smear anyone's name" (33). There is a long silence, and then Parks, completely broken, gives the names of Morris Carnovsky, Joe Bromberg, and five others. He is grilled about another seventeen people of whom he knows nothing, as his lawyer pleads, "I wonder if we can proceed a little faster so he doesn't suffer so much" (34). At the end of the grilling, a Committee member says, "I think you could get some comfort out of the fact that the people you mentioned have been subpoenaed. If they do appear here, it won't be as a result of anything you have testified to." Parks replies: "It is no comfort whatsoever" (35). When the Investigator tells the Chairman that he is finished, one of the Committee members comments, "I'd like to say, Mr. Chairman, that Mr. Parks' testimony has certainly been refreshing!" (35). It is the sentiment of a bird of prey, sated with its measure of blood. If the HUAC interrogation was a scapegoating ritual, or, as Victor Navasky suggests, a "degradation ceremony,"[29] Larry Parks was the perfect victim. Only the hardest of hearts could fail to be moved by his victimization. Only the most ruthless of Red-baiters could take pleasure in his persecution.

From this intense moment of pathos, Bentley goes on to "Act 3," which is the exhibition of a series of friendly witnesses, each juxtaposed with, and ironically undercut by, their own or others' statements. Sterling Hayden's testimony, ending, "my appearance before this committee could serve a very useful purpose!" (38), is followed by a statement from his autobiography: "I was a rat, a stoolie, and the names I listed – some of those, close friends – were blacklisted and deprived of their livelihood. . . . I don't think you have the foggiest notion of the contempt I have had for myself since the day I did that thing" (38). This is followed by the testimony from the second appearance of Ed Dmytryk, when he agreed with the Committee that the best test of a witness's credibility is the willingness to name names; by José Ferrer fervently seeking the Committee's advice on how to warn other actors of the dangers of Communism; by Abe Burrows trying to talk his way around the issue by appearing the innocent naif who only entertained at parties and by saying that he was not a Communist "in [his] heart"; by an excerpt from Elia Kazan's *New York Times* ad, and his statement to the Committee that he will "be glad to do anything you consider necessary"; by Jerome Robbins eagerly naming his associates and being advised to "use that great talent which God has blessed you with to put [Americanism] into ballets in some way, to put into music in some way, that interpretation" (54–5); by Martin Berkeley naming "my old friend Dashiell Hammett, now in jail in New York for his activities, and that excellent playwright Lillian Hellman" (56); and by Marc Lawrence identifying Lionel Stander as recruiting him into the Communist Party with the promise, "Get to know this stuff and you will make out more with the dames" (58). Provided as counterpoint to their testimony are various statements such as Tony Kraber's on being reminded that Kazan had testified that he had recruited him into the Party: "Is this the Kazan that signed the contract for $500,000 the day after he gave names to this Committee . . . would you sell your brothers for $500,000?" (53); Elliot Sullivan's statement about "the long, tired list of men who have sold their honor and dignity for a mess of pottage, for a job, for a movie contract" (55); and Lillian Hellman's famous letter to the Committee.

The momentum of this sequence accrues through irony. The self-proclaimed "American values" of the Committee are shown to be a fraud, as the Committee members and the informers are revealed as self-serving and weak, unmindful of the injury they do to others, while the resisters are honorable and noble. The melodramatic action of the play reaches its low point at the end of this sequence, as the forces of evil seem to be overpowering the forces of good. With "Act 4" – the testimony of Stander, Miller, and Paul Robeson – the action takes an upward turn, suggesting that there is hope for American society after all. In Stander, Bentley presents the strategy of resistance, the refusal to accept the Committee's definition of the ritual in which they are participating. Rather than address the Investigator's questions, Stander describes his victimization at the hands of the Committee and the blacklisters. "I have knowledge of subversive action!" he says. "I know of a group of fanatics who are trying to undermine the Constitution of the United States by depriving artists of life, liberty, and the pursuit of happiness without due process of law! I can cite instances! I can tell names. I am one of the first victims, if you are interested. A group of ex-Bundists, America Firsters, and anti-Semites, people who hate everybody, Negroes, minority groups, and most likely themselves – " (62). The testimony of Miller provides a reprise of the ethical issue as it is presented in the Hellman letter: "I am trying to – and I will – protect my sense of myself. I could not use the name of another person and bring trouble on him. . . . My conscience will not permit me to use the name of another person" (66).

In ending the play with the testimony of Paul Robeson, Bentley presented the witness who perhaps had the clearest sense of the ritual in which he was being forced to participate, and who used the most direct strategy of resistance to it. Bentley begins with a quotation from Robeson outside the context of the hearings:

I am not in any conspiracy. It should be plain to everybody and especially to Negroes that, if the Government had evidence to back up that charge, they would have tried to put me *under* their jail. They have no such evidence: In 1946 I testified under oath I was not a member of the Communist Party. Since then I have refused to give testimony to that fact. There is no mystery in this. I have made it a matter of principle to refuse to comply with any demand that infringes upon the constitutional rights of all Americans (67).

In the course of his testimony, Robeson takes the Fifth Amendment in response to questions about Communism, but undermines the Committee's power somewhat by demanding that his interrogators identify themselves and, when informed of witnesses who named him as a Communist, asking: "Why don't you have these people here to be cross-examined? Could I ask whether this is legal?" (70). Whenever possible, he breaks out of the Committee's discussion of Communism to suggest that the real issue is not his membership in the Communist Party but his outspoken criticism of the United States's treatment of "the Negro people of this land" and the treatment of indigenous peoples in colonial African countries: "I am not being tried for whether I am a Communist. I am being tried for fighting for the rights of my people who are still second-class citizens in this United States of America" (71). The play ends with Robeson's final exchange with Chairman Walter:

Investigator: While you were in Moscow, did you say Stalin was a great man?
Mr. Robeson: I wouldn't argue with a representative of the people who, in building America, wasted the lives of *my* people. You are responsible, you and your forebears, for sixty to one hundred million black people dying in the slave ships and on the plantations. Don't you ask me about *anybody*, please.
Investigator: I am glad you called our attention to that slave problem. While you were in Soviet Russia –
Mr. Robeson: Nothing could be built more on slavery than *this* society, I assure you. Can I read my speech?
The Chairman: You have *made* it without reading it. The hearing is adjourned.
Mr. Robeson: You should adjourn this forever (75).

In establishing the Committee as the agent of racism and slavery as well as blacklisting and informing, Bentley was doing some scapegoating of his own. In the context of the melodrama that is *Are You Now or Have You Ever Been*, it is clear that adjourning the Committee forever will purge a great source of evil from American society and allow the good American qualities of decency, loyalty, honesty, equality, and fair play to prevail once again. In its way, the play's representation of the world is as simple as *Big Jim McLain*'s. If the structure and the level of discussion are more sophisticated, the presentation of good and evil, and the moral choices between them, are just as clear. They are just reversed.

Are You Now had its premiere at the Yale Repertory Theatre in November 1972. It was produced Off-Broadway in late 1973, and then followed a six-month run in Los Angeles to capacity audiences. The production moved from there to Washington for a five-week run at Ford's Theater. The concurrence of the play's production with the breaking of the Watergate scandal in 1972 and 1973 gave its representation of the Congressional investigation an immediate context and its characterization of politicians a certain verisimilitude, but that was clearly not the only source of its popular appeal. It was revived successfully in London in 1977 and was considered dangerous enough to be banned in South Africa in 1978. An Off-Broadway revival ran from October 1978 until February 1979, thanks partly to the caché of celebrity attached to a revolving list of stars who did a turn at reciting the Lillian Hellman letter for Equity minimum: Colleen Dewhurst, Rosemary Murphy, Frances Sternhagen, Tammy Grimes, Barbara Baxley, Peggy Cass, Joan Copeland (the sister of Arthur Miller), Marcella Markham, and Liza Minnelli.

The play's strengths and its weaknesses were evident from its first production, when Zero Mostel, whose testimony is featured briefly, declared it to be "a public insult." Mostel and Ring Lardner, Jr., attended the premiere, and afterwards, it was reported, on the sidewalk outside the theater, "as a crowd gathered, Mostel ripped into the play and Lardner calmly declared that it was not theater or history."[30] In an interview years later, Bentley said that Mostel had gotten "so nervous" that the segment featuring his testimony was later dropped from the production.[31] As produced at Yale, the play had been presented as "documentary drama," a form that was in vogue during the early seventies with plays such as *In the Matter of J. Robert Oppenheimer*, *The Trial of the Catonsville Nine*, and *Inquest*. The press release on the play noted that "[Michael] Posnick's production will evoke the harsh reality of the hearings, which were held amid popping flashbulbs before a nation watching on television. Over a hundred slide projections and an extensive display of photographs in the theatre's lobby and lounge will show the original witnesses on the stand, and in some of their best-known works."[32] Despite the attempts to provide the historical context, criticism of the lack of context in the script itself came from both Right and Left. John Beaufort complained: "Literally faithful though it is, the documentary provides too little of the context of the ideological strife

in which Communists and their compliant fellow travelers used existing organizations or specially created 'front' groups to win a power
struggle and a propaganda wa. . . . 'Are You Now . . .' presents a limited
view and pleads its own special cause."[33] On the other hand, Jules
Chametzky wrote that in the Yale production, "not enough of this historical material – the political climate of the time – was presented. Nor
was the intellectual support and respectability lent to informing, or the
prevalence of crude Cold War shibboleths among presumably sophisticated thinkers."[34] What's more, he contended that the style of the Yale
production, which tended toward the abstract and "timelessness,"
worked against its putative "documentary" agenda:

> The acting, set, style all contributed to an appreciation of the ritual-
> istic nature of the HUAC proceedings themselves. The approach pre-
> sumably was an effort to emphasize the "timelessness" of the issues,
> and it may explain the curious distant quality about the produc-
> tion. . . . A small but vital element in the show was the stenotypist,
> silent, unobtrusive, ceaselessly recording it all. She too was somewhat
> abstract and a little spooky, but her task pointed to our real connec-
> tion with the events: The record exists, and we must study it carefully
> if in answer to the play's title we are to find out truly who we are.[35]

In the London production, a similar Brechtian distancing was achieved
by staging the play as "one of the first of what are now known as media
events."[36] Anton Rodgers achieved this effect by using closed-circuit
television monitors, which created a simulated telecast of the hearings
for the audience, complete with network identification and commer-
cials.[37] Thus the spectators simultaneously perceived the events of the
play as if they were the audience for, and thus in a sense, participants
in, the hearings and the general public watching a media event in their
homes. This dual representation provided a sense of historicity that was
missing from the script, as well as a more sophisticated sense of theatricality. Presumably the audience was led to consider the implications
of Bentley's play as yet another layer of theatricality through which they
were perceiving the event of the hearings. But this metatheatre did not
alter the fundamental melodrama that was being presented, and it still
left spectators with an inadequate sense of history. One British critic
wrote that the play "leaves me aching to know more about the real feelings and beliefs of the participants on both sides, particularly on the
committee side, where it is impossible to distinguish between alarmed

democrats, possible new-fascists and opportunists jumping on the witch-wagon."[38]

The early viewers of the play were divided on the question of the effectiveness of Bentley's strategy of "arrangement." Chametzky noted approvingly that

> the play is not merely a chronicle or recitative of "facts." Beyond telling us what happened – which it is necessary to know – the playwright (if that's the right word here) has shaped his material so that the human and political drama of the process might emerge. Through their words and actions we come to understand why the Committee acted as it did, why the witnesses performed as they did, the interplay of individual and public morality, our own stake in the outcome.[39]

A few years later, however, a more skeptical critic wondered "about the order of the witnesses: is it merely a habit of production that builds the story to nicely timed climaxes – with Lionel Stander and Paul Robeson – toward the end? And that allows Robeson to close the play by making the issue racism rather than communism and anti-communism?"[40] Several critics thought the play, and particularly the Robeson segment, too long. *Variety* complained that it was "a story with no real suspense . . . basically static."[41] Most reviewers, however, found that the play succeeded in provoking the audience to consider the implications of the hearings. "It does add up to a most forceful consideration of human values and attitudes,"[42] wrote one British critic. In *The Sunday Times* (London), John Peter declared that "the show is a test of conscience for aggressive liberals and complacent conservatives . . . the central core of Bentley's documentary play is to ask how political power should be used and how far people's conscience can or should resist it." At its simplest, it is "a warning that your freedom depends on guarding the freedom of others, and that the humanity of the law survives in the conscience of individual men."[43] Eric Bentley could hardly have said it better himself.

Blacklist

The Defenders, "Blacklist" (1964)

The first direct representation of the blacklist occurred, fittingly, in a television series. *The Defenders* was one of the few serious dramatic series on an American network in the early sixties to take on contemporary social issues and problems. At a time when such topics were scrupulously avoided by producers for fear of being "controversial," *The Defenders* offered dramatizations of the conflicts around book-burning, loyalty oaths, civil disobedience, and euthanasia. Although the show's main characters, father-and-son legal team Lawrence and Ken Preston, played by E. G. Marshall and Robert Reed, were idealized as unwaveringly ethical and altruistically devoted to their clients – and they almost never lost a case – the series attempted to present genuine issues that were grounded in the reality of American life. In addition to the producer's commitment to serious treatment of contemporary issues, the show's star, E. G. Marshall, had personal experience with the blacklist. Having originated the role of the Rev. John Hale in Miller's *Crucible* on Broadway in 1953, Marshall had been blacklisted along with Beatrice Straight, who had played Elizabeth Proctor. After this production, the roles the actors had been offered in television productions were mysteriously withdrawn. The pressure came from Laurence Johnson, the owner of four grocery stores in Syracuse, New York, who managed to make the television and advertising agency executives who controlled the industry adhere to his blacklist by threatening to place signs next to the sponsors' products in his stores, saying that they employed Communist sympathizers. Straight later said that she was "cleared" only after she paid a Catholic priest a fee of $500.[44]

On 18 January 1964, *The Defenders* aired an episode entitled "Blacklist," which was written by Ernest Kinoy and directed by Stuart Rosenberg. Kinoy has explained that he intentionally created a plot that "paralleled the situation with Johnson," avoiding the use of a big star. "We created an ordinary working actor, and when he's blacklisted he's finished." When Kinoy and the producers chose the actor to play the lead, however, "CBS said, 'You can't hire him.' They were still blacklisting him!"[45] The show concerned an actor, Joe Larch (Jack Klugman), who had been blacklisted in 1952 for contributing to Spanish War Relief in the thirties and for opposing HUAC in the forties. It was loosely based on Arthur Miller's experience with the making of a film about the New York City Youth Board in 1955. Miller had been hired by a small television producing firm to write a script about the efforts of social workers to civilize New York City's street gangs. After an exposé on Miller's leftist past and an editorial calling for the city to get him fired from the film was printed in the *New York World-Telegram*, a HUAC staff member summoned a member of the Youth Board and demanded that it sever its connections with Miller. The board met and voted eleven to nine to drop its association with the film. This was the occasion for the often-quoted remark by one of the board members: "I'm not calling him a Communist. . . . My objection is he refuses to repent."[46] The *World-Telegram* provided the rationale for the board's action in a lead editorial: "The question was not whether Mr. Miller is talented – or whether he could write an unbiased script on the work of the Youth Board. It was simply whether the city should enhance the playwright's prestige and diminish its own by indirectly hiring a man with such a questionable political background."[47]

As "Blacklist" opens, George Veigh, who is going to produce a documentary film about a city's youth program, decides to defy the blacklist and hire Joe Larch for the film. Scenes of celebration by Joe, who now clerks in a shoe store, and his family are juxtaposed with the scene in an office where two women are turning out a mimeo "bulletin" for the National Security Vanguard League, which alerts its members to the fact that Joe has been hired. When this hits the papers, the mayor says he will "look into" the situation before the city's final approval is given for the film. When his teenage son urges him to fight the blacklist this time, Joe goes to the Prestons for advice. They tell him that the Vanguard League has been careful to avoid a libel suit by stating only things that were a matter of public record, or "alleged" to be true, in their bulletin. The scene shifts to the mayor's office, where the mayor tells an aid he has enough problems without a "Red issue." Larch and the Prestons meet with Veigh, who tells them he will "fight all the way down the line" to keep Larch on the project.[48]

Lawrence Preston (E. G. Marshall) goes to talk with Judson Kyle, the power behind the Vanguard League, and the show's Laurence Johnson figure. Kyle reminisces about the early fifties and brags about the number of Communists who were "cleaned out" of their jobs by his group in 1952. He remembers with satisfaction that they produced 7,000 letters protesting the hiring of a woman who had belonged to a "front" organization. He tells Preston that Joe has "a record," but that he has never tried to pursue people like Joe though the courts because "They" have penetrated everywhere in American society: "parasites . . . vermin . . . rats . . . they'll swear to anything, you know. They'll lie" (109). He tells Preston to be careful, because Communism is poison and spreads like contagion. He says that other attorneys have been corrupted by Red clients and warns Preston: "There are only two sides, you know. . . . You're either for Them or against Them! Which side are you on . . . Mr. Preston, which side?" ("Blacklist," 109). As Preston leaves his office, Kyle's secretary tells him that she can help Joe to "rehabilitate" himself, if he's seen the error of his "Commie associations," through her brother's "consulting public relations service," the show's reference to the smear-and-clear agencies, for a fee of $200. The young Ken Preston (Robert Reed) is outraged by the idea of giving into the demand for a payoff. He says they should be attacking the whole system of blacklisting, not offering to cooperate with the blackmailers, calling Kyle's activity "a heresy hunt, a lynching for unpopular political opinions. And besides that, what right does Judd Kyle have to be judge, jury, and executioner?"[49] Representing the opinion of the younger post-McCarthyism generation in 1964, he says angrily that the blacklist is what's subversive, and that it is much more dangerous "than left-wing politics left over from 1937" (113).

The scene shifts to the city council meeting where the mayor maneuvers to avoid a vote on the film project, and the heat shifts to producer George Veigh. Then the scene shifts to the apartment, where the Larches tell Ken Preston that Joe has received a call from Veigh's office telling him he is being replaced because they have rewritten the part for a younger man. The casting director has told him, "personally, I'm going out now and getting a job poisoning orphans, it's cleaner" (118). Joe's wife asks, "Why does it hurt them for Joe to be an actor? . . . What kind of men are they?" (119). The scene shifts to the law office and a discussion between the Prestons about how little the law can do in the face of a blacklist. Ken decides to prepare an attack on the whole issue of the blacklist, while Lawrence tries negotiation with George Veigh and the mayor. Lawrence's strategy proves fruitless, as George explains that he can make the picture without Joe, or he can't make it at all, and the Mayor says he will lose the election if he "sticks his neck out" on this issue.

Ken has prepared a memorandum on a prima facie tort approach that attacks blacklisting as the violation of a property right. He would attack the "intermeddler," Judd Kyle, directly, as one who has induced George Veigh not to hire Joe Larch. Lawrence says that, although it is good law, the approach will never hold up in court. They can't prove that Kyle's action was directly responsible for Joe's firing. He says that the blacklist works like some "vague, poisonous fog." Nobody tells anyone anything; they "get the message. They know. . . . Everything is 'understood'" (132). There is no way to attack because they can't prove in court that pressure was applied. Disappointed, Joe decides to give up and go home to try to explain to his son why he can't fight the blacklist.

In an interesting metatheatrical reference to the series' approach to American society, Lawrence Preston tells Ken that maybe they've won too often, and it's made them arrogant: "The law is man-made and imper-

WILLIAM BENJAMIN   THE CHRISTIANFORM
No. 7   July 31, 1951   1740 K St., N.W., Wash. 6, D. C.

WHAT CAN I DO ABOUT COMMUNISM?
I'M JUST A SINGLE, ORDINARY PERSON;
WHAT CAN I DO?

MANY AMERICANS ASK THESE QUESTIONS EVERY DAY, PERHAPS EVEN YOURSELF.

J. Edgar Hoover has stressed the importance of exposing communism if we are to defeat it. YOU, as well as the F.B.I., can be in a position to expose the many fronts behind which it advances. THE CHRISTIANFORM is sending you a recently published document issued by the Committee on Un-American Activities of the United States House of Representatives. It is entitled GUIDE TO SUBVERSIVE ORGANIZATIONS AND PUBLICATIONS. Possession of this document will enable you to identify those groups and periodicals in America which are carrying forward the Communist program to destroy our country, the greatest bulwark of Christian civilization among nations.

SCORECARD! SCORECARD!
YOU CAN'T TELL THE PLAYERS WITHOUT A SCORECARD!

This is a cry as well known in the United States as these two old sayings:

YOU CAN TELL A MAN BY THE COMPANY HE KEEPS...and...
BIRDS OF A FEATHER FLOCK TOGETHER.

The GUIDE TO SUBVERSIVE ORGANIZATIONS AND PUBLICATIONS will not name Communists or identify fellow travelers for you, but it will clearly point out what TEAMS are opposing all loyal Americans right here in our own back yard. NOT ONLY WILL YOU BE AWARE OF THE TRUE NATURE OF SUCH GROUPS, BUT YOU WILL BE ABLE TO PASS THE INFORMATION ON TO OTHERS WITH OFFICIAL PROOF TO BACK YOU UP. Whenever you come across one of these organizations you can be sure that those working for it or with it are part of the enemy forces, either knowingly or unknowingly. Being so exposed really hurts the Communists. That's why they scream hysterically, "GUILT BY ASSOCIATION", in a terrific effort to obliterate the age-old truth contained in YOU CAN TELL A MAN BY...and...BIRDS OF A FEATHER...

Acquiring this knowledge of the enemy is an exceedingly important step which must be taken by anyone who asks what he can do about communism with honest intentions of doing what he can when he finds out what it might entail. WHAT CAN YOU DO RIGHT NOW? YOU can help THE CHRISTIANFORM distribute one GUIDE TO SUBVERSIVE ORGANIZATIONS AND PUBLICATIONS to every person on our mailing list which covers the entire United States.

25¢ will cover cost of handling and postage involved
in the distribution of two of these booklets.
$1.00 will send ten of them to other Americans who
will put them to very good use.
$5.00 will deliver sixty GUIDES.

YOU CAN HAVE A HAND IN THE EXPOSURE OF COMMUNISM URGED BY J. EDGAR HOOVER. YOU CAN HELP THE CHRISTIANFORM WEAKEN COMMUNISM BY HELPING IT DISTRIBUTE THIS OFFICIAL DOCUMENT WHICH STIGMATIZES COMMUNIST FRONTS FOR WHAT THEY ARE. Return blank below specifying the amount of your assistance. Many thanks for an act on your part in America's defense.

THE CHRISTIANFORM   1740 K St., N.W.   Washington 6, D.C.

Enclosed please find $...... to help defray cost of handling and postage involved in sending as many copies of the GUIDE TO SUBVERSIVE ORGANIZATIONS AND PUBLICATIONS to those on your mailing list as this sum will cover. Thank you for my copy.

NAME........................ADDRESS........................

Figure 5. An example of the "newsletters" put out
by the anti-Communist "Mimeo Press."

fect; not every story in life ends satisfactorily; neither does the law. Sometimes everything ends up in the air. No rescue, no climax, not even a good, rousing disaster. . . . There are injustices in the world, and they're not always solved by some brilliant point of law at a dramatic moment. Things don't always work out the way we want them to."[50] *The Defenders,* in the optimistic liberal spirit typical of the mid-sixties, suggested week after week that society's ills could be cured and that two smart and dedicated lawyers could make a difference on almost any issue. In this instance, however, Ernest Kinoy used the show's own formulaic character to suggest that the problem of blacklisting had no solution within the social system as it was then constituted. Producers needed funding; politicians had to be reelected. As long as the Judson Kyles could control public opinion, anyone they opposed could be deprived of employment. Kinoy gave the last word to Joe Larch. He says that blacklisting grows out of an atmosphere. "People are afraid – afraid of Communists and Socialists, folksingers – they're not sure who – anybody."[51] He says the situation will improve only "when people start believing in what they say they're defending . . . the Constitution" (134).

Ernest Kinoy won an Emmy for the writing of "Blacklist," as did Jack Klugman for his performance as Joe Larch. The show was the occasion for an editorial in *The Commonweal,* a liberal Catholic magazine, which noted that blacklisting was "a topic, as far as we know, that has not been treated in the last decade by the prime offenders: the film industry and the television industry." It went on to praise the program for demonstrating so effectively "how blacklisting works – how it functions through the marshaling of pressures that are difficult to see, and through the meshing of 'understandings' that frustrate most attempts to gain judicial redress."[52] The editorial did note, however, that by casting the story in terms of the documentary film industry, the show "avoided discussing the kind of pressure from sponsors that keeps blacklisting a problem in television today." It went on to make clear that "vigilantes and the vigilante mentality, so often written off as a highly forgettable aspects of the nineteen-fifties, are still with us," listing several recent products of the "mimeograph press": "48 Ways President Kennedy Helped the Communist Party," "9 Ways the Warren Court Defends Communists," and "The Commie-Front Listings of 57 Ministers."

Fear on Trial (1975)

Television's second treatment of the blacklist was more self-critical. *Fear on Trial* was an adaptation for television of John Henry Faulk's autobiographical account of his blacklisting and successful libel suit against anti-Communist Laurence Johnson, "clearance" specialist Vincent Hartnett, and Hartnett's agency, Aware, Inc. In 1962, Faulk was awarded $3.5 million in damages (later reduced to $550,000) after persevering for five blacklisted years in his effort to bring the suit to trial. Aside from the lawsuit, Faulk's story was a typical one. Having neither Communist membership nor Communist sympathies in his past, he was accused in an Aware, Inc. Newsletter of nine counts of "Communist front" activity, including entertaining at a State Department dinner at the request of CBS. With the help of lawyer Louis Nizer, Faulk decided to take on the whole issue of blacklisting by suing Johnson and Hartnett for libel, and, although he won the suit, his career and his marriage were destroyed in the process.

The television dramatization of Faulk's experience by David W. Rintels centers on the trial, using the forensic techniques of Louis Nizer, played by a forceful George C. Scott, to convince the television audience, as well as the jury, of Hartnett's guilt and the evil of the blacklist. The drama opens with Faulk (William Devane) at work, doing his down-home radio show, "Johnny's Front Porch," in which he entertains his audience with anecdotes about his old Texas friends and relatives, stories in the Garrison Keillor vein that embody a gentle humor and a wholesome folk wisdom. Faulk then watches with approval while Edward R. Murrow broadcasts his famous *See It Now* episode, "A Report on Senator Joseph R. McCarthy," with film clips of McCarthy at his most repulsive, and ending with Murrow's forthright attack on McCarthy and the other Red-baiters, and the American public for not taking action against their activities:

> The line between investigation and persecuting is a very fine one, and the junior senator from Wisconsin has stepped over it repeatedly. His primary achievement has been in confusing the public mind as between the internal and the external threat of Communism. We must not confuse dissent with disloyalty. We must remember always that accusation is not proof and that conviction depends upon evidence and due process of law. . . . We will not be driven by fear into an age of unreason if we dig deep in our history and our doctrine and remember that we are not descended from fearful men, not from men who feared to write, to speak, to associate and to defend causes that were for the moment unpopular.
>
> This is no time for men who oppose Senator McCarthy's methods to keep silent, *or* for those who approve. We can deny our heritage

and our history, but we cannot deny responsibility for the result. . . . We cannot defend freedom abroad by deserting it at home. . . . [McCarthy] didn't create this situation of fear, he merely exploited it, and rather successfully. Cassius was right. "The fault, dear Brutus, is not in our stars, but in ourselves."[53]

Watching with his colleagues, Faulk says, "Good on Ed, and good for CBS for lettin' him do it." Faulk soon finds out that CBS's opposition to McCarthyism does not run very deep, however. He is shaken when he learns of the suicide of Philip Loeb, who had been blacklisted and fired from the popular show *The Goldbergs*. Then he learns that he has been accused by Aware, Inc., of Communist sympathies, obviously because he has run for vice president of his union on an anti-blacklisting platform. When he talks about suing for libel, his producer urges him to write an answer to the "charges" against him, and not to make waves. Members of AFTRA, the union, at first offer to pay the legal charges of a challenge to the blacklist, but back off when they are reminded that the union will be attacked if it spends its money to defend Faulk. A scene follows in which Faulk's friend Harry explains that he can't support him because he has already been a target of Hartnett and Johnson, and he knows his career will be destroyed if he goes up against them again. Faulk's producer tells him that Johnson is visiting his sponsors and they are dropping the show. Faulk consults Louis Nizer about suing for libel, and the lawyer warns him that, although the suit might end the blacklist, Faulk will be taking a severe personal risk. Nizer says that the suit will bring everything about him into the open, and in making him "controversial," might itself make him unemployable to networks, which are concerned about pleasing sponsors, who in turn are concerned about pleasing customers. He also warns him that it will be very expensive to sue, that it will take a great deal of time, and that, in the end, he may lose.

Faulk goes to talk with a former Communist friend (John Houseman) who has been blacklisted. He tells him his experiences, and says that John has the right to sign anything he "has the stomach for," since he wasn't a Communist. John says that he doesn't want to "roll over for 'em either, like a whipped dog," and that he's going to sue. John's wife fails to support him, saying that he wants to sue because he wants to be a hero, and he doesn't stop to think that he will be ruining his family's lives as well as his own: "All I want is a happy, peaceful life with you and the children." John is given $8,000 by Edward R. Murrow for his legal costs, a check which Murrow tells him "is not a loan, but 'an investment in America.'" John and Nizer begin work on the case as he is fired from his job at CBS and conducts a fruitless and finally desperate search for employment on radio and television throughout the country. His marriage breaks up, and he spends five years doing jobs like selling encyclopedias and driving a cab while his suit makes its way through the courts.

The issue comes to a climax in the trial scene, where Nizer asserts that Faulk's career was cut off by Vincent Hartnett, "a man who sold people's names at five dollars a throw" to the networks. The defense lawyer presents Hartnett as having performed a service for the networks and advertisers: "Mr. Hartnett is not a terrorist. He is a dedicated, sincere man who is painstaking in his research, and as you will see, he is scrupulously honest." He suggests that the lawsuit is a publicity stunt by Faulk to cover up his own incompetence, to gain a little sympathy, to glorify himself, and to harass the defendants, "whose political position you do not like." The defense lawyer asks Faulk, "Are you now or have you ever been a member of the Communist Party?" and proceeds to question him about gatherings he attended at people's houses, just as if he were a HUAC investigator. Faulk answers "absolutely not" to all questions about membership in the Communist Party or "front" groups, establishing him as a completely "innocent" victim of anti-Communist Red-baiting, and thus assuring the sympathy of both the jury and the television audience.

In an unusually candid gesture by CBS, after an advertising executive testifies to the pressure Laurence Johnson exerted on him not to hire John Henry Faulk, two unwilling participants in the blacklisting procedure were allowed to portray themselves in testifying about the smear-and-clear procedures at the network. David Susskind explains the clearance procedure that made it necessary to find replacements for a number of actors who were considered politically subversive, including an eight-year-old child. Mark Goodson describes the blacklisting of potential participants in his panel shows and describes the blacklisting of a panelist who was mistaken for an actress with a similar name. Although the misidentification was cleared up, the panelist was still blacklisted because, now that she had been named in anti-Communist publications, she might be unpopular with the viewers. The pièce de résistance of the trial scene is the testimony by actress Ann Claibourne. She explains tearfully that she was blacklisted for three years after she refused to pay Hartnett a fee of $200 to clear her. She got off the blacklist only by agreeing to speak in favor of Hartnett and Aware, Inc., at a union meeting when there was a motion to condemn the blacklisting. Hartnett is portrayed as a robot-like functionary whose only emotion is a sweaty discomfort when activities like his clearing of Santa Claus and his devious methods for getting money from corporations are exposed. He writes constantly in a little black book during the trial, which is revealed to contain a list of the names of people who attended the trial. Nizer further discredits him when he misidentifies a woman in the courtroom as "Mrs. Faulk."

There is a triumphant moment in the drama, when the jury comes in and the foreman asks if they are permitted to award more in damages than the plaintiff asks for. Faulk is vindicated when the jury awards him $3.5 million rather than the $500,000 in damages that he sued for. The triumph of innocence over evil is undercut, however, when, in the midst of the victory celebration at Nizer's elegant New York apartment, he tells one of Faulk's supporters that Laurence Johnson has died, and turned out not to have been very wealthy despite his chain of supermarkets. Faulk will not be able to collect more than "five cents on the dollar" of his damages. A voice-over reveals that Faulk returned to Texas and found employment at a Dallas radio station. It does not reveal that, in payment of the later much-reduced award of damages, Hartnett, who was not rich despite his entrepreneurial skills in the smear-and-clear industry, spent the rest of his life sending small checks to Faulk to pay the debt.[54]

Nonetheless, the mood of the ending was suitably anticlimactic. Although the television drama had the key elements of melodrama in its innocent victim (Faulk), its inexplicably malevolent villain (Hartnett), its avenging hero (Nizer), and a society that needs to save itself from evil by destroying the villain, its mood was more complicated than this formula would imply. In trying to suggest the larger implications of the blacklist, Rintels wrote a different kind of script. He took his text from Shakespeare, by way of Ed Murrow: "The fault, dear Brutus, is not in our stars, but in ourselves." The trial scene in the television drama was itself a media event in the United States of 1975. It allowed the network to assume its share of the guilt, as personally did Susskind and Goodson, two of CBS's most successful producers. Through them, the television audience was invited to repent as well, for, as the defense lawyer says, Hartnett and Johnson could only operate in the entertainment industry because "the American public doesn't want Communist fronters appearing on their programs." The implication was that we all shared responsibility for this shameful episode in our past, and that, in order to purge the evil from our society, we had, like Ann Claibourne and David Susskind and Mark Goodson and CBS, to acknowledge our guilt and repent. Even in victory, John Henry Faulk remains a victim, as in their ways are Hartnett and Johnson. The subtext of the piece is perhaps Dalton Trumbo's famous statement about the blacklist in his speech to the Screen Writers Guild in 1970:

> The blacklist was a time of evil, and . . . no one on either side who survived it came though untouched by evil. Caught in a situation that had passed beyond the control of mere individuals, each person reacted as his nature, his needs, his convictions, and his particular circumstances compelled him to. There was bad faith and good, honesty and dishonesty, courage and cowardice, selflessness and opportunism, wisdom and stupidity, good and bad on both sides; and almost every individual involved, no matter where he stood, combined some or all of these antithetical qualities in his own person, in his own acts. . . . It will do no good to search for villains or heroes or saints or devils because there were none; there were only victims.[55]

The insistence on social responsibility and the denial of individual guilt was perhaps an expression of the times in the United States of 1975. It was recognized that the simple bipolar conflict of good and evil, persecutor and victim, innocent and villain, within the melodramatic paradigm was an inadequate explanation for a phenomenon that had gripped the country in an atmosphere of fear and suspicion for so long. It was a time to acknowledge shared guilt for social conditions that the whole country had allowed to come about.

The Front (1976)

Director Martin Ritt and writer Walter Bernstein were both blacklisted during the fifties. After being named in *Red Channels*, Bernstein was unable to sell a television script under his own name for eight years. Ritt, who had begun his career acting with the Group Theatre, was blacklisted from 1951 to 1957. Working together on *Paris Blues* (1961), the two spent a good deal of their spare time thinking about a film that would convey the experience of the blacklist. "Neither of us wanted to do it head-on, or in a documentary-type fashion," Bernstein said in an interview, "because we didn't want it to be a polemic."[56] The break-through came when Bernstein thought of using his personal experiences as a blacklisted television writer as the basis for a screenplay about "fronts." The result was what Ritt has called "a comedy in the classic sense," which "probes one of showbiz's most unfunny periods," a film that left Ritt describing its "ironic comedy" in one breath and its depiction of "how savage the system is" in the next.[57] "What the audience will get," he told an interviewer, "is a film filled with a bitterness and irony that reflect the ludicrousness of the time of the blacklist." [58] Bernstein agreed. "I guess what I've written is a serious comedy," he said.[59]

In his *Report on Blacklisting,* John Cogley provides an explanation of the use of "fronts" by blacklisted television writers as it had evolved by 1956:

> In the early days of blacklisting, it was possible for a writer to submit scripts under an assumed name. After a while, the system was tightened up. It is now necessary for a writer to have a "front" in order to continue working. The "front" must be a person who can convincingly carry off the role of a writer. He attends all conferences on the script which he is supposed to have written. He has to be coached on how to react to suggestions, how to take notes on the changes which the producer or director requests, etc. If the front has some acting experience, so much the better.[60]

Cogley describes a number of problems that arise for the front. He must accept public credit for another person's work. His family and friends assume he is making a great deal of money. His employer may object to his moonlighting. What's more, Cogley suggests, "Ego problems develop. The 'front' begins to act like a first-rate writing talent and resents the actual writer." There was even a case where a front was blacklisted after he had achieved "a certain ersatz prominence." Cogley noted that the television industry often took advantage of a writer's blacklisted status to buy "high-priced talent" at "cut-rate prices." Some talent agencies and "packagers" of shows went along with the arrangement, taking kickbacks for the scripts they sold for the blacklisted writers.[61] While he was blacklisted, Bernstein had made a living along with his blacklisted colleagues, Abraham Polonsky and Arnold Manoff, by writing scripts for the television programs *You Are There* and *Danger* with the help of various fronts.[62]

In their movie, Bernstein and Ritt took advantage of the screen persona that Woody Allen had already established in such films as *Take the*

Money and Run and *Love and Death,* in presenting the character of the front. As Robert Asahina noted, "Howard Prince is one more example of the wheedling and whining neurotic, the self-serving and self-mocking opportunist whose two imperatives are, in the words of Vivian Gornick, to 'get laid and stay alive.'"[63] With Woody Allen's name above the title, the film's association with Allen's sleazy but somehow eminently likeable schlemiel antihero was inevitable, establishing the film's comedic framework from the beginning. The dark humor of the film's treatment of the fifties is conveyed quickly through its opening montage of black-and-white film clips from the period, to the accompaniment of Frank Sinatra singing "Young at Heart." The montage begins with the wedding of Senator Joe McCarthy, as he emerges beaming from the church, and later clowns over cutting the cake with his new bride. In the rest of the sequence, images of soldiers returning from Korea, of bombs dropping and tanks rolling, of General MacArthur's retirement parade, of Presidents Truman and Eisenhower joking with army officers, of a suburban family proudly displaying their atomic bomb shelter, of the Rosenbergs in handcuffs, are juxtaposed with images of the era's escapism and frivolity. Fifties icons such as Joe DiMaggio, Marilyn Monroe, and Rocky Marciano are displayed along with Mrs. America of 1952 and various models showing off the latest swimwear in high heels. The montage has a simple message. The fifties were filled with war – both cold and hot – Red-baiting, and mass fear as well as the escape from those things through hero worship, sex, mythicizing the family, and materialism. Bringing the two poles of reality into a rather bizarre juxtaposition is the image of McCarthy cavorting in his wedding garb, just another American family man.

The mood of irony that is established in the opening sequence informs the audience as it is confronted with Howard Prince (Woody Allen) at work as a cashier and taking small bets as an unsuccessful bookie, and with his response to the request of his boyhood friend Alfred Miller (Michael Murphy) that he serve as a front for him. Howard is happy to do it, both to help out his friend and to make a little money, as Alfred insists on paying him 10 percent of his fees. Howard quickly begins to enjoy his reputation as a writer and talks Alfred into arranging for him to front for two more blacklistees. The movie's plot follows a simple comedic structure, as Howard falls in love with Florence Barrett (Andrea Marcovicci), an assistant producer who is equally devoted to leftist politics and good writing, loses her when he refuses to risk his new-found success to fight the blacklist with her, and gets her

117

back again when he refuses to cooperate with the Committee. In terms of comic structure, the movie is deeply ironic. There is barely a "happy ending." The fundamental corruption in American society that manifests itself in Red-baiting and blacklisting is the same at the end of the film as at the beginning. Yet the change in the character of Howard Prince suggests that there is some hope for the future. As a result of his experience, and of Florence's love, Howard moves from a state of almost pure self-interest and willful ignorance about society to a position of moral responsibility and resistance to oppression.

The portrayal of the blacklist is carried out in a series of incidents related to Howard's "career" and to a subplot involving the actor Hecky Brown, played by Zero Mostel and loosely based on his and Philip Loeb's experiences with the blacklist. Alfred explains the blacklist to Howard in simple terms: "You're on the list, you're marked. You don't work." He tells Howard, "I'm a Communist sympathizer." When Howard says he always was, he replies, "It's not so popular anymore." In the course of the film, the blacklisted writers don't suffer all that much. Although they have to sell their work at reduced rates and to put up with Howard's increasing self-importance, they manage to work. The only indication of the stress they are under is that Alfred's ulcer flares up when Howard is subpoenaed. The film's pathos is invested in the character of Hecky Brown, and the evil of the blacklist is displayed most prominently in his interviews with Hennessy, the proprietor of the "Freedom of Information Service," which is a version of Vincent Hartnett's Aware, Inc. Sent to Hennessy to find out how to clear himself by his producer, Phil Sussman (Herschel Bernardi), Hecky admits that he once marched in a May Day parade, that he has subscribed to the *Daily Worker*, and that he has signed petitions for Loyalist Spain and Russian War Relief. He says he only got involved with these activities because he was attracted to a Communist girl. Hennessy tells him to write a letter explaining that he has seen the error of his ways and deeply repents his activities. He tells him the letter must "come from the heart," and that "sincerity is the key." The proof of sincerity, of course, is that he has to name the names of the other people who were involved with him.

Hecky writes a letter, but Phil is told by a network executive that the letter doesn't go far enough, and that he has to fire Hecky. In a scene in Hecky's dressing room, Phil tells Hecky that his character isn't working, that his personality is too dominant for an ensemble show, and that he's throwing the balance off. He will try to work with him on a show of his own. Hecky and Florence immediately recognize what is happening, and Hecky demands to know what more he is supposed to do, after he has written "what that snake asked me to write." Hecky is shown being shunned by his old friends in a restaurant, and then a second scene with Hennessy shows him getting desperate. He tells Hennessy he can't get work. His agent of thirty years will not answer his calls. Hennessy demands that he give names if he wants to be rehabilitated. Hecky says he is "terrible with names." Hennessy says that the others "remember you," meaning that they have named him. Hecky replies that then he doesn't need him to name them. Hennessy comes back with the Informer Principle: "Your sincerity is important, your desire to cooperate fully." Hennessy suggests that Hecky can show this by "getting to know" Howard Prince better, by finding out who his friends are, what he does in his spare time, and "where he stands on the issues of the day." Hecky responds, "You want me to spy on Howard Prince." Hennessy tells him they are "in a war against a ruthless and tricky enemy who will stop at nothing to destroy our way of life." Hecky says, "You mean, if I spy on Howard Prince, I can work." Hennessy replies, "I don't do the hiring. I only advise on Americanness," but "as the sign of a true patriot, it would certainly help" if he gave them information on Howard Prince.

Hecky gets Howard to drive him to the Catskills for a performance, and on the way asks about his friends and tries to get him to talk about friends who are "in the same position" as Hecky. Then follows an incident that was drawn from Zero Mostel's own experience. The owner of the resort has already offered Hecky a much smaller fee than he would have paid him before the blacklist. On the spot, he cuts the fee from $500 to $250. Hecky does the show, an immense success, but gets drunk afterwards and attacks the owner, who has him removed by bouncers, shouting, "You'll crawl in the gutter, you Red bastard, you Commie son of a bitch!" Howard takes Hecky home to stay with him, and he goes through Howard's papers while he sleeps.

This is followed by a party scene, where Howard and Phil are introduced by a network executive to a version of Laurence Johnson, the supermarket owner. As Walter Bernstein knew only too well, Johnson and his daughter, Eleanor Buchanan, made it their business to collect information on actors from sources such as *Counterattack* and *Red Channels* and to apply pressure on networks and sponsors not to hire them. For example, when two such actors appeared on the TV series *Danger*, the "Veterans Action Committee of Syracuse Super Markets" wrote to Leonard A. Block of the Block Drug Company, which manufactured the show's sponsor, Amm-i-dent toothpaste, acquainting him with the actors' "records" as listed in *Counterattack*. The letter went on to threaten:

> If you plan to continue the use of Communist Front talent wouldn't it be a good idea if you were to send a representative from the Block Drug company or Cecil & Presberey, Advertising Agency, since both companies are aware the Communist Fronters are allowed in Amm-i-dent advertising. Perhaps we could work out a questionnaire to be given to the people who buy from our cosmetic displays. A question-naire could be drafted reading, for instance, as follows:
> Do You Want any Part of Your Purchase Price of Amm-i-dent to be Used to Hire Communist Fronters?
> Yes ❏ No ❏
> Indicate your choice by **X** in the appropriate box.
> We are sending this letter to you by registered mail because our ear-lier correspondence you on May 28th evidently went astray since no answer has been forthcoming.[64]

In the film, Phil and Howard are introduced by a network executive to Hubert Jackson of Jackson supermarkets on Long Island. He complains that some of the actors being used on the show are "pretty pink." The executive says they are as concerned as he is about the politics of the actors they employ and assures him that "we take every precaution" against hiring Communists. Jackson tells him that his customers don't buy the products of sponsors who employ Reds. When Howard asks him how they know, Jackson says, "I put signs right up over the prod-ucts to tell them." The executive tells Phil he should send Jackson a list of actors he wants to use and let him look it over and "give you any ideas he has." When they leave, Howard asks Phil how many stores Jack-son has. Phil says, "Three or four." Howard says, "He's got three stores, he tells a whole network who to hire." Phil says, "Who wants trouble?"

Howard now becomes a target himself, as an investigator is shown dogging him and taking pictures of his meetings with the blacklisted writers and with Florence. Howard is subpoenaed, and Phil tells him that he doesn't like it, but Howard has to testify: "You gotta go. If you don't do it, you don't work." Howard gets Phil to protest this, but he quickly knuckles under to the network executive. Howard meets with the network's lawyer, Hennessy, and the investigator who has been fol-lowing him. He tries to get the lawyer to buy off the Committee – "How much could it cost? They're just Congressmen" – but ends up agreeing to read the statement that is written for him. Then Howard goes with the other writers to see Alfred in the hospital. Alfred tries to get him to see that he is being used by the Committee if he cooperates, not using it, as Howard claims: "They don't care about names. They care about getting people to name names." The other writers disagree. One says Howard should take the Fifth, and the other says he should cooperate and save himself, since there is no further harm that could be done to them. Howard and the audience are thus presented with the three options open to the subpoenaed witnesses.

Hecky comes to Howard's apartment to apologize for his behavior and tells him, "take care of yourself. The water is full of sharks." This is followed by Hecky's suicide scene. Then, as Howard watches Hecky's funeral from across the street, in the shadow of a brick wall, the investigator is shown taking pictures of the mourners and of Howard with a telephoto lens, a scene reminiscent of the funeral of J. Edward Bromberg, whose death was attributed by many on the Left to his treatment by the Committee. (Bromberg's funeral became something of a leftist event, and a number of show-business people were blacklisted because of their attendance.) Howard goes to see Florence and tells her that he is a front. He says that he is not going to cooperate with the Committee because "Howard Prince is his own man," and that he can beat the Committee in his own way. The penultimate scene in the movie is the Committee hearing, which is a typical subcommittee arrangement, with a few Committee members and no audience. The network lawyer makes an unctuously ingratiating statement of thanks to the Committee for allowing Howard to appear and agrees profusely with the Chairman's statement, "We are here to keep this country just as pure as we possibly can." Howard tries to evade the Committee's questions with double-talk, a strategy reminiscent of the Hollywood Ten's claims to be answering the questions "in their own way." The Committee decides to play hardball by asking Howard about his activities as a bookie, thus opening him to criminal prosecution. The lawyer talks the Committee into taking a single name and suggests to Howard that he "give them Hecky – he's dead anyway. What difference does it make?" After a moment of soul searching, Howard responds to the question of whether he knows Hecky Brown: "Fellas, I don't recognize the right of this Committee to ask me these kind of questions. And furthermore, you can all go fuck yourselves."

As Peter Biskind wrote, the ending was "an Old Left wet dream, where the hero gets to say 'Fuck You' to HUAC, and is rewarded with a

big kiss from his beautiful girlfriend."[65] Howard wins Florence's
respect along with her love and is cheered off to prison by admiring
fans, in a scene reminiscent of the early days of the Hollywood Ten.
Howard is condemned by the corrupt society depicted on the screen,
but is rehabilitated in the eyes of the audience, having resisted the
oppression of the Committee and somehow discovered the values of
loyalty and altruism. The response to the film suggests, however, that
Bernstein and Ritt were not successful in their attempt to blend dark
comedy in the Howard Prince story with melodrama and pathos in the
Hecky Brown story. Robert Asahina complained, "instead of the mixture of tragedy and farce that would have been appropriate, the film
offers empty moralism, the cheapest of ironies and little bitterness – or, indeed, any other genuine feeling. It is a hash of pathos and
low humor that turns 'the plague years' into a laughing matter: What
comes off as ludicrous is the movie's own foolishness, not the time of
the blacklist." The film's weakness, according to Asahina, was in its
simplistic moral scheme: "The actual tragedy and complexity of the
McCarthy era are completely obscured," and what we have is "a grossly
simplified tale that approaches blatant propaganda in the guise of
humor."[66] Asahina claimed that the film reduced all politics to the
strengths and failings of individuals, pitting the good guys – Florence
and the blacklisted writers, who are "virtuous, idealistic human-
ists" – against the bad guys – the studio bosses, the Committee and its
investigators, the pressure groups, and the cooperative witnesses, who
are "selfish, cold-blooded fanatics." Those caught in the middle, such
as Hecky, Phil, and Howard, are "spineless cowards." In this scheme,
"the essence of the film's drama lies in Howard's movement from the
last group to the first." From the perspective of 1975, Asahina rejected
the melodramatic vision that had informed the representation of the
events of the fifties from both the Left and the Right, contending that
Howard's struggle does not correspond to "the real choices made by
real people during the McCarthy madness, when refusing to testify did
not automatically signify innocence and 'friendly' witnesses were not
necessarily craven grovelers." On the other hand, he suggested, "it is
unpleasant to have to say it – and painful to think of being misunderstood – but there were plenty of ethical cowards who deceived themselves and others about the horrors of Stalinism, who hid behind the
very Constitution and system of laws they had previously regarded with
contempt. Ambition and egotistic cynicism were hardly confined to
the bad guys: many of the good guys were opportunistic martyrs."[67]

Asahina seems to have been speaking for a generation of critics for whom the vision of the "Old Left" was simplistically clear-cut. Andrew Sarris wrote that "*The Front* takes dead aim at the television blacklisters of the 1950s and shoots loads of buckshot at these baddies."[68] Geoff Brown wrote of the "old-fashioned charm" of Ritt's directing style and suggested that "the patterning of scenes is frequently revealed as baldly melodramatic and conventional."[69] Peter Biskind remarked that "the film reduces itself, in the last analysis, to a morality play about good guys and bad guys. . . . a pious reminder that it did happen here, but it furthers our understanding of the period not an iota." For Biskind, "if it works at all, it does so as a black comedy about Making It."[70] From the point of view of the "Old Left," however, and old liberals too, the film did its work. As Robert Hatch expressed it in *The Nation*: "*The Front* is full of laughs, full of tears, keeps you cheering for the home team. It doesn't tell you how bigotry gets a hold on this country from time to time, but what it does, which more serious discussions never quite seem to do, is make you sense how it would feel to be played with by jackals. And, being entertainment, it ridicules evil. That, of course, is not the only way to fight it, but laughter is a useful tool in the cause of virtue."[71]

Guilty by Suspicion (1991)

While Kinoy and Bernstein, writing in the mid-sixties and the mid-seventies, were uneasy about casting their representations of HUAC in terms that were too straightforwardly melodramatic, there were no such qualms for the makers of *Guilty by Suspicion*, which is easily identifiable as a film of the early nineties: a straightforward melodrama that casts the Committee as the source of evil – the persecutors – and the witnesses as tortured scapegoats. As David Denby suggests, "the movie is about a Man of Conscience – it's just the kind of film once concocted by the screenwriters among the Hollywood Ten."[72] The project began, interestingly enough, with a French director, Bertrand Tavernier, who was interested in making a film about blacklistees like Joseph Losey, Jules Dassin, and Jack Berry, who chose self-exile in Europe, where they could work, to life in the United States. Tavernier brought together producer Irwin Winkler and Abraham Polonsky, whose importance as a writer, in the words of the *Dictionary of Literary Biography*, "rests both on his body of work – one of the strongest, continuously radical political statements in commercial American film – and on his role as symbol of the oppressed Hollywood writer, driven underground by Cold War hysteria, only to reemerge undaunted, still creative, and still radical."[73] Although Polonsky is the first to say that he survived the blacklisting well enough, writing novels and making money from his blackmarket television scripts, his calm, unwavering, and articulate expression of the leftist position and his fundamental decency have made him the chief spokesman for the post-Ten blacklisted writers.

Polonsky wrote a screenplay that began with a hearing scene which "Mr. Winkler and Mr. Tavernier both felt . . . was too climactic for the beginning of the film. It belonged at the end, they thought, lest the rest of the picture appear anticlimactic." Polonsky decided that, in that case, "it's no longer a survival-in-Europe story. It should be a picture about Hollywood. And if it's a picture about Hollywood, it will have to be a picture about the political controversy."[74] Tavernier eventually dropped out of the project, and Winkler signed himself on to direct the film, his first effort in that role. Then Winkler decided to rewrite the screenplay himself, turning the protagonist, David Merrill (Robert De Niro), from a Communist to a political naif who had attended a few Party meetings in the thirties and been thrown out for "arguing too much." He also changed Ruth Merrill (Annette Bening) from an independent woman with a degree in microbiology to a Hollywood ex-wife who is living on alimony until Merrill's blacklisting forces her to go back to teaching. Winkler told a reporter that if the movie was "about a Communist, the end result would be perceived as a defense of Communism." Instead, he "chose to do a story about a nonpolitical person because I find that much more interesting . . . a moral man who got too caught up in his career – the glitter, the fancy car, the lavish apartment." "What's interesting about David Merrill's character," he said, "is that as his success and the symbols of his success start to slip away, the values of friendship and being with his family and those he loves begin to reassert themselves. He regains his morality."[75] So Irwin Winkler turned Polonsky's political script into a movie about the fall and rise of David Merrill, a story that has been rooted in American culture as long as there has been an American success myth, and that was told very effectively in 1884, when William Dean Howells wrote *The Rise of Silas Lapham.* Nevertheless, the movie is still a film about the fifties, about HUAC and the show-business blacklist, and it still has what one reviewer called a "primal horror"[76] about it.

In the style of fifties pseudodocumentary, notably *Big Jim McLain*, the film is preceded by a statement about the blacklisting:

In 1947 the House Committee on Un-American Activities began an investigation into Communism in Hollywood.

Ten men who refused to "cooperate" with the committee were tried, convicted, and sentenced to prison terms after the Supreme Court refused to hear their case.

Thereafter, no one called to testify, either in public or in secret, could work unless he satisfied the committee by naming names of others thought to be Communist.

The action begins as Polonsky had originally conceived it, with the trope of the Committee hearing, but instead of David Merrill, it is Larry Nolan (Chris Cooper), an amalgam of Larry Parks and director Richard Collins, who is testifying. The spectator sees a long shot of a dingy room where a makeshift subcommittee is holding an "executive session," hearing testimony in secret. A caption reads "House Committee on Un-American Activities Los Angeles, California September 1951, Executive Session." With the camera angle from the point of view of the interrogators, the spectator sees a small table where an ashen-faced and sweaty Larry Nolan sits with his lawyer, Felix Graff, a version of studio lawyer Martin Gang. The atmosphere is dark and murky, with a smoky appearance supplied by large quantities of dry ice. Indeed, this is the case throughout the film, which Michael Ballhaus, the director of photography, shot in a consciously *film noir* style in order "to convey a sense of the era's bleakness."[77]

A loutish character who turns out to be the Committee's investigator, Ray Karlin, a version of Roy Cohn, hovers over the Committee members, a fat, cigar-chomping Chairman Wood and a bulldogish "Congressman" Tavenner, promoted from Committee Counsel for the purposes of the film. The congressmen are berating Nolan for defending the Communist Party. Wood says that Communists should wear some kind of identification, like a bumper sticker or a pin, so the Committee wouldn't have to go through this. Nolan gives the inevitable Larry Parks line: "I beg of you, please don't make me do this. Don't make me crawl through the mud. You know who they are. They're my friends." Wood replies that they are Communists, and "we need to protect this country from the ideas they're spreadin' through their films and their television shows." When Parks says that he doesn't want to be an informer, Wood says, "Real Americans have appeared before this Committee and they have demonstrated their loyalty. Now, how do you think we got your name in the first place. . . . Will you speak up, please, son. There's nothing to be ashamed of here."

Having clearly established the identities of the persecutors and scapegoat, Winkler goes on to give a portrait of Hollywood in the time of the great fear. David Merrill, played by Robert De Niro with a distinct resemblance to Elia Kazan in the early fifties, right down to the hair style and the clear-rimmed glasses, arrives from a two-month trip to Europe unaware of the terror that has gripped the film community as a result of the 1951 hearings. At a welcome-home party, Larry's wife Dorothy (Patricia Wettig), based on Dorothy Comingore, who played Susan Kane in *Citizen Kane* and was married to Richard Collins, gets drunk and accuses them all of hiding from the reality of the persecution. David takes her home to find Larry burning his books, while Dorothy throws his belongings out the window and asks if he named her too. Larry says, "I did what any scared, loyal American would have done." David's writer friend Bunny Baxter (George Wendt) says, "Welcome home, David."

David's own troubles begin when he is called in by Darryl Zanuck (Ben Piazza) and told to see the lawyer Felix Graff (Sam Wanamaker) and get himself "straightened out" so he can make his next picture. David meets with his agent, who says, "Zanuck likes you, David, don't louse that up." Then he meets with Graff in a sleazy hotel room. Ray Karlin emerges from another room and tells him he's been named as a Communist sympathizer. David tells him he went to a couple of meetings, and that was it. Karlin tells him he will have to testify to his own associations and "those of others" in order to "purge himself." David refuses to inform on people, and Karlin says he will be subpoenaed to appear at a public hearing. Then follows a series of scenes in which David discovers that he is blacklisted and witnesses the effects of the blacklist on his friends. His agent tells him not to come to the agency. He is called in the middle of the night by Joe Lesser, a version of Joseph Losey, played by Martin Scorsese, who wants him to finish the film he is making because he is about to depart for Europe in order to duck a subpoena. David is called to the set to do something about Dorothy, who is dead drunk and weeping because Larry has taken their son away from her on the grounds that she is a Communist and an unfit mother.

David is increasingly unsettled to find that Joe Lesser, Ruth, and Bunny all think that he will cooperate with the Committee because everyone knows that his movies mean more to him than anything else. He goes to New York, planning to find work in the theatre, and is at first welcomed, but then shunned by his old friend Abe Barron, a version of Abe Burrows, and his wife. He is shown failing to get work with the advertising agencies because they have to "check around about a couple of things" first. Finally, he is working in a small camera shop when two FBI agents come to ask the owner if he is working there – "just a routine check-up" – which makes the owner so nervous that David quits. David goes back to Los Angeles, where he moves in with Ruth and his son. Driven to desperation over the loss of her son and being blacklisted, Dorothy Nolan kills herself. In a sequence that pays homage to Carl Foreman and *High Noon*, David gets a black-market job filling in on a picture, but loses it quickly when the executives find out who he is. David's moral dilemma builds to a climax as he goes to see Felix Graff, who asks him whether it is "worth all this pain" to resist the Committee. He says a lot of people think the Committee is doing a good thing, "just think of yourself. Don't confuse it with one of your movies." His friend Bunny, who has been subpoenaed, comes and asks for David's permission to name him, on the theory that, since they already have his name, he can't be hurt further. David replies, "You want my permission to inform on me . . . that's the whole point of this hearing, isn't it – nail your best friend." Ruth throws Bunny out of the house, and she and David consummate their reconciliation. Zanuck calls him in and offers him a bribe in the form of a good script if he will cooperate with the Committee. David is finally brought to ask rhetorically, "Is it so wrong to do what they want?"

The film ends with David's appearance at a public hearing. As he and Ruth enter the hearing room, Abe Barron, who has just cooperated, is being exhibited for the press by a triumphant Congressman Velde. David is called. In testimony that is loosely based on Arthur Miller's, he tells the Committee about the meetings he attended, but refuses to give the names of others. When Graff advises him, "They want the names, David. That's why we're here," he says, "Forget 'em," a polite form of Howard Prince's epithet. The lawyer asks to be excused, and gets up and leaves David, who engages in a shouting match with Wood and Tavenner, echoing at different times Miller – "I'm not gonna let you hurt innocent people" – and Joseph Welch in the Army-McCarthy hearings – "Don't you have an ounce of decency?" David is removed from the stand, shouting, "Shame on you!" As he and Ruth leave the hall, Bunny Baxter is called to the stand and refuses to answer questions, invoking the First Amendment. David and Ruth walk out smiling and the film ends with the statement:

Thousands of lives were shattered and hundreds of careers destroyed by what came to be known as the Hollywood blacklist.

People like David and Ruth Merrill faced terms in prison, suffered the loss of friends and possessions, and were denied the right to earn a living.

They were forced to live this way for almost 20 years.

It was not until 1970 that these men and women were vindicated for standing up – at the greatest personal cost – for their beliefs.

The press kit for *Guilty by Suspicion* contains a forthright statement of Winkler's thematic aim: "From the project's outset, Winkler's point of view was to overlay a powerful morality tale on the palette of the hearings and the blacklist era. 'In David Merrill we have a man who, in order to gain worldly possessions, compromised his morality. As those possessions started slipping away, he regained that morality.'"[78] Thus the fall and rise of David Merrill. The Committee is not so much the source of evil as its occasion. The evil is in the greed, the materialism, and the blind ambition of the movie business, as well as the drive for power and publicity that motivates the Committee members themselves. The Committee hearing provides the stage on which each individual moral dilemma is enacted. While the weaker ones, such as Larry and Dorothy, are destroyed by the test of their moral mettle that the Committee occasions, the stronger ones, such as David, and even Bunny, are ennobled by it. As in all effective melodrama, the force of good, and innocence, triumphs over evil in the end. But there is more than a touch of darkness about this imitation *film noir* movie. The forces of evil remain in control in the persons of the Committee and the studio executives, as the heroes go off to face blacklisting and possible prison terms.

The response to the movie was in keeping with its straightforwardly melodramatic presentation of the subject. David Denby wrote that the movie does not "escape certain consoling simplicities that so often taint liberal attempts to understand the period. . . . This is the kind of thesis movie in which each episode illustrates some moral point – the scenes are borderline clichés."[79] Victor Navasky, who was aware of Polonsky's history with the film, conceded that it did "capture the grotesquerie of the great fear," but still questioned the choice of "a political tourist" rather than a Communist as protagonist.[80] There were attacks on the film's liberal politics from both Right and Left. Pat Buchanan complained on the television program *Crossfire* that it exaggerated the anti-

Communist menace and downplayed the "real" menace, Joe Stalin and his minions.[81] Another critic wrote that the film was not half as effective as *The Front*: "There is sorrow and there is some fear but there is very little rage. . . . It seems just a little too detached. Maybe you had to be there. Maybe you had to suffer it yourself. Or maybe Winkler and company aren't quite willing to extend their range and see the ways in which we are all still suffering it now."[82]

These representations of the Committee and the witnesses were created in varying historical contexts, and they differ widely in aesthetic technique and quality as well as political perspective. Nevertheless, they all begin with a perception of the hearings that is rooted in the social drama itself, a ritual confrontation of the forces of good and evil which, in these times, finds its most natural artistic expression in melodrama. The identification of good and evil might be at opposite poles, as in *Big Jim McLain* and *Guilty by Suspicion*, but one set of values must be affirmed and validated, and another condemned and somehow defeated. Even the attempts by writers such as Kinoy and Bernstein to suggest a more complex moral field by subverting the melodramatic formula through metatheatre or irony must begin with the framework of melodrama in order to subvert it. The social drama of the hearings had created a perceptual field of persecutors and victims, a good side and an evil side. Representations of HUAC, even by those who come after it, must begin with a reality that has been constructed within this perceptual field. The objects might be moved around and their characteristics reversed, but the field remains. The metanarrative has been set, and it is a melodrama.

PART TWO

MAKING ANALOGIES

4

Witch Hunt

Mr. Arens: Are you cognizant of the fact that your play *The Crucible*, with respect to witch hunts in 1692, was the case history of a series of articles in the Communist press drawing parallels to the investigations of Communists and other subversives by Congressional Committees?
Mr. Miller: The comparison is inevitable, sir.

HUAC Hearings, 21 June 1956

Marion L. Starkey's popular psychosocial history of the Salem witch hunt of the 1690s, *The Devil in Massachusetts* (1949), contained no direct references to the Red-baiting activities of the American Legion, the FBI, and the House Committee on Un-American Activities, but the author made the connection unmistakably clear. Her concluding paragraph invited the reader to meditate on the similarities between the 17th Century and the 20th:

> Moral seasons come and go. Late in the nineteenth century, when it was much the fashion to memorialize the witchcraft delusion, honest men discussed it with wondering pity as something wholly gone from the world and no longer quite comprehensible. But such condescension is not for the twentieth century. . . . Our age too is beset by ideological "heresies" in almost the medieval sense, and our scientists have taken over the office of Michael Wigglesworth in forcing on us the contemplation of Doomsday. What one feels now for deluded Salem Village is less pity than admiration and hope – admiration for men whose sanity in the end proved stronger than madness, hope that "enlightenment" too is a phenomenon that may recur.[1]

Although it would be liberal journalists who brought the similarities into sharp relief, Starkey suggested most of them simply by her presentation of the situation in Salem. Her analysis of the community's emotional condition at the beginning of the witch hysteria, for example, described not only the mental set of the persecutor as defined by René Girard, but the mood of many Americans at the beginning of the Cold War:

> The nearly universal belief in devils and witches could not alone explain the capitulation of reason which took place. The fact was that the commonwealth no less than the girls craved its Dionysiac mysteries. A people whose natural impulses had long been repressed by the severity of their belief, whose security had been undermined by anxiety and terror continued longer than could be borne, demanded their catharsis. Frustrated by the devils they could not reach, they demanded a scapegoat and a full scale lynching. And they got it (Starkey, 29–30).

In her careful presentation of the narrative, Starkey implied many of the specific similarities between the two historical events that reviewers were to notice and develop. Of the confessors, for example, she noted,

> whatever their eventual fate the confessors would in the meantime be given full opportunity to repent and prove their repentance by informing on their fellow witches. Their willingness to do this provided a very utilitarian reason for keeping them alive. By means of the confessions, round every witch on the roster was woven a web of spectral evidence which in the end became more damaging than the original charges (Starkey, 191–2).

HUAC's equivalent, of course, was what Victor Navasky has named the "Informer Principle," the demand for proof of repentance through a willingness to name names, which was made of every witness who had been accused of anything in exchange for rehabilitation. Seventeenth-century "spectral evidence," which consisted of the charge that the accused had "sent out their Shapes" to witnesses in visions, either to torment or to tempt them, was the equivalent of the twentieth-century accusation that a witness had seen someone at a meeting or that he "talked like a Communist." In her account of the expressed reservations of one brave magistrate, Richard Pike of Salisbury, Starkey reflected HUAC's abrogation to itself of the roles of investigator, prosecutor, judge, and jury, and its refusal to allow the accused the benefits of cross-examination or the mounting of a defense. After witnessing the activities at Salem, Pike wrote a letter to one of the judges, expressing his opinion that "the present handling of the trials left the lives of innocent people 'to the pleasure and passion of these that are minded to take them away. . . . The witnesses were not only informers . . . but sole judges of the crime'" (Starkey, 223).

Starkey's veiled allusion to the anti-Communist crusade was made clear and definite by reviewers for liberal periodicals in the fall of 1949. McAlister Coleman began his *Nation* review with the observation that "the hysterical babblings of two nasty little Puritan maids started the whole horrid business," asserting that "these precocious gossips" were "the spiritual ancestors of Elizabeth Bentley, Whittaker Chambers, and J. B. Matthews."[2] He concluded it with a rather pessimistic prediction: "In this time of the prevalence of witch-hunters the book should serve as a horrible warning, but it won't be read by those who most need warning – that is, unless it should have the good luck to be suppressed in Boston."[3] *New Republic* addressed the connection head-on with a review essay on Starkey's book and Merle Miller's novel about the hounding of a former Communist by the FBI and HUAC, *The Sure Thing*. "The common subject," wrote James R. Newman, "is witch hunt-ing: the irrationality that besets men's minds, the follies to which they are driven when they are afraid."[4] Newman remarked that one expected to see similarities in "these two interludes of social hysteria," such as "their epidemic quality, the kind of evidence against accused persons to which credence is given, the incalculable injury inflicted on the life of the entire community by even a limited indulgence in per-secution," but was particularly distressed that not only did the belief in witchcraft persist, but "the Devil does a better business on the Potomac in the twentieth century than on the Bay in the seventeenth" and that "there is no sign of the recantation and repentance which, coming soon after the Salem sickness, at least partially redeemed the men and women – judges, juries and townspeople – who had succumbed to it" (Newman, 17). Newman pointed out two "interesting principles" that were established in the Salem witch trials and survived, perhaps because of their "elegant simplicity," in the HUAC hearings. First, "Salem Village adhered to the legal and scientific theory that defined a witch as any person cried out upon, that is to say anyone whom anyone else denounced as a witch. . . . Once cried out upon, there was little the accused could do in his own defense." Second, "since it was assumed that the Devil could not 'assume the shape' of an innocent person, it followed that anyone accused of wizardry, provided only the accuser howled and writhed sufficiently during the crying out, was probably guilty of *something*." The analog in the hearings, of course, was with anyone named as a Communist or "Communist sympathizer" by an informer. In the Salem of the 1690s, as in the Washington of the 1940s, the fundamental presumption of innocence in English common law was ignored: "In a community hungering for scapegoats, the innocent – as we are daily reminded – must prove their innocence." As for informers, "that unhappy group of psychotic maidens," Newman noted, "in her own person each was safe enough, the theory being that accusers could not be accused." In the end, "they all came to repentance, or worse." But in their "brief glory they had known attention and admiration beyond a paranoid's dreams and had wielded the delicious power of destroying anyone on whom their malicious fancy might light" (18). Inviting the reader to ponder the implications of the similarities between the two persecutions, Newman asserted that "nothing that occurred in Massachusetts in 1692, except for the actual application of the rope to the neck and the *peine forte et dure*, is lacking in the purges of Washington." The difference is that, "after a year of madness, Salem Village recalled the vision; the stupidity and folly of our own day have not yet been so relieved" (19).

Arthur Miller was already a target of the Red-baiters when he began to think about the connections between Salem and HUAC. Miller had made a direct assault on the Committee in *You're Next*. For this and for his support of a long list of "popular front" causes, he had already been placed on the lists of subversives. *Death of a Salesman* had been picketed by the American Legion on Long Island and by Catholic anti-Communists in Dublin, who quoted Cardinal Spellman against Miller. Fearing attacks from the Right, Columbia Pictures had nearly undermined the movie of *Salesman* with an accompanying short subject praising Big Business and the life of the salesman.[5] At the request of Fredric March and Florence Eldridge, Miller had adapted Ibsen's *An Enemy of the People* in 1950, pointing up the persecution of the truth-tellers by the corrupt politicians in our midst. He had known about the Salem witch trials since college, but thought of them "as one of those inexplicable mystifications of the long-dead past." Then, as Miller reports, "as though it had been ordained, a copy of Marion Starkey's book *The Devil in Massachusetts* fell into my hands."[6]

Miller's reading of Starkey's book could hardly have been an accident. Its effect, as he recalls in his memoir *Timebends*, was to bring back "the bizarre story" of the witchcraft phenomenon "in remarkably well-organized detail" (*Timebends*, 330). Miller's engagement with the mate-

DEATH of a SALESMAN
by
===== ARTHUR MILLER =====

"Some shows are hotbeds of left-winged agitation and the focus of comrade acclaim out front. The current "Death of a Salesman" is a good example", quoted from "Red Footlights" an article by George A. Maguire in 'The Sign', November, 1949. *(Published by the Passionist Fathers, Union City, New Jersey, U.S.A.)*

According to The Fifth Report (1949) of the Senate Fact-Finding Committee on Un-American Activities in California, Arthur Miller is a member of the following organisations :

AMERICAN YOUTH FOR DEMOCRACY. CONTEMPORARY WRITERS. CIVIL RIGHTS CONGRESS. PEOPLES INSTITUTE OF APPLIED RELIGION, INC.	Cited as subversive by the Attorney General.
PROGRESSIVE CITIZENS OF AMERICA. STAGE FOR ACTION.	Cited as subversive by the California Committee on Un-American Activities.
WORLD FEDERATION OF DEMOCRATIC YOUTH.	Cited as a "part of the Communist International solar system" by the California Committee on Un-American Activities.
VOICE OF FREEDOM COMMITTEE.	defending pro-communist Radio Speakers.

SUPPORTERS OF COMMUNIST BOOKSHOPS.

"The party is content and highly pleased if it is possible to have inserted...A LINE, A SCENE, A SEQUENCE, conveying the communist lesson and more particularly, if they can keep out anti-communist lessons."
J. Edgar Hoover, Chief F.B.I.

"Communism is intrinsically wrong and no one who would save christian civilisation may give it any assistance in any undertaking whatever."
(Encyclical Letter DIVINI REDEMPTORIST on Atheistic Communism, Pope Pius XI.)

Issued by the Catholic Cinema & Theatre Patrons' Association, 85-86 Grafton St., Dublin

Figure 6. This anti-Communist handbill was distributed to theatre-goers attending the Dublin production of *Death of a Salesman* in 1951.

rial was both intellectual and deeply emotional. On the one hand, it was clear to him that "the hearings in Washington were profoundly and even avowedly ritualistic. . . . The main point of the hearings, precisely as in seventeenth-century Salem, was that the accused make public confession, damn his confederates as well as his Devil master, and guarantee his sterling new allegiance by breaking disgusting old vows – whereupon he was let loose to rejoin the society of extremely decent people" (331). The heart of the drama's social significance lay in this analogy. The play's emotional germ was more personal, however, for, as Miller has acknowledged, "even in the first weeks of thinking about the Salem story, the central image, the one that persistently recurred as an exuberant source of energy, was that of a guilt-ridden man, John Proctor, who having slept with his teen-age servant girl, watches with horror as she becomes the leader of the witch-hunting pack and points her accusing finger at the wife he has himself betrayed" (332).

Miller's own narrative of the time he was conceiving *The Crucible*, recounted in his memoir, provides the elements from which his characterization of John Proctor was constructed. In 1951 and 1952, Miller's life was closely connected with that of Elia Kazan, the director of *All My Sons* and *Death of a Salesman*, who had, as Miller puts it, "entered into [his] dreams like a brother, and there [they] had exchanged a smile of understanding that blocked others out" (333). Miller and Kazan had been at work on a movie project, *The Hook*, which was to be about the infiltration of the Brooklyn waterfront unions by organized crime. The script was turned down by Harry Cohn of Columbia Pictures on the advice of Roy Brewer, who suggested that Cohn should do the movie only if Kazan and Miller agreed to change the crime bosses to Communists. Of course they refused. According to Miller, just as he was deciding to go to Salem to do some preliminary research towards a possible play about the witch trials, Kazan confessed to him that he planned to name names before HUAC. Kazan had already acknowledged his own brief Party membership during the thirties in a private "executive session," but the Committee demanded names in exchange for getting him off the blacklist. Kazan gave them seven. Miller remembers feeling "my sympathy going toward him and at the same time I was afraid of him. Had I been of his generation, he would have had to sacrifice me as well. And finally that was all I could think of. I could not get past it" (333).[7]

Further complicating the situation was the fact that Kazan, who was rather legendarily promiscuous and had had an affair with Marilyn Monroe himself, was the one who had brought Miller and Monroe together when the two men had been in Los Angeles negotiating with the studio about *The Hook*. Guilt, sexuality, and a powerful sense of creativity had seemed to form the nexus of a new play as Miller had flown back to New York: "A retreat to the safety of morals, to be sure, but not necessarily to truthfulness. . . . I knew my innocence was technical merely, and the fact blackened my heart, but along with it came the certainty that I could, after all, lose myself in sensuality. . . . I sensed a new play in me, and a play was my very self alive" (307). As is usually the case with Miller, he was seeking through the writing of this new play a paradigm for behavior that was intensely personal as well as public. It is no surprise that his earliest thinking about the Salem story focused on a "central image, the one that persistently recurred as an exuberant source of energy . . . a guilt-ridden man, John Proctor" (332). He wrote in an early notebook: "The important thing is the process by which a man, feeling guilt for A, sees himself as guilty of B, and thus belies himself, – accommodates his credo to believe in what he knows is not true."[8] Miller could have been describing his friend Kazan, whose actions were constantly in his mind as he pursued his relationship with Marilyn Monroe and pondered his own strategy of response to the Committee when he faced a subpoena, which could be imminent.[9] As Christopher Bigsby has noted, Miller "was interested primarily in the creation of bourgeois tragedy, in the battle of an individual not only, or even primarily, with a world external to the self but with a personal fallibility and, beyond that, a deeply flawed human nature."[10] More specifically, in writing *The Crucible*, Miller was seeking a paradigm for behavior that would lay down a path of righteousness for a guilty man.

Miller spent three weeks in Salem in April 1952, reading in the records of Salem Village and the materials about the witchcraft outbreak and the trials of 1692 at the Essex Institute. Two major resources for him were Charles Upham's extensive two-volume history, *Salem Witchcraft*, published in 1896, and the typed transcripts of the official proceedings that were done by the WPA in the thirties, but he also read extensively in New England colonial literature and religious writings.[11] In these sources, Miller found the facts, events, and persons that would serve as the material from which he would shape *The Crucible*. According to Upham, in 17th-century Salem:

A witch was regarded as a person who had made an actual, deliberate, formal compact with Satan, by which it was agreed that she should become his faithful subject, and do all in her power to aid him in his rebellion against God and his warfare against the gospel and church of Christ; and, in consideration of such allegiance and service, Satan, on his part, agreed to exercise his supernatural powers in her favor, and communicate to her those powers, in a greater or less degree, as she proved herself an efficient and devoted supporter of his cause. Thus, a witch was considered as a person who had transferred allegiance and worship from God to the Devil.[12]

Witchcraft was a capital crime, for which citizens of Massachusetts were occasionally hanged throughout the 17th century, although the outbreak in Salem, during which, in the space of four months, nineteen people and two dogs were hanged, one man was pressed to death, and two people died in prison, was by far the most extensive instance of accusation and prosecution. Through the Devil's agency, witches were believed to have the power to "send out their Shapes," or spectral images, to torture people, causing them to waste away; to inflict any disease upon them; to throw them into convulsions; and to choke, bruise, beat, and pierce them with pins. It was a matter of theological debate, significantly so for the trials at Salem, whether the Devil could assume the Shape of an innocent person in order to afflict or tempt others, or whether the appearance of a specter was itself evidence that the corporeal person had "signed the Devil's book," and so become his minion. In the Salem trials, the testimony of the "afflicted" as to the identity of their afflictors, called "spectral evidence," was the primary evidence used to convict the nineteen people who were executed. Witches were believed to torture their victims by means of a malignant fluid from their eyes, which was drawn back into the witch's body when her hand touched the victim. In the Salem trials, the best test of guilt was taken to be the affliction of a victim by a "fit" when the defendant was allowed to look at her, and the subsequent cessation of the fit when the defendant's hand was touched to her body. It was also believed that witches could not weep, so that dry eyes when one was told to weep were a sign of guilt, as were the ownership of "puppets" or dolls that could be used as what are now commonly called "voodoo dolls" to afflict the victim.

The accusers in the Salem trials, the so-called "afflicted children," were Elizabeth Parris, 9 years old, the daughter of the Salem Village minister, Samuel Parris; Abigail Williams, 11, the niece of the minister, who lived in his house; Ann Putnam, 12, the daughter of wealthy landowner Thomas Putnam; Mary Walcot, 17, the daughter of former church deacon Jonathan Walcot; Mercy Lewis, 17, a servant of the Putnams; Elizabeth Hubbard, 17, who lived with her uncle Dr. Griggs; Susannah Sheldon, 18, who lived with her widowed mother; Elizabeth Booth, 18; Sarah Churchill, 20, a servant in the house of George Jacobs, Sr.; and Mary Warren, 20, a servant in the house of John Proctor. They were later joined in their "afflictions" by John Indian, a slave whom the Reverend Parris had brought with him from Barbados and who was married to another of his three slaves, Tituba; and occasionally by other adults, including Ann Putnam, senior, Thomas Putnam's wife.

The "affliction" began in the Parris family in February 1692, with little Elizabeth, who had begun to go into trance-like states, and to crawl around the house, sometimes barking like a dog. Soon her cousin Abigail was similarly afflicted. Parris and Dr. Griggs put their heads together. Mindful of the resemblance between the girls' behavior and the description of the afflicted Goodwin children of Boston that Cotton Mather had given in "Memorable Providences, Relating to Witchcrafts and Possession" (1689), they called in the Reverend Hale of nearby Beverly, who had recently dealt with accusations of witchcraft, including one against tavern-keeper Bridget Bishop in 1687. Under questioning, the girls revealed that they were indeed bewitched, and they named the Parris slave Tituba and two women of the village, Sarah Good – a vagrant with four children who lived on the charity of the villagers and was often turned away muttering from their doors – and Sarah Osborne, a woman who was widely known to have slept with her Irish indentured servant for many months before she married him and disinherited her two sons. Tituba, Good, and Osborne were examined by local magistrates, and, under questioning, as well as beatings by her master Parris, Tituba confessed to bewitching the girls and opened the door to further accusations by saying that there were five people who had hurt the children: Good, Osborne, two women she did not know, and a "tall man from Boston." The "afflicted children" were soon joined by the other young accusers, who "called out upon" an ever-increasing number of citizens, from an ever-widening geographical and socioeconomic circle, eventually naming the wives of the Reverend Hale and the governor, Sir William Phips. Parris quickly sent Elizabeth to stay with the Stephen Sewall family in Salem Town, where she was cured of her "fits" by the kind and sensible ministrations of Mrs. Sewall, but Abigail, along with Ann Putnam, became a central figure, and something of a ringleader among the "afflicted children."

A great deal has been written about the motives of the "afflicted" and the religious, psychological, and socioeconomic conditions that occasioned the phenomenon of the Salem witchcraft outbreak. At the time of the outbreak, the Reverend Parris was at odds with a large faction in his church, a group that had just attained power on the village committee, which was refusing to collect the taxes to pay the minister's salary. The younger son of a wealthy London merchant who had failed at business in Boston and in Barbados, he was keenly aware of the decline in his social status and jealous of every perquisite to which his position as minister in a small country church entitled him in this colonial theocracy. He had alienated a good part of the congregation by finagling the deed to the parsonage as part of his agreement with the church, and by his constant complaints about such things as his arrangements for firewood and the plain pewter tankards that furnished the church's communion table. Thomas Putnam, who, as the eldest son of the biggest landowner in the village, had expected to retain his father's position, found himself in considerably reduced circumstances when his father willed the bulk of his estate to his younger stepbrother and he received little from his wife's wealthy family. Putnam was also involved in a number of boundary disputes, including one with the Nurse family. Francis Nurse was a former tray maker, who, along with his four sons and four sons-in-law, was farming a large and valuable tract of land that he was in the process of buying. Francis had also been elected to the anti-Parris village committee. His wife Rebecca had never transferred her church membership from Salem Town to Parris's church in Salem Village. Although their mother had once been accused of witchcraft, she and her two sisters, Mary Esty and Sarah Cloyce, were church members and respected members of the community. Martha Corey was similarly respected, although manifestly independent in her thinking. She was one of the few members of the community to deny the existence of witches. Her blunt-speaking and litigious husband Giles, 80 years old in 1692, had only recently given up a life that was considered scandalous by Puritan standards to become a church member.

The case of the Proctor family is one of the clearest examples of the devastation that was wrought by the outbreak in Salem Village. John Proctor, 60 years old in 1692, was the father of a large family. He was a native of nearby Ipswich, where some of his older children were now established, farming the land he had inherited from his father. He and his wife Elizabeth lived on a large tract of land in Salem Town, just outside the Salem Village border, and were members of the Salem Town congregation. Their house, on the main thoroughfare, the Ipswich Road, was licensed as a tavern for wayfarers. Elizabeth and her daughter Sarah, 16, kept the tavern, while John farmed the land with his eldest son Benjamin, Elizabeth's stepson. The other Proctor children living in the house were William, 18; Samuel, 7; Abigail, 3; and a baby.

Upham describes Proctor as "a person of decided character, and, although impulsive and liable to be imprudent, of a manly spirit, honest, earnest, and bold in word and deed," contending that "he saw through the whole thing, and was convinced that it was the result of a conspiracy, deliberate and criminal, on the part of the accusers. He gave free utterance to his indignation at their conduct, and it cost him his life" (Upham, II, 304). Against his better judgment, Proctor had been compelled to allow his servant Mary Warren to take part in the proceedings against Rebecca Nurse in late March of 1692. Samuel Sibley of the Village later testified that, on the next morning, he had met Proctor on the road, and that Proctor had told him:

> He was going to fetch home his jade, he left her there last night and had rather given 40 c than let her come up, said Sibley asked why he talked so. Proctor replied if they were let alone sir we should all be devils and witches quickly they should rather be had to the whipping post, but he would fetch his jade home and thrust the Devil out of her and more to the like purpose crying hang them, hang them. And also added that when she was first taken with fits he kept her close to the wheel and threatened to thrash her, and then she had no more fits till the next day he was gone forth and then she must have her fits again forsooth.[13]

Apparently, the Proctors were early targets of the "afflicted." At Elizabeth Proctor's trial, one witness testified that he had been at Thomas Putnam's house on the 20th of March "a-helping to attend the afflicted Folks," when

> I heard them talking who the children complained of and I heard them tell Mercy Lewis that she cried out of Goody Proctor and Mercy Lewis said that she did not cry out of Goody Proctor nor nobody, she said she did say there she is, but did not tell them who and Thomas Putnam and his wife and others, told her that she cried out of Goody Proctor and Mercy Lewis said if she did it was when she was out in her head for she said she saw nobody. (Levin, 64)

Another said that he at been at Ingersoll's tavern, just down the road from the meeting house, on 28 March, when "there being present, one of the afflicted persons which cried out and said there's Goody Proctor William Raiment being there present, told the girl he believed she lied for he saw nothing then Goody Ingersoll told the girl she told a lie for there was nothing then the girl said that she did it for sport they must have some sport" (Levin, 64).

When Elizabeth Proctor was arrested for witchcraft early in April, John denounced the accuser in typically blunt fashion. He rather loudly told Joseph Pope in front of Ingersoll, to whom Parris had loaned the services of John Indian to help with the increased trade occasioned by the trials, that "if he had John Indian in his Custody, he would soon beat the devil out of him" (Levin, 52). At Elizabeth Proctor's trial, John Indian accused her of coming "in her shift" and choking him. The girls fell into their "fits" and sighted Elizabeth on a beam of the meeting house, saying that she was after them to sign her book. Eleven-year old Abigail Williams cried, "did you not tell me that your maid had written." (Mary Warren was not present in the courtroom.) Elizabeth replied, "dear child, it is not so. . . . There is another judgment, dear child." Abigail turned on John Proctor, who had come to support his wife, saying, "you can pinch as well as your wife and more to that purpose" (Levin, 51). On 11 April, Proctor was indicted for "Certain detestable acts called witchcraft and sorceries" against Mary Walcot, with Mercy Lewis and Ann Putnam attesting as witnesses. On 12 April, the day of Proctor's arrest, the clerk complained that he was met "with nothing but interruptions" while he was trying to prepare the warrant:

> By reason of fits upon John Indian and Abigail, and Mary Walcot happening to come in just before, they one and another cried out there is Goodman Proctor very often, and Abigail said there is Goodman Proctor in the magistrate's lap. . . . Then John cried out to the Dog under the table to come away for Goodman Proctor was upon his back; then he cried out of Goody Cloyce, O you old witch, and fell immediately into a violent fit that 3 men and the marshall could not without exceeding difficulty hold him. In which fit Mary Walcot that was knitting and well composed, said there was Goodman Proctor and his wife and Goody Cloyce helping of him, but so great were the interruptions of John and Abigail by fits while we were observing these things to notify them, that we were fain to send them both away that I might have liberty to write this without disturbance. (Levin, 52)

The Proctors, husband and wife, were remanded to the Boston jail on 12 April, along with Rebecca Nurse and her sister Sarah Cloyce, Martha Corey, and Dorcas Good, the four-year-old daughter of the hapless Sarah Good. Dorcas had been accused of sending out her Shape to bite the girls, who exhibited the baby-teeth marks to prove it.

Witches in 17th-century Massachusetts forfeited their property. Without waiting for a conviction in the case, the sheriff went out to the Proctor farm and confiscated everything he found, selling off the livestock, and even dumping the beer out of a barrel and the soup out of a pot. Shortly thereafter, three of the Proctor children, Benjamin, William, and Sarah were also arrested. On 23 July, John Proctor wrote from prison a strongly worded petition to the ministers of Boston, begging their assistance, "that if it be possible our Innocent Blood may be spared, which undoubtedly otherwise will be shed, if the Lord doth not mercifully step in," for "we know in our own Consciences, we are all Innocent Persons" (Levin, 62). He told the ministers that the "Confessed witches" who had accused them of being part of their coven, had been tortured, as had his eighteen-year-old son William, tied "Neck and Heels till the Blood gushed out of his Nose, and would have kept him so 24 Hours, if one more Merciful than the rest, had not taken pity on him, and caused him to be unbound." "These actions," Proctor warned the ministers, "are very like the Popish Cruelties" (Levin, 62), an accusation that was bound to hit home for ministers of a religion that had in a sense been born in opposition to the cruelties of the Inquisition.

Meanwhile, Samuel Parris and the magistrates, John Hathorne and Jonathan Corwin, were at work on the Proctors' servant, Mary Warren. After the arrest of the Proctors, Mary had recanted her earlier testimony, telling the court and others that the girls were lying, that there was no witchcraft. The other girls immediately "cried out upon" Mary, who was arrested and brought before the court in Salem Village on April 19, a week after the Proctors had been transferred to Boston jail. While Mary protested her innocence, the girls created pandemonium in the meeting house: "Now they were all but John Indian grievously afflicted and Mrs. Pope also who was not afflicted before hitherto this day, and after a few moments, John Indian fell into a violent fit also" (Levin, 53). In the midst of this, Mary herself fell into a fit, and for some time acted out a dramatic inner conflict within the court proceedings:

Now Mary Warren fell into a fit, and some of the afflicted cried out that she was going to confess, but Goody Cory and Proctor and his wife came in in their apparition and struck her down and said she should tell nothing.

Mary Warren continued a good space in a fit, that she did neither see, nor hear, nor speak.

Afterwards she started up, and said I will speak and cried out, Oh!

I am sorry for it, I am sorry for it, and wringed her hands, and fell a little while into a fit again and then came to speak, but immediately her teeth were set, and then she fell into a violent fit and cried out, oh Lord help me! Oh Good Lord save me! (Levin, 53)

Samuel Parris, serving as recorder that day, wrote at the end of his account, "note that not one of the sufferers was afflicted during her examination after once she began to confess though they were tormented before" (Levin, 53). Mary's fits were so violent that she was twice removed from the room that day, and under continued questioning on that and subsequent days in Salem jail she continued to be torn between telling the truth and "confessing," both to perjury and to witchcraft, to save her life. While she continued to tell the other prisoners that the girls were lying and dissembling, under interrogation she told Hathorne and Corwin that John Proctor had brought her a book, "and he told me if I would take the book and touch it that I should be well and I thought then that it was the Devil's book" (57). Touching a page with her finger, "she knew not that it was wet or whether it was wet with sweat or with Cider that she had be drinking of she knew not: but her finger did make a mark and the mark was black" (55). Asked what was in the book, she said that she had spelled out the word "Moses," but couldn't read the next word, so "her Master and Mistress bid her if she could not pronounce the word she should touch the book" (56). She said that she knew Elizabeth was a witch because "her mistress had many books and her mistress carried one book with her to Reading when she went to see her sister" (56).

By 12 May, Mary Warren had completely broken down under the questioning and was telling all sorts of wild tales, among them that she had stuck a pin in a puppet in Elizabeth Proctor's hand that was "for Ann Putnam or Abigail Williams, for one of them it was I am sure," and that John Proctor had brought her "an Image which looked yellow and I believe it was for Abigail Williams being like her and I put a thing like a thorn into it" (58). From a 20th-century vantage point, there is a clear sexual undertone to Mary's testimony about Proctor, and a hint of rivalry in her remarks about Elizabeth. "The first night I was taken," she said,

I saw as I thought the Apparition of Goody Cory and catched at it as I thought and caught my master in my lap though I did not see my master in the place at the time, upon which my master said it is nobody, but I it is my shadow that you see, but my master was not before me that I could discern but Catching at the apparition that looked like Goody Cory I caught hold of my master and pulled him down into my lap; upon which he said I see there is no heed to any of your talkings, for you are all possessed with the Devil for it is nothing but my shape. (58)

At another time she said that "her master had told her that he had been about sometimes to make away with himself because of his wife's quarreling with him" (56). After releasing a flood of accusations, not only about the Proctors and Martha Cory, but about the two latest defendants, Alice Parker and Ann Pudeator – from throwing one man off a cherry tree and drowning another at sea to impeding justice by bewitching the horses of magistrates Hathorne and Corwin – Mary Warren was deemed to have been saved from witchcraft. Unlike the other confessed witches, she was not imprisoned, but restored to her place among the "afflicted" to assist the witch-hunt.

At the grand inquest held on June 30, Mary Warren swore:

I have seen the apparition of John Proctor senior among the witches and he hath often tortured me by pinching me and biting me and choking me, and pressing on my Stomach till the blood came out of my mouth . . . and he hath also tempted me to write in his book and to eat bread which he brought to me, which I refusing to do, Jno Proctor did most grievously torture me with variety of tortures, almost Ready to kill me" (61).

Despite petitions by their neighbors in Ipswich and Salem that attested to their Christian and upright lives, John and Elizabeth Proctor were convicted of witchcraft and sentenced to hang. Elizabeth was saved by her pregnancy. John was executed along with four others on 19 August. On the morning of his execution, he asked for and was denied some more time to prepare his soul. After the hanging, his body is believed to have been removed from its shallow grave on "Witch Hill" by his children and buried in the family plot.

The outbreak came to a quick end in the fall, after the hanging of nine people convicted of witchcraft and the pressing to death of Giles Cory, *peine forte et dure* for standing mute and refusing to plead to the charge against him, in the space of three days in late September. The power of the girls met its limit when they "cried out" upon the wives of

Governor Phips and Reverend Hale. Hale, who had participated in the court proceedings up to this point, began to denounce the girls as perjurers. The Special Court of Oyer and Terminer that had been hearing the cases was replaced by Governor Phips with a Superior Court of Judicature, which met for the first time in January 1693. On the advice of Increase Mather and other prominent ministers, the use of "spectral evidence" was severely curtailed in the new judicial process, and only three convictions were secured on the next fifty indictments. These three were condemned, but not executed. Finally, in May 1693, Phips pardoned all of the remaining prisoners, about 150 in all, including Elizabeth, Benjamin, William, and Sarah Proctor. In 1715, when Massachusetts awarded compensation to the families of those executed for witchcraft, the largest share, £150, went to Benjamin Proctor on behalf of the family of John Proctor.

I have given this account of the Salem outbreak in such detail in order to make clear the extent of Miller's creative manipulation of his historical material in the writing of his play. His most significant creative act was of course the choice of what Bigsby calls "bourgeois tragedy" as the play's structure and of John Proctor as its protagonist. The next was taking the hints of sexuality in his relationship with his servant and of trouble in his marriage from Mary Warren's testimony and adding them to Proctor's troubled state on the morning of his execution to create the character of John Proctor. Miller needed to place Proctor at the center of his drama about a man who, "feeling guilt for A, sees himself as guilty of B, and thus belies himself." Much has been made of the changing of Abigail Williams' age from 11 to 17 in creating the character for the play. As Robert Martin has suggested, Mary Warren was a much more plausible candidate for an affair with Proctor than Abigail Williams.[14] In the context of his tragic paradigm, however, Miller needed two characters – characters in the Aristotelian sense of the collection of moral qualities that impels human action – to account dramatically for the behavior of the historical Mary Warren: John Proctor's wanton "jade" and the anguished young woman who placed her conflict of conscience so dramatically on the court record. Since Abigail was a conspicuous actor in the case against Elizabeth Proctor, Miller made her Proctor's temptress and the partner in his sin. Perhaps more significantly, Proctor's age was changed from 60 to "middle thirties" (Miller was 37 in 1952). The historical Elizabeth Proctor was a well-read, perhaps quarrelsome woman, who ran a tavern and a large household. It was she and not John who was tripped up by what the court heard as a faulty recitation of the Lord's Prayer – taken to be significant evidence of her bargain with the Devil. Miller's character is a "sickly," repressed, and pious young farm wife who cannot season a stew properly and is too "cold" to satisfy her husband sexually. Like Marilyn Monroe as Miller depicts her in *Timebends*, Abigail is imbued with sexual energy and promise. In the scene that Miller added to the Broadway production after it had been criticized as too "cold" and intellectually distanced, Abigail embraces her sexuality with a religious fervor:

> Why, you taught me goodness, therefore you are good. It were a fire you walked me through, and all my ignorance was burned away. It were a fire, John, we lay in fire. And from that night no woman dare call me wicked any more but I knew my answer. I used to weep for my sins when the wind lifted up my skirts; and blushed for shame because some old Rebecca called me loose. And then you burned my ignorance away. As bare as some December tree I saw them all – walking like saints to church, running to feed the sick, and hypocrites in their hearts! And God gave me strength to call them liars, and God made men to listen to me, and by God I will scrub the world clean for the love of Him! Oh, John, I will make you such a wife when the world is white again![15]

After Act 1, which establishes the basic facts and the background of the witchcraft outbreak, almost every event that happens in Acts 2, 3, and 4 of Miller's play is pure invention, for which the playwright drew on the historical existence of the characters to create a chilling verisimilitude. In Act 2, the Proctors discuss their marriage, John's guilt for having had sex with Abigail, the trials, and Abigail's desire to get Elizabeth out of the way. Mary Warren comes home from Salem Village with the announcement that 39 people are now in prison and that Elizabeth has been mentioned by the girls. She also presents her with a "poppet" she has made to while away the time in court. Reverend Hale comes in and questions the Proctors, finding grave cause for concern in John's inability to remember the Ten Commandments. Then the marshall arrives, searching for poppets, finds Mary's with a needle stuck in it, and arrests Elizabeth for witchcraft. Proctor tells Mary she must come to court with him to tell the truth and save Elizabeth. In Act 3, Proctor brings Mary to confess to Judge Danforth in an anteroom of the courtroom. The judges interrogate her and then bring in some of the girls to testify. Abigail denies that she saw Mary make the doll and stick her needle into it for safekeeping. Proctor accuses Abigail of dancing naked in the forest and other sins. When Mary breaks down under questioning by the judges and accusations of witchcraft from the girls, John finally names Abigail a "whore" and confesses to the sin of lechery. Having been told that Elizabeth never lies, Danforth arranges a test of the charge by summoning her to answer whether it was true that her husband was guilty of lechery. She lies to save him, restoring Abigail's credibility to all but the Reverend Hale. The girls then go into their fits, crying out upon Mary, and she retracts her statement, calling Proctor "the Devil's man."[16] Proctor is sent to jail along with Giles Corey, and Hale denounces the proceedings.

In Act 4, which takes place in Salem jail on the morning of John Proctor's execution, the Judges, trying to get him to confess to witchcraft and thereby save his life, allow his wife to speak with him. John tells her that he feels his innocence is pretense: "I cannot mount the gibbet like a saint. It is a fraud. I am not that man. . . . Let them that never lied die now to keep their souls" (*Crucible,*136). Elizabeth confesses to him, "I have sins of my own to count. It needs a cold wife to prompt lechery," and tells him, "do what you will. But let none be your judge" (137). Proctor decides to confess, but refuses to name the other people he has "seen with the devil." The judges are willing to settle for a signed confession they can nail up on the meeting-house door. But Proctor cannot bring himself to sign the confession because "it is no part of salvation that you should use me! . . . I have three children – how may I teach them to walk like men in the world, and I sold my friends? . . . I blacken all of them when this is nailed to the church the very day they hang for silence" (143). Refusing Proctor's plea to leave him his name, Danforth calls for the marshall, and Proctor goes off to hang, saying, "I do think I see some shred of goodness in John Proctor. Not enough to weave a banner with, but white enough to keep it from such dogs" (144). Thus Arthur Miller found the paradigm for behavior through which a guilty man might find righteousness.

It was the public significance of the play, the clear analogy it made between the Salem witch-hunt and the HUAC hearings, that gave this intensely personal search for the right way to behave its wider social meaning in the historical context in which it was written and produced. Looking back on the times more than thirty years later, Miller said that he had chosen the Salem outbreak for his play because "it was simply impossible any longer to discuss what was happening to us in contemporary terms. There had to be some distance, given the phenomena. We were all going slightly crazy trying to be honest and trying to see straight and trying to be safe. . . . It seemed to me that the hysteria in Salem had a certain inner procedure or several which we were duplicating once again, and that perhaps by revealing the nature of that procedure some light could be thrown on what we were doing to ourselves."[17] In 1953, three weeks after the play opened on Broadway, he told an interviewer: "Of course I intended it as a parallel for today. . . . It's insanity to think you can write anything good without a point or message."[18] Miller has treated the analogy with differing emphasis at different times, sometimes finding it necessary to insist that the play was not *only* about McCarthyism,[19] but he has never denied his original purpose or its implications. *The Crucible* was an attempt, he said in 1960, "to create the old ethical and dramaturgic order again, to say that one couldn't passively sit back and watch his world being destroyed under him, even if he did share the general guilt. In effect, I was calling for an act of will,"[20] an act of resistance, that is, like John Proctor's.

The analogy is made clear in its broadest sense in Act 3, when Reverend Hale begins to have doubts about the proceedings as Giles Corey is being pressured to give the name of a man who had spoken against Thomas Putnam:

Hale: We cannot blink it more. There is a prodigious fear of this court in the country –
Danforth: Then there is a prodigious guilt in the country. Are *you* afraid to be questioned here?
Hale: I may only fear the Lord, sir, but there is fear in the country nevertheless.
Danforth: *angered now.* Reproach me not with the fear in the country; there is fear in the country because there is a moving plot to topple Christ in the country!
Hale: But it does not follow that everyone accused is part of it (*Crucible*, 98).

Both the irony and the allusion to HUAC are clear in Danforth's response: "No uncorrupted man may fear this court, Mr. Hale! None! *To Giles:* You are under arrest in contempt of this court. Now sit you down and take counsel with yourself, or you will be set in the jail until you decide to answer all questions" (98).

As Miller noted, many of the parallels between the forensic procedures of the Court of Oyer and Terminer in Salem and the HUAC hearings were chillingly obvious. Like the charge of Communism as it was defined by the Committee, the charge of witchcraft became a definition of essence rather than of behavior. In the 1950s, an American citizen could be a Communist "in his heart," as the Committee liked to put it. In the 1690s, all it took to convince the court that a British subject had made a pact with the Devil was the screaming of a child, or an adult, that his invisible Shape was torturing her. Both operated on a presumption of guilt, and these charges were very difficult to disprove. The most often-quoted line in the early reviews of *The Crucible* was John Proctor's "Is the accuser always holy now?" (77). Both tribunals allowed the accused the option of confession and repentance in order to avoid punishment, but only on the condition that they name others. As Starkey puts it, the confessed witches were given "full opportunity to repent and prove their repentance by informing on their fellow witches. Their willingness to do this provided a very utilitarian reason for keeping them alive. By means of the confessions, round every witch on the roster was woven a web of spectral evidence which in the end became more damaging than the original charges" (Starkey, 191-2). In the case of Mary Warren, as we have seen, full rehabilitation was earned by providing sufficient evidence against others to convince the judges of her sincerity. Like Louis Budenz, Elizabeth Bentley, and Whittaker Chambers, she became something of a star witness for the prosecution and a model to hold up to the adamant.

Miller made a powerful subtext out of the confession/informing nexus, closing Act 1 with the guilty anxiety of the girls finding its ecstatic outlet in their chant of accusations:

Abigail: I want to open myself! . . . I want the light of God, I want the sweet love of Jesus! I danced for the Devil; I saw him; I wrote in his book; I go back to Jesus; I kiss His hand. I saw Sarah Good with the Devil! I saw Goody Osburn with the Devil! I saw Bridget Bishop with the Devil! . . .
Betty *calling out hysterically and with great relief:* I saw Martha Bellows with the Devil!
Abigail: I saw Goody Sibber with the Devil! *It is rising to a great glee . . .*
Abigail: I saw Goody Hawkins with the Devil!
Betty: I saw Goody Bibber with the Devil!
Abigail: I saw Goody Booth with the Devil! (48)

To emphasize this theme, Miller took the hint of Giles Corey's standing mute against his accusation to create the incident in Act 3 in which

Giles refuses to give the name of a man who supplied him with evidence against Thomas Putnam because he will not be the cause of his imprisonment: "I will not give you no name. I mentioned my wife's name once and I'll burn in hell long enough for that. I stand mute" (97). Miller's most significant development of the theme of "naming names," of course, is his placement of the issue at the center of John Proctor's climactic wrestling with the decision of whether to die or to make a false confession. When he breaks down and agrees to confess, Judge Danforth quickly asks him whether he has seen Rebecca Nurse with the Devil. When he denies it, Danforth asks about Mary Esty and Martha Corey, and when Proctor denies it, says "Did you ever see anyone with the Devil?" (140). Proctor says "I did not." The dialogue continues:

Danforth: Proctor, you mistake me. I am not empowered to trade your life for a lie. You most certainly have seen some person with the Devil. *Proctor is silent.* Mr. Proctor, a score of people have already testified they saw this woman with the Devil.
Proctor: Then it is proved. Why must I say it?
Danforth: Why "must" you say it! Why, you should rejoice to say it if your soul is truly purged of any love for Hell! (141)

Miller's Salem magistrates prove less exacting on the matter of naming names than HUAC did, agreeing to let Proctor incriminate only himself. Having refused to give them the names of others, however, Proctor gains a new respect for his own and recants his confession. When a repentant Hale tries to persuade Elizabeth to tell her husband to confess, "for it may well be God damns a liar less than he that throws his life away for pride," Elizabeth replies: "I think that be the Devil's argument" (132).

Some of the events in the play occurred in the HUAC hearings but not in the Salem trial. For example, when Francis Nurse presents the petition in favor of Rebecca that has been signed by 91 of his neighbors, the judges orders that all of the signers be arrested and brought in for "examination." When Nurse expresses his horror at having brought trouble on these people, Danforth answers: "No, old man, you have not hurt these people if they are of good conscience. But you must understand, sir, that a person is either with this court or he must be counted against it, there be no road between" (94). There is no evidence that suspicion rested on anyone in the Salem outbreak simply for signing a petition, which many did. It was only in the HUAC hearings that explanations were demanded for the signing of petitions. Similarly, Parris's accusation that the petition protesting the innocence of the accused is an "attack upon the court" was characteristic of HUAC, not of the Salem court: "All innocent and Christian people are happy for the courts in Salem! These people are gloomy for it" (94). Similar statements were used to imply anti-anti-Communism, and thus guilt, in the witnesses before HUAC who had participated in the movement to have the Committee abolished.

The analogy between HUAC and the Salem outbreak was palpable to the play's early audiences, and few reviewers failed to mention it, whether with approval or with outrage. John Gassner remembered in 1960 that, on opening night, "The strong impression on the audience was almost the impact of an *event* rather than of just one more serious play. Even while aware of some creakiness in the work, I shared a feeling of grief and anger with others."[21] *The Nation*'s reviewer wrote two weeks after the opening that he could not "shed the sense of having experienced simultaneously the anguish and heroism of Salem's witch hunt and of today's."[22] Eric Bentley expressed the sense of most critics when he wrote, "at a moment when we are all being 'investigated' or about to be 'investigated,' it is moving to see images of 'investigation' before the footlights. It seems to me that there ought to be dozens of plays giving a critical account of the state of the nation, but the fact of one such play, by an author who is neither an infant, a fool, or a swindler, is enough to bring tears to the eyes."[23]

The affirmation of Miller's historical analogy was far from unanimous, however. *Time* complained of what it called the play's "bifocal nature, its linking of 'witch-hunting' past & present, its absorption with parallels – despite the axiom that parallel lines never meet."[24] Brooks Atkinson sounded the keynote of the reservations when he wrote in the *New York Times* that "the difference between the Salem trial and the current hysteria is a fundamental one. There never were any witches. But there have been spies and traitors in recent days. All the Salem witches were victims of public fear. Beginning with Hiss, some of the people accused of treason and disloyalty today have been guilty."[25] Miller answered this objection directly in the published text of the play, calling it "a snobbish objection and not at all warranted by the facts. I have no doubt that people *were* communing with, and even worshiping, the Devil in Salem, and if the whole truth could be known in this case, as it is in others, we should discover a regular and conventionalized propitiation of the dark spirit," citing as evidence Tituba's confession and the behavior of the children who seemed to have learned something about sorcery from her (35).[26] Another complaint was that the Salem outbreak was treated as a melodrama in which the prosecution was completely evil, and foolish beyond credence.[27] Miller answered this in 1957, in the introduction to his volume of *Collected Plays*, noting that "some critics have taken exception to the unrelieved badness of the prosecution in my play." He answered:

> I understand how this is possible, and I plead no mitigation, but I was up against historical facts which were immutable. I do not think that either the record itself or the numerous commentaries upon it reveal any mitigation of the unrelieved, straightforward, and absolute dedication to evil displayed by the judges of these trials and the prosecutors. After days of study it became quite incredible how perfect they were in this respect. . . . There was a sadism here that was breathtaking.[28]

In a 1958 interview, he said that his mistake was that he had not made the judge evil enough. The behavior of the historical models had been far more calculatedly evil than that of his characters.[29] To the complaints about Miller's raising Abigail's age, which he acknowledged in the published text, and other historical "inaccuracies," Miller replied that "a playwright has no debt of literalness to history. Right now I couldn't tell you which details were taken from the records verbatim and which were invented. I think you can say that this play is as historically authentic as *Richard II*, which took place closer to Shakespeare's time than *The Crucible* did to ours."[30]

The most hostile critique of Miller's play came from Robert Warshow, who wrote that *The Crucible* "offers us a revealing glimpse of the way the Communists and their fellow-travelers have come to regard themselves" in its suggestion of a connection with the men and women of Salem who "were upholding their own personal integrity against an insanely mistaken community."[31] Calling the use of historical analogy an "evasion" of Miller's real subject, he said that the main point of the play was that "'witch trials' are always with us, and especially today; but on the other hand do not hold Mr. Miller responsible either for the inadequacies of his presentation of the Salem trials or for the many undeniable and important differences between those trials and the 'witch trials' that are going on now."[32] Although Warshow chose not to specify those "undeniable and important differences," he berated

Miller for not addressing what he called "the present atmosphere" directly in his play, accusing him of a lack of clarity in his statement about the present, and implying that he had sought the cover of a historical analogy out of cowardice. For the most part, Warshow's article amounted to a string of charges and innuendos implying that Miller, who, like most self-proclaimed liberals, was really a shifty Communist, was hiding behind a misuse of history for political ends. It is significant, however, in that it attacked Miller for the very aesthetic strategy of historical analogy, for Miller's lack of "responsibility" in using it. In calling the play "a drama of universal significance," Warshow said, the liberal critics were causing the audience to think about contemporary events without discussing them openly. Describing the final scene of Proctor's confession and recantation, for example, he wrote, "now it is very hard to watch this scene without thinking of Julius and Ethel Rosenberg, who might also save their lives by confessing." His complaint against Miller was that he brought the audience to think these thoughts without making an argument:

> Does Mr. Miller believe that the only confession possible for them would be a false one, implicating innocent people? Naturally, there is no way for him to let us know, perhaps he was not even thinking of the Rosenbergs at all. How can he be held responsible for what comes into my head while I watch his play? And if I think of the Rosenbergs and somebody else thinks of Alger Hiss, and still another thinks of the Prague trial, doesn't that simply prove all over again that the play has universal significance?[33]

This of course was precisely what the play was meant to do. What Warshow found so infuriating was that Miller's depiction of the Salem outbreak impelled even right-wingers like him to think of the analogy with contemporary Red-baiting without the playwright's needing to draw any overt parallel. The analogy came to the audience's minds because they recognized the similarities. The play was the more powerful because it was the spectator who constructed its meaning in the context of contemporary events. And the writer was safe from attack because he wrote only about historical events. In Miller's hands, it was a far more effective subversive strategy than the revolutionary realism of *You're Next* or the satire of "A Modest Proposal for the Pacification of the Public Temper." It was about the only one that was possible in the Broadway theatre of the fifties.

One could be more precise in print than on stage, however. In the published text of the play, Miller included copious notes that supplied his interpretation of the social, economic, and psychologcial context of the Salem outbreak, and made its analogy with contemporary events unmistakably clear:

At this writing, only England has held back before the temptations of contemporary diabolism. In the countries of the Communist ideology, all resistance of any import is linked to the totally malign capitalist succubi, and in America any man who is not reactionary in his views is open to the charge of alliance with the Red hell. Political opposition, thereby, is given an inhumane overlay which then justifies the abrogation of all normally applied customs of civilized intercourse. A political policy is equated with moral right, and opposition to it with diabolical malevolence. Once such an equation is effectively made, society becomes a congerie [*sic*] of plots and counterplots, and the main role of government changes from that of the arbiter to that of the scourge of God. (34)

The outbreak of McCarthyism moved so swiftly through American history that just four years later, in the introduction to his *Collected Plays*, Miller was able to discuss it as a historical event that had passed, much as he discussed the Salem outbreak:

It was not only the rise of "McCarthyism" that moved me, but something which seemed much more weird and mysterious. It was the fact that a political, objective, knowledgeable campaign from the far Right was capable of creating not only a terror, but a new subjective reality, a veritable mystique which was gradually assuming even a holy resonance. The wonder of it all struck me that so practical and picayune a cause, carried forward by such manifestly ridiculous men, should be capable of paralyzing thought itself, and worse, causing to billow up such persuasive clouds of "mysterious" feelings within people. It was as though the whole country had been born anew, without a memory even of certain elemental decencies which a year or two earlier no one would have imagined could be altered, let alone forgotten. Astounded, I watched men pass me by without a nod whom I had known rather well for years; and again, the astonishment was produced by my knowledge, which I could not give up, that the terror in these people was being knowingly planned and consciously engineered, and yet that all they knew was terror. That so interior and subjective an emotion could have been so manifestly created from without was a marvel to me. It underlies every word in *The Crucible*.[34]

The Crucible was by far the most influential and effective literary statement that was made about McCarthyism in the fifties. A number of writers took their hint from Miller's strategy of historical analogy to create their own statements about the issues it raised through historical analogs. Others who had been working along these lines became bolder and more overt. A good example of this is the trio of blacklisted film writers who were writing the popular television series *You Are There* under the cover of their various fronts. *The Crucible* opened in New York on 22 January 1953. In the spring of that year, *You Are There* broadcast its pseudo-news reports on *The Boston Tea Party* (15 February), *The Execution of Joan of Arc* (1 March), *The Crisis of Galileo* (19 April), *The Death of Socrates* (3 May), and *The First Salem Witch Trial* (29 March). Written by "Kate Nickerson," a front for Arnold Manoff, one of the trio of blacklisted writers, with Abraham Polonsky and Walter Bernstein, the program on the trial and execution of Bridget Bishop managed to cram a number of historical issues with contemporary implications into its half-hour format.[35] While it focuses on the Bishop trial, it features several interviews from other venues, including one of Dorcas Good in prison, who says, "My name is Dorcas Good. I'm five years old, and I love our good Lord." In another interview, Cotton Mather explains why spectral evidence must be accepted by the court.[36] The Reverend Samuel Willard disagrees, arguing that he "cannot accept a proof against which there is no disproof. A person can have no fair defense against another's hallucinations, dreams, or fancies, if these be all the evidence required for the court." When Mather counters that there have been more than a hundred confessions, Willard says that confessions obtained under duress are not worthy of trust. Willard says there is no such thing as a witch in scripture, and that the persecution exists because "our lives are somber and lonely. We work in the dark forests. For days we may hear naught but the animals as they prowl over moldering leaves, the sudden shriek of wild birds; our fears and imaginations are the constant prey of strange fancies and excitements." He wonders if the afflicted girls are not suffering from their difficult lives and their parents from "further taxation, Indian Wars, and the uncertainty of the ownership of the land," asking, "are we destroying [the Evil One] at this trial, or are we destroying each other?"

In the trial scene, after Dr. Griggs acts as expert witness, explaining how the girls have been bewitched, Bridget is urged to confess. She says, "I cannot confess to what I do not believe." Several witnesses present rather fanciful spectral evidence against her, and then the girls feign attack from a bird in the rafters. Bridget says, "There is no bird. The children are demented." The scene shifts to the jail, where Constable John Willard, imprisoned for refusing to arrest any more suspects, says that he believes the girls are the ones who should be hanged, since "they are the ones that are stirring up all this horror on us." At the trial, Bridget's son Edward Bishop tries to introduce a deposition from Mary Warren saying that the girls are lying, but the girls cry out against him, and he and his sister are taken off for interrogation. Urged once more to confess, Bridget says, "I cannot confess for what I have not done . . . who will answer to God if I, in fear of my life, do lie." While Miller wrote a bourgeois tragedy that focused on the fate of an individual in the context of social and political events, the attempt in *You Are There* was to portray a social atrocity whose victims were innocent women and children and citizens who tried to do right. The emphasis on the general atmosphere of paranoia and fear, and on accusation without proof, on false confessions, on attacks on witnesses for the defense, on reliance on the testimony of "experts" on witchcraft, as well as the defendant's refusal to confess, are all calculated to suggest an analogy with the HUAC hearings. As with *The Crucible*, the construction or "discovery" of analogical parallels is left to the viewers, who must then deal with the recognition of similarities between the actions of their own government and those of a colonial government in the distant past that was acting on what they can only see as a misguided and horrible delusion. A similar strategy was used in the *You Are There* programs on Galileo, Socrates, and Joan of Arc.

In 1956, Louis Coxe's *The Witchfinders* was produced at the Provincetown Playhouse. An earnest play with a three-hour running time, Coxe's effort attempted to move beyond the parallels that were already in the public mind as a result of *The Crucible* and Starkey's *Devil in Massachusetts*, as well as more popular efforts like the *You Are There* program and novels such as Esther Forbes's 1928 *A Mirror for Witches*, reissued in 1954, and Lyon Phelps's *The Gospel Witch* (1955). As in his better-known *Billy Budd*, Coxe was interested in examining the more fundamental questions of good and evil and the vagaries of human motivation in *The Witchfinders*. As one reviewer expressed it, Coxe was "exploring the motivation of the heresy hunters and suggesting that behind the righteousness lurked personal greed and the dank New England winter."[37]

Unlike Miller, Coxe did not use historical figures to anchor his play in reality. He noted that "none of the people in the play is real in the sense that he or she is copied from an historical portrait. . . . The effort has been to set in conflict certain forces and to make these forces human by means of character."[38] The only significant historical name that is used is Tituba's, but her role is altered from accused witch to former "witchfinder" in her native Barbados, and she tells the three daughters of the Calef family how to recognize a witch rather than teaching the girls to conjure. Like Miller, Coxe associates the threat of witchcraft with sexuality. Elizabeth Calef, the 23-year-old stepmother of the adolescent Calef daughters, has a passionate affair with Jonathan Bayles, an ideologically liberal minister. The play concerns this sexual violation on the one hand, and, on the other, the ideological issues that are dividing the community.

As Elizabeth's doctrinaire husband Roger puts it: "The time has come for the folk of the land to choose – between the free-thinking godless and the solid men of God's word." The witch trials, he says, will not try the accused witches alone, but "Jonathan Bayles, the Newtonian, the Deist, the hanger-on of rationalists and Arminians, shall go on trial with all of his like" (II.3.3). With a rhetorical turn that was familiar to those who followed the HUAC hearings, Calef declares that what had recently seemed a humanistic desire for a better world was the evil of Satan masked as good. Tarring all deviants from Puritan orthodoxy with the taint of witchcraft, Calef declares that "Satan shifts his shades like the chameleon, and what you have thought to be promise of a better world, your deism and your rationalism and I know not what, all these gauds were the cast skins of the old serpent" (II.4.7). Now that Satan has been unmasked, Calef declares, "all true men and believers must turn out and gird for the right" (II.4.7), a call for all good Christians to join the witch-hunt. Although the play makes a significant commentary on the ideological element in the hysteria surrounding any witch-hunt, it finally focuses less on the ideological issues than on the themes of sexual guilt and revenge, and the greed for land that motivates much of the witch-baiting. The thematic strands were never fully integrated in the script. In the end, as the reviewer of the Provincetown production put it, "'The Witchfinders' hunts hard after its theme, but the quarry is never really completely trapped."[39]

All of these treatments reflect a shared awareness by author and audience of the obvious parallels between the outbreak of public hysteria over witchcraft that occurred in Salem Village in 1692 and the anti-Communist frenzy of some segments of the American populace in the late forties and early fifties. Whether the observer stood in the ideological Left, Right, or Center, the image of the misguided witch-hunt of their seventeenth-century forebears loomed large and terrifying in the cold-war imaginations of the spectators of these dramas. Miller's *Crucible* touched a nerve in the body politic, and the effect was heightened with every new manifestation of the drama of the witch-hunt. The social drama being enacted on the public stages of America's public buildings had found its most potent metaphor in the most horrific social drama of its colonial past.

5

Inquisition

To hurt innocent people whom I knew many years ago in order to save myself is, to me, inhuman and indecent and dishonorable. I cannot and will not cut my conscience to fit this year's fashions, even though I long ago came to the conclusion that I was not a political person and could have no comfortable place in any political group.

Lillian Hellman to John S. Wood, 19 May 1952

Mr. Stripling: Are you now or have you ever been a member of the Communist Party of any country?

Mr. Brecht: Mr. Chairman, I have heard my colleagues when they considered this question not as proper, but I am a guest in this country and do not want to enter into any legal arguments, so I will answer your question fully as well as I can. I was not a member, or am not a member, of any Communist Party. . . .

Mr. Stripling: Have you ever made application to join the Communist Party?

Mr. Brecht: No, no, no, no, no, never.

HUAC Hearings, 30 October 1947

Joan of Arc, Unfriendly Witness

Joan of Arc is probably the best-documented woman of the Middle Ages. Not only is the extensive record of her trial for witchcraft and heresy readily available, but there are enough historical records to pinpoint her whereabouts and her activities almost daily throughout her public career, from March 1429, when she arrived at the court of the dauphin Charles VII in Chinon, through 30 May 1431, when she was executed in Rouen. What has made her particularly useful for analogical purposes, however, is that, as Marina Warner has amply demonstrated, "Joan of Arc was an individual in history and real time, but she is also the protagonist of a famous story in the timeless dimension of myth, and the way that story has come to be told tells yet another story, one about our concept of the heroic, the good and the pure."[1] Despite the extraordinary documentation of her words and her actions, Joan has for more than five centuries been a cultural cipher to which the ideals for feminine virtue and for patriotism have been attached by men as different as Friedrich Schiller and Mark Twain. That she was appropriated as a visual symbol by both the French Resistance and the Nazis in World War II is evidence enough of the freedom with which various schemas of cultural values and diverse political ideologies have been imposed on her life. For writers who were looking for a positive historical analogy through which to address the issues surrounding HUAC's unfriendly witnesses, Joan of Arc provided the perfect combination of martyred innocence and ideological tenacity.

Over the centuries, the "story" of Joan's life has been conventionalized into a set of events from a variety of sources, some of which have the status of historical "facts," originating in the records of Joan's trial or written documents such as letters and official communications, and some of which come from literary accounts, hearsay and oral tradition, and more remote historical sources such as the testimony of witnesses in the trial for Joan's rehabilitation by the Pope in 1456. Strictly speaking, there was no "Jeanne d'Arc" or "Joan of Arc" in history, the name itself being a creation of later chroniclers who wanted to add a suggestion of nobility to the name of Joan's father, Jacques Darc.[2] Joan herself was illiterate, but occasionally she took the trouble to trace her full name on an official document rather than making her mark, and when she did, she signed herself "Jehanne la Pucelle" (Joan the Maid). The name was a key to her self-constructed identity. Joan grew up in the small village of Domremy, on the river Meuse, in the frontier between Lorraine and Champagne, at a particularly chaotic time during the Hundred Years War between France and England. As Jules Michelet pointed out in his 1841 study of Joan:

> The unfortunate inhabitants of the borderlands had the honor of being the direct subjects of the king; that meant in fact that they belonged to no one, were supported by no one, were spared by no one: their only liege, their only protector, was God. . . . They know that their hold on goods or life is precarious. They till the soil, the soldiery take the harvest. Nowhere is the peasant more deeply concerned with the affairs of the whole country.[3]

When Joan was growing up, the area was the site of constant pillaging by freelance soldiers attached to both the Armagnac supporters of

Charles VI and the Burgundian supporters of the English claimant to the French throne, Henry V. When both Henry V and Charles VI died in 1422, the fighting began to heat up, as the Burgundians supported the infant king Henry VI, who had been declared the heir to the French throne by the Treaty of Troyes in 1420, and the Armagnacs proclaimed Charles VII King of France. Domremy was an Armagnac village, its inhabitants the direct subjects of Charles VII.

Joan first heard the voices she later identified as those of St. Michael the Archangel and Sts. Margaret and Catherine in 1425, when she was about 13 years old. A prophecy current in the area predicted that, since a woman, Isabella of Bavaria, had destroyed France by disinheriting her son Charles VII with the Treaty of Troyes, a virgin would come out of Lorraine to save France. In June of 1428, Joan's family was forced to flee Domremy with the rest of the villagers, who took refuge at Neufchâteau from a Burgundian attack, returning to find their village sacked and burned. In October of that year, the Duke of Bedford, English regent in France, laid siege to Orleans, the last stand of the Armagnac supporters of Charles VII. Joan's "voices" told her that she must go to Robert de Baudricourt, the captain of nearby Vaucouleurs, and get him to give her a horse so that she might go to Charles in Chinon in order to raise an army to save Orleans and bring Charles to Rheims, where tradition dictated the official coronation must take place. Somehow, Joan persuaded Baudricourt to equip her and send her with a small escort through enemy territory to Chinon. When she arrived there in the late winter of 1429, the legend is that Charles tried to trick her by hiding among the courtiers, but that she picked him out of the crowd and, by a sign from God, convinced him that her mission was genuine. To satisfy those who insisted that her voices came from the devil, Joan was sent to the University of Poitiers to be examined by a phalanx of theologians and Church dignitaries, who were convinced that she was not a witch, and that it was lawful to use her services. Returning to Chinon, Joan was equipped as a knight, with a noble squire, a page, two heralds, a steward, and two valets, as well as a personal confessor. She rode a black charger given her by the king, and commissioned the crafting of a suit of white armor and the standard she was to carry in battle, a white background with the *fleur du lys* of France, at the center God holding the world in his hands, and on either side an angel holding a lily, with the motto "Jesus Maria." For her sword, Joan sent to the monks at the shrine of St. Catherine of Fierbois, where a sword was found, miraculously according to legend, behind the altar, bearing her motto "Jesus Maria."

Joan rode with the army to Orleans, and entered the city on 29April. In the first week of May, the army took Fort St. Loup and Les Tourelles, where Joan was wounded, as her voices had predicted, and drove the English forces to retreat from Orleans on 8 May. After a series of victories in May and June, Joan rode with army to escort Charles from Sully across the Loire, into what had been enemy territory, and on to Rheims for the coronation. City after city acknowledged and welcomed Charles as he made his triumphant progress to Rheims, several changing allegiance on the spot. When he was crowned king on 17 July, Joan stood next to him bearing her standard, the only one displayed at the ceremony. One legend is that Joan told Charles she had accomplished her mission with his coronation and now wished only to resume her feminine identity and return to the pastoral life of Domremy. Another is that she dedicated herself to peace after the coronation, leaving her armor at the church of St. Denis. After traveling with Charles back in triumph to the Loire, however, the historical record shows a Joan who was eager to keep fighting. Even after Charles had signed a truce lasting until Christmas, Joan made a failed assault on Paris, damaging her military reputation, and, since it was held on the feast of the birthday of the Blessed Virgin Mary, her reputation for sanctity as well. After a winter of inactivity and a few indecisive battles, Joan was captured on 23 May 1430, while defending Compiègne from a siege by John of Luxembourg, and sold to the English Earl of Warwick for a king's ransom. While imprisoned at Compiègne, she jumped from the tower into the moat in an attempt either at escape or at suicide, and could not, or refused to, eat for three days. In November she was handed over to Pierre Cauchon, Bishop of Beauvais, for trial as a witch and a heretic, but was kept in an English prison, guarded by soldiers who slept in her cell and tried unsuccessfully several times to rape her. She was eighteen years old.

Joan's trial was held in Rouen, presided over jointly by the Bishop of Beauvais and a representative of the Pope's Inquisition, although it was Cauchon who controlled the proceedings. After two weeks of a public trial, in which Joan steadfastly maintained that her voices came from God, that she was not a witch, and that she was not a heretic, but refused to accede to the demand that she resume wearing women's clothing (and thus give up the outward sign of her knightly identity), Joan became violently ill, it was said, from eating a carp that was sent her by the Bishop of Beauvais. Private sessions were held in her prison cell, in which she was constantly urged to admit that her voices were not from God and to resume wearing women's clothing, a point on which Joan was adamant, insisting that she would not be "safe" in her prison if she wore a dress, and asking repeatedly to be transferred to an ecclesiastical prison. When threatened with torture, she told the judges it was no use, for she would say anything they wanted under torture, but then take it back as soon as she was released. At one point, the judges tried to bribe her into assuming women's dress with the promise that they would allow her to hear Mass and take the sacraments. On 24 May, in the marketplace next to the cemetery of St. Ouen, Joan was set up on a scaffold and induced to sign a recantation, acknowledging that she had been in error and heretical. She was condemned to life imprisonment and agreed to assume women's clothes. Rather than sending her to the ecclesiastical prison she expected, however, Cauchon ordered, "take her back to the place you brought her from."[4] Three days later, she resumed her men's clothing and withdrew her recantation. Many legends surround these events, such as that the documents were switched on her; that she signed the recantation as a joke; and that her women's dress was stolen by the soldiers and she resumed her men's clothing out of modesty.

On 28 May 1431, Joan was condemned as a heretic by the Church and handed over to the English to be burned. The execution took place on 30 May. The pyre was made especially high so that she would literally be burned to death, instead of strangled by the executioner before the flames reached her body, as was customary. A miter bearing the words "heretic, relapsed, apostate, idolater" was placed on her head. She asked for a cross, and an English soldier handed her one he had made of two sticks, which she placed under her robe. As was his duty, Cauchon came to the foot of the pyre and urged her to abjure. She reportedly answered, "Bishop, my death is your doing. . . . If you had placed me in a prison of the Church, this would not have come to pass."[5] The Church's official witness, the Augustinian monk Isambart de la Pierre, who stood closest to the pyre, said that she prayed to her saints as the flames rose, and that her last word was the single cry, "Jesus!" John Tessart, secretary to the King of England, cried, "We are lost; we have burnt a saint."[6] A number of legends surround the burning. It is said that ten thousand people, French and English, wept at her death, that an English soldier who ran up to add fuel to the fire saw a white dove fly out of the flames toward France at her death, that the soldiers saw "Jesus" written in the flames, that her heart refused to burn and was thrown into the Seine by the executioner. In 1456, the

1431 verdict was rescinded by the Church. In 1920, Joan of Arc was canonized a saint.

As Marina Warner has noted, the life of Joan of Arc is "organised by dramatists and by historians and biographers with a dramatic sense, according to Aristotelian theory: first the glory of the hero with an overarching conviction of personal mission, then reversal, the destruction of hopes and, usually, extinction." The difference, however, is that in Joan's case, the meaning generated by the paradigmatic placement of events is closer to the salvation and redemption of Jesus Christ than the fatalism of the Greek tragic hero:

> The moral message of the form resembles that of the Catholic Mass. There is no hubris in the strict sense, for the drive toward self-destruction lies in a laudable consent to the divine will and God's call, which raises up the hero-victim, paschal lamb or virgin girl, for the time required to accomplish the vocation. There is no defiance of the gods, nor is the destruction of the hero a defeat, but a victory.[7]

The story of Joan has in fact become conventionalized over the years into an antitragedy, a martyrdom in which Joan dies for truth and to preserve her own integrity against the monstrous hypocrisy of Church and State.

At the time of the HUAC trials, the image of Joan of Arc was fresh and vibrant in the United States. Her canonization in 1920 and the success of George Bernard Shaw's *Saint Joan* in 1923 had revived her image and recast her legend. Shaw presented Joan as a straightforward country girl, an independent thinker who confounds the scheming churchmen and politicians through her courage and common sense – "the first Protestant and the first nationalist." The canonization, Shaw's play, and the quincentenary of Joan's death in 1931 occasioned a number of serious studies of Joan in English during the thirties, including the publication of the records of her trial and biographies by Vita Sackville-West and Milton Waldman.[8] More popular treatments, such as Frances Winwar's *The Saint and the Devil* (1948), Julian Green's translation of Charles Péguy's *Mystère de la Charité de Jeanne d'Arc* (1950), Albert Guérard's translation of Michelet's *Jeanne d'Arc* (1957), and Lucien Fabre's *Joan of Arc* (1954), followed in the forties and fifties, along with a stream of treatments on the stage and in film and television. Shaw's *St. Joan* was revived successfully on Broadway by the Theatre Guild in 1951 and Off-Broadway by the Phoenix Theatre in 1956. Even a partial list of the new

American dramatic treatments shows the tremendous extent to which the story of Joan of Arc had permeated the American imagination at the time of the HUAC hearings: *Joan of Lorraine* (Maxwell Anderson, stage,1946); *CBS Is There: The Execution of Joan of Arc* (CBS radio, 1948); *Joan of Arc* (RKO film, based on the Anderson play, 1948); *The Miracle of the Bells* (film, 1948); *Joan of Arc* (Hallmark Hall of Fame, NBC TV, 1952); *You Are There: The Execution of Joan of Arc* (CBS TV, 1953 and 1957); *Joan of Arc at the Stake* (film, 1954); *The Lark* (Jean Anouilh, 1953; trans. Lillian Hellman, 1955); *The Lark* (Hallmark Hall of Fame, NBC TV, 1957); and *Saint Joan* (Columbia film, based on Shaw's play, 1957).

These representations of the Joan of Arc story reflect a wide range of political agendas related to the abuse of political power and the repression of individual thought. Uta Hagen, who played Joan in the 1951 production of Shaw's play, has said that it was easy for her to find a conception for the character in the trial scenes because, at the time, "Joe McCarthy was reigning. People were being hounded nigh unto death for their unpopular convictions and beliefs."[9] Hagen was herself a target of HUAC for having made a speech in favor of Henry Wallace in 1948, and she was finally called to testify in 1953. Asked why the Theatre Guild had cast her, she answered, "Well, they were considered to be 'liberal.' In any event, the whole notion of heresy and loneliness and having your beliefs challenged was terribly easy for me to identify with."[10]

In fact, the Theatre Guild was less forthcoming about the contemporary American application of Joan's martyrdom than Hagen suggests. In a carefully phrased article for the *New York Times*, Guild Director Lawrence Langner coached audiences and critics on how to read the historical analogy so as to suggest a "universal" application and to anticipate the charge that the Theatre Guild was attacking HUAC by establishing its firmly anti-Communist position. "'St. Joan' is a play about the timeless subject of personal integrity and freedom of conscience," he wrote, and "its story is more applicable to today's events than when it was first written . . . no saint in the catalogue has more of a message, with the Kremlin relentlessly applying the principle that only people rendering submission to the Stalin line have a right to existence."[11] After laying out his anti-Communist framework, Langner suggested gingerly that "there is also a lesson for the free part of the world in Joan's integrity." Proposing that Joan is a saint of "free conscience" and "the kind of patriotism we still honor," he suggested that the play has a message for "the young people of America" and "even more of a message for those adults who seem to have shed the garment of integrity and have fallen victim to the error that 'the big lie,' oft repeated, can readily become confused with truth."[12] Langner left the reader to determine the content of "the big lie," thus presumably appealing to both anti-Communists, for whom it was Communism, and leftists, for whom it was anti-Communism. The strategy seems to have worked. The *New York Times* critic Brooks Atkinson, who was to shy away from the political implications of *The Crucible* two years later, wrote that if Shaw were living, "he would find his thesis monstrously confirmed in the savage intolerance and the wild persecutions for heresy that have paralyzed our society. . . . There is a grandeur about 'Saint Joan' that was less apparent twenty-eight years ago. Tolerance was not so hamstrung then."[13] On the other hand, Joseph Wood Krutch wrote of "the obvious parallel between the premises of the Inquisition and those of the rulers of even the more mild-mannered totalitarian states."[14] Many critics noted contemporary parallels, and both Shaw's play and the Theatre Guild's production were ideologically indeterminate enough that each could appropriate the analogy to express his or her political viewpoint.

To the Frenchman Jean Anouilh, Joan was a leader of the French Resistance victimized by the corrupt collaborators of the Vichy government. *Time* described his play *The Lark* as "a sort of poetic recruiting poster, as a medieval Marianne waving the *bleu-blanc-rouge* and calling all Frenchmen to their former greatness."[15] Anouilh has Cauchon say to the Earl of Warwick:

> We shall go as far as ever we can to save Joan, even though we have been sincere collaborators with the English rule, which seemed to us then the only reasonable solution to chaos. It was very easy for those who were at Bourges to call us traitors, when they had the protection of the French army. We were in occupied Rouen. . . . We were men, with the frailty of men, who wanted to go on living, and yet at the same time to save Joan if we could. It was not in any way a happy part that we were called upon to fill.[16]

During the trial, Cauchon tries to persuade Joan to give up her allegiance to Charles VII and accept the English King Henry VI as king of France: "The useless resistance of the man you call your king, and his absurd pretensions to a throne which isn't his, appear to us to be acts of rebellion and terrorism against a peace which was almost assured. The puppet whom you served is not our master, be certain of that."[17] Joan replies: "Say what you like, you can't alter the truth. This is the king God gave you. Thin as he is, with his long legs and his big, bony knees."[18]

As the *Catholic World* reviewer put it, "unfortunately, Anouilh has rewritten the Trial to suit his own purpose; substitute Pétain for Cauchon and his conciliatory speeches could be the head of the Vichy Government pleading the cause of collaboration with the soul of Free France (Joan)."[19] She went on to complain that "to give substance to this allegory . . . Anouilh was forced to distort historical truth."[20] The question of the establishment or existence of "historical truth" aside, this raises one of the immanent difficulties in the literary use of historical analogy. To make the analogy meaningful, the events represented as past must be recognizable to those who are familiar with the traditional story, but to make the point the writer wants to make about the present, the audience must affirm the resemblance between these events and the current situation. Every playwright who has made use of the Joan of Arc legend has represented enough of the events of Joan's life as they were recorded to make the audience affirm the verisimilitude of the representation. It is generally in the episodes that depart from the written record, however, that the writer's most important implications about the present are invested. Hence, to complain about a failure to reflect the historical record accurately is to misunderstand the whole project of historical analogy.

In her adaptation of *The Lark*, as Richard Moody has shown in detail, Lillian Hellman "reduced the discursive arguments, dramatized rather than reasoned her way through the sacred mystery, changed the ending, added a biting briskness, and energized the proceedings with an emotional charge that was absent in Anouilh."[21] She also developed Anouilh's play as an analogy for her own well-known refusal to "cut [her] conscience to fit this year's fashions" when asked to name names before HUAC. In an interview she said that Anouilh had had Joan offer to go to the stake instead of retiring to a convent because she could not face the idea of growing old, "an unimpressive woman among ordinary people, of finishing her life a fat, sallow, sterile mediocrity."[22] Hellman said that "Joan was too big to be so concerned with vanity. Death, as I see it, is the most dramatic choice a person can make. Very few have made it. I just couldn't see Joan going to the stake out of arrogance."[23] Hellman developed her ending from Joan's statement to the Inquisitor in Anouilh's dialogue: "What I am, I will not denounce. What I have done, I will not deny."[24] As in Anouilh's original, and as in the historical record, Hellman's Joan gives in to Cauchon and abjures, but then recants the abjuration, becoming in the eyes of the Church a relapsed heretic, and is handed over to the English to be burned. The motive that Hellman gives to Joan is significantly different from that in Anouilh's version, however. She says to Warwick, "Monseigneur, I have done wrong. And I don't know how or why I did it. (*Slowly, bitterly.*) I swore against myself. That is a great sin, past all others – (*Desperately.*) I still believe in all that I did, and yet I swore against it. God can't want that. What can be left for me?" (53). She looks forward to a future of "cast-off brocade," and after her death, of being remembered "as a crazy girl who rode into battle for what she said she believed, and ate the dirt of lies when she was faced with punishment" (54). After contemplating this future, she addresses her God: "You are silent, dear my God, because you are sad to see me frightened and craven. And for what? A few years of unworthy life. . . . Forgive me and take me back for what I am" (54). Joan's execution follows swiftly, but the play ends with the triumphant legend rather than the tragic denouement. Cauchon admits that the burning of Joan was "a monstrous sin"; Warwick says that it was a "grave mistake," for "we made a lark into a giant bird who will travel the skies of the world long after our names are forgotten" (56). Ladvenu, Joan's confessor, whom Anouilh made into her champion during the trial, says "the true story of Joan is not the hideous agony of a girl tied to a burning stake. She will stand forever for the glory that can be. Praise God" (56). The play ends with a recreation of Joan's "happiest day," the coronation of Charles VII.

By rewriting the ending, Hellman succeeded in remaking Anouilh's existentialist play into a historical tragedy that conveyed some of her central convictions in the context of the McCarthyist pressures of the fifties – the primacy of the individual conscience and the importance of being true to one's word, regardless of the consequences. In her hands Joan the martyr became a witness to truth and individual responsibility similar to the Lillian Hellman who wrote to HUAC: "To hurt innocent people whom I knew many years ago in order to save myself is, to me, inhuman and indecent and dishonorable. I cannot and will not cut my conscience to fit this year's fashions."[25] Not surprisingly, it was Eric Bentley who recognized the contemporary application of *The Lark* as adapted by Hellman, but he complained that the analogy could have been more overt: "It is high time," he wrote, "that a Catholic dramatist should write a Joan play and remind the public, first, that the trial was as shameless and corrupt a frame-up as anything in Soviet annals and that, as for character, Bishop Cauchon was in all probability about as likeable, enlightened, and highminded as Senator McCarthy."[26]

As if in answer to remarks like Bentley's, Hellman made the analogy between the Inquisition and the HUAC hearings unmistakable in her libretto for the comic opera *Candide* the following year. *Candide* openly burlesques HUAC in its depiction of the Inquisition, which Candide observes on his travels. One man is hanged for "eating ham and eggs and throwing away the ham, as his people did before him,"[27] an obvious allusion to HUAC's anti-Semitism. Another is charged with "the overbuying of candles for the overreading of books in subversive association with associates" (Hellman, *Collected Plays*, 659), an allusion to the Smith Act. The witness admits to being "a tool and a fool," having learned to read as a very young man, and is required to name his "associates." He responds: "Yes, sir. Well, there was Emmanuel, Lilybelle, Lionel, and Dolly and Molly and Polly, of course. And my Ma and my Pa and my littlest child. A priest, deceased, and my uncle and my aunt. The president, his resident, and the sister of my wife." The Inquisitor responds, "All right, All right. Thank you for your splendid cooperation." The Inquisitor asks the crowd whether the witness should be given five or ten years, and they respond with "ten," singing: "At first he lied and tricked us,/ But now he's sung his tale./ So bid him Benedictus/ and let him sing in jail." Hellman's open ridicule of the Committee and its methods partly reflected the fact that she felt she had nothing left to lose in 1956, but her associates, Leonard Bernstein and Richard Wilbur, her director Tyrone Guthrie, and her producers, Ethel Linder Reiner and Lester Osterman, all had to go along with her. Opposition to the Committee was possible on Broadway in 1956, although it was daring.

From the opposite point of view, Maxwell Anderson made his Joan of Arc play into an apologia for collaborators, like the witnesses who took a pragmatic view of cooperating with the Committee so they could get on with their work, but, Anderson would contend, stopped short of compromising their essential integrity. Anderson had taken the position in 1941 that, after the Nazi-Soviet pact, American Communism was "a conspiracy to overthrow our democratic government and [was] at present working in cooperation with the Nazi war on civilization."[28] Believing along with J. Edgar Hoover that Communists were "enemy agents, engaged in wrecking us from within,"[29] Anderson later supported the right of motion-picture studios and television networks to blacklist them, declaring that Communists "should be ousted from any position of influence or honor which they hold."[30] Nevertheless, he deplored the *tactics* of HUAC.[31] In other words, Anderson's views were closer to those of middle America than those of Hellman or the Hollywood Ten. His Joan of Arc play, *Joan of Lorraine*, was written before the Show Business hearings began in the fall of 1947, but well after HUAC was established in 1939 and made permanent in 1945.

In an article detailing his conception of the play, Anderson wrote that it was about "the question that has been my own torment – along with most of the human race – during the last decade. The problem of what to believe, and how a man defends his belief in a world of power politics and disillusion."[32] His play is also a metatheatrical study of the rehearsal process, in which he hoped to capture the "first magic, this first flash of fire," that happens when a play first comes to life in rehearsal and to give an audience "a glimpse of that first miracle."[33] The frame of the play is the rehearsal process for a Broadway play about Joan of Arc, in which the actress who is to play Joan disagrees with the director and the author about her character. The actress, Mary Gray, complains that the play had begun as a simple chronicle of Joan's life, but in revision has been turned into a play "about how she finds that she must compromise with the world, and even work with evil men, and allow evil to be done, before she can accomplish her task."[34] She objects to the script's implication that "we all have to compromise and work with evil men – and that if you have a faith it will come to nothing unless you get some of the forces of evil on your side" (20). The director responds that he wouldn't necessarily call them the forces of evil, but "you have to get some of the people who are running things on your side – and they're pretty doubtful characters mostly" (21). Mary finds it a "desecration" of Joan to use her character in this way. She believes that "the great things in this world are brought about by faith – that all the leaders who count are dreamers and people who see visions," while the play is being rewritten "to say that nobody can be sure he's right about anything . . . that we have to tolerate dishonesty in high places in order to get things done" (46). The director shows her that the theatre world itself, including their own production, is full of corruption and compromise, but contends: "I still think it's worth while to put on a play about Joan of Arc – in the middle of all this. The human race is a mass of corruption tempered with high ideals. – You can't sacrifice your integrity, but short of that – " (47).

The plot of the frame play mirrors the traditional Joan of Arc story, as Mary makes a decision to leave the production, mirroring Joan's abjuration, but is persuaded to continue in her role for the rest of the rehearsal. The Joan play within the frame play is a chronicle representing Joan's career, from Domremy to Vaucouleurs, Chinon, Orleans, Rheims and the coronation of Charles the VII, and Joan's renunciation of her armor before the statue of the Blessed Virgin in the cathedral of Saint Denis. The emphasis in these scenes is on the corruption of the court and the Church, and the political power-struggles surrounding the events of Joan's career. After a scene from the frame play, the Joan play is taken up at the trial scene, through Joan's abjuration, where she is represented as signing the articles renouncing her visions and her military career in a moment of despair: "I don't know what is true. I don't know what is good. Bring me a dress to wear and leave me alone in my prison. I will do as you say. I will believe no more in my visions. I will let the church decide" (74). In this play, Joan is tricked into breaking her vow to renounce her Voices, to wear women's clothes, and to submit to the authority of the Church. Cauchon allows the English guards to remain in her cell, and she does not change into women's clothing for fear of being raped. Her Voices visit her, however, giving her the confidence not to take the second chance that is offered: "It won't help now to change my clothes. I've heard my Voices again, and I trust them, and they are good. I'm sorry that I denied them" (79). When the Inquisitor reminds her that she had been convinced the day before that her Voices were evil, her line is, "I have an answer now" (79). Mary interrupts the rehearsal to say that she has an answer as well. "Are you getting revelations, too?" asks the director. Mary responds: "Maybe. Anyway, I knew the answer. It's true that she would compromise in little things. You were right. But it's also true that she would not compromise her belief – her own soul. She'd rather step into the fire – and she does" (79).

Anderson's is an unusual statement for a Joan of Arc play to make. One of the few playwrights to place her temporary abjuration at the center of the play, he emphasizes Joan's pragmatism rather than her idealism or her victimization. Somehow, he suggests, Joan represents the possibility of compromising one's integrity and yet maintaining it, making use of political corruption without being tainted by it – a unique use of the Joan of Arc legend if finally an unconvincing one. That it was deeply felt is evident in an article Anderson wrote while the play was in production, called "Compromise and Keeping the Faith." In it he argued for the necessity of making "concessions" in the theatre, for "unless you are willing to make nearly every possible business and artistic concession to the play-producing setup, you'll probably never get your play on at all."[35] Making the political analogy overtly, he wrote:

Figure 7. Ingrid Bergman as Mary Gray in a rehearsal scene
from Maxwell Anderson's *Joan of Lorraine.*

Suppose you are a statesman or popular leader, trying to take a
nation with you through a crisis in its destiny. Your first essential is a
conviction about what must be done. The second essential is a willingness to bargain with every cheap local politician you need to get
your measure through. Lincoln bargained in such fashion, and so
did the second Roosevelt. But if in your bargaining you forget your
convictions and sacrifice the thing you were trying to attain, then you
become a run-of-the-mill politician yourself; your work is worth nothing, and the world will forget you gladly.[36]

Anderson and the Playwrights Company walked a fine line between
compromise and principle with the production itself, when it allowed
the Washington premiere to proceed over protest demonstrations
against "the exclusion of Negroes from the audience," yet had leaflets
distributed to the patrons that quoted statements from the star, Ingrid
Bergman, and the Playwrights Company opposing racial discrimina-
tion.[37] Anderson's position on HUAC, deploring its methods while sup-

175

porting any legal means, including the blacklist, to attack Communists, was a similar piece of casuistry. It was a brilliant stroke to place his apology for compromise in a play about the figure who represented to her audience not only innocence, but truth, integrity, and tenacity. If Joan of Arc could compromise with the evil statesman surrounding Charles VII in order to save France, then surely the average American citizen could cooperate with the Committee in eradicating the evil of Communism.

Along with scenarist Andrew Solt, Maxwell Anderson was given credit for the screenplay of the motion picture that was supposedly based on *Joan of Lorraine*, RKO's *Joan of Arc* (1948). The film's director, Victor Fleming, said in an interview that the plan had been to base the screenplay directly on the play script, deleting the "rehearsal interludes," but, "as Anderson had amassed a great deal of fresh research material, we decided to scrap it and concentrate on a straight Joan story."[38] The screenplay he decided to use, Fleming said, was Anderson's third completed script. Anderson dissociated himself from the film rather vehemently after it was produced, claiming that his screenplay had been completely mangled in production. He responded to John Mason Brown's criticism of the dialogue with typical asperity toward Ingrid Bergman – who was not only the star of the film but one-third owner of the production company – and the whole movie-making process:

> I didn't write that dialogue you objected to in "Joan of Arc." It was probably stuck in at the last moment during the shooting. You evidently don't know what goes on in the film business. The writer has no control whatever. If Ingrid hadn't insisted on taking out all human touches and making Joan a plaster saint the thing might have had some quality. She wrecked that one. She had the power to wreck it and she did. Moreover, she's completely unscrupulous. She doesn't keep her word and she has no respect for a writer's work.[39]

It is no wonder that Anderson disowned *Joan of Arc*. The film is missing not only the metatheatrical framework of the play, but the moral complexity of its conflict over the question of compromising with evil in order to do good. The film is simply a narrative chronicle of Joan's career, "the routine, sixth-grade reader version of the noble story of the Maid of Orleans," as one reviewer put it.[40] The film is structured as a straightforward melodrama of martyred innocence, as the forces of corruption in Church and State, represented by Cauchon (Francis L.

Sullivan), the dauphin's advisor Georges de La Tremouille (Gene Lockhart), the Earl of Warwick (Alan Napier), and John of Luxembourg (J. Carroll Naish) combine with the weakness and cupidity of Charles (José Ferrer) to destroy Joan, who is represented as a rather bland vessel of innocence, purity, and idealism.

In the film, Tremouille undermines Charles's faith in Joan by arguing that she is as corrupt as they are: "This girl is both ambitious and unscrupulous. And if the war goes on and her military party keeps the ascendant, she, not you, will rule in France, whether you're crowned or not."[41] Charles defends Joan at first, but, when the cheers for Joan outnumber the cheers for him at the coronation, he agrees to the truce with Burgundy for 100,000 gold crowns. When Joan tells him his action looks like "betrayal or stupidity, or both," he responds, "What do you know of the expedients to which heads of nations must stoop? What do you know of statecraft? A ruler has to rob, murder, compromise, lie, cheat, steal – and bargain with the lowest sort of people – even the enemy. Men have been governed by corruption since the invention of government. They like it!" (Anderson and Solt, *Joan*, 100). When Joan answers that "men hate corruption and God hates it," he responds, "I don't know about God, but men take to it very naturally" (104). Thus the film places the acceptance of compromise with corruption not in Joan's hands, as the play does, but in those of the dauphin, expertly played by José Ferrer as a well-meaning but weak man, with a love of pleasure and comfort and an essentially frivolous soul.

The film has Cauchon himself come to bargain with John of Luxembourg to buy Joan with £10,000 from the Earl of Warwick. When Luxembourg taunts him for working for the English, Cauchon retorts, "Whose side are you on, my friend," and Luxembourg replies: "The same side we're all on. The me-side. What's in it for me? That's my side and it's your side and it's the English side and the French side and the Burgundian side. Of course, that girl – she's the only one I know who's not on the me side" (122). Similarly, Cauchon is given a purely political motive for seeking Joan's abjuration:

> I know what must be done here in the interests of our king. She's a heretic, an apostate, and a sorceress, and she will go to the stake, but we must discredit her before she dies. For she is not just a sorceress. She's a symbol – adored by the people of France. If we burn her now we make a martyr of her. And that's exactly what her king wants us to do. But if we can force her to recant, to abjure – to renounce her

177

mission, her Voices and her king – the people will lose faith in her and in the king who was crowned by a heretic. They will accept our Henry as the lawful king of France. (142)

To make sure the audience doesn't miss the point, the film introduces the Bishop of Avranches (Taylor Holmes) into the trial scene to denounce the proceedings and make their historical consequences clear: "I warn you, you the so-called judges – you may succeed in sending her to the stake, but one day your English king will be ashamed of these proceedings. Rome will declare the truth about this girl, and France will praise the Maid for its birth as one nation!" (144). As for Cauchon, Avranches declares him a traitor who has betrayed his country and his Church. Although Joan abjures in what appears to be a state of near delirium, the film sends her to her death a martyr, ascribing the motive for her recantation purely to her having heard her Voices and repented her lapse of faith in them. The film's final statement about the meaning of Joan's life is placed in the mouth of her confessor, Father Massieu (Shepperd Strudwick):

Oh, mistaken men, traitors to yourselves and your country. You have thrust greatness and an undying name upon your chief enemy. . . . The winning of a few victories – that could be put aside as a nine-days' wonder. But you have made her a symbol – and her ashes and her words will blow like seeds and take roots on deserts and pavements. They will flower in heralds and prophets to spread her fame. This will be her age, her century, and all the rest of you – priests and kings – will be minor figures in her tragedy (162-8).

Thus, much against Anderson's will, his play, which attempted to justify cooperation with political corruption, was turned into a melodrama that defined it as evil, setting against it the symbolism of Joan as martyred innocent and pure patriot. Ideologically speaking, the screenplay could have been written by Lillian Hellman.

Reaction to the adaptation was "mixed," with critics responding more to the reduction in complexity than the change in ideological stance. The *Baltimore Sun* film critic declared *Joan of Arc* "a marked improvement over the play by Maxwell Anderson . . . from the viewpoint of entertainment and spectacle. The character of *Joan* has been simplified," and although "the plots hatched around this pious and candid country girl by greedy courtiers and noblemen engaged in the sordid power politics of the time are as complicated as they are base," they serve to point up "the conflict between them and the direct, dedicated *Maid*."[42] The New York *Daily News* noted with approval that Bergman's screen performance was uniformly ardent and sincere, "free of the changes of pace and mood that handicapped her interpretation of Joan in the Anderson play, in which she was more the actress than the Saint."[43] On the other hand, the more sophisticated critics, such as Bosley Crowther in the *New York Times*, Leo Mishkin of the *Morning Telegraph*, and John McCarten of the *New Yorker* complained that the screenplay was a childishly oversimplified version of Joan's story and bore little resemblance to Anderson's play. The *New Yorker* complained that the film was "overburdened with scenery, employs a cast that must run into thousands, and never departs from its fifteenth-century locale. Awash in Technicolor, it staggers from one unlikely scene to another, while Ingrid Bergman, who was so triumphant as Joan on the stage, wanders about the premises urging all hands to cut out gambling, wenching, and swearing."[44]

Otto Preminger's *Saint Joan* (1957), a screen adaptation of Shaw's play that was written by Graham Greene, was not quite the extravaganza that *Joan of Arc* was, but it managed a similar feat of simplification by compressing the action into 110 minutes and eliminating Shaw's "talkiness" to the extent that little remained of his ideas. The film's publicity campaign focused on Preminger's "talent search" for a young actress to play Joan, which yielded the 17-year-old Jean Seberg, who was "discovered" in her high school in Marshalltown, Iowa. With only one season of summer stock behind her, Seberg was thrust into the most demanding female role in the repertoire of modern drama. It is not surprising that Preminger decided to use her primarily as a visual icon of youth and innocence, cutting all of her substantial speeches and leaving the debates to John Gielgud, who played Warwick, with occasional support by the churchmen. Richard Todd played a rather romantic Dunois, who is clearly a temptation for the ardent Joan to abandon her mission, and Richard Widmark overacted as a silly Charles. The film makes use of Shaw's epilogue as a frame – Charles is visited by the spirits of Joan and several of the other characters in 1456, when Joan has been rehabilitated – and it ends with Shaw's well-known lines, "O God that madest this beautiful earth, when will it be ready to received Thy saints? How long, O Lord, how long?" The ending is one of reverent pathos, however, rather than Shavian irony. The Joan in this film is a victim of political corruption rather than a participant in a historical dialectic, and the focus is on personal greed and self-interest rather than on corrupt institutions or social forces.

Despite the increasing threat to the broadcast industry that was emanating from HUAC, CBS allowed radio writer Max Ehrlich and "Jeremy Daniel," a front for Abraham Polonsky, to treat its three *You Are There* dramatizations of Joan's execution as analogies for contemporary political corruption and the attempted subjugation of the individual conscience to a dominant ideology. The day treated in both the radio play, first broadcast in February 1948, and the teleplay, first broadcast in March 1953, was "May 30th, 1431: The Execution of Joan of Arc." The radio program begins with a summary of Joan's career, ending with her trial by the Inquisition, and stating that today, Joan "can renounce her visions and live, or hold to her faith and die." The authorities, the reporter says, "will make one more effort to break Joan's will . . . she must confess that the visions and the voices she has heard did not come from God, and sign an abjuration to that effect" if she hopes to avoid being burned at the stake.[45] There is no mention of the historical fact that Joan of Arc had signed an abjuration a week before her execution, but later recanted, the reason for the charge "relapsed heretic" among the many made against her. The program then switches to the reporter "covering" the procession to the marketplace where the execution will take place. The reporter interviews Cauchon, who has the responsibility of handing Joan over to the secular officials to be burned. Asked about the accusation that the trial was illegal, Cauchon claims that it was fully legal and refuses to comment on the question of whether the trial was politically motivated. He says that Joan's heresy was that she did not consult with the Church about her visions, and that, because she did not submit them to the Church's authority, they must have come from the Devil.

The reporter then interviews the Earl of Warwick, who, as the governor of the castle at Rouen where the young Henry VI was in residence, had the authority to execute Joan. He says that he doesn't know about Joan's being a witch, but that she will not abjure and will burn. As a military man, he predicts that France will continue to fight under Joan's name as a symbol, and says, "what a pity she was not born an English woman." The scene switches to the Great Hall, where Joan is described as entering in chains, wearing women's clothes. She is described as pale, and showing the marks of five months in prison. The oath of abjuration is read, and Joan refuses to sign – all in French, as the reporter describes the action in English. The reporter comments that "she did not seem to waver for a moment."

The scene then switches to the outside, where some members of the crowd call "burn the witch," but most are silent. The paper miter with the words "heretic, relapsed, apostate, idolatress" is placed on Joan's head and she is turned over to the English, who place her in a cart. She leans against the side of the cart and prays. The reporter says she looks on the jeering crowd with pity. Warwick moves at the head of the procession to the stake, where, as the reporter says, the Burgundian crowd "want to see Joan burn." A reporter interviews the executioner, who says he has no feeling about burning Joan, that it's "a matter of business." Another reporter interviews Alfredo Firenzi, who is there as a collector of manuscripts for the Medici library in Florence. He comments on Joan's probable role in history, saying that she will initiate a new political era in Europe, that she has been condemned for "political heresy" against the Church, that she has helped to create "a new state," and that she is being burned because the only way to "uncrown" the new king of France is to discredit him by declaring Joan a witch so the people will rise against him. The reporter thanks him for his unusual perspective on the event.

Joan is then led to the stake and chained by the waist and feet. The Bishop asks her again to abjure, and she raises her head and answers: "It was God who sent me, and tonight I am going back to him. Tonight I will be with him in Paradise." As she cries, "for the love of God, a cross," the mood of the crowd changes. An English soldier runs up and hands her a cross; Joan is described as "ecstatic." A man cries in terror: "God help us, we are burning a saint." The reporter describes the crowd as crying out, weeping and praying, falling to the ground, "overcome with guilt and horror." The dramatization ends as the crowd erupts in panic, realizing its error immediately and repenting it.

There is no doubt in this dramatization that Joan is a martyr, executed for her beliefs by a corrupt and politically motivated court. The spine of the radio play is the question, "Will Joan abjure?" In other words, will Joan save herself by renouncing her beliefs – the central question for the "unfriendly" witnesses in the HUAC hearings. Refusing to abjure, Joan becomes a martyr for truth. Because of her steadfastness, the crowd is converted to her side. To make this analogy clearly, it was important not to allude to Joan's earlier abjuration, but to present her as an unwavering witness for truth. In presenting Joan as a visionary who instituted a new era of civilization by envisioning the nation state of France, the radio play also alludes to another central issue prompted by the HUAC hearings – the suppression of original thought leading to political change by the coercive power of existing institutions, such as the United States Congress.

Polonsky's 1953 teleplay has the same format as the radio play, and many of the same scenes, but a slight shift in emphasis. Again, the spine of the action is the question, "Will Joan abjure or burn?" and there is no mention of Joan's earlier recantation. A substantial scene in Joan's cell is added, where Joan first appears lying on the stone floor, very pale and frail, chained to a huge wooden pillar. The scene consists of a final interrogation of Joan by Cauchon and several monks, a compendium of most of the famous answers that Joan gave to her inquisitors. This is a weak and hysterical Joan, however. She falls on her knees weeping uncontrollably when she is told she will be burned, and she is prostrate before Cauchon when she says, "Bishop, I die through you."[46] When the churchmen leave her cell, she crawls to the pillar and clutches it, screaming. At the marketplace, the reporter interviews the executioner, who has nothing but contempt for the crowd that has come to watch. He says that there is "nothing so revolting that they won't watch," and that there is a bigger crowd than usual there today because they like to see the mighty fall and to see a woman suffer. Joan is dragged in by a soldier and she prostrates herself before Canon Midi, who preaches to her. Cauchon calls on Joan to abjure, but she says she can never abjure because it would be a lie. Joan is tied to the stake and calls on Jesus to save her. She asks Ladvenu, her confessor, where she will be that night. He asks her if she is in the state of grace, and she replies that by God's will she will be in paradise. When the flames rise, she calls on Jesus and screams. The whole crowd, with the exception of Warwick, turns and looks away. A voice from the crowd cries "Death to the English," and Warwick orders the soldiers to find the man.

The characterization of Warwick in the teleplay differs markedly from that in the radio play. Rather a foppish courtier than a military man, he has no regard for Joan whatever, saying that he wants her to burn because he bought her for £10,000, and she is nothing but a "little witch," a charlatan, a camp follower. Thus Polonsky made the political motive for the execution and the manipulation of the trial even more overt than the radio play did. Another addition in the teleplay is a subtext involving La Hire (Etienne de Vignolles), one of Joan's favorite captains. He is shown at the execution in disguise, first praying for Joan in the church, and then watching the execution. At the end of the dramatization, La Hire makes a speech to his soldiers that signifies the beginning of Joan's mythicization. Describing the execution, he says: "They reviled her, but she was proud. She walked slowly and solemnly to the stake." This description is played against the visual representation of the scene that the spectator has just viewed, in which the soldiers have roughly and unceremoniously dragged a weeping Joan to the stake, clearly establishing the divergence from historical reality of the myth that is being created. La Hire continues:

> She was not afraid. . . . The crowd fell back in terror, but she was not afraid. She stood in the flames and prayed to her Lord. She did not cry out. She felt no pain. Her Lord was with her in the flames. Her soul shot like a silver arrow to heaven. . . . She called out "Jesus" to her Lord. The English fell back in fear, terror. People of France. What shall we do with these murderers of the Maid of France? Our friend, our saint, our love?

The crowd cries out, "Kill them!" which is clearly the response La Hire was looking for. He responds: "Her soul is in heaven, but we will make the English lives a hell on earth." The camera shifts to the host, Walter Cronkite, who says, "This was the beginning of the legend of Joan of Arc. What La Hire saw was not a young girl in agony dying by fire, but he saw what his heart wanted to see, a heroine of the ages." He adds that with Joan's canonization in 1920, "her truth prevailed over the lies." Thus Polonsky affirmed simultaneously the essential nature of truth and the power of cultural symbolism and legend to effect major changes in national and political structures.

With the Hollywood Ten hearings of the previous fall a strong unspoken presence, the emphasis in the radio play of February 1948 had naturally been on Joan as witness. Would she give in to the Inquisition and give up her faith, or would she compromise her faith and save herself? In 1953, in the context of the Rosenberg executions and the blacklisting that resulted from the sweeping Show Business hearings of 1951–2, the emphasis shifted slightly. Joan became less the witness and more the victim. Her frail helplessness was made to contrast the cold political cynicism of her judges even more strongly, and the emphasis was on the effect that both her refusal to abjure and her victimization by the Inquisition and the English would have on the future through the creation of her legend and its transmission through the people. The McCarthyism issue here was not so much the crisis of the individual conscience when faced with a coercive power as the process and effects of victimization of the innocent by powerful institutions.

The teleplay also invited the American people to empower themselves by rejecting the victimization of innocence and fighting for their ideals against corrupt and oppressive political institutions.

Galileo, Cooperative Witness

If Joan served as the perfect representation of victimized innocence in the period of McCarthyism, the great Renaissance mathematician and astronomer Galileo Galilei became the cultural symbol of choice for cooperation with oppressive political institutions and pragmatic recantation of one's beliefs. Born in Pisa in 1564, Galileo was a brilliant mathematician who had been convinced by the 1590s that the new theory of Nicholas Copernicus about the solar system was scientifically valid. In keeping with its theology, which derived its natural philosophy from Aristotle, the Catholic Church's official teaching on astronomy at the time was based on the geocentric Ptolemaic model for the universe, which was directly contradicted by Copernicus's heliocentric model for the solar system. In the Ptolemaic model, the earth is the center of the universe, and around it, fixed in translucent globes of an immutable substance called "quintessence" or "ether," revolve the moon, the planets, and the sun. All is encased in a globe of fixed stars, and beyond it, the empyrean, or Heaven. Through empirical investigation, Copernicus had determined that it was the earth itself that moved around the sun, as did the other planets, and his theory was winning increasing support from astronomers throughout the late sixteenth and early seventeenth centuries. The problem for Catholics was that the heliocentric theory called into question the literal truth of the story of the Creation in Genesis and the whole Catholic theological system that had been built upon the Bible and Aristotelian natural philosophy in the four centuries since Thomas Aquinas had written his *Summa Theologiae*. If people were convinced that the earth moved, it was thought, the whole elaborate structure of Catholic theology and philosophy might collapse, and with it the Church's ideological and moral authority, at a time when it was fighting its great battle against the Protestant Reformation.

Strengthening the power of the telescope that had been invented by the Dutchman Hans Lippershey in 1608 and training it on the skies in 1609, Galileo made a discovery that placed him firmly in the Copernican camp. The next year, Galileo published his *Starry Messenger*, which reported the existence of four moons of Jupiter. Since these bodies moved not around the earth but around Jupiter, they called into question the existence of the Ptolemaic revolving globes and tended to support the Copernican theory. Galileo's later writing on sunspots confirmed his Copernican stance and distanced him further from the Church's sanctioned positions on natural philosophy and astronomy. In 1611, Galileo came to Rome, where his astronomical discoveries were confirmed by astronomers from the most powerful conservative intellectual force in Rome, the Society of Jesus. Two years later, however, his writings on sunspots were attacked as heretical by these guardians of the Church's official philosophy. In 1616, when the Church censured Copernican opinion as heretical, it also issued an injunction to Galileo, forbidding him to hold or defend Copernicus's theory, or, according to some sources, to discuss it in any way. This was conveyed verbally to Galileo by Robert Cardinal Bellarmin, cardinal inquisitor, and Galileo later obtained a written statement of the injunction from Bellarmin that contained no reference to a ban on *discussing* Copernicus's ideas as hypothesis, but forbade him to *defend* the Copernican theory.

Although Galileo obeyed the injunction to the letter, he continued his scientific studies, which tended to confirm the Copernican theory of the solar system. When his friend and well-educated exponent of the "new science," Maffeo Cardinal Barberini, became Pope Urban VIII in 1623, Galileo immediately seized his chance, going to Rome from Florence, where he was attached to the Medicean Court as philosopher and mathematician, to try to get his censure lifted. After six long discussions with the Pope, the ban was not lifted, but Galileo was given encouragement to write about these ideas within the limits of a hypothetical treatment. In 1630, Galileo completed work on his *Dialogue on the Two Great World Systems,* which ridiculed the Ptolemaic theory and implied that the Copernican theory was the only scientifically tenable view of the solar system. In that same year his most powerful patron in Rome, Prince Cesi, died.

At this point, Galileo misjudged the power and loyalty of his protectors, the Duke of Florence and the Pope's nephew, Francesco Cardinal Barberini. In the spring of 1631, when the *Dialogue* was published in Florence, Pope Urban VIII was being attacked by the powerful Jesuits, who thought him too open to the new scientific ideas. The medieval threat of the Black Plague had reemerged in Europe and seemed to be at the gates of Rome. The Protestant army of the Swedish King Gustavus Adolphus was threatening the European balance of power and the political independence of the papacy. Urban VIII could not afford to stick his neck out for Galileo. Sales and publication of the *Dialogue* were halted by order of the Papal Holy Office in August 1632, and a secret commission composed of three theologians was established to examine Galileo's works for evidence that he had advocated the Copernican theory. In 1616, a similar examination had resulted simply in the admonition of Galileo to stop writing about the heliocentric theory, but things were different in 1631. Galileo was summoned to Rome, where he arrived in February, waiting in a guest house in the Palace of the Holy Office for his trial. Although his friend Sagredo Niccolini, the Florentine ambassador, intervened on his behalf with the Pope, his trial for heresy proceeded.

As Pietro Redondi has pointed out, "the Galileo affair was an affair of state, a very serious affair of state. If it were to come out that the pope's official scientist was a suspected heretic against the faith, it would be scandalous."[47] Galileo's allies intended to stage a trial at which he would retract and repent his Copernican errors and then be treated leniently by the Church. Galileo surprised them, however, by producing Bellarmin's handwritten statement of his censure in 1616, which informed Galileo that the works of Copernicus had been placed on the Index as heretical but contained no injunction against Galileo's writing about Copernicus's ideas per se. As Galileo told the court: "It was merely announced to me that the doctrine attributed to Copernicus of the motion of the earth and the stability of the sun must not be held or defended, but that, beyond this general announcement affecting every one, no trace of any other injunction intimated to me appears there."[48] Since Galileo's new work did not advocate the Copernican theory, but merely discussed it in the form of a "dialogue," the case against him was in danger of going up in smoke. Galileo was then summoned to a private interview with his judge, Father Maculano Firenzuola, without lawyers or any other witnesses present. It has been suggested by some historians that the 70-year-old Galileo was threatened with, as Redondi puts it, "greater legitimate procedural rigor"[49] during this session – the tools of the Inquisition. It is true that, according to the records of the Holy Office, the Pope "decreed that the said Galileo is to be interrogated with regard to his intention, even with the threat of torture,"[50] and he was threatened with torture during his trial. At any rate, the judge was persuasive, for Galileo abandoned his sound line of defense at the next meeting and confessed, telling the court that he had reread the *Dialogue* and realized that he had indeed defended Copernicus's ideas there, and he recanted his Copernicanism. Firenzuola wrote to Cardinal Barberini that "the court will maintain its reputation, and the defendant will be treated benignly. His Holiness [the Pope] and Your Excellency will be satisfied."[51]

Galileo was sentenced for being "vehemently suspected of heresy" in believing "the doctrine which is false and contrary to the Sacred and Divine Scriptures, that the sun is the center of the world and does not move from east to west and that the earth moves and is not the center of the world,"[52] and ordered to repeat the seven penitential psalms once a week for three years and to be confined to prison "subject to our judgment." In a greater ritual humiliation than the circumstances required, Galileo knelt to recite his formal abjuration, declaiming "with sincere heart and unpretended faith I abjure, curse, and detest the aforesaid errors and heresies. . . . I swear that in the future, should I know any heretic or person suspected of heresy, I will denounce him to this Holy Office or the Inquisitor or Ordinary of the place where I may be,"[53] a warning to future heretical astronomers. By order of his friend Pope Urban, Galileo was treated very leniently by the standards of the Inquisition. His daughter, a Carmelite nun, was allowed to say his psalms for him, and he was confined to his home in Florence under the care of his son for the rest of his life rather than to any ecclesiastical prison. He carried on his research in the "new science" as before, although he stayed away from astronomy, and in 1638 he published his *Discourses on Two New Sciences,* which many consider to be his most important contribution to the "new thought," preparing the way for Newtonian physics. In 1992, after a thirteen-year investigation of Galileo's case, Pope John Paul II formally proclaimed that the Church had erred in condemning Galileo. In his speech, John Paul said that there are two realms of knowledge, distinct but compatible, "one which has its source in Revelation and one which reason can discover by its own power,"[54] a validation of Galileo's life and work and a rejection of the authoritarian conception of knowledge that was enforced by the Inquisition.

Bertolt Brecht, the shadowy eleventh witness at the Hollywood Ten hearings, had arrived in Santa Monica, California, in July of 1941, after a seven-year flight from the Nazis. During this journey he had lived temporarily in Skovbostrand, Denmark, Stockholm, and Helsinki, and had traveled frequently to Paris, London, Moscow, and throughout Europe supervising productions of his plays. By 1941, Brecht had had at least twenty plays produced in Europe, including *The Threepenny*

Opera, Baal, Mahagonny, The Mother, and *Mother Courage.* Nevertheless, he was all but unknown in the United States, having had only a production of *The Mother* by the Theatre Union of New York in 1935 to represent his work in this country. If he was an obscure German playwright in New York, in Los Angeles his name was known, if at all, as that of Kurt Weill's librettist. Brecht quickly sized up the situation and set about two tasks: getting his plays produced in America and getting some high-paying work in the film industry that would finance long periods of writing on his own work. He was not particularly successful at either of these, although he did make enough for his family to live on from his work on the Fritz Lang film *Hangmen Also Die* (1943) and a couple of other film projects. The major theatrical project of his Hollywood period was the English adaptation he did with Charles Laughton of *Life of Galileo,* a play he had originally written with Elizabeth Hauptmann in 1938.

By all accounts both Brecht and Laughton treated the *Galileo* collaboration as their most important work during the period they were engaged in it, from December of 1944 until the Los Angeles production in July and August of 1947, although they had to take time out for Laughton's film engagements. They worked painstakingly, as Brecht wrote in his journal: "l[aughton] had first met the play in very inadequate translations, which we set aside. now I translated it into english myself, sentence by sentence (l. doesn't know a word of german) and he wrote it down verbatim. then he would make suggestions and act everything out until he got it right, in other words until the gest was there."[55] After some frustrating and finally fruitless negotiations with big-time producers Orson Welles and Mike Todd, Brecht finally entrusted the play to Pelican Productions, a new producing venture founded by John Houseman and Norman Lloyd, which was planning its first season in the newly renovated 255-seat Coronet Theatre in Los Angeles. It was one of several theatre groups formed by Hollywood people to allow film actors to practice their art on stage. The board of directors, which included Joseph Mankewicz, Nicholas Ray, Howard Da Silva, and Kate Drain Lawson besides Houseman and Lloyd, was definitely left-leaning. Joseph Losey, whom Brecht had met in New York when he was directing a Living Newspaper for the Federal Theatre Project, was hired as director, although the actual direction was pretty much done by Brecht and Laughton.

With Laughton as Galileo, rehearsals for a July opening began in May. Meanwhile, one of Brecht's collaborators and close friends, the composer Hanns Eisler, was undergoing questioning by HUAC, primarily because his brother Gerhart, also a friend of Brecht's, was suspected by the FBI and the Committee of being an important Soviet agent. An FBI file had long been active on Brecht, and he was suspected of engaging in espionage with Gregory Kheifetz, a Soviet diplomat whom the FBI suspected of being an NKVD agent. Throughout the summer, Brecht was making plans to leave the U. S. and settle in Switzerland as HUAC investigators moved in on Hollywood and intimations of hearings and subpoenas began to circulate. *Galileo* opened in Los Angeles on 31 July 1947. On 19 September, Brecht, along with the other eighteen witnesses who were called to testify at the hearings in October, received his subpoena. After testifying on 30 October, Brecht left the next day for New York, to catch a plane to Paris, and then went on to Zurich. He did not return for the New York production of *Galileo* in December.

Walter Benjamin's well-known comment that in Brecht's *Galileo*, the hero is the people, sums up the play's focus, and its use of the Brechtian techniques of epic theatre. Rather than dramatizing the conflict between the individual Galileo and the forces of the Inquisition, the play dramatizes the effects of Galileo's actions on "the people" – whether directly, as in the carnivalesque Scene 9, or indirectly, as when the "Little Monk" explains the effect of the new science on the faith of his peasant parents in Scene 7. As a good Marxist, Brecht is most concerned with the life of Galileo as a historical development and with the play as a reflection of reality, both historical and contemporary. He had no compunction, for example, about changing the play's whole "message" about science when the dropping of the atomic bomb seemed to change the meaning of scientific research for the contemporary world. In 1939, he wrote that the play was about "Galileo's heroic struggle for his modern scientific conviction."[56] In 1946, he wrote: "The 'atomic age' made its debut at Hiroshima in the middle of our work. Overnight the biography of the founder of the new system of physics read differently. The infernal effect of the great bomb placed the conflict between Galileo and the authorities of his day in a new, sharper light."[57] Brecht and Laughton rewrote the play to reflect not the heroism of scientists, but their lack of responsibility.

The political climate of the United States, and particularly of Hollywood, in the mid-forties is reflected as well. The methods of the Inquisition are implicitly likened to those of the FBI and HUAC investigators when, during Galileo's seemingly casual conversation with Cardinal Bellarmin at a masked ball, two "secretaries" appear. Bellarmin at first tells them not to write anything down. "This is a scientific discussion among friends" (*Galileo*, 228). When Galileo displays a certain tenacity in holding to his views, Bellarmin gestures to the secretaries to write down his warning to Galileo to abandon the Copernican theory. They also begin to write down Galileo's statements. As the Cardinals put on their masks and go back to the ball, the secretaries commune conspiratorially:

First Secretary: Did you get his last sentence?
Second Secretary: Yes. Do you have what he said about believing in the brain?
(Another Cardinal – the Inquisitor – enters)
Inquisitor: Did the conference take place?
(The First Secretary hands him the papers and the Inquisitor dismisses the Secretaries. The Inquisitor sits down and starts to read the transcription). (229)

The method of "investigation" calls to mind the activities of Bill Wheeler and other agents on the Hollywood party circuit, who often turned casual party talk into evidence.

In the play's final scene, in which Andrea Sarti smuggles Galileo's new manuscript across the border, the trope of the witch-hunt was developed significantly from the 1938 version to the 1947 one, with obvious reference to the HUAC hearings. In the earlier version, some boys tell Andrea that a witch lives in the hut he is sitting next to, and he tells them they have to learn to use their eyes when they say she has bewitched a box he was sitting on. In the later version, the boys tell him they are stealing the woman's milk because she is a witch. Andrea replies, "and because she is a witch she mustn't have milk. Is that the idea?" (264). When the boys affirm that, he asks how they know she is a witch, and they show him her shadow on the wall, looking large and menacing as she stirs a pot. A boy says that she rides a broomstick and that she has bewitched the coachman's horses – he knows this because his cousin heard the horses coughing when he looked through a hole in the roof of the stable. Andrea asks how big the hole was, "because maybe the horses got sick because it was cold in the stable" (264). The boy evokes an authoritarian model for knowledge: "You are not going to say Old Marina isn't a witch, because you can't." Andrea replies with the fundamental principle of the new science: "No, I can't say she isn't a witch. I haven't looked into it. A man can't know about a thing he hasn't looked into, or can he?" The boy agrees, and Andrea boosts him

Figure 8. Charles Laughton as Galileo (center), in his adaptation
of Brecht's *Galileo,* is questioned by Cardinals Barberini (Rusty Lane, left)
and Bellarmin (Lawrence Ryle, right).

up so he can see the real Marina and not her shadow. When Andrea
asks what he sees, the boy replies, "just an old girl cooking porridge"
(264). Andrea and the boy examine the shadow and see that the boys
had taken a soup ladle for a broomstick. As Andrea goes off, having
been cleared by the customs officer, the boy calls after him, "She *is* a
witch! She *is* a witch!" and Andrea replies, "you saw it with your own
eyes: think it over!" The play ends with the boys singing:

> One, two, three, four, five, six,
> Old Marina is a witch.
> At night, on a broomstick she sits
> And on the church steeple she spits. (265)

The ending suggests that science has a long way to go to overcome the
prejudicial fantasies of the people and get them to trust their own
observations. It also suggests the blind tenacity of the anti-Communist
witch-hunters.

On the issue of Galileo's recantation, Brecht had already changed his mind by 1944. The 1938 version of the play suggests that Galileo's act is that of a clever pragmatist, who sees that he offers the world more in the continuation of his scientific work than he would in the heroism of resisting the Inquisition. In the earlier version Andrea Sarti condones his action by saying "science makes only one demand: contribution to science." Galileo agrees, with a statement of their mutual corruption:

> Welcome to the gutter, brother in science and cousin in betrayal! . . . I sell out, you are a buyer. O irresistible glimpse of the book, the sacred commodity! The mouth waters and the curses drown. The great whore of Babylon, the murderous beast, the scarlet woman, opens her thighs and everything is altered. Blessed be our horse-trading, whitewashing, death-fearing community. (107)

Although Galileo says that he has betrayed his profession, Andrea responds that he "cannot think your devastating analysis will be the last word" (109). In his journal for 6 April 1944, Brecht wrote:

> to my dismay, I am given to understand that I thought it right for him to recant in public in order to carry on his work in secret. this is too cheap and shallow. g[alileo] destroyed not only himself as a person, but also the most valuable part of his scientific work. the church (ie the authorities) defended the biblical doctrine simply in order to maintain itself, its authority, its capacity to oppress and exploit . . . g[alileo] jeopardised true progress when he recanted, he let the people down[58]

Brecht has been accused by his most severe critics of playing before HUAC "the part of the scoundrel Galileo."[59] His strategy was in fact similar to Galileo's. As James Lyon explains, "Brecht recognized the Committee as a threat to individual freedom. He himself planned to oppose it through an outward show of cooperation that was really a brand of cunning."[60] In doing so, Lyon suggests, Brecht was rejecting the course of the Ten as misguided martyrdom, and demonstrating that "outsmarting a powerful enemy was to him a valid form of opposition" (319). Lyon has offered a convincing explication of Brecht's testimony as "a polite exercise in cunning and duplicity that lasted a full hour" (329). In his testimony Brecht denied forcefully that he was a member of the Communist Party of any country and that he had ever applied for membership, which was probably the truth. Brecht was not exactly a joiner. Most of his testimony was evasion and misrepresentation, however. He bought himself extra time in answering the questions by pretending that his English was far worse than it was and that he needed an interpreter. The interpreter, David Baumgardt, who was a consultant in philosophy for the Library of Congress, turned out to have a heavier accent than Brecht, so that Chairman Parnell Thomas complained at one point, "I cannot understand the interpreter any more than I can the witness."[61] Brecht obligingly consulted with Baumgardt about the translations of his plays and poems when asked about them, and managed to evade their obvious Marxist implications, which had been thoroughly explicated in his FBI file, essentially by putting them down to bad translations. He represented his relationship with Hanns Eisler as purely artistic, and with Gerhart Eisler as purely social. He affected to barely know the most dangerous of his associates as far as the Committee was concerned, Gregory Kheifetz. Brecht did outwit Robert Stripling and the congressmen, who were entirely out of their literary depth here, but most of his testimony was not all that important to them. Having secured Brecht's forthright denial of his Party membership after the wrangling and confrontations with the Ten, the Committee was content with the appearance of cooperation, whether the substance was there or not. At one point, when Brecht's attorney, Robert Kenny, tried to clarify a question for Brecht, Thomas told him, "He is doing all right. He is doing much better than many other witnesses you have brought here" (503). And when the questioning was finished, he said, "Thank you very much, Mr. Brecht. You are a good example to the witnesses of Mr. Kenny and Mr. [Bartley] Crum" (504).

In his journal, Brecht noted that when asked whether he belonged to the Communist Party, "I, as a foreigner, answer the question with 'no,' which also happens to be the truth." He also noted that he had benefitted "from having had almost nothing to do with hollywood, from never having participated in American politics and from the fact that my predecessors refused to give evidence," adding, "the 18 are very pleased with my statements as are the lawyers."[62] Lester Cole, who rode back to the hotel in a taxi with Brecht, said that Brecht had become emotional and asked him to try to understand his lack of solidarity with the other witnesses, saying, "I'm not a citizen. They can hold me for months before deporting me." Dalton Trumbo remembered that Brecht had apologized to some of the other witnesses for his stand, which is remarkable if Trumbo's memory is accurate, since Brecht made a point of never apologizing.[63] He did, however, offer a kind of explanation to his friend Hanns Eisler, commenting in a letter: "I see from some newspaper cuttings that certain journalists thought I behaved arrogantly in Washington; the truth is that I simply had to obey my six lawyers, who advised me to tell the truth and *nothing* else. Not being a citizen either, I could no more refuse to testify than you could."[64] Brecht had two lawyers, not six, and he was not required to "obey" them. The fact is that he followed an effective strategy for getting himself off the hook and on his way to Paris rather than sacrificing himself to a gesture of solidarity with his fellow witnesses, and he seems to have felt somewhat guilty for it.

The plans for the New York production of *Galileo* continued despite Brecht's departure, and it premiered under the auspices of the Experimental Theatre wing of the American National Theatre and Academy (ANTA) at Maxine Elliott's Theatre on 7 December 1947, running for a limited engagement of six performances. Although Brecht tended to intimate that Charles Laughton was fearful about the potential effect on his career of associating with Brecht, Losey, and others under suspicion by HUAC, Brecht's subpoena did not stop Laughton from playing Galileo in New York. According to the biography approved by his wife Elsa Lanchester, Laughton "was fully aware of what he was doing and fully aware that the play's meaning increased in significance throughout each day of its performance, each day it lay under the shadow of the inquisition."[65] There is no doubt that the New York audience was attuned to this dimension of the play's meaning. Richard Watts praised the production for not emphasizing "any possible modern parallel" with Galileo's case. "Official intolerance and thought control," he wrote, "has a way of repeating itself, but it is more effective to let it go by implication."[66] Irwin Shaw brought out the parallel unmistakably in his review for *New Republic*:

The story of Galileo's martyrdom by Authority is bitterly apposite for today's audiences. The heresy hunters are almost as busy today in Washington as they ever were in Florence, and recantations fill the air in a medieval blizzard of fear. *Time, Life* and Hearst have replaced the rack, and the Representative from New Jersey [Parnell Thomas] has donned the Inquisitor's dark satin. The sobbing "I was wrong" of the matinee idol is now to be heard, instead of the "I have sinned" of the old astronomer, but the pattern, as Brecht bleakly points out, is the same. Truth dies with conformity, this year or last.[67]

Figure 9. Peter Capell's tortured, visionary Galileo in the New York production of Barrie Stavis's *Lamp at Midnight* was clearly intended as an historical portrait of the scientist.

Barrie Stavis's *Lamp at Midnight* had its New York premiere on 21 December 1947, just two weeks after Brecht's *Galileo*. The Experimental Theatre had actually planned to produce *Lamp at Midnight* and had even announced it as part of its 1947-8 season, but had discarded it in favor of the play on the same subject by the internationally recognized Brecht and the stage and film star Laughton. Thus Brecht's Marxist *Galileo* had six performances at Maxine Elliott's Theatre on Broadway, while *Lamp at Midnight*, a new play by an unknown academic, was quickly chosen as the inaugural production for the new cooperative Off-Broadway venture New Stages and had 48 performances at its newly renovated theatre on Bleeker Street in Greenwich Village. New York critics

195

were primed for both the comparison of the two plays and the use of Galileo's trial and silencing as an analogy for the HUAC hearings in Hollywood that were staged the previous October. In the words of the usually cynical show-biz paper *Variety*, *Lamp at Midnight* was seen as "a moving outcry against the crushing of the human spirit by dogmas armed with torture wracks and, as a parable, it is pointed against modern totalitarianism. It's not accidental that the play is a striking parallel to Arthur Koestler's novel, 'Darkness at Noon,' even to the title."[68] The critic for *Women's Wear Daily* noted that "Galileo's struggle is the struggle for free thought, a conflict which has persisted down through the ages. In its case for freedom of thought and its implied condemnation of heresy hunting, the play has many contemporary nuances."[69]

Stavis's Galileo is a far cry from Brecht's hedonistic and weak pragmatist. His struggle is not for survival and avoidance of pain but to reconcile the two driving passions of his life, his search for truth as a scientist and his religious faith and loyalty to the Church. For him, science is a way to religious faith: "Let man penetrate the secrets of nature. Each new law of nature learned by man will be additional proof of the infinite greatness and infinite wisdom of God."[70] This Galileo recants not out of fear, out of the desire for self-preservation, or out of the pragmatic desire to go on with his work, but out of obedience to his Church and faith in its dogma. Firenzuola gets him to confess not by showing him the instruments of torture but by adducing the habit of doubt that is the tool of the scientist. He tells Galileo that, in refusing to sign the confession the Inquisitors have written for him, he has become "a man of chaos" (*Lamp*, 87). In a Christian world whose unity depends on "a series of beliefs about the relationship of God, man and the world," Firenzuola says, "the man who threatens this unity threatens the world" (86). He says that Galileo's innocence depends on a truth in his own mind: "And if it is wrong? And if the Prince of Darkness has fastened himself upon you and at this very moment you are his servant, performing his work? Is there no doubt at all in your mind? Somewhere, deep, deep, there *is* the shadow of doubt" (87). When Galileo signs the paper and allows himself to be humiliated by reading it aloud on his knees, as the *Daily Worker* put it, "Galileo here is a lamb being propelled to, and then led to, the slaughter."[71]

Stavis gives the Church two arguments for its position: that the faith of the common people will be weakened by Galileo's scientific teachings, resulting in heresy, apostasy, atheism, and the weakening of the Catholic Church; and that, in the words of Bellarmin, "Truth is a philosophic fiction . . . where the salvation of the soul is concerned, the Church teaches that there is no absolute truth. Something is true in proportion to the good or evil it does" (41). Neither is defended very forcefully in the play. Stavis also makes crystal clear the analogies between the corrupt and unscrupulous methods of the Inquisition and those of the Un-American Activities Committee. When Bellarmin is described as having "one guiding passion – the salvation of Christian souls," Sagredo Niccolini says, "through the Inquisition he has the power to reach out and force Christian salvation down a man's throat whether he wants it or not" (31). Firenzuola, a sadistic and scheming little henchman in the play, explains the necessity of obtaining a confession despite the powerful evidence Galileo has brought forth in the signed injunction from Cardinal Bellarmin:

> We will accomplish little without a confession. The misguided may even place a halo around his head – a martyr to science. But if he confesses freely, this trial will be a great success. We will show Galileo weak, insincere, of no integrity. We will wreck his influence. One more danger to the Church will be eliminated. I must have his free confession! I will be satisfied with nothing less" (84).

Firenzuola's lack of humanity is represented as a direct result of his job, extorting confessions from witnesses before the Inquisition:

> The understanding of pressure – how to apply it – when – to what degree – these are the fine techniques of a craft attained only by deep study of the inner workings of a man's heart and brain. To understand the mixture of fear and courage, hope and despair – to make a man's mind war with the fear which is mixed with the marrow of his bones. This subject . . . has been my constant study (66).

Like the members of HUAC, Firenzuola makes a distinction between "those who quickly confess and throw themselves on our mercy" and "those who do not confess, who when examined and questioned at length with all the facilities and ingenuity of this Holy Office . . . are found guilty and convicted of heresy" (78–9). To the first the Church can be merciful. The second, like Joan of Arc and Giordano Bruno, are handed over to the secular authorities to be burned. The consequences to such stiff-necked behavior before HUAC were less dire, but no less distinct.

Stavis also suggested the similarities between the procedures of the Inquisition and those of the Committee. After Bellarmin first warns Galileo against teaching the Copernican theory in 1616, he calls a monk to him, saying "Clerk of the Inquisition, open up a file for one Galileo Galilei, an astronomer. Let it be looked into if he has ever had any dealings with anyone accused of heresy" (35), an allusion to the collusion between the FBI and HUAC. Later, when the unsigned notes of a clerk of the Inquisition are adduced against Galileo, with the claim that he was admonished not to speak of the Copernican theory either as fact or as hypothesis, Sagredo objects, "why, this paper doesn't even have a signature. Not of Cardinal Bellarmin, or any of the witnesses, or of Galileo" (68). Sounding for all the world like an FBI official, Pope Urban cautions him, "do not speak lightly of memoranda from our official files. . . . This document is enough to hand the entire matter over to the Inquisition" (69). During the trial, when Galileo produces the signed letter from Cardinal Bellarmin, which stops short of forbidding him to discuss Copernican theory as hypothesis, Firenzuola is only temporarily discomforted. Holding Bellarmin's letter in one hand and the notes of the Inquisition in the other, he asks Galileo: "Here are two sets of records. Whose are to be relied upon? Yours or ours?" (81). To a stunned Galileo, he orders, "we will proceed," simply setting aside the evidence – an effective evocation of HUAC's reliance on its own records of unsupported allegations by informers and spurious Party "membership cards" to make its accusations against witnesses.

Stavis even replicates the advice of the attorney to the witness who is brought before the Committee for ritual humiliation, having Sagredo advise Galileo on his response to the judges:

Sagredo: Be acquiescent. Be humble. Be submissive. When they say Yes, you say Yes. When they say No, you say No.
Galileo: But if I cannot say Yes to their Yes, or No to their No?
Sagredo: Then say – "Perhaps it is so," or "I do not remember."
Galileo: "Perhaps it is so." "I do not remember."
Sagredo: Do not cross them – pacify them. Do not defend your work – if you do they will be all the more certain to condemn it. Remember, be acquiescent – be submissive. Be humble. (72)

Like the cooperative witness that he is, Galileo follows this advice, choking back a strong desire to defend his work, and he reads on his knees the confession in which he abjures and curses his "errors" and swears that he will not in the future "say or write anything which may raise similar suspicion against me" and that he will denounce any heretic or "anyone suspected of heresy" to the Inquisition (94), the equivalent of naming names to HUAC. Stavis is more forgiving of Galileo's cooperation than Brecht is, however. When Galileo returns to his daughter after the trial, he says, "All my life I've needed only two things. My Bible and my telescope. I have betrayed them both. I put my hand on the Bible – on the Bible! – and swore falsely about my science!" (98). Sister Maria Celeste offers him the comfort of pragmatism that Brecht had not allowed: "You were right to choose life. Religion may need martyrs, but science needs the living. . . . What you have done and what you will do may help another scientist many years from now" (99). Of course Galileo's future work did prepare the way for Newtonian physics and a new scientific era. Whether this principle could be used to justify the testimony of cooperative witnesses before HUAC, such as Bertolt Brecht, who denied his Marxist and Communist political philosophy under questioning, is another matter. But it enabled Brecht, for one, to get out of the country and on with his work.

The reception that New York audiences and critics gave to *Lamp at Midnight* was overwhelmingly positive. Audiences interrupted the trial scenes with applause again and again, and often got to their feet when Galileo cried in the closing scene: "I say that if a man takes away reason to make room for revelation he puts out the light of both. Help me, Oh God. Give me a measure for the truth! . . . It does move!" (101). In the contest with Brecht's *Galileo*, it was the decisive winner, largely because New York audiences did not take well to Brecht's epic theatre or to his ironic alienation effect in creating the character of Galileo. As one critic put it, "this play by Barrie Stavis is a potentially better play, about a decidedly better person."[72] The Catholic press preferred Stavis to Brecht, although it was none too pleased with either play. *The Catholic World* noted that, while "Mr. Stavis has made Galileo's personal faith completely sincere he has drawn a lurid picture of clerical tyranny, dissimulation and the Inquisition," commenting, "it is the strength of the Church that she is not ashamed to acknowledge with full publicity the mistakes of her clerics and prelates. She canonized the girl who defied the French Inquisition to the end."[73]

After its brief engagement in New York, *Lamp at Midnight* was sent on a tour of college theaters. It was produced at the Bristol Old Vic in 1956, and on television as part of the Hallmark Hall of Fame series in 1966, with such veterans of the blacklist as Melvyn Douglas playing

Galileo and Kim Hunter playing his daughter. Although producer-director George Shaeffer was willing to defy the blacklist in casting the production, he was more careful about offending the Church. The production was done with the "special assistance" of Rev. John S. Banahan, the director of the Communications Center of the Archdiocese of Chicago, and it was introduced by no less a figure that John Patrick Cody, Archbishop of Chicago, who told the viewers that sometimes the results of the thirst for knowledge "were ill-received by their contemporary age, yet in time, the judgement of mankind mellows and turns from the vinegar of prejudice to the wine of wisdom." This, he said, "is the lesson of tonight's play. It is the story of a man whom our Holy Father Pope Paul has called 'a great spirit of immortal memory.' In the light of his words, I commend to you tonight's performance of *Lamp at Midnight*, the story of Galileo Galilei."[74]

This was not the first television dramatization of Galileo's life. The blacklisted trio of Abraham Polonsky, Walter Bernstein, and Arnold Manoff had teamed up with director Sidney Lumet and producer Charles Russell to make its *You Are There* version, "The Crisis of Galileo," in April of 1953. Before the script was approved for production, the executive producer, William Dozier, cleared it with the Archdiocese of New York. According to Charles Russell, Dozier told him which lines in the script must be changed and insisted that writer "Jeremy Daniel" (Abraham Polonsky) eliminate all references to the Church's torture of Galileo, or the show would not go on the air.[75] Russell and Polonsky went over the script, cutting references to the torture of Galileo and "softening" the figures of the Holy Office, although this did not prevent Russell and Lumet from filming the important scene in which Barberini urges Galileo to submit on a set representing a dungeon with torture instruments hanging from the wall.[76]

In the teleplay, Polonsky presented the trial in the context of the opposition of two systems of thought: the appeal to authority, represented by the syllogistic reasoning of Scholastic philosophy, and the "new science," based on empirical observation. In the teleplay, one of the reporters interviews Chiaramonti, an old-fashioned astronomer who uses syllogistic arguments against the existence of "the four new planets" (the moons of Jupiter) and the movement of the earth, taking Aristotle's views as fact and reasoning from there. Another interviews William Harvey in London, who is introduced as a former pupil of Galileo's and praises him as "an experimenter. He looks for facts and he goes where the facts lead him."[77] According to Harvey, his opponents are "metaphysicians. They use words, not facts." He says, "There can be no progress in the world and no advance in science without freedom of the mind, freedom of thought and of work" ("Crisis," 84). Galileo's friend, Francesco Cardinal Barberini, shows him the prison cell to suggest the consequences of rebellion and makes the argument that anything Galileo does to weaken the faith of the "common man" weakens the Church. Galileo responds that he has no "doctrine," that he merely tells the facts as he sees them, and that no common men have yet complained that he has weakened their faith. Barberini reminds him that he must recant in full faith to keep the Pope's protection. Galileo remembers the burning of Giordano Bruno and fingers the instruments of torture. In response to Barberini, he cries, "I want to live" (87), saying that he has much more to discover before he dies. Barberini tells him to think of his life in eternity rather than his momentary life on earth. A reporter interviews Galileo's students, one of whom says he will leave Italy if Galileo is forced to recant: "How will it seem if we must admit that the universe revolves about the earth, when we know the earth is but a speck in the vastness of time and space? The world will laugh at the Italians if they do not live and die for their truth" (90).

The trial scene in the teleplay proceeds much like a HUAC hearing. Firenzuola questions Galileo about his previous admonition by the Holy Office, seventeen years earlier. The court challenges him with his letters written to fellow scientists Castelli and Kepler years earlier, demanding, "have you returned to such opinions in the interim?" (92). Pressed to answer, Galileo finally responds, "What I wrote then is not my opinion." The Bellarmin injunction is not made into an issue here. Instead the questioning proceeds relentlessly, the judges forcing Galileo to acknowledge his previous "errors" and recant them. He says that he was wrong in making the argument in the *Dialogues* stronger on the "false" Copernican side than on the "true" one, and when challenged, "you no longer hold the opinion, then," he responds: "I am here to obey. I have not held the opinion since the command was given to me to abandon it" (94). Galileo is shown reading his recantation on his knees, with the statement "but, that if I shall know any heretic, or anyone suspected of heresy, I will denounce him to the Holy Office, or the Inquisitor and Ordinary of any place that I might be" (96) featured clearly and prominently.

After the recantation, Chiramonti says that the verdict was welcome and that it justifies his work. Harvey says, "if it is true . . . I reject the action of Galileo Galilei as a betrayal of the work of his life" (97). When Galileo returns to his students at the Florentine Embassy, one of them kisses his hand, and he pulls it away, weeping with his head on his arms. In the final scene with his daughter, which is not in the published script, he says, "I wonder if the stars heard me today," but is comforted by the fact that the telescope and the sky will remain, whatever he has done, and "men will look through this and see what is up there." Overall, Polonsky's teleplay is a gentle treatment of the cooperative witness, a demonstration of the folly of authoritarian repression of the freedom of thought rather than a commentary on the judges or the witness.

Eric Bentley was a houseguest of the Brechts during the Los Angeles production of the Brecht-Laughton *Galileo*. He has admitted that the play "has always irked" him, and that "it is a work that goads [him] into talking back." After writing two extensive essays on Brecht's play, Bentley wrote his own *Recantation of Galileo Galilei*, a work which he says was "begun in the fifties, finished in the sixties, produced and published in the seventies."[78] Bentley's play was first produced at the Bonstelle Theatre, Wayne State University, for the 1973–4 season. Having written his *Are You Now* the previous year, and edited the thousand pages of testimony in *Thirty Years of Treason* the year before that, Bentley had HUAC much in his mind as he wrote the Galileo story, and his version emphasizes the political process of the Inquisition more than the others. Since the danger of criticizing HUAC was pretty much a thing of the past by 1973, he could be more overt in his allusions to the events of recent history than could the writers who were living them.

The analogy between the Inquisition and the HUAC hearings is first made clear in a rather darkly humorous scene entitled "The Investigation," in which an Inquisitor interrogates Galileo's assistant Castelli. In an allusion to the ignorance of the officials who were passing judgment on witnesses, Bentley has the Inquisitor ask Castelli about Copernicus:

Inquisitor: *consulting papers.* The science taught by Galilei is based on the work of one Hibernicus, correct?
Castelli: Copernicus.
Inquisitor: A Russian?
Castelli: A Pole.
Inquisitor: Are you quibbling with me?
Castelli: It isn't a quibble. The Poles are Catholic, the Russians aren't.
Inquisitor: Hibernicus's book is called *On Revolution*. Is that a Catholic title?
Castelli: It's called *On Revolutions*. Plural. Of the globe, that is.

Inquisitor: What globe?
Castelli: This one.
Inquisitor: Are you telling the Holy Roman Inquisition that we are sitting on a globe, and that it revolves?
Castelli: I am reporting that Copernicus believed this; and that he was a Pole and a Catholic.[79]

In the course of questioning that reminds the knowing spectator or reader unmistakably of that undergone by HUAC targets, the Inquisitor tries to get Castelli to say that Galileo believes in the Copernican theory, and he questions him about the legitimacy of Galileo's children and his "sex habits in Florence," implying that he is suspected of homosexuality. Finally, he threatens Castelli himself: "You are not very cooperative, Father Castelli. This is serious: a priest who is not willing to fight heresy" (*Recantation*, 112).

Bentley makes the Inquisition resemble a congressional hearing as much as anyone could. He expands the number of judges at Galileo's trial from three to six, and by establishing the Cardinals as three Jesuits and three followers of Pope Urban VIII's more liberal views, makes them appear to be members of political parties. The scenes of the trial are staged so that the Cardinals *"look like a bench of judges"* (132). In the stage directions, Bentley queries, *"What manner of men are they? Are they religious? Are they recognizably ecclesiastical, even?"* He answers, *"It is debatable. What is certain is that these are men in important positions in an organization that dominates the life of the time. They resemble other such men"* (132). In his representation of the function of such an arm of the Inquisition, Bentley summarizes the two political points of view that characterized the members of HUAC. When one Cardinal proposes to actually examine the evidence of his innocence that Galileo offers, another replies, "we're here to find this man guilty, not hold student debates on the English model!" (135). The one liberal Cardinal of the tribunal suggests tentatively that the methods of the Inquisition might backfire:

I wonder if our true objective should not be stated thus: *At all costs avoid a public crisis. One Giordano Bruno was enough.* More than enough. For an *auto da fé* which was supposed to deter heretics and help us only aroused indignation among heretics and made us repellent. Today, certainly, such an execution would serve only the Lutherans. If I am right, what follows? That, instead of making the name of

Galilei a rallying point for our enemies, we should come only to con-
clusions which he himself will voluntarily accept (135).

Bentley makes Rev. Christopher Scheiner into Galileo's scientific
rival and the chief accuser at the trial. When Galileo produces his document with Cardinal Bellarmin's signature, he casts doubt on the truthfulness of Scheiner, who, it happens, was the one taking notes for the
Inquisition at his original meeting with Bellarmin in 1616. Thus
Scheiner plays the combined role of investigator, informer, and inter-
rogator in the play. Like an Elizabeth Bentley or a Whittaker Chambers, he complains of his own victimization by the witness who denies
his accusations. Once Galileo has been brought to recant, Scheiner
presses for a worse punishment than silencing for his own justification:

> During the early stages of the hearing, Galilei pleaded total inno-
> cence. If there was any guilt at all, he was at pains to attach it to my
> humble self. Which would have little importance, except that I was
> the main source of evidence against him. The thesis of the *poisoned
> source* being not only useful but *necessary* to him, I was guilty of men-
> dacity, even of forgery. If he was innocent, his accuser had to be
> guilty. If he spoke truth, his accuser had to be a liar. But now Galilei
> has pleaded guilty and the positions are reversed. He is guilty, his
> accuser is innocent (154).

Although he knows Galileo's "confession" is a sham, Scheiner is compelled to seek his own vindication through Galileo's destruction, a common enough pattern in the HUAC hearings, and a disturbing
reminder of the relativity that the concepts of truth and justice had
assumed in the era of McCarthyism. After Scheiner's uninterrupted
two-and-half-hour indictment of him, Galileo responds with a reminder
of how truths were constructed during such hearings: "As Father
Scheiner spoke I was reminded of Roman Law – in which the omission
of relevant truths coupled with the cunning suggestion of untruths con-
stitutes lying. At no point did Father Scheiner weigh the pro and con;
at no point did he let the relevant fact and falsehood confront each
other; at no point did he attempt to measure differing degrees of relevance" (137). Like the witnesses before HUAC, Galileo is denied the
right to cross-examine his accuser. In the decision to punish Galileo,
the trope of contamination is evoked, as it often was in the HUAC hearings, so that no citizen might be tainted by thinking forbidden

thoughts: "That the book is to be suppressed is already agreed. Next: The heretic Galileo Galilei must be isolated from the community. A condition of *quarantine* is indicated. Such an infection must not be allowed to spread. If not in jail, this man must be under life-long house arrest" (155). The same impetus that motivated the blacklisting of Communists is clear here, as is the suppression of free thought and the expulsion of the thinker from an authoritarian society.

Bentley treats the subject of Galileo's recantation much more positively than Brecht does in his 1947 version of *Galileo*. In fact Bentley attempts to turn Galileo into a Joan of Arc figure by having him sign a confession when he is in the depths of despair because "nothing mattered anymore" (158) and then tear it up because he is willing to die, saying "today I don't want to die, but if it is the best way to fight you, my lords, I will do it" (159). He agrees to the final recantation when he overhears the Cardinals speaking of the dangers of having writers under house arrest, who tend to become "a thorn in the flesh" of the authorities: "They have hangers-on, you see. Visitors. Admirers. Hardly surprising that their writings circulate in manuscript . . . the notoriety of such manuscripts sometimes gives them a wider circulation than books" (160). As in the first version of the Brecht play, Bentley's Galileo is seen as a hero of pragmatic action who recants in order to finish and disseminate his work, an activity the historical Galileo certainly pursued avidly after his condemnation. By implication, the cooperative witness, a Bertolt Brecht, for instance, might be justified in taking a public pose of submission to the Committee in order to pursue his Marxist agenda in private.

6

Informers

I have come to the conclusion that I did wrong to withhold these names before, because secrecy serves the Communists, and is exactly what they want. The American people need the facts and all the facts about all aspects of Communism in order to deal with it wisely and effectively. It is my obligation as a citizen to tell everything I know.

Elia Kazan, Statement to HUAC, 9 April 1952

I want you to understand that I am not protecting the Communists or the Communist Party. I am trying to, and I will, protect my sense of myself. I could not use the name of another person and bring trouble on him.

Arthur Miller, Testimony, HUAC Hearing, 21 June 1956

With the royalties from his first Broadway success, *All My Sons* (1947), Arthur Miller bought a house in Brooklyn Heights and moved his family from their small city apartment to this comfortable middle-class neighborhood on the hills above the Brooklyn waterfront. His new proximity to Red Hook, the Italian-American neighborhood surrounding the piers, brought Miller into contact with the longshoremen who lived there and made him aware of their Mafia-ridden waterfront unions. Intrigued by the graffiti he saw everywhere on his walks through the area – "Dove (where is) Pete Panto?" – he began to investigate the circumstances of Panto's death and its relationship to organized crime's hold on the maritime unions, with an eye to writing about it. Panto, a young rank-and-filer who was trying to lead a revolt against the local leadership of the International Longshoreman's Association (ILA), had been lured away from his home by a telephone call and never heard from again. While studying the situation of the longshoremen, Miller met up with two unlikely candidates to lead a reform of the union: Mitch Berenson, a young labor organizer who was interested in carrying on Panto's effort, and Vinny Longhi, a young lawyer who was interested in establishing a political career by wresting the waterfront district away from the organizations that were controlling it, the Democratic Party machine and the forces of organized crime. Under their tutelage, Miller became intrigued enough by their struggle against the feudal operations of the waterfront unions to work on a screenplay, called at different times "Shape-Up," after the procedure by which the men were hired, and "The Hook" after the neighborhood, Red Hook, and the sickle-shaped tool that was the longshoreman's occupational symbol.[1] Meanwhile, in 1949, reporter Malcolm Johnson wrote a series of articles for the *New York Sun* entitled "Crime on the Waterfront," which detailed many of the abuses that Miller was hearing about and placed them in the context of the corrupt business, union, political, and organized crime agendas that were at work on the New York waterfront. Published in book form as *Crime on the Labor Front* in 1950, Johnson's work provided detailed descriptions of the longshoremen and their work as well as the various rackets by which they were exploited.

As the germ of material for both Kazan's *On the Waterfront* (1954) and Miller's *A View from the Bridge* (1955), Miller's "Shape-Up" needs to be considered in some detail. In Miller's screen treatment, Pete Panto became "Pete Banta," a brave young labor leader who is taken away by two anonymous men in the night and shot after he makes a speech against the contract that has been negotiated by the union boss, Wally Hackett, warning the men that none of the things they really cared about, like the establishment of a hiring hall and the institution of various safety regulations, have been included. Mitch Berenson has become Pete's younger brother Danny, who is inspired by Pete's death to find out the facts by working as a longshoreman. Danny quickly becomes embroiled in the fight against the crooked union bosses, making speeches in favor of a hiring hall and against kickbacks to the hiring bosses. Danny learns about speed-ups on the job when he is working in the hold and the foremen overload the sling, injuring one of the men. After Danny saves the man, "One-Eyed Pop," who, unknown to Danny, was an eyewitness to his brother's murder, from being crushed, One-Eye is tortured throughout the film by the decision of whether to risk turning in the killers or to keep the longshoreman's time-honored code of silence. Danny urges the men to refuse to work until the slings are reloaded with half the tonnage they are carrying, and he leads them off the ship in a walkout. Danny meets with Ralph, the local union Mafia stooge, who was his boyhood friend. When Ralph tries to get Danny to sell out to the mob, Danny reminds him that he is Hackett's stooge, eminently expendable, and works on his sense of guilt by saying he oppresses his own people. Ralph in effect declares war, and Danny accepts the challenge, rising in the union as he pursues the reforms the men want.

Danny is called to a meeting at Hackett's home in the suburbs, where Hackett offers to produce Pete's murderer if Danny will give up on the union reforms and let the contract be voted in as is. Danny refuses, and when Hackett addresses the men about the new contract, Danny stands up and demands a contract that includes the hiring hall and a number of safety measures including safe weights in the slings. When Hackett's thugs go for Danny, the other workers protect him, responding to his call for a strike with a walk-out then and there. At the wharf, Danny urges the men not to go back to work and, hoisted on the shoulders of the men, leads them in a mass wave to the warehouse, where the crowd of workers collectively fights off the thugs. One-Eye is shot by Ralph as he is about to sign a statement identifying Pete's killers. The treatment ends rather abruptly, as Danny makes a speech against Hackett from the top of One-Eye's hearse and then proposes to Pete's widow Beatrice, telling her not be afraid because they are sure to win a better future with all the longshoremen behind them.

Miller's friend Elia Kazan, who had directed *All My Sons* and, in 1949, the phenomenally successful *Death of a Salesman,* on Broadway, was eager to work with him on a film about the waterfront material. In January 1951, with the films *A Tree Grows in Brooklyn, Gentleman's Agreement, Pinky,* and *Panic in the Streets* behind him, and on the verge of completing *A Streetcar Named Desire,* Kazan was a powerful figure in Hollywood, under contract with Twentieth-Century Fox and Darryl F. Zanuck. He did not think that Zanuck would be interested in such gritty naturalistic material as the New York waterfront, but he was pretty certain of getting a hearing from Warner Brothers or Harry Cohn of Columbia. Although Kazan thought that Miller "had done a half-ass job finishing the script, that it was not 'ready to go' and would require considerably more work," he thought that the two of them could work on it together and have a strong screenplay in a few weeks.[2] The two men took the train from New York to Los Angeles, planning to work on the script and conduct negotiations with the studios simultaneously. They moved into the house of Kazan's *Streetcar* producer Charley Feldman and proceeded to concentrate more on Marilyn Monroe, a round of Hollywood parties, and Feldman's swimming pool than on the script, but they did produce a new version.

In the screenplay of "The Hook" that was completed in early 1951, the Mitch Berenson character is called "Marty." Instead of the death of his brother, it is the incident in the hold of the ship that radicalizes him. On his way to work, he watches Phil, the hiring boss, toss the two remaining brass checks, which mean work, on the ground for the men to fight over after he has picked out the ones who have paid their bribes.[3] Farragut, the union boss, finds this amusing. Later, as a result of the speed-up in the hold, one of the men is killed. The men form a reverent circle around the body in the ship, and each crew stops and stands still as at the passing of a hearse when the ambulance slowly makes its way along the piers. When Rocky, the pier boss, tries to get the men back to work, Marty calls the union bosses "finks" and confronts them with speeding up the work at the behest of the shipping company. At first Marty tries to leave the union behind him by going in with the mob and getting an easy job, and more money than he'd ever imagined, as a bookie. His conscience gets the better of him, however, and he decides to go back and fight the corrupt union leaders. He is blacklisted from working on the waterfront and suffers from poverty and fear of violence, but he pursues his fight. Later, when Rocky spits in one of the organizers' faces as he tries to make a speech, Marty tells him he will never have a good name because he has spit in his own father's face by spitting on a working man. Rocky later joins with Marty and the reformers, saying that all he wanted was his good name. In the end, Marty succeeds in discrediting the corrupt union leadership.[4]

After Fox and Warner Brothers had turned down "The Hook," Harry Cohn showed some interest in it, but he was concerned about its "controversial" material. According to Kazan, a meeting of Cohn, Miller, Kazan, and anti-Communist labor leader Roy Brewer ensued, at which Brewer insisted that the threat to the union should come not from organized crime but from Communists and suggested a scene or two that should be inserted to show this. Kazan has written:

> As we left the meeting, Art and I didn't know if we had an agreement or not. I wondered about Cohn's reaction. It had been a dreadful scene. A man we'd never met, who had nothing to do with the artistic values of our script, seemed to believe he had the power to decide whether or not we could go ahead with the film. We felt humiliated, so much so that we couldn't discuss the problem. . . . The next day, Art suddenly left California and went back east." (Kazan, *A Life*, 412)[5]

Kazan remembers that Miller continued to work on the script, sending him revisions along with personal letters about his growing feelings for Marilyn Monroe, and then, in the middle of the budget meeting on the film, Kazan was called to the phone to hear from Miller that he had decided to withdraw "The Hook."

According to Miller, he and Kazan met with Harry Cohn without Brewer, and Cohn said that the script had to be checked with the FBI: "They've got a good man here, I'd like him to look at it. Being it's about the waterfront."[6] Miller has written that, hearing nothing from Cohn, he flew back to New York after a few days. Then he got a phone call:

> It was Kazan speaking in his softest tone, I thought, almost as though others were in an office with him, which was probably not true at all; I may simply have caught a kind of public apprehension in him.
>
> Cohn wanted some change; if I agreed, the film would be doable, he said. The main one was that the bad guys in the story, the union crooks and their gangster protectors, should be Communists. I started to laugh even as my heart froze. Kazan said he was merely transmitting what Cohn had told him, in the belief that I should have it uninflected by his own comments. Roy Brewer, the head of all the Hollywood unions, had been brought into the matter – by the FBI, presumably; he had read the script and said flatly that it was all a lie, that he was a personal friend of Joe Ryan, head of the International Longshoreman's Association, and that none of the practices I described took place on the piers. (*Timebends*, 308)

Miller remembered that Brewer had threatened a strike by all the projectionists across the country if the movie was made as written, and had said that the FBI "regarded it as a very dangerous story that might cause big trouble on the nation's waterfronts at a time when the Korean War was demanding an uninterrupted flow of men and matériel. In effect, unless [racketeer] Tony Anastasia was turned into a Communist, the movie would be an anti-American act close to treason." Miller has written that he told Kazan there were "next to no Communists on the Brooklyn waterfront," and that depicting the rank and file of the union as revolting against Communists rather than racketeers would simply be idiotic. He remembers that, "in an hour or two I wired Harry Cohn that I was withdrawing my script as I was unable to meet his demands" (*Timebends*, 308). In any case, the film project of "The Hook" ended early in 1951.

Meanwhile, probably unbeknownst to either Kazan or Miller, Harry Cohn's nephew, Joseph Curtis, had founded a production company for the sole purpose of making a film of Malcolm Johnson's Pulitzer Prize–winning newspaper series on the waterfront, for which he had bought the rights. Writer Budd Schulberg had spent considerable time investigating conditions on the waterfront himself, as well as getting to know some of Johnson's contacts, in preparing to write his script, *Crime on the Waterfront*, which was also completed early in 1951. Curtis's production company had failed financially, however, and the script was gathering dust when Schulberg was called to testify before HUAC in May 1951. A disaffected former Communist, Schulberg cooperated with the Committee, naming names. Kazan's own testimony in January and April of 1952 having placed him in the same camp, he contacted Schulberg shortly afterwards about his idea to make an "eastern," a film about corruption in an eastern city that would be filmed on location. Discovering their mutual interest in the waterfront material, and with the rights to *Crime on the Waterfront* having now reverted to Schulberg, the two decided to pursue the story idea that united union corruption and organized crime on the New York waterfront. After a tortured writing process in conjunction with producer Sam Spiegel, which included eight separate versions of the script, *On the Waterfront* was finally filmed on location in Hoboken in the fall of 1953.[7]

In addition to the testimony of Schulberg and Kazan before HUAC, a significant event in the waterfront situation contributed to the refining of the film's focus. In 1951 and 1952, the congressional investigating committee headed by Estes Kefauver had followed the lead of the Johnson exposé in bringing to light the relationship between organized crime and the waterfront unions, particularly the ILA. It was no longer possible for a Roy Brewer to pretend that the trouble on the waterfront came from Communists. Further, as Thomas Pauly has noted, the Kefauver Committee and the subsequent investigations of union corruption by the New York State Crime Commission complicated the issue of informing for the American public. While most of the union men feared to break the protective code of silence by turning in their unions bosses, a few brave men risked death to do so. As Pauly suggests, "Now the public sentiment was solidly on the side of the man who dared to reveal what he knew. . . . Rather than the cowards the HUAC 'friendlies' had been branded, these were heroes, standing against injustice and oppression, actions befitting 'men of individual conscience.'"[8] It was now possible to present the informer's side of the issue, constructing an informer who was not only scapegoat but hero, the basic elements of both the classic protagonist of Greek tragedy and

Terry Malloy of *On the Waterfront*. Terry defies the "Deaf & Dumb" code of the longshoreman to testify against the corrupt union-boss Johnny Friendly for having killed Joey Doyle, who had been about to testify, and Terry's brother Charley, who had refused to turn Terry over to Friendly's thugs. Terry is ostracized by the men until he leads them to see that it is Johnny who is the betrayer: "I'm glad what I done – you hear me? – glad what I done! . . . I was rattin' on myself all them years and didn't know it."⁹

While Miller had focussed on Pete Panto, the real-life heroic leader who had resisted the union bosses, Kazan and Schulberg discovered Tony Mike de Vincenzo, the informer as hero. In Kazan's words, "Tony Mike told the full truth as no one had before. He named names. When he did that, he broke the hoodlum law of silence" (Kazan, *A Life*, 499). Kazan and Schulberg identified intensely with this witness who was called "a rat, a squealer and stoolie. He was ostracized, then threatened. Friends he'd had for years didn't talk to him" (499). Kazan has written that, after his testimony, he found he was notorious, "an 'informer,' a 'squealer,' a 'rat.' I'd become the star villain for 'progressives'; just as they'd expected me to be the staunchest defender of their position, they now labeled me the most treacherous of traitors" (468). In telling de Vincenzo's story, Kazan and Schulberg were able to effect their own moral redemption.

Kenneth Hey has recognized three ritual scenes in *On the Waterfront*: the "shape-up," a scene of ritual degradation; the death of Kayo Dugan and the eulogy of Father Barry, a scene of martyrdom; and the scene when Terry testifies before the Crime Commission, a scene of testimonial, in which "the legal institutions received reinforcement, and Terry confesses to society his complicity."¹⁰ To these should be added the final sequence of the film, which is Terry's ritualistic redemption scene. Having redeemed himself by his testimony, he redeems the rest of the men by suffering a beating at the hands of the thugs and showing them by example that it is possible to stand up afterwards and claim their "rights" by going to work against the union boss's orders. The Christ symbolism with which Schulberg and Kazan invest Terry Malloy (Marlon Brando) is well known, and although Kazan thought some critics had gone too far in their analyses, he did not deny it when asked about it by an interviewer.¹¹ The allusions to Christ are fragmentary in earlier scenes, as when Terry sustains a stigmata-like wound while trying to protect Edie Doyle (Eva Marie Saint) from the thugs, but they are unmistakable in the final scene, as Terry, beaten and weak, with blood streaming down his face, shoulders his longshoreman's hook, as Christ did the cross on which he would be crucified, and stumbles along the path between crowds of the longshoremen he is trying to save, climbing at last to the enormous door that marks the entrance to work and dignity for the men. The final scene establishes the film as a melodramatic enactment of the Christian salvation myth, as Terry triumphs over his persecutors and brings the longshoremen with him into a community of brotherhood and honest work, while the evil Johnny Friendly (Lee J. Cobb) is expelled from the community, left alone on the dock, beaten and bloody and still vowing revenge. This ending was "a last minute change Kazan himself developed."[12] Schulberg's final shooting script called for Terry to be beaten to death for his attack on Johnny Friendly, establishing a tragic rather than a melodramatic mythos for the film. Pauly has suggested that "Terry's bloody staggering walk was an insistent parade of anguish that commented on the state of mind of the man who staged it. It was almost as though, deeply injured by the consequences of his decision to testify, Kazan was calling attention to both his wounds and his own refusal to be defeated."[13] Kazan once told an interviewer that *On the Waterfront* had been shot "surrounded by people, by spectators. It was great, it was like a public trial."[14] It was a trial in which both Kazan and Schulberg were seeking vindication.

While the Christian myth carried a heavy freight of signification in the film, Kazan has affirmed that it was not its central thematic concern. Speculating on the film's immediate box-office popularity, achieved with little studio publicity and before the reviews had appeared, he wrote:

> My guess is that it's the theme, that of a man who has sinned and is redeemed. . . . Terry's act of self-redemption breaks the great childhood taboo: don't snitch on your friends. Don't call for the cop! Our hero is a "rat," or for intellectuals, an informer. But that didn't seem to bother anyone in the audience, not given our villains, those whom Terry was fingering. Which is proof that Budd Schulberg struck a deep human craving there: redemption for a sinner, rescue from damnation. Redemption, isn't that the promise of the Catholic Church? That a man can turn his fate around and by an act of good heart be saved at last? (Kazan, *A Life*, 528)

While the film's melodramatic structure offered the spectator a simple sense of satisfaction through emotional identification with the designated "good guy," it also suggested the complexity of the issue of informing through a number of subtexts, visual and verbal. Playing off against Terry's growing awareness of the complexity of his moral decision – "There's a lot more to this whole thing than I thought, Charley"(*On the Waterfront*, 101) – are the two codes that the film exposes as simplistic and childish, the longshoremen's policy of "D & D" and the Golden Warriors street gang's commitment to never holler "cop" on a criminal, even if the injured party is one of your own.

As Victor Navasky has pointed out, however, Schulberg and Kazan pulled something of a sleight of hand in the plot. Perhaps with Tony Kraber's well-known attack on Kazan, "would you sell your brothers for $500,000?" ringing in the background, one of the film's major motifs is the betrayal of and by brothers. One of its best-known scenes is in the taxicab, when Terry gently accuses Charley (Rod Steiger) of selling him out: "It was you, Charley. You was my brother. You should of looked out for me. Instead of making me take them dives for the short-end money" (*Waterfront*, 104). When Glover, the Crime Commission investigator, visits him on the roof, Terry explains just how Johnny Friendly and his brother betrayed him and destroyed his fighting career. In this context, Terry's testifying to the Crime Commission could be seen partly as a justified act of revenge on his brother, similar to the justifications both Kazan and Schulberg have given for their testimony against the Communist Party, by which both of them felt ill-used. As Navasky has pointed out, if Terry's informing had meant he would be sending his brother to prison, the dilemma posed by the act of informing would have been real, but Kazan and Schulberg have the mob kill Charley for his ultimate act of loyalty to Terry, thus giving Terry a "socially sanctified personal motive (revenge) for testifying against the mob, as well as the political one (anti-corruption)."[15] This enfolding of the act of informing into the melodramatic mythos of the film empties the issue of its complexity and relieves the spectators from experiencing their own emotional and moral ambivalence about it with any intensity. As Navasky notes, "'Squealing' may be relative, but in *Waterfront* it is mandatory."[16]

Through their combination of the melodramatic structure and the Christian symbolism that bears the burden of meaning in *On the Waterfront*, Kazan and Schulberg managed, as Stephen Whitfield has put it, to "convert a Judas figure into a Christ symbol,"[17] thus establishing a cultural rallying point for the anti-Communist position without conflating Communists with criminals, as the film moguls wanted them to do, or even mentioning them in the film. Schulberg, and particularly

Kazan, also emphasized the scapegoating of the informer by society at large. In the screenplay, Terry is called a "canary" by the police who are assigned to protect him and a "pigeon" by his hitherto admiring young fan, Tommy of the Golden Warriors, who destroys Terry's pigeons in a crudely symbolic act of repudiation. Kazan inserted a little scene after the Crime Commission hearing, in which a friend walks by Terry on the stairs, refusing to acknowledge his greeting, as had happened to Kazan many times in New York. Establishing Terry's victimization for performing what the film insistently defines as a moral act is a crucial preparation for the redemptive symbolism of the ending. By turning in to the authorities the people who threaten evil to the community, the film makers imply, the informer does a social good for which he is unjustly persecuted by a populace that blindly follows a simplistic code of loyalty and silence. The film suggests to all humane spectators that they should rethink their simplistic positions on this issue at the same time that it stacks the moral deck in favor of the informer.

Arthur Miller's play, *A View from the Bridge*, was first presented in New York on 29 September 1955. Its protagonist, the longshoreman Eddie Carbone, turns in two illegal immigrants who are related to his wife because he is desperate to stop one of them from marrying his niece and ward, for whom he harbors an unconscious but driving passion. In the play, Miller establishes the enormity of Eddie's treachery in the eyes of the Italian-American community of Red Hook by foreshadowing it with the story of a similar incident. In the original one-act version of the play that was produced in New York, Eddie's wife Beatrice explains to her niece Catherine that Vinny Balzano, a boy of sixteen, "snitched on somebody to the Immigration. He had five brothers, and the old man. And they grabbed him in the kitchen, and they pulled him down three flights, his head was bouncin' like a coconut. . . . And they spit on him in the street, his own father and his brothers. It was so terrible."[18] In response to Catherine's question about what happened to Vinny, Eddie responds, "Him? Naa, you'll never see him no more. A guy do a thing like that – how could he show his face again?" (96). After Eddie turns them in to the authorities, one of the immigrants, Marco, spits in his face and then shouts, "That one! I accuse that one! . . . He killed my children! That one stole the food from my children" (150). When the lawyer Alfieri tells him he must not take revenge by killing Eddie, he replies:

Marco: Then what is done with such a man?
Alfieri: Nothing. If he obeys the law, he lives. That's all.

Marco: The law? All the law is not in a book.
Alfieri: Yes. In a book. There is no other law.
Marco: *his anger rising:* He degraded my brother – my blood. He robbed my children, he mocks my work. I work to come here, mister!
Alfieri: I know, Marco –
Marco: There is no law for that? Where is the law for that?
Alfieri: There is none. (153)

Unable to accept the law's restrictions on his primal desire for revenge, Marco challenges Eddie, who demands that he take back his accusation, crying like John Proctor, "I want my good name, Marco! You took my name!" (159). Marco demands instead that Eddie go on his knees to him. They fight, and Marco ends up killing Eddie with his own knife.

Eric Bentley began his review of *A View from the Bridge* for *New Republic* by remarking, "Not long ago Elia Kazan made a movie about the New York waterfront, and now Arthur Miller has brought out a play about the New York waterfront. The climax of both movie and play is reached when the protagonist gives the police information which leads to the arrest of some of his associates."[19] Bentley suggested that it would surprise no one that "in the movie, the act of informing is virtuous, whereas, in the play, it is evil," and contended that "both stories seem to have been created in the first place for no other purpose but to point up this virtue and that evil, respectively," complaining that the issue of informing had been reduced in both works to "mere melodramatic preachment" (21). He went on in the review to suggest that Miller seemed in his reface to the published play (his article, "On Social Plays") to have made "an effort to transcend the outlook on which this author was, so to speak, raised. The only single word for that outlook is 'Stalinism' yet it should only be used if we understand that its adherents weren't usually Communists but only progressivists whose feelings were hurt if anyone said anything against Russia" (21). He implied that Miller's aesthetic was fundamentally Marxist – "though one may not see any synthesis, one certainly sees the thesis and the antithesis" (22). Praising Robert Warshow's article on Miller, he suggested that Miller was deceptive about his ties to the Communist Party: "The ambiguity of 'Is he or isn't he?' is inherited from *Children's Hour*, and *Cat on a Hot Tin Roof*: much is made of false accusation, yet we don't feel sure that the accusation is false" (22).

Bentley was to change his mind about Miller, and about the anti-Communist position of someone like Warshow, but he was not the only one to suggest that *A View from the Bridge* was intended as a rebuttal of the Kazan-Schulberg representation of the informer in *Waterfront*. Reporter Murray Kempton even went so far as to print in the *New York Post* as "theatre gossip" the rumor that Miller had sent *View* to Kazan, and, when Kazan wrote back that he would like to direct it, sent him a wire that said, "I didn't send it to you because I wanted you to direct it. I sent it to you because I wanted you to know what I think of stool pigeons."[20] Miller answered Kempton's piece with an angry denial of the story, remarking, "I do live in New York, and Kempton could easily have checked the facts with me." Miller went on to clarify the facts for the reader:

> I never offered Kazan "A View from the Bridge," and if I had, and he had accepted the job of directing it, I cannot conceive a more boorish act than Kempton ascribes to me, namely to then refuse him the project. I don't have time or the inclination for such idiocy and I am amazed that he could have judged me such a stupid man as to do such a thing. . . . I will offer Kazan a play of mine to direct when I have one which I believe would be best served by his kind of talent. And I am sure he will accept or reject the job on the merits.
>
> I would add but one further fact. "A View Form [sic] the Bridge" is not about a political informer. When I write a play about a political informer he will be called a political informer. The situation in the present play is not analogous, is not even pertinent to that kind of dilemma. In this, as in Kempton's acceptance of the "theatre gossip," he has fallen prey to the wish fulfillment assertions of Left dogmatists who join with the Right in finding secret plots, angles, and smirking analogies wherever it serves them to do so.[21]

When Elia Kazan was asked in 1971 about the suggestion by the French film critic Roger Tailleur that Miller had written *View* to answer *Waterfront*, he replied, "I don't think Arthur Miller is that small a guy. He meant to write a play about the waterfront many times before. . . . But that he wasn't affected somewhat by one of his best friends doing something he disagreed with is bullshit, isn't it? It's a colouration, a degree, rather than the whole thing."[22] When Miller was interviewed by Nora Sayre in the late seventies, he told her that he had been disturbed because "'the idea of informing' was 'turned around' in *On the Waterfront*: 'At the time, I felt that it was a terrible misuse of the theme.'"[23] His play, he told her, "was a kind of attempt to throw a different light on the whole informing theme. . . . I suppose the passions of the

moment cast it in that mold.' . . . I have never ceased to blame the
Committee first and foremost. . . . I never felt a *fraction* of my antago-
nism for the Committee toward any person who [appeared] in front of
it.' And he added that sympathy should not be withheld from the
informers."[24]

There is not so much an ambivalence as a divided sympathy in
Miller's statements that pervades the play itself as well. Eddie Carbone
is as helpless to resist his fate as any of the Greek tragic protagonists he
has been deliberately constructed to resemble. Alfieri, who serves the
function of a Greek chorus in the play, observes that Eddie was the victim of "a passion/ That had moved into his body, like a stranger" (*View*,
115), and, as if he were listening to an ancient myth:

> I could have finished the whole story that afternoon.
> It wasn't as though there were a mystery to unravel.
> I could see every step coming, step after step,
> Like a dark figure walking down a hall toward a certain door (121).

Eddie is driven by his passion to destroy Catherine's lover Rodolpho,
even if it means violating one of the elemental taboos of his community, just as Marco is driven to take his revenge on Eddie, even if it violates the law. The spectator is brought to feel sympathy for Eddie, even
if his death seems the result of a primal justice that precedes the laws of
civilized society, whatever Alfieri may say. In a newspaper article in
1965, Miller explained his view of the issue of justice in the play:

> What kills Eddie Carbone is nothing visible or heard, but the built-in
> conscience of the community whose existence he has menaced by
> betraying it. Whatever both plays [*View* and *A Memory of Two Mon-
> days*] are, they are at bottom reassertions of the existence of the com-
> munity. A solidarity that may be primitive but which finally
> administers a self-preserving blow against its violators. In both plays
> there is a search for some fundamental fiat, not moral in itself but
> ultimately so, which keeps a certain order among us, enough to keep
> us from barbarism.[25]

Coming from Arthur Miller, who is preoccupied enough with the law
to have a lawyer in nearly every one of his plays, this statement is somewhat startling. He seems to be endorsing the position of Marco – "All
the law is not in a book" (*View*, 153) – rather than that of Alfieri, who

takes his stand for civil order against primal justice: "Most of the time now we settle for half,/ And I like it better" (159). Miller was far from condemning the informer, perhaps because he was keenly aware of the anguish that many of the people he considers weaker than himself endured during and after their decisions to give names to HUAC. He had offered the part of Eddie Carbone first to Lee J. Cobb, who had cooperated with HUAC, noting in *Timebends* that, "cynically or not, [he] had thought that under the circumstances Lee would bring the pain of the harried longshoreman onto the stage rather than some studied impersonation" (394).

Miller's most open treatment of the informer came in *After the Fall* (1964), a play that has been widely criticized for its candor about the playwright's life, particularly his relationship to his second wife, Marilyn Monroe, who died in 1963. The play is deeply rooted in Miller's personal relationships, among them his friendship with Elia Kazan. Although he had been working on the idea for some time, the play began to take shape when he was approached by producer Robert Whitehead about contributing a play for the inaugural production of the new Lincoln Center Repertory Theatre where Whitehead and Kazan had agreed to serve as co-directors. Although Miller and Kazan had been estranged since Kazan's testimony in 1952, they both wanted to work together. It took only the diplomacy of Whitehead to effect their reconciliation, although their relationship was to remain self-conscious ever after. As Kazan has described it:

> A reconciliation happened through Bob; it could not have happened through me, not yet. But once brought together, Art and I got along well – even though I was somewhat tense in his company, because we'd never discussed (and never did discuss) the reasons for our "break." I believed he was the playwright closest in character to me and that I was the natural director for him. I admired the effort he made to come together with me again, an effort that could not have had the endorsement of a number of his closest friends. I responded equally – against the inclination of some of my closest friends. (Kazan, *A Life*, 586)

Miller has written that he had not changed his opinion that Kazan's "testimony before the Un-American Activities Committee had disserved both himself and the cause of freedom, and I had no doubt that he still thought himself justified" (*Timebends*, 529). In his view, what it came down to in the early sixties was whether Kazan should be black-listed from working in the theatre with those of differing political views. And he also thought Kazan "the best director for this complex play" (530). The somewhat uneasy spirit of compromise on personal, political, and moral fronts was in keeping with the play itself.

After the Fall is about the capacity for evil that exists in all of us, and about the process by which its protagonist, Quentin, stops protesting his innocence through the self-justifying blaming of others and accepts his own culpability for what can only be called his sins. As Gerald Weales puts it, Quentin learns in the course of the play that "he has spent his life trying, one way or another, to establish his innocence" and the guilt that he feels about his family, his two failed marriages, and his reluctance to defend his old friend Lou against HUAC "has always been transferred to the other person in the relationship. At the end, he accepts that it is after the fall, that there is no innocence, that the guilt is his."[26] And Christopher Bigsby has suggested that the Un-American Activities Committee and the Holocaust are used in the play as a kind of public symbolism for "the examples of personal cruelty and love destroyed by egotism which abound in Quentin's past." In his view, the symbols "gain their particular effectiveness from the realization that both institutions derive their power from the ready complicity not only of the 'innocents' who stand by and watch but also of the victims who succumb still naively believing in the folly of opposition and the virtue of inactivity."[27] In Bigsby's view, the innocence in the play is simply another form of guilt, which stems from a wish for noninvolvement. In any case, Miller has left the simple oppositions of *The Crucible* far behind in this play. If the act of informing is morally confusing for Eddie Carbone, it is a symbol of moral complexity for Quentin.

Miller establishes the moral issues surrounding HUAC through Quentin's relationship with two characters, Mickey, a close friend of Quentin's, and Lou, a law professor who was a kind of mentor to Quentin and Mickey in the leftist days of their youth. Miller has indicated that Lou is partly based on Louis Untermeyer, a poet and friend of Miller's who was blacklisted from television for his support of the Waldorf Conference, after being told by the producer of *What's My Line?* that "The problem is that we know you've never had any left connections, so you have nothing to confess to, but they're not going to believe that. So it's going to seem that you're refusing to be a good American." According to Miller, Untermeyer locked himself in his apartment for almost a year and a half afterwards: "An overwhelming and paralyzing fear had risen in him. More than a political fear, it was really that he had wit-

Figure 10. The design for the traveling production
of *After the Fall* by Jo Mielziner emphasized the Holocaust symbolism
through the watchtower and its barbed wire, but otherwise kept
the bare platforms of the original production.
Reprinted by permission of the Estate of Jo Mielziner.

nessed the tenuousness of human connection and it had left him in terror" (*Timebends*, 264). Although he called Untermeyer several times on
the telephone, Miller did not see him during that period. In the play,
Quentin has agreed to represent Lou when he is called to testify before
HUAC, and he finds himself immensely and guiltily relieved when Lou
commits suicide, letting him off the hook. Mickey, who is based on
Kazan, appears in the play just as he is about to testify and asks Lou's permission to name him, for which Lou denounces him.

Miller brought an unfinished script to the first rehearsal of *After the
Fall*, partly because the repertory company was an experiment, and its
four-month rehearsal period afforded an opportunity for a more collaborative production than was possible in the usual three-to-four weeks
of rehearsal time that was typically provided by the commercial New
York theatre, and partly because he did not yet have complete control
of the play, for which he had written thousands of manuscript pages.
A version of the play was published by Viking and in the *Saturday
Evening Post* just as the play premiered in January 1964, but so great
were the changes that occurred during this first production process
that Miller published a second version of the script, a "Final Stage Version," in April 1964 – the version that is currently published by
Viking/Penguin. Despite the fact that Kazan was fully aware that he was

directing a version of himself in the scene, however, the dialogue in the scene with Lou and Mickey went almost unchanged during the rehearsal and production process.[28]

The Director's Notebook that Kazan compiled throughout 1963 as he was working on his conception of *After the Fall* shows that he had definite ideas about the character of Mickey. He described him there as "The Guiltless Man (as vs. Quentin)" and "A great and natural hedonist, full of energy and pleasure . . . because he is not crippled with puritanism and the consequent guilts,"[29] which is very much the way Kazan describes himself in distinction to Arthur Miller. He also noted that Mickey recognizes Quentin as a "killer" and expects Quentin to destroy him, and that he is no more sure of his position emotionally than Lou is. In other words, Kazan directed Ralph Meeker, who played Mickey, pretty much as a version of Elia Kazan, a self-proclaimed amoral hedonist who is constantly suspicious and wary of others, and unsure of himself philosophically and morally. During rehearsals, Kazan was uncharacteristically passive. This was partly because of the sudden death of his first wife Molly, which took place during the rehearsal process. He was deeply affected by the death of the woman he had always regarded as his guide on issues of morality, aesthetics, taste, and even politics. His passivity was also a measure of his relationship with the play and its author. William Goyen, who observed the rehearsal process as a writer-in-residence at Lincoln Center, noted that as the actors rehearsed, "Arthur would interrupt and explain something – with glee and childlike relish." Kazan, who as director would normally be the one advising the actors, "waited, watched, relished. He seemed to let Arthur have his full say without interfering, except occasionally to agree heartily with Arthur or even to embellish Arthur's comments. I don't ever remember hearing Gadg [Kazan] take a stand or express a point of view contrary to Arthur's."[30] Always a director who worked one-on-one behind the scenes with his actors, Kazan could produce the interpretations he wanted without demonstrating them publicly at rehearsals, but his deference to Miller's opinion was a significant gesture by this director, who was known to bar big-money producers from Broadway rehearsals and once ejected Tennessee Williams from the rehearsal of one of his plays for talking to an actor about her part.

As it is written, Miller's script is carefully even-handed in its representation of the positions of Lou, the uncooperative former-Communist witness; of Mickey, the cooperative former-Communist witness; and of Quentin, the liberal who wants to help victims of injustice, but shrinks

from getting involved. Miller establishes the duplicity of the former supporters of Stalin by having Lou explain that he had lied in a study of
Soviet law that he had written in the thirties: "I left out many things I
saw. I lied. For a good cause, I thought, but all that lasts is the lie. . . . I
have never been a liar. And I lied for the Party, over and over, year after
year."[31] Lou has now written a book in which he wants above all to be
true to himself: "You see, it's no attack I fear, but being forced to defend
my own incredible lies!" (*After the Fall*, 26). Nevertheless, he and his wife
Elsie are terrified that he will be called before the Committee and asked
not only to tell the truth about the past but to name names.

Mickey, in almost a direct representation of the scene between Kazan
and Miller in 1952, has come to Quentin to explain why he has decided
to name names. Miller places in Mickey's mouth a speech that is a far
more eloquent defense of Kazan's position than his own "Statement" to
the *New York Times* had been, as he tries to explain himself to Lou:

> I despise the Party, and have for many years. Just like you. Yet there is
> something, something that closes my throat when I think of telling
> names. What am I defending? It's a dream now, a dream of solidarity.
> But the fact is, I have no solidarity with the people I could
> name – excepting for you. And not because we were Communists
> together, but because we were young together. Because we – when
> we talked it was like some brotherhood opposed to all the world's
> injustice. Therefore, in the name of that love, I ought to be true to
> myself now. And the truth, Lou, my truth, is that I think the Party *is* a
> conspiracy. . . . And I don't think we can go on turning our backs on
> the truth simply because reactionaries are saying it. (35)

Like a number of the friendly witnesses, Mickey proposes to Lou that
they go together to the Committee and tell the truth about their pasts.
Lou responds as many of Kazan's friends did: "You may not mention
my name. . . . And if you do it, Mickey, you are selling me for your own
prosperity. If you use my name I will be dismissed. You will ruin me.
You will destroy my career" (36). Lou goes on with the familiar theme
of loyalty to the brotherhood: "If everyone broke faith there would be
no civilization! That is why that Committee is the face of the Philistine!
And it astounds me that you can speak of truth and justice in relation
to that gang of cheap publicity hounds! Not one syllable will they get
from me!" (36). When Lou accuses Mickey of having sold his soul to
the Committee for his eleven-room apartment, his car, and his money,

he responds, "And yours? Lou! Is it all yours, your soul?" (37). He reminds Lou that it was his wife Elsie who made him throw his first, presumably factual, account of the Soviet legal system into the fireplace: "I saw you burn a true book and write another that told lies! Because she demanded it, because she terrified you, because she has taken your soul" (37). Lou condemns Mickey and Elsie calls him a moral idiot, but the hypocrisy beneath their self-righteousness has been exposed. They have remained loyal to their friends, but their lies have served to support a regime that murdered thousands of innocent people. On the other hand, Mickey may be truthful, but he is also self-interested, mercenary, and disloyal.

Between these two extremes stands Quentin. Miller makes it clear that he has already failed Mickey before he tells him about the Committee:

Mickey: Yes. I wish you'd have come into town when I called you. But it doesn't matter now.
Quentin: I had a feeling it was something like that. I guess I – I didn't want to know any more. I'm sorry, Mick. *To Listener:* Yes, not to see! To be innocent! (32)

Quentin is a bystander in the scene between Mickey and Lou, culpable only in that he withdraws his friendship from Mickey, even before he knows about his testimony. Although he agrees to defend Lou before the Committee, he feels guilt when Lou kills himself. Telling his Listener that Lou had told him he was the only friend he had left, he says:

It was dreadful because I was not his friend either, and he knew it. I'd have stuck it to the end but I hated the danger in it for myself, and he saw through my faithfulness; and he was not telling me what a friend I was, he was praying I would be. . . . Because I wanted out, to be a good American again, kosher again – and proved it in the joy . . . the joy . . . the joy I felt now that my danger had spilled out on the subway track! (59).

It is not only the guilt of the friendlies and the unfriendlies that is exposed here, but the guilt of all the good liberals who stood by with their mouths shut and prayed not to become "involved." Although Miller refused to name names, thus avoiding a sin of commission, he implies that he felt some guilt for what might have been a sin of omission in not going more vigorously to the aid of those who were made to suffer unjustly. The play exonerates no one. Like John Proctor, Quentin accepts his lack of innocence in the end, but unlike Proctor, Quentin is not transformed into a hero by his refusal to do harm to others. He does not have his "goodness" at the end of the play. What he has is something like knowledge. Kazan wrote in his notebook that the spine of *After the Fall* was "A Man Recognizes His Humanity!"[32] What Quentin discovers is that it is possible to live after one realizes that no one who is human is innocent, that sin and guilt are part of life, and that he, personally, is guilty. Only then can he look his third wife in the eye as he greets her, an image for Miller of the possibility of a future life for adults after the loss of innocence. In *After the Fall*, by ending his protestations of righteousness, Miller embraced the common guilt, and thus common humanity, of friendlies, unfriendlies, and bystanders, everyone involved in the HUAC hearings – except maybe the Committee.

7

Forensics

Mr. Arens: Mr. Chairman, I respectfully suggest that the witness be ordered and directed to answer the question as to who it was that he saw at these meetings.

Mr. Jackson: May I say that moral scruples, however laudable, do not constitute legal reason for refusing to answer the question.

HUAC Hearings, 21 June 1956

Must the citizen ever for a moment, or in the least degree, resign his conscience to the legislator?

Henry David Thoreau, Civil Disobedience

The Self and Others

The period during and immediately following World War II was a time of colossal political trials, not only in the United States, but throughout the world. Here we had the trial of Alger Hiss for perjury, the trials of Julius and Ethel Rosenberg and Judith Coplon for espionage, the trials of American Communist Party officials under the Smith Act, and the numerous trials of uncooperative witnesses before the Un-American Activities Committee – those who refused either to name names or to take the Fifth Amendment – for Contempt of Congress. In Europe there were the Nuremberg Trials of those accused of atrocities under the Nazi regime and the Moscow "purge" trials, the humiliating rituals of self-abasement and "confession" in which former Communist leaders participated before they were executed for crimes against the state. With the awareness of these public trials pervading the intellectual atmosphere of the forties and fifties, it was perhaps inevitable that the forensic mode would be employed in the plays of the time. As Victor Turner has noted, the trial serves as a redressive or remedial procedure within the process of social drama. What's more, it is itself a species of ritual theatre, during which the jury of spectators judges the performances of the antagonists partly by their forensic skills, awarding the victory to the most effective debater, and, by its very decision, giving the victory a concrete effect on the community. During a time of ever-widening ideological schism in the country, the trial play provided an arena in which the Right and Left were brought together, if only to exhibit their differences and battle for ideological influence over the direction that post-war American culture and politics were to take.

The most propagandistic of the trial plays was Sidney Kingsley's adaptation of Arthur Koestler's novel about the Moscow trials, *Darkness at Noon* (1951). Koestler, a former Communist who was firmly anti-Communist by the time he wrote the novel, produced a penetrating and horrifying study of the intellectual and emotional process by which the former revolutionaries could have been brought to repudiate their old beliefs and actions, and abase themselves before Stalin's "court" before they were executed. Koestler demonstrated that it was possible for this to have taken place without the drugs and torture that most Americans imagined, simply through the manipulation of deeply held ideological convictions. A *tour de force* of fictional technique, the novel details the thinking of Rubashov, "ex-Commissar of the People," as he endures his imprisonment and three "hearings" for his crimes against the state. Kingsley's adaptation had none of the subtlety of Koestler's probing novel. As he said in an interview, he had simply seen the novel as "the most powerful literary weapon against communism that he knew about and felt strongly that a play should be made of it."[1] In doing his research for the play, Kingsley read the works of Stalin and other Soviet Communists, and simply put in the mouths of his characters "dialogue straight from the tongues and pens of the Communist leaders." He told his interviewer, "This is a play for liberals who know that one must be anti-Communist in order to be whole-heartedly anti-Fascist." Not surprisingly, the critics were not impressed with Kingsley's play. Brooks Atkinson wrote: "For Arthur Koestler's haunting terror, Sidney Kingsley has substituted a complicated melodrama . . . somewhere between the novel and the theatre the intellectual distinction has gone out of the work. . . . His melodrama comes with elements of the glib propaganda play that we find so distasteful when it is on the other side."[2] Harold Clurman noted that the play had been pieced together "from the surface of Koestler's novel, from quotes out of the writings and speeches of various Soviet spokesmen, and from the editorial repetitiousness of innumerable contemporary journalists," suggesting, "the result is a sort of *Reader's Digest* melodrama, intricate without suspense, psychological without characters, philosophical without mind, violent without effect."[3]

Although *Darkness at Noon* was not directly related to the HUAC hearings, it was used as a touchstone, and something of a talisman, for witnesses whose political ideology was viewed as suspect by the Committee. Edward G. Robinson, who found himself in the difficult position of having been named by a friendly witness, and therefore blacklisted in the film industry, but of having no former Communist or even fellow-traveling activities to confess and repudiate, made use of his touring with the play to establish his anti-Communist credentials. He told the Committee: "While you have been exposing Communists, I have been fighting them and their ideology in my own way. I just finished appearing in close to 250 performances of Darkness at Noon all over the country. It is, perhaps, the strongest indictment of communism ever presented. I am sure it had a profound and lasting effect on all who saw it."[4]

Two plays that clearly allude to the dilemma of the HUAC witness are Lillian Hellman's *Montserrat* (1949), an adaptation of the play by Algerian playwright Emmanuel Roblés, and Arthur Miller's *Incident at Vichy* (1964). Hellman saw Roblés's play in Paris at the height of her period of political activism. In 1948, she was deeply involved in Henry Wallace's campaign for the presidency and in the founding of the Progressive Party. In October of that year, she interviewed Marshall Tito in Prague, and in March 1949, she was to be a principal speaker at the Congress of World Peace at the Waldorf, sponsored by one of HUAC's *bêtes noires*, the National Council of the Arts, Sciences, and Professions. In June 1949 she was named by Jack Tenney's California "baby HUAC" for "having followed or appeased some of the Communist party-line programs."[5] When she saw *Montserrat* in Paris, in October 1948, she immediately recognized it as a philosophical dramatization of her heartfelt views at the time. She got herself introduced to Roblés and bought the English-language rights to the play; then she proceeded to drop her activity on the Wallace campaign and spend the next four months working on her adaptation, which was finally produced by Kermit Bloomgarden in October 1949, and directed, not very successfully, by Hellman herself.

In adapting the play, Hellman worked from a literal translation and made few substantial changes. She added an opening scene to the play and cut some of the characters' philosophizing, on the theory that

American audiences have far less tolerance for lengthy speeches than European ones. The effect was to foreground the play's rather thin plot device, clearly incidental to the existentialist drama of soul that Montserrat undergoes in the Roblés version, but too insistently melodramatic in the Hellman version. The play concerns an incident that occurred during the revolutionary struggle headed by Simon Bolivar against the Spanish Colonial forces in Valencia, Venezuela, in 1812. As the play opens, Bolivar has escaped from a patrol headed by the elegantly sadistic Colonel Izquierdo, who has sworn revenge against the colonial revolutionaries because they humiliated him when he was taken prisoner in an earlier battle, burying him up to his chin in the sand and urinating on his face. It is quickly revealed that it is Captain Montserrat, a liberal young man who opposes the cruel imperialism of the Spanish regime, who has enabled Bolivar to escape, and that he, presumably, knows where Bolivar is. Rather than conventional torture, which Izquierdo knows will not work on Montserrat, he conceives the idea of taking six people at random from the town square and giving them an hour to convince Montserrat to inform on Bolivar in order to save their own lives. Since the cause of Montserrat, and Bolivar, is to save the people from Spanish oppression, Izquierdo reasons, and Montserrat is a man of honor and deep conviction, it will be very difficult for him to watch six people die, one by one, in order to save the one man Bolivar, regardless of what happens to Montserrat himself.

As the hostages try their arts of persuasion on Montserrat, it is clear that Roblés had a social microcosm in mind when creating his characters. At one end of the spectrum is the rich merchant Salas Ina, a completely self-interested capitalist who at first tries to bribe his way out of the situation, and then offers his young wife, whom he has claimed to love better than life itself, to Izquierdo in exchange for his freedom. Next is a character called "Matilde" in Hellman's version, and more tellingly "LaMère" in Roblés's, who cares about nothing but the two children she has left at home, and would be happy to sacrifice not only Bolivar, Montserrat and the revolution, but everyone else in the room including herself if only her children would be fed and be safe. Two artists, Salcedo, a royalist actor who is newly arrived from Spain, and Luhan, a "half-breed" carver of wood, whose works have been bought systematically for a pittance by the Spanish officers and then sold at a great profit to museums, suggest a level of contribution to civilization beyond the simple instincts of survival for self and offspring represented by Salas Ina and Matilde. Salcedo is not a very good actor, but he is capable of enacting a representation, however flawed, of Ascascio, a character who is "based on a large philosophic concept . . . most serious and profound . . . deeply Spanish, most exalted, large, noble in motive, filled with charity."[6] The value of this contribution to human culture, however, is left in doubt, for it is clear that the import of Salcedo's artistry has had little effect on Izquierdo, who has seen his performance, and thought it merely "a pleasant evening." The play, he says was "overacted, in places, too much talk, far too long. I don't think myself a judge of art, even bad art" (*Montserrat*, 442). Art, good or bad, the play reminds us, has little effect on the Philistines. Luhan, whose native art has been plundered by the colonial invaders, views it and himself with far less arrogance than Salcedo: "I work, I carve all day, most of the night. I make good things, I know it. . . . And what happens to them? You steal them. You steal everything. . . . You steal from us, you live from us, and you kill us if we try for another piece of bread" (449). Luhan had spent three months when he was a boy plotting to kill a man who had called him a "dirty half-breed," and then didn't do it because he was "too frightened," but his fondest hope, even after the exploitation he has suffered, is still to have his name carved in the pedestal of the two statues he has made for the cathedral at Cadiz. Both the value of his art and the recognition of his worth have been entirely dependent on the whims of a few powerful men in a colonial regime who, he knows, despise him for being what they have created, a "half-breed," both physically and culturally.

The other two hostages, Ricardo and Felisa, are barely more than children, but it is they who have enough belief in the revolution as a cause to give up their lives for it. Ricardo, a boy who has lost his father and two brothers in the revolution, says, "I am not afraid to die, if it serves a purpose" (456). He goes bravely to his death. Felisa refuses Izquierdo when he offers to let her go if she will promise to return to him that night. When Montserrat is about to lose his resolve as Matilde pleads with him to spare her life so that she can care for her babies, it is Felisa who convinces him not to give in: "It's too late. Four people have died. What will you make it – that they have died for nothing? Stay with what you believe. (*Furiously*) Yes. It's bad about her babies. But death is death, no better for one than another" (475). Montserrat suffers the anguish that Izquierdo expected of him throughout the killings, but he does not betray Bolivar, telling Izquierdo, "there is no one man, and therefore no only man. You take the best man you find. That is what I have done" (478). If he is wrong, Izquierdo reminds him, he has killed six people for nothing. When Izquierdo is about to bring in another six, Montserrat finally gives in, telling Izquierdo that Bolivar was never in hiding, and his strategy had been a delay tactic: "I promised I would give him as long as I could. . . . Now either you've taken him, or he's joined his people" (479). When the patrol comes back with the news that Bolivar has gotten through, Montserrat is beaten by the soldiers and executed, without "repenting."

Montserrat's analogy with several of the inquisitions of the forties was clear, and it was noted by reviewers. For Hellman, of course, the most immediate application was to the HUAC hearings. The interrogation of the Hollywood Ten had taken place the previous year, and both Hellman and her long-time companion Dashiell Hammett were prime targets for future hearings. Montserrat's dilemma is similar to that of the witness who must either inform on those who were fighting for the leftist cause in the United States or bring harm on all sorts of people who had no connection with the Left, and perhaps no interest in politics – families who would suffer from the witness's blacklisting and unemployment, friends and associates who would be tainted by association. On the other hand, the interrogation and execution of the six innocent witnesses in the play was a reminder of the parade of witnesses before HUAC, many of whom lost their jobs for doing nothing more dangerous to the national security than marching in a May Day parade or contributing to Spanish War Relief, and some of whom went to jail for their refusal to put other citizens in the same predicament. The position that Hellman was to take in her letter to the Committee in 1952 has its roots in *Montserrat*: "I am not willing, now or in the future, to bring bad trouble to people who, in my past association with them, were completely innocent of any talk or any action that was disloyal or subversive."[7]

Hellman did a poor job of directing the play, and those who knew the Roblés original agreed that she had reduced the complexity of his existential tragedy to straightforward American melodrama. Nevertheless, some of the critics did take note of the play's American political implications. Writing in *The Nation*, Margaret Marshall commented:

> The play, it will be seen, touches upon all the themes that are so dear to the hearts of leftists committed to the class struggle: the dilemma of either-or and the necessity of choice between absolutes, the imminence of crisis, class behaviorism, the leader principle, the sacrifice of the present to the future, the unimportance of the individual, and

above all the principle that the end justifies the means. These themes are not as fresh as they once were. They have become shopworn in the theater, and in the real world they have been exploited so systematically as a means to an end no more inspiring than power that they arouse suspicion rather than belief. It will take a better play than "Montserrat" to reinvest them even with their actual limited validity.[8]

In his magisterial way, Harold Clurman, who was to take over the direction of the play, explained that Lillian Hellman misunderstood *Montserrat*'s content. "Miss Hellman seems to have believed that she was dealing with a 'revolutionary' play in our 1930 sense of a play in praise of the struggle for freedom," he wrote. "'Montserrat' is not such a play. It is primarily a drama of moral issues – its plot association with Bolivar's fight for South American independence is almost accidental."[9] Montserrat, Clurman declared, "sacrifices his life and that of others with entire consciousness of his individual responsibility. What distinguishes his choice of action is that it is undertaken in behalf of millions of others. This is the essence of the existentialist ethic."[10] Clurman did not choose to notice in this case the connection between existentialism and Marxism, particularly in Paris, where this play originated. Roblés was a compatriot and close friend of Albert Camus and a committed leftist, in both philosophy and politics. In 1948, his existentialism was of the Sartrean Marxist variety. Clurman, who had studied French literature at the Sorbonne, was well aware of intellectual developments in Paris in the forties. That he found it necessary in domesticating this play for American audiences to empty it of the political implications that had attracted Hellman to it in the first place is a good measure of the ideological tightrope on which liberal intellectuals were trying to balance in 1948.

When Arthur Miller wrote *Incident at Vichy* for Lincoln Center in 1964, the political times had changed dramatically. It was so unnecessary to hide the analogy the author was making between Vichy France and the United States that Miller spelled it out for an interviewer in 1967:

We discovered after the war . . . that there was an immense social pressure to conform, a chilling of the soul by the technological apparatus, the destruction of the individual's capacity for choosing, an erosion of what used to be thought of as an autonomous personality – all this was carried to its logical extremes by the Nazi regime, which ended up by controlling not only Man as a social ani-

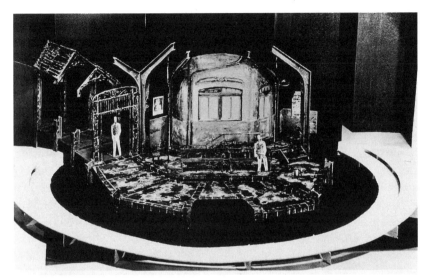

Figure 11. The model for the set of *Incident at Vichy*
as produced at Lincoln Center is suggestive of a Sartrean Hell.

mal in his job and on the assembly line or in his office or in the Army
but in his bed, in his relationships to his children, who were taught to
carry any expression of opinion by him to the authorities as a patriotic act, until you had created a nation of people who could be said
to have lost or given up or been robbed of what for two thousand
years was supposed to have been the – their human nature. They
now existed to carry through a social program. In my opinion we
have inherited this.[11]

Incident at Vichy uses Nazism as a touchstone for all dehumanizing governmental oppression in the 20th century. Despite the almost universal
understanding by early critics that *Vichy* is a kind of suspense play about
the Nazis with moral overtones, Miller tried to make the point that he
was using Nazism as a vehicle for a broader statement about human
beings. "The occasion of the play is the occupation of France," he told
an interviewer in 1964, "but it's about today. It concerns the question
of insight – of seeing in oneself the capacity for collaboration with the
evil one condemns. It's a question that exists for all of us."[12]
    Although both plays are based on historical incidents, the dramatic
structure of *Vichy* is remarkably similar to that of *Montserrat.* In his play,

Miller collects ten people in a room where they are waiting to be interrogated. They discuss their captors, the motives for their interrogation, its probable outcome, and their possibilities for survival. One by
one, they are called for interrogation, and, with one exception, disappear behind the door that becomes one focal point of the set, the
other being the corridor that leads to the street and freedom. As the
men talk, it becomes clear that they have been picked up because they
are suspected of being Jews, or, in one case, a Gypsy, and they are
about to be examined and either released or sent to concentration
camps. Like Roblés and Hellman, Miller assembles a social microcosm, developing his characters as representations of sociocultural
attitudes rather than as complex psychological individuals. Marchand,
a businessman who is closely tied to the Vichy regime, is examined
first and released. He is constantly preoccupied with his business
appointments and resists the approaches of the other men. The next
to go is Bayard, an electrician with knee-jerk Marxist opinions on
everything. He does not return from his interrogation. Neither does
Lebeau, a self-involved painter who can not see beyond his own
predicament, or Monceau, an actor who has left Paris at the height of
his career to take refuge in "unoccupied France" because he believes
he has inadvertently tipped off the authorities that he is a Jew. A
waiter, a fourteen-year-old boy, a Gypsy tinker, and a silent "old Jew"
with a bundle of feathers are also taken away. The central conflict
involves an unnamed Major in the regular German army who has
been placed in charge of the Racial Program police proceedings very
much against his will; Von Berg, an Austrian aristocrat who has been
picked up by mistake; and Leduc, a psychiatrist and former captain in
the French army who is in hiding with his family and seems to be
fighting in the French Resistance.

When the Major escapes to a local bar for a few minutes, he warns
Leduc on his return not to attempt the escape plan he knows he is contemplating because the place is too well guarded. He says to him: "Captain, I would only like to say that . . . this is all as inconceivable to me as
it is to you. Can you believe that?"[13] Leduc replies: "I'd believe it if you
shot yourself. And better yet, if you took a few of them with you" (*Incident*, 280). When the Major asks him why he thinks he deserves to live
more than the Major does, Leduc says, "Because I am incapable of
doing what you are doing. I am better for the world than you." The
Major asks him, "If you were released, and the others were
kept . . . would you refuse?" The scene continues:

Figure 12. The Major (Hal Holbrook) confronts Leduc (Joseph Wiseman) in the Lincoln Center production of *Incident at Vichy.*

Leduc: No.

Major: And walk out of that door with a light heart?

Leduc: – *he is looking at the floor now.* I don't know. *He starts to put his trembling hands into his packets.*

Major: Don't hide your hands. I am trying to understand why you are better for the world than me. Why do you hide your hands? Would you go out that door with a light heart, run to your woman, drink a toast to your skin? . . . Why are you better than anybody else?

Leduc: I have no duty to make a gift of myself to your sadism.

Major: But I do? To others' sadism? Of myself? I have that duty and you do not? To make a gift of myself?

Leduc – *Looks at the Professor and the Police Captain, glances back at the Major:* I have nothing to say.
Major: That's better. (282)

Von Berg, on the other hand, continually expresses his outrage at the atrocities of the Nazis and explains how he has suffered at their hands, although he realizes that he is not in danger as the others are. When Leduc asks him to stop talking because "it's difficult to listen to amelioration, even if it's well-meant," Von Berg says that he had no intention of ameliorating. Leduc replies: "I think you do. And you must; you will survive, you will have to ameliorate it; just a little, just enough . . . you see, this is why one gets so furious. Because all this suffering is so pointless – it can never be a lesson, it can never have a meaning. And that is why it will be repeated again and again forever." Von Berg says, "Because it cannot be shared?" And Leduc answers, "Yes. Because it cannot be shared" (285).

This scene prepares for the climactic moment of the play, when, all the others having been called for interrogation, only Von Berg and Leduc are left in the room. When Von Berg says that he would like to leave with Leduc's friendship, Leduc demands that he recognize that, like most gentiles, he harbors "somewhere hidden in [his] mind, a dislike if not a hatred for the Jews" (288). Von Berg says that this is not possible, and Leduc tells him with "wild pity" in his voice:

> Until you know it is true of you you will destroy whatever truth can come of this atrocity. Part of knowing who we are is knowing we are not someone else. And Jew is only the name we give to that stranger, that agony we cannot feel, that death we look at like a cold abstraction. Each man has his Jew; it is the other. And the Jews have their Jews. And now, now above all, you must see that you have yours – the man whose death leaves you relieved that you are not him, despite your decency. And that is why there is nothing and will be nothing – until you face your own complicity with this . . . your own humanity. (288)

When Von Berg is called and emerges from the room with the pass that will bring him freedom, he puts the pass in Leduc's hand and urges him to take it and go. Leduc backs away, momentarily covering his eyes against his own guilt, saying, "I wasn't asking you to do this! You don't owe me this!" (290), but he takes the pass and goes out, leaving Von

Berg. As the police and the soldiers take off in pursuit of Leduc, Von Berg rises to face the Major. "*A look of anguish and fury is stiffening the Major's face; he is closing his fists. They stand there, forever incomprehensible to one another, looking into each other's eyes*" (291). As the Austrian and the German stand facing each other, another group of prisoners is brought in, signifying the continuity of the interrogation.

Miller has said that he was unaware of Jean Paul Sartre's description of the existentialist Theatre of Situation when he wrote *Incident at Vichy*, but he has acknowledged that it seems to fit the play.[14] Lawrence Lowenthal has demonstrated that *Vichy* is not only an excellent example of the Theatre of Situation, it is "an explicit dramatic rendition of Sartre's treatise on Jews."[15] Sartre described situational drama as short and violent, suited to the dimensions of a single long act, with "a single set, a few entrances, a few exits, intense arguments among the characters who defend their individual rights with passion."[16] Here Sartre could be describing Miller's one-act play, with its severely restricted action, its claustrophobic set, its tense rhetorical structure, its life-and-death stakes, and its enormous moral issues. In Sartrean existentialism, the freedom of the will is a central concept. Rejecting essentialism, Sartre holds that each person is a free being, entirely indeterminate, who achieves transcendence over determinism by re-creating the dehumanized self through a succession of choices that represent the assumption of responsibility for one's own being. Sartre's version of the Fall is the presence of the Other. As human beings, we lose our freedom when we allow ourselves to become Beings-for-Others, selves constructed by the subjective gaze of the Other – in other words when one's self is determined by another's view of it. In the Jew–anti-Semite confrontation, as Lowenthal puts it, "the anti-Semite sadistically objectified the Jew in order to justify his own existence, while the Jew often submits to this manipulation in order to escape the struggle toward transcendence" (Lowenthal, 34). The Jew in this situation can act inauthentically by submitting masochistically to the anti-Semite's "gaze," or he can take on the risks and responsibilities of the situation and defy the gaze of the anti-Semite, thus acting authentically. The first, an escape into cowardice and an *a priori* ideological system, is an example of Sartrean "bad faith," or the "lie of the soul" by which one flees the responsibility of freedom by accepting determinism in one form or another.

Miller provides a number of examples of bad faith in the play. The businessman Marchand, of course, denies his Jewishness, allowing himself to be completely defined by the ideology of the Nazi. Lebeau admits to feeling guilty: "Maybe it's that they keep saying such terrible things about us, and you can't answer. And after years and years of it, you . . . I wouldn't say you believe it, but . . . you do, a little" (*Incident*, 278). He gives in to the Nazi "procedure" as he gives in to the Nazi's definition of him. Monceau, the actor, hopes to flee from the crisis by placing the illusion of a role between him and the gaze of his oppressors. This proves hopeless because he cannot act away his fear. As Leduc tells him, "your heart is conquered territory, mister." The "old Jew" submits silently to oppression, the immemorial Hebrew victim. Bayard, the Communist, is guilty of bad faith for, as Lowenthal puts it, "dissolving his individuality in a collective mass" and for "turning his back on the existential present for the theoretical proletarian revolt in the future" (35). In the service of his saving lie, he ignores Von Berg's reminder that most of the Nazis are from the working class. The oppressors, of course, are the strongest examples of bad faith in the play. "The Professor," the civilian who is in charge of the Racial Program, is what Sartre calls a "salaud," one who claims special rights to existence through an *a priori* system of values and beliefs. He holds a degree in "racial anthropology" and believes that certifies him to decide who deserves to live and who to die. Like Bayard, he dissolves his individuality, and thus his individual responsibility, in a faceless ideology. As a Nazi, he has all of the rights that the Reich confers on him and no responsibility for its actions. The Major, on the other hand, insists that the Nazi system has taken away all of his freedom, and therefore his responsibility to act. Turning on the helpless old man, he displays the sadistic behavior his self-imposed moral entrapment has bred in him.

In the end, it is only Von Berg and Leduc who act with what Sartre would consider authenticity. Although he feels guilt for it, Leduc chooses to accept the gift of self-preservation that Von Berg gives him. As Lowenthal explains, "Leduc is now stained by Von Berg's gift of life and must carry on the existential cycle of transmuting his guilt into redemptive action. He is free, like all men, to transcend his present action by choosing a new and redeeming project." Presumably, Leduc will go back to fight in the Resistance, and "the death of the weak aristocrat will then be justified by the services of the strong combat officer" (38). If he does not make this choice, he is no "better for the world" than the Major, who also survives by allowing others to be killed. Von Berg, of course, makes the most active choice among the characters. In choosing to change places with Leduc, he *becomes* "the Jew," thus expiating the guilt he had for even his distant complicity with the Holocaust. He contributes to the anti-Nazi cause by exchanging one decadent and useless aristocrat for one potentially useful Resistance fighter. Thus his sacrifice is not a passive submission to the Other, but an active resistance of it. Through Leduc's help, Von Berg has been led to a moral awakening in which he has seen his complicity with evil and has transcended his guilt through a positive action chosen because of his acceptance of individual responsibility for his life. As Lowenthal points out, the play "represents in its total action the essence of Sartre's philosophy, which was, and still is, the demand for authenticity, or the moral awakening to individual responsibility" (38).

As Miller has made clear, *Incident at Vichy* is not just a play about Nazis. "The occasion of the play is the occupation of France, but it's about today."[17] The play's thematic statements about individual responsibility and resistance to oppression, about the reality of evil, the acceptance of guilt, the awareness of prejudice have manifold implications for the post-war world. Closest to home and to Miller's experience, of course, was the experience of those who were involved in some way with the HUAC hearings, whether as interrogators, witnesses, or spectators. The play has several implications about witnesses. When Monceau explains that he hopes to convince the interrogators of his "innocence" by acting – "after all, you are trying to create an illusion; to make them believe you are who your papers say you are" (*Incident*, 264) – Leduc responds, "That's true, we must not play the part they have written for us," an articulation not only of the danger of accepting the definition of self through the gaze of the Other, but of the theatrical nature of the interrogation. One of the central questions of all interrogations is who controls the script. In the theatre of the HUAC hearings, the struggle for power was a forensic one: what the interrogators could get the witnesses to say, and what the witnesses could say to deflect the most dangerous questions and avoid saying the fatal lines that would bring trouble on others or land them in prison. The freedom to write your own part, even if it meant keeping silence, was an essential element of authenticity for the HUAC witness. A second application to HUAC is the conflict between the law and justice. Part of Monceau's bad faith is that he escapes personal responsibility by fleeing to the assumption that the law is always just: "I go on the assumption that if I obey the law with dignity I will live in peace. I may not like the law, but evidently the majority does, or they would overthrow it" (*Incident*, 279). Leduc points out to him that this position is absurd. In

Vichy France, he is now about to be condemned by the law to hard labor or death because he has been circumcised: "In short, because the world is indifferent you will wait calmly and with great dignity – to open your fly" (279). Where the law is unjust, Miller implies, the individual's responsibility is to oppose the law, not to obey it passively because he is a "good citizen."

The play's most significant analogy with the HUAC hearings, however, is not related to the participants, but to the spectator Von Berg, the equivalent of the "liberal bystander" during the hearings. Miller is most concerned here with the guilt of complicity and the responsibility of the passive observer to take action against state-sanctioned injustice. Von Berg has always found the ideas of the Nazis abhorrent, and their anti-Semitism insupportable. He has sheltered people against them, and even contemplated suicide. Leduc brings Von Berg to see that his typical liberal reactions to injustice are not enough. Sheltering a few people from oppression – like contributing to defense funds and signing petitions – is not enough to resist evil. Unless the suffering itself is shared, Leduc says, "it can never be a lesson, it can never have a meaning. And that is why it will be repeated again and again forever" (*Incident*, 285). It is only when Von Berg *becomes* the Jew by taking his place that his opposition to anti-Semitism becomes meaningful. And taking an action of resistance that puts one in the same danger that the victim of oppression faces, Miller suggests, is the only way to rid oneself of the guilt of complicity.

The Individual and the State

Herman Wouk's novel *The Caine Mutiny* won him the Pulitzer Prize in 1951 and had sold over 5 million copies in various American and British editions by 1955. Its 500 pages recount the story of the USS *Caine*, a destroyer-minesweeper assigned to the Pacific during World War II, from the viewpoint of Willie Keith, a young man who rises from spoiled mama's boy to mature Navy lieutenant in the course of the narrative. While the novel has the requisite love story required of a best-seller in the fifties, its primary focus is the ship, and the reaction of the Naval officers to their captain, Lieutenant Commander Philip Francis Queeg. Disliked at first for being a rigid, petty tyrant and capricious disciplinarian, Queeg later displays cowardice in battle and finally seems to the officers to have broken down entirely. In one incident, he neglects all other ship's business to spend three days in pursuit of an illicit key to a food locker. He believes that use of this key is the only possible explanation for a missing quart of strawberries, ignoring the fact that several people tell him they have seen the stewards eating them. Finally, in the midst of a typhoon, Queeg freezes in terror, insisting blindly on following his original orders for the fleet's course, despite evidence that the ship is foundering and will have a better chance of surviving if it reverses course and steams directly into the wind.

Steve Maryk, the ship's executive officer, has been encouraged by resident "intellectual" Tom Keefer to think that Queeg is psychotic and is compiling a medical log to document the captain's insanity. In the typhoon, he decides that Queeg has finally gone off the deep end, and relieves him under Navy Regulations, Article 184, which states: "It is conceivable that most unusual and extraordinary circumstances may arise in which the relief from duty of a commanding officer by a subordinate becomes necessary, either by placing him under arrest or on the sick list." The other officers and men obey him, and Maryk successfully navigates the ship through the typhoon. Maryk is subsequently tried, not for mutiny, but for "conduct to the prejudice of good order and discipline." His defense counsel, Lieutenant Barny Greenwald, succeeds in winning him an acquittal by bringing out Queeg's paranoid fantasies through questioning and causing him to break down on the stand, thus suggesting to the Naval officers who are judging the case what his behavior during the typhoon might have been like. Greenwald, who had taken the case reluctantly, then goes to the combination party for Maryk's acquittal and the publication of Keefer's novel. There he makes a drunken speech in which he says that Queeg was a hero to him because Queeg and the other officers of the regular Navy had kept Hitler from coming to the United States and melting his Jewish mother down into a bar of soap. He tells Maryk that he and Keith were guilty and that he had gotten him off by "making clowns out of Queeg and a Freudian psychiatrist – which was like shooting two tuna fish in a barrel – and by 'pealing very unethically and irrelevantly to the pride of the Navy."[18] The real guilt, however, he lays at the feet of Keefer, who had planted the idea of Queeg's insanity in Maryk and then refused to back him up when he wanted to tell Admiral Halsey about it, and did not have the guts to testify about it in the court martial. He gives Keefer a "little verbal reprimand":

> I defended Steve because I found out the wrong guy was on trial. Only way I could defend him was to sink Queeg for you. I'm sore that I was pushed into that spot, and ashamed of what I did, and

thass why I'm drunk. Queeg deserved better at my hands. I owed him a favor, don't you see? He stopped Hermann Goering from washing his fat behind with my mother. (*Caine Mutiny*, 448)

Stephen Whitfield has remarked that "what can be inferred from the runaway success of *The Caine Mutiny* is how smoothly popular taste could accommodate an authoritarian ideology, justifying submission to a demented superior."[19] The stage and film adaptation of the book only made that ideology clearer.

Wouk sold the film rights to Stanley Kramer, an independent producer who had a financial association with Columbia Pictures. Kramer and Columbia executive Harry Cohn secured the cooperation of the Navy to do the film. Meanwhile, Wouk had interested Charles Laughton and producer Paul Gregory in doing a stage version of the novel's trial section. When Gregory found out that Henry Fonda wanted to play Greenwald, Wouk put together a four-hour script in three weeks. The production originated in San Diego, with actor Dick Powell as director, but Powell could not handle Fonda or the four-hour script. After two weeks it became clear that something would have to be done. Gregory persuaded Laughton to assume direction, and he used his considerable skills as play adapter to help Wouk cut the script down to a playing time of two and one half hours.

The resulting play centers on Greenwald and Maryk, Keith being only a minor character, and it assumes the familiar forensic structure of the courtroom drama. First the prosecution presents its case, with Queeg appearing at his most convincingly rational. Keefer testifies evasively, failing to support Maryk. Keith bungles his testimony. Greenwald then discredits the testimony of two psychiatrists who have pronounced Queeg fit to command, getting one to testify that Queeg had exhibited "rigidity of personality, feelings of persecution, unreasonable suspicion, withdrawal from reality, perfectionist anxiety, an unreal basic premise, and an obsessive sense of self-righteousness,"[20] and another to say that Queeg is "sick," although not "disabled for command" and demonstrating to the Naval officers of the court that the psychiatrists have no idea of the stress involved in commanding a ship at sea during wartime. Act I ends with a conversation between Maryk and Greenwald. When Maryk says that Queeg was "nuts," Greenwald responds:

Greenwald: You heard Dr. Lundeen. It's a question of degree. If you're in a war and your command personnel is stretched thin, maybe you've got to use him because he's got the training. I'll grant you that Captain Queeg was a mean, stupid, son of a bitch . . . if that was grounds for deposing your superior officer we wouldn't have an army or a navy. That's a widespread opinion of superior officers.

Maryk: They're not all Queegs.

Greenwald: Superiors all tend to look like Queeg from underneath. It's an unflattering angle.

Maryk: What do you do when you really get a Queeg?

Greenwald: You fight the war. (*Caine Court-Martial*, 79)

Act I, Scene I consists of the defense case, in which Maryk explains, simply and straightforwardly, what happened during the typhoon and describes some of Queeg's craziest behavior, and the judge advocate shows that Maryk did not have the competence to make any psychiatric diagnosis. Then Greenwald calls Queeg to the stand, confronting him with incident after incident of his past behavior until he breaks down in a long monologue of paranoid fantasy and self-justification, trying to show that Keith and Maryk were two incompetent officers who had combined against him from the beginning. Greenwald then has him read his latest fitness report on Maryk, in which he has described him as "consistently loyal, unflagging, thorough, courageous, and efficient," fully qualified for command of a destroyer-minesweeper. Maryk is acquitted.

Act II, Scene Two consists of the scene in the restaurant that occurs in the book, with Greenwald's speech about Queeg's having saved his mother from the Nazis. In the play, Wouk anticipates the argument that the ship would have foundered and been lost if Maryk had blindly followed Queeg's orders and kept on the fleet's course by having Greenwald tell Keefer: "If you hadn't filled Steve Maryk's thick head full of paranoia and Article 184, why he'd have got through to the south, and the *Caine* wouldn't have been yanked out of action in the hottest part of the war" (127). The play ends with Greenwald throwing a glass of wine in Keefer's face and saying, "You can wipe for the rest of your life, Mister. You'll never wipe off that yellow stain" (128), a reference to the officers' nickname for Queeg of "Old Yellowstain," coined by Keefer when Queeg had insisted on throwing a yellow dye marker out and steaming away instead of escorting some unprotected landing-craft to their line of demarcation for a beach that was under fire.

According to Charles Laughton's biographer, producer Paul Gregory opposed the final scene, which is "exasperating, since it forces the audience to go back on its own judgment. By using the specious argument that any mutiny is wrong, that Queeg should never have been deposed, Wouk comes to the edge of Fascism."[21] In a *New York Times* interview a few days before the play opened on Broadway, Laughton said that Wouk intended for audiences to see beyond the "courtroom melodrama" in the play to "certain fundamental ideas he holds about authority, about defiance of authority, about respect for our Navy – and by implication, about respect for the other institutions of authority in American Society today."[22] Spectators and critics were thus well-prepared for Wouk's message when the play opened in New York. While Laughton's skillful adaptation and the brilliant acting of Henry Fonda as Greenwald and Lloyd Nolan as Queeg absorbed most of the opening night critics' attention, there were some doubts expressed about the play's ideological message. Richard Watts wanted to put on record that he was among those who thought Queeg deserved to be removed from command, that "the alleged mutiny was entirely justified" and that Greenwald's speech "didn't convince me in his rather mystical advocacy of the sacredness of discipline."[23] In his Sunday follow-up article on the play, Brooks Atkinson declared that "there is no easy way out of the dilemma Mr. Wouk has raised in this trenchant play." If you accept Greenwald's position that "the authority of a regular Navy commander should not be challenged at sea, you are left with some plausible evidence that the Caine would have foundered in the typhoon if the executive officer had not taken over."[24] Atkinson also pursued an issue that had not yet been mentioned in the discussion of the play: the issue of the ends justifying the means, which, he observed, came up three times in the course of the play. Did the end of saving the ship justify the "alleged mutinous behavior of Lieutenant Maryk"'? Did the end of acquitting his client justify the "tricky court technique" of Lieutenant Greenwald? And then the "big question": Did "the end of keeping the Nazis away from our shores justify the authoritarian system of command implicit in all professional fighting organizations? Is incidental injustice tolerable in a good cause, and are small men heroes in great crusades?"

Atkinson merely posed the questions, but the magazine critics who weighed in shortly afterwards had clear positions on the play's authoritarian ideology. On the liberal side, in *The Nation*, Harold Clurman wrote that the play suggested "a decrepit orthodoxy full of implications which are certainly anti-democratic" and "a state of mind which regards any and all criticism of established orders as unwarranted and villainous."[25] His review provoked such a flood of letter- writing that the magazine printed a mini-symposium from among the letters, adding one from Clurman defending his position.[26] In *The New Republic,* Eric Bentley, referring to "the claim [Wouk] made in the NY *Times,* through his director, that the play is no mere psychological thriller but a tract for the times telling us to respect authority," suggested that "Mr. Wouk's retort to sentimental radicalism is in order, yet cannot the New Conservatism – for surely his play belongs in this current of opinion – be equally sentimental, equally ambiguous?"[27] Bentley's criticism of Greenwald's speech, however, was primarily on aesthetic grounds:

> We spend three quarters of the evening pantingly hoping that Queeg – the commander – will be found insane and the mutineers vindicated. When, in the very last scene, Mr. Wouk explains that this is not the right way to take the story it is too late. We don't believe him. At best we say that he is preaching at us a notion that ought to have been dramatized.

In the liberal Catholic magazine *Commonweal,* Richard Hayes pronounced it "lamentable" that Wouk "has seen fit to append the notorious epilogue, with its indefensible abrogation of the values we have previously been led to accept," and contended that "the very fact that he should have ruptured the texture of his work to enjoin so irrational a surrender to a mindless mystique of discipline is, in itself, symptomatic, and appalling. . . . Mr. Wouk has inexplicably chosen to sacrifice the intimate truth and rigorous compassion of these scenes for the poor triumph of a vulgar ideological *frisson.*"[28]

From a less tendentious position, the *New York Times Magazine* printed a lengthy article on the play by Hanson Baldwin, the *Times'* military editor, with the subtitle, "A military expert examines a dilemma raised by a hit play: How far does unquestioning obedience to order go?"[29] Noting that "unreasoning, unquestioning acceptance of orders has been a foundation stone of many of the world's military organizations," he wrote that it had "produced in the past both disastrous stupidity and Homeric deeds." Agreeing with what he saw as Steve Maryk's position that there must be a "rational limit" to obedience, even in military organizations, he wrote, "yes, not only a rational limit but a moral, ethical and philosophical limit and a legal one" (13). He also raised the delicate issue of the war crimes trials, noting that we refused to accept obedience to orders as a defense for committing such acts as the taking of hostages and shooting of individuals, and he denounced Greenwald's (and Wouk's) rhetorical trick of evoking the Holocaust as an easy emotional justification for his position: "Because Greenwald is a Jew, he wants to beat Hitler and save his mother from being 'cooked down to soap.' Greenwald seems to lend allegiance to any authority that can stop that. This is a dangerous generalization, for the same principle of unquestioning obedience, of submission to constituted authority, could be applied to Hitler's officers: they would carry out any orders that promised victory" (42). Baldwin thought this was the reason for the "vague dissatisfaction" many have felt with the play, after all "a man when he dons a uniform does not lose his soul or shed his conscience." By the time the play opened in London in 1956, the liberal position was clear-cut enough for Kenneth Tynan to deliver his critique in several brisk sentences. *"The Caine Mutiny Court-Martial,"* he wrote, "is a fine ephemeral play disfigured at the end by a brute stroke of tendentious illogic. . . . The inferences from [Greenwald's] tirade are extremely nasty: that the egghead ought to have run away from school and joined the Navy, that a truculent paranoiac is a better citizen than pacific intellectual, and that a wartime commander must be blindly obeyed even when he is demonstrably gaga and a danger to the lives of his men." He judged that "Mr. Wouk's standards of human conduct differ from those of the Nazi Party only in that Mr. Wouk is not anti-Semitic. One wonders, neither idly nor for the first time, just how many thinkers of his stamp would have opposed Hitler if Hitler had not indulged in racial persecution."[30]

Conservative magazines, of course, approved wholeheartedly of the play, particularly the final scene. Theophilus Lewis summed up their responses when he wrote in *America*:

> Mr. Wouk makes some pertinent, trenchant and highly original observations on the iconoclasts who rouse the intellectual rabble. As Keefer undermined the confidence of the crew in their commander, the civilian image-breakers are continually magnifying the flaws in venerable traditions, discrediting the motives of men in authority and disparaging their efforts. By sniping at every man who climbs to a conspicuous place in society, they create an atmosphere of distrust of all authority and a spirit of revolt against discipline.[31]

When *Time* featured Wouk on its cover for 5 September 1955, the occasion was the publication of his next novel, *Marjorie Morningstar,* but its generous cover story dealt mainly with *The Caine Mutiny*. In both book and play, the story suggested, "Wouk defied recent literary fashion and loosed some real shockers by declaring his belief in 1) decency – in language as well as deeds, 2) honor, 3) discipline, 4) authority, 5) hallowed institutions like the U. S. Navy. . . . His chief significance is that he spearheads a mutiny against the literary stereotypes of rebellion."[32] Maxwell Geismar responded with a piece in *The Nation* in which he examined the reasons for what he saw as *Time*'s establishment of Wouk as "the House Author of the American Way at the middle of the twentieth century."[33] He suggested that the Luce publications *(Time* and *Life)* were consciously laying down a program for "a new slap-happy optimism mingled with a proper respect for whatever exists and a species of domestic drama that will avoid all bad language and all serious human issues." The new literature, he wrote, will be based on the "principle of 'Woukism' . . . 'Peace, Prosperity, and Propaganda' will be the grand theme of the new literature, and all deviants from the norm, whether biological or esthetic or ethnic, will be tolerated so long as they do what they are told" (Geismar, 400).

In short, *The Caine Mutiny* became a major ideological touchstone in the mid-fifties, a safe cultural site for battles over several of the issues that were polarizing Left and Right, and that were being brought before the public daily in the proceedings of HUAC and the Senate Internal Security Committee. Among them were the conflict between the responsibility of following one's individual conscience and obedience to institutional authority; the issue of using the end of national security to justify the undemocratic means being used to extract information from citizens; the questions of the place of the intellectual and of the military in American society; the manipulation of forensic tactics; and the capacity of judicial proceedings to discover the truth about human experience or the morality of any human act. Given the cultural significance of *The Caine Mutiny*, it is not at all surprising that the motion picture that Stanley Kramer made from it, with the direct interference of Harry Cohn, attracted a good number of artists who had been shunned by the Hollywood Left for their cooperation with HUAC. Kramer himself had broken with his partner Carl Foreman in 1951, when Foreman refused to testify. To direct the film, he hired Edward Dmytryk, the only one of the Hollywood Ten to be "rehabilitated" by naming names to HUAC, which he did in 1951 after his release from prison. As writers, Kramer hired Stanley Roberts and Michael Blankfort; both were former leftists who testified cooperatively,

Roberts giving the Committee 29 names. To play Greenwald, Kramer cast José Ferrer, one of the most conspicuously cooperative of HUAC witnesses. He was delighted to have Humphrey Bogart call and ask if he could play Queeg. Bogart had been named by John L. Leech and cleared in "executive session" by Martin Dies in 1940. After this experience, he had been a conspicuous supporter of the nineteen witnesses who were subpoenaed in 1947, but he, like many of the Hollywood members of the Committee for the First Amendment (CFA), had grown cool toward the Ten as their obstreperous tactics emerged. When the CFA itself became a target of HUAC, Bogart wrote an article for *Photoplay* magazine entitled "I'm No Communist" in which he said that he was a "dope," fooled by the Communists into fellow traveling, and thereby saved his career.

Thus, to make the film, Kramer managed to assemble a group of talented liberal artists who had in one way or another bowed before the authority of HUAC. They could be expected to make a most effective case for Wouk's position that blind obedience to authority was sometimes necessary, even in a democracy, and to have a deep sympathy with the positions of Lieutenant Greenwald and Captain Queeg. Bogart, in fact, wrote an article entitled "The Way I See Queeg," in which he said that he had liked Captain Queeg from the time he had first read the book in 1951: "I felt I understood the guy," he wrote, "he was not a sadist, not a cruel man. He was a very sick man. His was a life of frustrations and insecurity. . . . In peacetime Queeg was a capable officer. But he could not stand the stress of war."[34] Kramer had no trouble securing the cooperation of the Navy, a prerequisite for making a movie about the armed services in the fifties, for without the military's help it would be prohibitively expensive to film. Within a week of submitting Roberts' screenplay to Rear Admiral Lewis Parks for approval, Kramer said later, he got "a 'delighted' okay."[35]

The film, which was dedicated to the United States Navy, made Queeg a more sympathetic character than he is in either novel or play and made Keefer into a weak, smart-alecky cynic rather than the introspective and troubled writer he is in the novel. The film's Keefer, Fred MacMurray, constantly undermines Queeg's authority with knowing looks of smug superiority and delivers rather sophomoric one-liners, such as his motto that the Navy was designed by geniuses to be run by idiots. To make Queeg more sympathetic, Roberts inserted a scene in which he reassures Willie Keith after having chewed him out, telling him that command of men is a difficult job and that it's only human to make mistakes. In the novel, after the Yellowstain incident in which Queeg shows his cowardice, he acts characteristically by demanding from his officers minute attention to details like breaking codes and making out reports. In the film, Roberts gives him a speech about the Navy's being like a family, in which he makes an implicit plea for the officers' support. The officers maintain a stony silence, causing Queeg to withdraw further into himself and deepening his paranoia. Greenwald uses this incident in his final speech to get Steve Maryk and Willie Keith to accept guilt for Queeg's later breakdown. In the battle scenes, Bogart appears more shell-shocked than cowardly, and in the typhoon, although he freezes in terror at one point, he remains on the bridge after Maryk relieves him. In short, the film shows more of Queeg's illness than his tyranny, and in Bogart's skilled hands, the character evokes considerable sympathy.

Since the film is an attempt to represent the whole novel, including, of course, the love story, the trial scene is considerably truncated. It moves swiftly through the testimony of Willie Keith and the sailors, the betrayal of Maryk by Keefer through his failure to admit his collusion, and Maryk's well-meaning but inarticulate account of the captain's behavior. Although Greenwald makes his point about the psychiatrist's not knowing about conditions at sea, Roberts has the judge advocate win points by demonstrating that the psychiatrist has worked with men under great stress in civilian life. In the film, Queeg's breakdown is not the much-anticipated and satisfying confirmation of the officers' case that it is in the play, but rather a pathetic scene in which everyone is embarrassed. As Greenwald, José Ferrer makes his dislike for his job and for Keefer so clear throughout the trial that there is not the sense of reversal when he makes his speech at the dinner that there is in the play. The audience is emotionally ready for it, and the climax of the film comes, not in the courtroom scene, but when the glass of wine hits Fred MacMurray's face and the other officers walk out in a body. What's being punished here is the smart guy who made trouble by stirring things up with his "advanced ideas" and attacking authority, and now is going to get off scott free while Maryk, the poor slob who listened to him and did the dirty work, is going to lose his career in the Navy. The bitterness of the HUAC cooperative witness who felt he had been sold down the river by smooth-talking Communists is evident here, and it is not hard to understand the attraction of the film makers to *The Caine Mutiny*. Maryk and Queeg are both victims in the film, and Keefer is the villain who gets his just deserts when the men turn on their heels and leave him alone with his cake in the shape of a book.

José Ferrer was offered another chance at dramatizing the conflict between individual conscience and obedience to authority when he directed *The Andersonville Trial* in 1959. Saul Levitt's play is based on the court records of the trial of Captain John Wirz, whose job it had been to oversee one of the worst horrors of the Civil War, the Confederate prison camp in Andersonville, Georgia. The camp was an unprotected stockade, 1,000 by 800 feet, in which up to 40,000 prisoners had been confined, and in which 14,000 had died in the space of a year and a half of untended wounds, malnutrition, exposure, and various diseases arising from the filthy conditions under which the men were forced to live. The prisoners were given no clothing, no shelter against the 100-degree Georgia heat or the winter cold, and, despite an abundant harvest in the countryside surrounding the prison and the willingness of civilians to contribute food, they were issued only starvation rations of coarsely ground cornmeal to eat. Conditions were so extreme that the men were reduced to eating rats, and cases of cannibalism were reported. Levitt's play concerns the trial of Captain Wirz in August 1865 for "criminal conspiracy to destroy the lives of soldiers of the United States in violation of the laws and customs of war."[36]

Even the title of the play, *The Andersonville Trial* echoes that of *The Caine Mutiny Court-Martial*, and Levitt clearly structured his play as an answer to Wouk's defense of blind obedience to authority. Like Wouk's play, it is in two acts, the first presenting the judge advocate's case and the second Wirz's defense, and it ends with Captain Wirz's breaking down on the stand. The difference is that Wirz is being tried essentially for obeying the orders of his superiors, and he is judged guilty and hanged for doing so. The play's protagonist is the judge advocate, Lieutenant Colonel Chipman, who faces a moral dilemma in prosecuting the case. He knows that Wirz was only executing the orders of his superior, General Winder, who is dead, and therefore cannot stand trial for the offense. As Defense Counsel Otis Baker points out, the government's charge of conspiracy is an excuse to hang a man for obedience to orders because "on that charge the accused may be convicted without any direct evidence against him" (*Andersonville*, 34). In short Wirz is being used as a scapegoat for the crimes of the Confederacy. After the first day of testimony, Baker asks Chipman how his role in the court differs from that of Wirz at Andersonville: "You know in your heart that you condemn him only for carrying out the orders of his superior. . . . You have as much as said so. But this Court will have no part of that argument. And what then do you do but withdraw it? You obey, as Wirz obeyed." He insinuates that Chipman is following through on the case to promote his career, asking "how does it feel to be an instrument of policy, nothing more?" (46). After Baker leaves, Chipman debates with his assistant Major Hosmer about calling a witness who they know is lying because he will make an effective presentation. Hosmer says, "Good God, what difference does it make in the end, Chipman? Wirz is doomed anyway" (47). Chipman responds, "if there's a moral issue here – I mean if we feel that Wirz should have disobeyed – and if we evade that issue – if we're afraid to raise it – how are we actually any better than that creature was at Andersonville? Are we all Wirz under the skin? Feeding where we're kept alive? At a trough?" (48). Hosmer appeals to the principle that the ends justify the means: "The government has a point to make too you know – it struggles to pull together a divided country. Isn't that a worthy, and important thing? At least as important as the purity of your soul?" Chipman agrees that "there are larger issues than a man's own convictions" (49).

In Act II, however, Chipman is finally driven to confront the court with the issue, basing his argument on an appeal to "the broader, more general code of universal international law" (67). In a rather extraordinary move, Levitt has the president of the court, General Lew Wallace, concede that soldiers have "the human right" to judge the commands of their military superiors, but say that "in practice one does so at his peril." Wallace then asks what a man fights for when he takes up arms for his country: "Is it the state or the moral principle inherent in that state? And if the State and the principle are not one, is he bound not to fight for that state and indeed to fight against it?" (68). The general gets Chipman to agree that if the United States had stood for slavery, he would have felt bound to follow his conscience and take up arms against the government. Wallace reminds Chipman that he is imperiling his career by pursuing this line of reasoning: "The Colonel understands, of course, that a man must be prepared to pay the penalties involved in violating the – let us say – the code of the group to which he belongs. In other societies that has meant death. In our society it can mean merely deprivation of status – the contempt of his fellows – exile in the midst of his countrymen" (68). Chipman makes it clear that he understands, but he pursues the issue anyway, asking Wirz, "as that situation had become a grossly immoral situation and as General Winder was not your moral superior, you did not have to obey him. So the questions remains, *Why did you obey?*" (70). Wirz, who goes through the trial lying on a couch because he is so weak from his war wounds and a recent suicide attempt, tries to defend himself by saying that he would have been court-martialed and probably executed for disobeying orders in war time, bursting out: "What heroic thing do you demand I should have done at Andersonville? I – an ordinary man like most men?" (70). He accuses the court: "You are all the victors here and you make up a morality for the losers!" (71). Chipman works away at Wirz until he sets aside all external considerations, asking him, "why – *inside* yourself – couldn't you disobey?" (73). Wirz replies "*(In a low relieved exhalation.)* Simply – I – could not. I did not have that feeling in myself to be able to. I did not have that feeling of strength to do that. I – could – not – disobey" (74). Wirz is convicted, and Baker tells Chipman it was a political verdict, no matter how he tried to shape the case: "It was a worthy effort though it hasn't anything to do with the real world. Men will go on as they are, most of them, subject to fear – and so subject to powers and authorities. And how are we to change *that* slavery? When it's of man's very nature?" (74) . Chipman can only answer, "We try. We try" (75).

The response to the play was positive, and critics noticed from the beginning its debate with *The Caine Mutiny*. In his opening night review, John McClain wrote that Levitt "chose to make the familiar case (echoes of Nuremberg) that he was merely acting on orders from his superior, that (echoes of 'Cain [sic] Mutiny') the military law of command is irrevocable. He manages finally, and I thought with unusual skill, to join the issue of when the responsibility of the individual to his conscience transcends anything else. And this, of course, is the crux of the play."[37] Critics noted the immediate relevance of the play to contemporary events, particularly the recent trial of Adolf Eichmann in Israel and the Nuremberg Trials. When George C. Scott, who played Chipman in the original production, directed a television production of *The Andersonville Trial* in 1970, viewers saw that the implications of the play's probing of the moral limits of obedience to authority went far beyond the immediate social and political context of the fifties. As Robert Lewis Shayon wrote, "it was a play for the times, echoing Dachau, Auschwitz, and more recently Mylai, as well as moral issues raised by students dissenting from the war in Indochina while facing the barrels and bayonets of rifles in the hands of National Guardsmen 'obeying orders.'"[38] The play was an effective expression of the opposition to "Woukism" in American culture of the fifties, but it had deeper implications than its simple dictum that it is sometimes necessary to disobey, oppose, and even to take arms against a government that is acting against one's fundamental moral principles. In a thoughtful magazine review, Tom F. Driver noted that neither *The Caine Mutiny* nor *The Andersonville Trial* faced the implications of its stand for contemporary social and political order:

> One can escape the tragic dilemma inherent in the demand for personal accountability from soldiers by facing and accepting the anarchical consequences that action according to individual conscience would lead to. If one continues to maintain, however, that the military is indispensable, one should recognize that the demands of the military and the demands of personal conscience will inevitably conflict. The individual is subject to contradictory sanctions and there is nothing for it but his destruction, physically or morally or both.[39]

Driver concluded that *Andersonville* "fails in its moral task for lack of examination of the bases for acts of moral heroism," finding its failure very much within the climate of the fifties. "In all the talk about the moral fibre of the nation, which is very popular these days, very few persons seem to be asking what basic assumptions must underlie a moral stance," he wrote.

One play that did confront the implications of the conflict between the necessity of absolute obedience in an effective military organization and the demands of individual moral responsibility was Louis Coxe and Robert Chapman's *Billy Budd* (1951), a *success d'estime* which had hung on and achieved a respectable Broadway run of 105 performances after producer Herman Shumlin, who had no financial interest in the play, had saved it from a quick end with a publicity campaign. The play is an adaptation of Herman Melville's novel about a young sailor who strikes and kills Claggart, the master at arms on his warship, because he stutters so badly that he cannot protest verbally when Claggart accuses him of urging the other sailors to mutiny. Melville focuses on the agony of Captain Vere, who knows that Billy was innocent and Claggart was evil, but feels he must convict and hang Billy under the Mutiny Act in order to preserve order on his ship. In the play, Vere says that "no man can defy the code we live by and not be broken by it."[40] In the deliberation about the verdict on Billly, he declares that "laws of one kind or other shape our course from birth to death. These are the laws pronouncing Billy's guilt; Admiralty codes are merely shadows of them" (*Billy Budd*, 65). When one of the officers objects, "that's tyranny, not law, forcing conformity to wrongs, giving the victory to the devil

253

himself!" Vere responds, "without this lawful tyranny, what should we have but worse tyranny of anarchy and chaos? . . . Oh, if I were a man alone, manhood would declare for Billy" (65). Billy shouts "God bless Captain Vere" (87) as he goes to his death, thus accepting his Christ-like scapegoat's role and confirming Vere's position that law and order must supersede justice as well as individual conscience when one is acting for the nation's greater good.

The appeal to individual conscience on the part of witnesses and the appeal to the necessity of obedience to authority to ensure law and order on the part of the Committee were central to the forensic ritual of the HUAC hearings throughout the fifties. Although they could not make the claim for the necessity of absolute obedience that the military could in time of war, the cold warriors on the Committee insisted that their battle against Communism was like a state of war in which individual citizens had to give up the rights they normally assumed in a democracy to assure a greater good: the preservation of the nation against what anti-Communists saw as the imminent threat of subversion from "the enemy within" and the ultimate destruction of democracy. The moral heroes of the Left were those who, like Arthur Miller, took full responsibility for their own actions but refused to bring harm on other citizens, on whose part they had witnessed no illegal activity, by naming them to the Committee. The moral arguments on the Right were similar to those of Barny Greenwald and Captain Vere. As Chairman Francis Walter put it in commending Budd Schulberg, who gave fifteen names, for his cooperative testimony: "It can only come through the lips of people who have had the experiences that you have had, the information that the American people should have, so as to bring home to everybody in every community of America an awareness of the menace of this world-wide conspiracy, and in our efforts to enlighten our people you have made a very fine contribution."[41]

CONCLUSION

Further Fields

In this realm mystification is a method, a fine art practiced for definite ends and on a gigantic scale.

Eric Bentley, "The Missing Communist"

What *[High Noon]* was about at that time was Hollywood and no other place but Hollywood.

Carl Foreman, *Take One* Interview

While history provided the most fertile analogical field for dramatizing the moral, political, and cultural issues that emerged from the activities of the House Committee on Un-American Activities, it was far from the only one. To be aware of the Committee's presence in the national psyche is to find implications of these issues throughout the whole range of the United States's cultural self-representation during the post-war and early cold-war periods. The broad scope of these analogical fields can be suggested by two popular films, *High Noon* (1952) and *Panic in the Streets* (1950). Each is deliberately ahistorical, and each is a distinguished example of a fundamentally American film genre: *High Noon* of the Western, and *Panic in the Streets* of the *film noir* crime thriller.

The better known of these texts is certainly *High Noon*, a 1952 United Artists film that was produced by Stanley Kramer, directed by Fred Zinnemann, and written by Carl Foreman. It is well known to students of film that Carl Foreman was a target of the HUAC investigations that took place during 1950 and 1951, in preparation for the round of Hollywood Hearings that took place from April to June and in September of 1951. Foreman, who had been a Communist Party member from 1938 to 1942, was finally called to testify in September, during the actual filming of *High Noon*. He took a version of the "diminished Fifth," refusing to confirm or deny his Communist Party membership. After the hearing, Stanley Kramer promptly cut off his association with Foreman, forcing him to relinquish his associate producer credit on *High Noon*, and buying out Foreman's interest in the film. Shortly afterward, Foreman went into self-imposed exile in England, where he had a successful film career, finally returning to the United States in 1975, when the blacklist was breaking down, to form his own independent company.

It is curious that the most influential political reading of *High Noon* has been Harry Schein's 1955 argument that the film is an "explanation for American foreign policy," an allegory for the United Nations' fear of the Soviet Union, China, and North Korea, and its failure to support the United States in its intervention in Korea.[1] Foreman has made it clear that, for him, *High Noon* was about "Hollywood and no other place but Hollywood and about what was happening in Hollywood and nothing else but that . . . that was perfectly recognizable to people in Hollywood when they saw the picture."[2] He told Nora Sayre that the film was a parable about the Committee's onslaught on Hollywood and "the timidity of the community there," and that he had been "morosely pleased" when he received many letters letting him know that his political imagery had been understood.[3] Foreman's message was in fact widely understood in 1952 and was articulated publicly as well as privately. In his *New York Times* review, Bosley Crowther called *High Noon* "a drama of moral courage in the face of bullying threats, a drama of one man's basic bravery in the midst of a townful of cowards." It is a story, he noted, "that bears a close relation to things that are happening in the world today, where people are being terrorized by bullies and surrendering their freedoms out of senselessness and fear." Calling the film's hero, Will Kane (Gary Cooper), "a man with the sense to meet a challenge, not duck in the hope that it will go away," he suggested that "this marshal can give a fine lesson to the people in Hollywood today."[4]

High Noon is set in the fictional town of Hadleyville, an obvious reference to Mark Twain's "The Man That Corrupted Hadleyburg." Mark Twain's story is a darkly satiric indictment of the moral hypocrisy of a town that considered itself "the most honest and upright town in all the region around about" and prided itself on being "incorruptible."[5] The tale describes the testing of the town's moral probity by a stranger who had been offended during an earlier visit there. He manages to puncture the town's vanity by demonstrating that its reputation for virtue will not hold up to temptation, proving to its citizens that "*the*

weakest of all weak things is a virtue which has not been tested in the fire"
("Hadleyburg," 380). Foreman's Hadleyville is a town of 400 people,
"located in a Western territory still to be determined, a town just old
enough to have become pleasantly aware of its existence, and to begin
thinking of its appearance."[6] Foreman explained in his introductory
notes that Hadleyville has recently been terrorized by Frank Mitchell
("Miller" in the film) and his retainers, who had ruled the town "ruth-
lessly and cruelly" (Foreman, *High Noon*, 148) until Will Kane had broken the gang and arrested Miller for murder. Five years later, Kane has
made Hadleyville a safe place for women and children. The town has a
school and a church, and some of the more prominent citizens have
built themselves houses, complete with lawns and flower gardens.

In the course of the film, Hadleyville shows its true colors as Kane,
newly married and about to leave town with his bride to start life as a
storekeeper, learns that Miller has been released from prison, and is
due to arrive in town on the noon train to exact his revenge on Kane
for arresting him. At first Kane's wife Amy (Grace Kelly), a Quaker, persuades him to leave town as planned, avoiding Miller and the inevitable
violent confrontation that would occur at high noon. After a few minutes on the road, however, Kane decides that he must return and face
Miller. Despite Amy's plea that the town's safety is no longer his concern, and her threat to leave on the train if he goes through with the
gunfight, Kane is determined to stay and face Miller. "I'm the one who
sent him up,"he says (171). Kane begins with great confidence in the
town's gratitude and loyalty: "This is my town. I've got friends
here. . . . I'll swear in a bunch of special deputies. With a posse behind
me, maybe there won't even be any trouble" (172). As he goes about
trying to find his deputies, however, pressured by the clock's relentless
progress toward 12 o'clock, he finds that his confidence is built on
sand. One after another, the townspeople refuse to help him, out of
motives ranging from professional jealousy to cynicism to simple fear.
Having tried the saloon for volunteers and found the crowd there
ready to support a new Miller regime, he goes at last to the church,
where the solid citizens are gathered in prayer. After debating the question of whether or not to help Kane for a few minutes, the citizens turn
their attention to Jonas Henderson (Thomas Mitchell), who, after praising Kane's bravery and goodness, argues that the town will be better
off if he leaves and a new marshal takes over, because Miller's quarrel is
with him and not with the town. Turning to Kane, he says, "Will, I think
you ought to go while there's still time. It's better for you – and better

for us" (221). A stunned Kane turns and leaves the church, passing the town's children, who are engaged in a game of tug-of-war in the churchyard.

After refusing offers of help from an old drunk and a fourteen-year-old boy, the only ones in the town who are finally willing to stand by him, Kane faces the Miller gang himself, with Amy coming to his aid at the last minute when she thinks he has been shot. The two of them subdue the Miller gang, and then leave town, after the film's most famous scene, when Kane takes off his marshal's badge and drops it in the dust at his feet.

It is difficult to imagine a more effective representation of the emotional state of a HUAC target like Carl Foreman than the relentless progress of *High Noon*. The film is a painfully detailed dramatization of the social process of scapegoating, as Kane, the erstwhile first citizen of the town, is perceived to be the source of its danger and is shunned and expelled by the populace out of a motive of self-preservation. Carl Foreman was undergoing the same process as he was writing and filming the screenplay, being marked as a HUAC target of investigation and then shunned and blacklisted as an unfriendly witness. The bewilderment, anger, fear, desperation, and grim determination of Carl Foreman's experience is embodied in Will Kane through Foreman's script and is fully realized in the most effective performance of Gary Cooper's career.

Foreman's scapegoat drama departs radically from the traditional tragic mode, however. Rather than taking the evil that threatens the community on his own shoulders, and being expelled by the populace with the responsibility for evil branded on him like the mark of Cain, Foreman's Kane vanquishes the source of evil and rejects the community, repudiating its badge of honor and its regard. When Kane throws the tin star that is the marshal's badge on the ground and leaves without a backward look, he abrogates any responsibility for the town and rejects the role of scapegoat, placing the responsibility for the town's future troubles precisely where it belongs. Carl Foreman's indictment of Hollywood's desertion of HUAC's targets is an indictment of the community, its group cowardice and its individuals' failure to assume responsibility for their actions. Perhaps the most telling reference to the situation in Hollywood is the character Baker (James Millican), the man who is all ready to join Kane in fighting the Miller gang as long as thinks he will be part of a big posse from the town. When he discovers that it is just he and Kane against the four men in the Miller gang, he immediately gets cold feet: "This is different. This ain't like what you said it was going to be. . . . This is just plain committing suicide, that's what it is! And for what? Why me? I'm no law-man – I just live here! . . . I got nothing personal against anybody – I got no stake in this!" (235). Finally pleading his wife and kids, he deserts Kane, having made all the arguments that were familiar to Foreman and the others in his position.

The final mood of *High Noon* is misanthropic disgust with the human community and a conviction of the individual's right and responsibility to enact a personal morality against the will of the community. As Peter Biskind has suggested, it "attacks both centrist models of the community: the federally focused, top-down model favored by the corporate liberals and the more bottom-up, populist model favored by the conservatives."[7] Its politics may have originated in a condemnation of the ultraconservatism of HUAC, but the film's position on society is decidedly anti-Left as well. In its review of the film, the *Daily Worker* criticized its cynicism and misanthropy, calling it "a classic restatement of the anti-human theme of nearly all cowboy and detective yarns: in this world all you can rely on is yourself and the power in a pair of guns: don't trust your neighbors, people are no damn good. Again Hollywood has employed a fine combination of talents [with] the [aim] of destroying a man's faith in his fellow man."[8] Among the many ironies surrounding this film, it is significant that one of the few Hollywood people who stood by Carl Foreman publicly after his testimony was the conservative Gary Cooper, who had testified as a friendly witness in 1947 that he never took any "pinko mouthing" very seriously because he didn't feel it was "on the level." In a sense, Cooper was living out the film's individualist ideology, rejecting the tyranny of Hollywood's scapegoating mentality and making his own moral judgments about how to act in this world. Having enacted Foreman's experience by proxy, Cooper was fully capable of supporting him, despite their differing politics.

Panic in the Streets (1950) is in some sense the mirror image of *High Noon*. If *High Noon* derives from the most romantic of American popular film genres, the Western, *Panic* is a good example of one of the most pessimistic, the *film noir* crime thriller, such as *The Naked City* (1948), *Double Indemnity* (1944), and *The Killers* (1946), that was popular during and after World War II. *Panic* was immediately recognizable to its reviewers as a "chase film."[9] In a more sophisticated analysis of popular genres, Peter Biskind has classified it as a "docs and robbers therapeutic thriller" substituting "illness for crime, and cure for punishment."[10] In any case, like *High Noon's*, its cinematic idiom was a popular one, familiar to post-war American audiences. The world they expected it to depict was a dark and threatening one, pervaded, as Philip Kemp has argued, with "fear and paranoia" and "hopeless fatalism."[11]

Like Carl Foreman, Elia Kazan was a former Communist, who might have been a target of the 1947 Hollywood hearings if he had been important enough at the time. Prior to 1947, however, he had directed only one Hollywood film, *A Tree Grows in Brooklyn* (1945). This sentimental Twentieth Century–Fox film was not enough to bring its director before the Committee. By 1950, however, Kazan was the most famous stage director on Broadway, having directed the premieres of *A Streetcar Named Desire* (1947) and *Death of a Salesman* (1949). He had won an Oscar for *Gentleman's Agreement* (1947), which, with its attack on anti-Semitism, was considered suspiciously "pink" by anti-Communists, and he had just earned the directing credit for the then daringly anti-racist film *Pinky* (1949). (He saved *Pinky* for Darrel F. Zanuck after John Ford had walked off the set in a disagreement with Ethel Waters.) In 1950, Kazan's Hollywood career was picking up steam, and he had more to lose with each assignment.

Unlike Foreman, however, Kazan was a deeply disaffected former Communist. By his own account, his political thinking had evolved into a cross between liberalism and "individualism" by 1950, a stance which put him at odds not only with his former Communist friends, but with most Americans who considered themselves left-of-center:

> I was not part of any group except the biggest one; I was an ordinary American. I began to have some idea of what that was. Like the rest of the country's men, I was independent and needn't fear anyone. I didn't have a cellmaster or a *führer*. All around me were my fellow citizens, people, not stars with their plump, soft-skinned, indoor faces. I was in the land of the free and I was free and could do whatever I wished.[12]

Along with this newfound sense of individual freedom, Kazan had the feeling that post-war Communism had become an increasing threat. One of the film projects he was working on in the late forties was a script about a colony of Greek sponge fishermen whose way of life is threatened by an approaching red tide. The symbolism is obvious.

It was his collaborator on this project, Richard Murphy, who had also done the screenplay for Kazan's film *Boomerang* (1947), and whom Darryl

Zanuck had assigned to take on the screenplay of what was then called *Outbreak*. The script had already been through many drafts, starting with the Oscar-winning story by Edna and Edward Anhalt, and passing though the hands of Daniel Fuchs, who was credited with the adaptation. Kazan was persuaded to work on the film with the promise that he could film it all on location, changing the scene from San Francisco to New Orleans. The script was a real collaboration between Kazan and Murphy, with changes and rewrites being made on the set every day. Kazan made full use of the city and its people, giving many of the smaller parts to its citizens, and often allowing them to improvise their lines. In the end he gave parts to 114 non-actors.[13] This was important because it is the city's people who create the tension of the film, and Kazan has a brilliance for creating depictions of ordinary people. Unlike a Marxist film-maker, however, Kazan's intention was to establish the people not as protagonist, but as antagonist. The hero of his film is an individual, an "expert," a member of the knowledge-elite, although Kazan makes it very clear that he is a member of the middle class in economic terms through a subplot about the tension his lack of money creates in his home life. "The people" are in the film chiefly to get in his way. He has to save them from themselves by keeping them in ignorance and secretly applying his special expertise to their problem.

Like the Thebes of *Oedipus Rex*, the New Orleans of *Panic in the Streets* faces an epidemic. An illegal Armenian immigrant has come ashore from a ship where he was a stowaway and been killed by three low-life gangsters after he cheated them in a card game. The pathologist who does the autopsy finds that the dead man had pneumonic plague, a disease that is sure to cause an epidemic if those who come in contact with it are not inoculated within 48 hours. The film's hero, Clint Reed (Richard Widmark), is a Navy doctor who is attached to the Public Health Service. He must find out who had contact with the dead man within the last 48 hours of his life and inoculate them if he is to save the city. In order to do this, he has to battle the Mayor's office and the police, who have a hard time taking the threat seriously, as well as a nosy reporter, Neff, who wants to print the story. Several times throughout the film, Reed has to take action in order to keep Neff from breaking the story because, as he explains several times, if the public finds out there is a threat of plague, everyone will leave town and spread the disease all over the country.

While the main plotline is the detective story of finding the killers, and therefore the disease, a subplot develops around the relationship between Reed and Police Captain Warren (Paul Douglas). Warren is at first suspicious of Reed as a "college man" whom he suspects of stirring up trouble over nothing in order to appear important, but he comes to respect Reed's knowledge and, more importantly, to acknowledge his authority. For his part, Reed comes to admire Warren for his "guts." The incident that elicits his admiration is a revealing one. When reporter Neff finally figures out that something big is going on, he confronts Reed: "You and the Public Health Service are turning this town upside down. . . . I want to know why this story wasn't released to the press." Reed tells him that he can't "allow" him to print the story, saying "I represent the public health." Neff responds: "Well I represent the public, and they have a right to know what's going on." Captain Warren has Neff arrested, and he is dragged out by two policemen, threatening that he will have Warren's badge for this. When Reed asks a policeman if Neff can make good on his threats, he replies that, if Neff's newspaper decided to "make trouble" for Warren, he'd be lucky to get a job mopping floors. Thus reporter Neff, who is the subject of false arrest for exercising his right, indeed his duty as a reporter, to inform the public, becomes the persecutor, and Warren, the public official who has just abused his power, becomes the victim. In a later scene, the mayor complains about the arrest, and his assistant says that the only chance for full cooperation with the investigation is to inform the public fully. When Reed reminds them that the killers will leave town if they're informed, and that they can be anywhere in the world in ten hours, infecting the populace there, the mayor says that he agrees with Reed, but that he couldn't hold Neff. It seems to be a case of the pesky Constitution interfering with the efficiency of the expert.

The use of the disease and contamination imagery in this film could not be more obvious. Like the mind-disease of Communism as depicted by J. Edgar Hoover, the contamination of the plague spreads instantaneously from person to person without the knowledge or volition of its carriers or victims. Dr. Reed, the lone individual who possesses the special knowledge that can save the country from this plague, is caught between the suspicion and ignorance of the institutions of authority on the one hand and the potentially hysterical public's "right to know" on the other. His conviction that secrecy and covert detective work is necessary to root out the plague is constantly being thwarted by the desire of the politicians on the one hand and the press on the other to expose the threat to the public. Foreman depicted the individual as the lone target of HUAC investigators who is deserted by the people. Kazan depicted him as the expert who could help to rid the country of Communism if only he were not exposed to public view. This is in keeping with Kazan's own response to the Committee. He testified in secret in January 1952 and in private executive session in April of that year, and the Committee made his testimony public the next day. The film celebrates the individual expert, placing his usefulness to society above that of both established institutional authority and the people, as well as the people's representative, the press.

Along with the contamination imagery, the film makes full use of anti-Communism's other metaphoric arsenal, xenophobia. As Peter Biskind has pointed out: "the smelly morass of working-class ethnics – Greeks, Italians, Armenians, and Eastern Europeans that make up the waterfront community – incubate, nurture, and spread the plague; in fact, they *are* the plague, which becomes, finally, a metaphor for the threat the lower orders pose to the higher ones, that foreigners pose to the native-born."[14] The plague is brought into the country by an illegal Armenian immigrant and is spread to his cousin, who brings it to a Greek restaurant, whose proprietors, a husband and wife, refuse to give information until the wife dies. The implications of this trope, coming from two Greek immigrants, Kazan and Spyros Skouras, the executive president of Twentieth Century–Fox, are unmistakable. Good Americans cooperate. Foreigners who resist what's good for them may not survive. Skouras was soon to pressure Kazan into testifying before HUAC as a friendly witness.

The other potential source of contamination is the ship that brought the stowaway. In a scene aboard the ship, Reed's men find rats and a sick Asian cook, equally dangerous, it seems, as sources for the plague. The captain at first resists Reed's desire to inoculate the men, but Reed persists despite the fact that he is told by a Navy officer that he has no authority on the ship: "We're in International waters. This man is master of the vessel. We have no authority here." When he finally persuades the captain that the cook suffers from plague, and that everyone on the ship may have been infected, the captain agrees to put himself in Reed's hands, quarantining the ship under his command. Thus the expert's inherent authority extends beyond national borders to anywhere the contamination may strike, and the threat from rats and foreigners is contained.

In the end, Reed thwarts the disease through his scientific knowledge and the force of his character, persuading those infected to agree to inoculation and/or quarantine. The only ones who resist him, the two surviving gangsters who killed the original victim, are caught in the end like rats, as they race through the waterfront trying to escape from Reed and Warren. Finally Fitch (Zero Mostel) is shot by Blackie (Walter [Jack] Palance) in the back. Blackie is prevented by a rat-shield from climbing up a rope to get onto a ship, falls in the water, and is fished out by the police, like a drowned rat. Again the anti-Communist imagery is unmistakable: the carriers of disease, the rats, must be destroyed if the community is to be saved from contamination. The film ends on a note of community, as Reed and Warren, friends now, drive up to Reed's house on his tree-lined suburban street, a marked contrast to the dismal waterfront of the previous scene. They bid each other a cheerful farewell as Reed goes to join his family, having purged the community of contamination and made it safe for the middle class once more. The implication is that the anti-Communist "experts" can save the country, if the institutional authorities cooperate, and if the press can be effectively muzzled and kept from letting the people know just what they are up to.

These two examples show the extent to which the issues surrounding the activities of the House Committee on Un-American Activities penetrated the collective Hollywood consciousness in the late forties and early fifties. Films that treat Communism directly, such as *The Red Menace* (1949), *I Married a Communist* (1950), *I Was a Communist for the FBI* (1951), *My Son John* (1952), *Big Jim McLain* (1952), *Walk East on Beacon* (1952), and *Storm Center* (1956), are less revealing than those that convey meaning through the imaginative techniques of image, metaphor, allegory, and analogy. The same is true for the New York theatre, where the history plays that have been discussed here present the social, moral, and political issues arising from the Committee's activities more powerfully and more provocatively than such direct treatments of Communism as Wouk's *The Traitor* (1949), Theodore Apstein's *The Innkeepers* (1955), Fast's *Thirty Pieces of Silver* (1954), Robert Ardrey's *Sing Me No Lullaby* (1954), and Donald Freed's *Inquest* (1969) ever do.

In singling out the treatments of the Un-American Activities Committee and focusing on the aesthetics of historical analogy, I have tackled only a modest corner of this potentially enormous field of study. There is much work to be done if we are to understand the political and cultural implications of the plays, films, and teleplays that were written by Americans who lived through this politically and ideologically charged period. Each year brings more information in the form of declassified documents, memoirs and biographies, interviews, and historical studies. Many more cultural texts will reward further reading, viewing, study, and analysis.

Notes

Introduction

1. Quoted in Christine Doudna, "A Still Unfinished Woman: A Conversation with Lillian Hellman," *Rolling Stone* 233 (24 February 1977: 52–7; rpt. Jackson R. Bryer, ed. *Conversations with Lillian Hellman* (Jackson: UP of Mississippi, 1986): 196.
2. The term "McCarthyism," coined by cartoonist Herbert Block, is defined as "(1) The political practice of publicizing accusations of disloyalty or subversion with insufficient regard to evidence. (2) The use of methods of investigation and accusation regarded as unfair, in order to suppress opposition" (*The American Heritage Dictionary of the English Language*, New College Edition, ed. William Morris [Boston: Houghton Mifflin, 1978]).
3. See, for example, Larry Ceplair and Steven Englund, *The Inquisition in Hollywood* (Garden City, N.Y.: Doubleday, 1980); John Cogley, *Report on Blacklisting*, 2 vols. (New York: Fund for the Republic, 1956); Robert Vaughn, *Only Victims* (New York: Putnam, 1972); Griffin Fariello, *Red Scare* (New York: Norton, 1995); Dalton Trumbo, *The Time of the Toad* (New York: Perennial Library, 1972); "Midsection: Notes on the Blacklist," *Film Comment* 23 (November/December 1987): 37–59, and Herbert Mitgang, *Dangerous Dossiers* (New York: Donald I. Fine, 1988). The best single history of the Committee is Walter Goodman, *The Committee* (New York: Farrar, Straus and Giroux, 1968). Eric Bentley's *Thirty Years of Treason* (New York: Viking, 1971) contains nearly 1,000 pages of edited testimony from the hearings. Good general treatments of the politics can be found in Stephen J. Whitfield, *The Culture of the Cold War* (Baltimore: Johns Hopkins UP, 1991); Stefan Kanfer, *A Journal of the Plague Years* (New York: Atheneum, 1973); David Caute, *The Great Fear* (New York: Simon & Schuster, 1978); David Halberstam, *The Fifties* (New York: Villard, 1993); and I. F. Stone, *The Haunted Fifties* (London: Merlin, 1963). Among the most important of the memoirs for this study are Lillian Hellman, *Scoundrel Time* (Boston: Little, Brown, 1976); Arthur Miller, *Timebends: A Life* (New York: Grove, 1987); Elia Kazan, *Elia Kazan: A Life* (New York: Knopf, 1988), Abraham Polonsky, "The Effects of the 'Blacklist' on a Writer" (*New York Times* Oral History Collection, Part I, No. 16); Walter Bernstein, *Inside Out* (New York: Knopf, 1996), Edward Dmytryk, *Odd Man Out* (Carbondale, Southern Illinois UP,

1996); and Howard Fast, *Being Red* (Boston: Houghton Mifflin, 1990).

4. See, for example, Eric Bentley, *The Theatre of Commitment* (New York: Athenaeum, 1967); C. W. E. Bigsby, *Confrontation and Commitment: A Study of Contemporary American Drama, 1959–1966* (Columbia: U of Missouri P, 1968) and *A Critical Introduction to Twentieth-Century American Drama.* Vol. 2. (Cambridge and New York: Cambridge UP, 1984); and Joseph Wood Krutch, *American Drama Since 1918* (New York: Braziller, 1957).

5. For a broader perspective, see Albert Wertheim, "The McCarthy Era and the American Theatre," *Theatre Journal* 34.2 (1982): 211–22; Richard G. Scharine, *From Class to Caste in American Drama: Political and Social Themes Since the 1930s* (Westport, Conn.: Greenwood, 1991); and Gerald Weales, "Arthur Miller and the 1950s," *Michigan Quarterly Review* 37.4 (Fall 1998): 635–51.

Chapter 1: The Stage is Set

1. *New York Times,* 14 September 1948: 1.
2. *New York Times,* 14 September 1948: 1.
3. Walter Goodman, *The Committee: The Extraordinary Career of the House Committee on Un-American Activities)* New York: Farrar, Straus and Giroux, 1968), 17.
4. Alien Registration Act of 1940, Section 2 (a) 3.
5. Goodman *Committee*, 326.
6. McCarran Internal Security Act, Section 103 (a).
7. John Wexley, *The Judgment of Julius and Ethel Rosenberg* (New York: Cameron & Kahn, 1955), 148.
8. Larry Ceplair & Steven Englund, *The Inquisition in Hollywood: Politics in the Film Community 1930–1960* (Garden City, N.Y.: Anchor/Doubleday, 1980), 216.
9. Goodman, *Committee*, 265.
10. "Theatre Project Faces an Inquiry," *New York Times,* 27 July 1938: 19.
11. "Dies Inquiry Gets Income Tax Books," *New York Times,* 10 August 1938: 6.
12. Goodman, *Committee*, 45.
13. House Special Committee on Un-American Activities (HUAC), Public Hearings, Vol. 4, 6 December 1938; rpt. Eric Bentley, *Thirty Years of Treason: Excerpts from Hearings Before the House Committee on Un-American Activities, 1938–1968* (New York: Viking, 1971): 25.
14. Hallie Flanagan, *Arena: The Story of the Federal Theatre* (1940; rpt. New York: Limelight, 1969), 342.
15. HUAC Hearings, 6 December 1938.
    So powerful was this moment as a crystallization of some of the most ridiculous aspects of the Committee's investigation of the arts, that it became a touchstone for critics of the Committee and defenders of the witnesses. When a similar embarrassment threatened during the examination of Joseph Papp in 1958, Staff Director Richard Arens was quick to intervene:

Mr. Moulder: Do you have the opportunity to inject into your plays or into the acting or the entertainment supervision which you have, any propaganda in any way which would influence others to be sympathetic with the Communist philosophy or the beliefs of communism?

Mr. Papirofsky: Sir, the plays we do are Shakespeare's plays. Shakespeare said, 'To thine own self be true,' and various other lines from Shakespeare can hardly be said to be subversive or influencing minds. I cannot control the writings of Shakespeare. . . .

Mr. Arens: We are not concerned with the plays, and you know we are not, and there is no suggestion here by this chairman or anyone else that Shakespeare was a Communist. That is ludicrous and absurd. That is the Commie line. The inquiry of this Committee is solely with reference to Communist activities, Communist propaganda, the extent to which Communists, people in the Communist Party, have used their prestige in the theater to promote Communists; and for you to twist this testimony in the presence of the public press here to give an implication that the chairman is trying to elicit information from you that Shakespeare was subversive, or this committee is investigating Shakespeare, investigating that type of thing, is not only ludicrous, but it is highly unfair.

Mr. Papirofsky: I am sorry. I think you misunderstand me.

Mr. Arens: I did not misunderstand you.

[HUAC, Public Hearings, Communism in the New York Area, 19 June 1958: 2556–7.]

16. Flanagan, *Arena*, 362.
17. Ibid. 334.
18. "Pinks Plan to Stalinize Studios," *Variety*, 16 September 1933: 1, 3.
19. Goodman, *Committee*, 106 and Ceplair & Englund, 156–7.
20. Ceplair & Englund, 157.
21. "Links Movie Chiefs to 'Big Plot on U. S.,'" *New York Times*, 1 July 1945: 20.
22. Goodman, *Committee*, 213.
23. Ceplair & Englund, 289.
24. "The combination of subpoenas, contempt citations, and blacklists pried 250 names of 'Communists' from the mouths of 'friendly witnesses.' Another 40 to 50 Party members had died, had left Hollywood early on, or were overlooked by the FBI and the informers" (Ceplair & Englund, 65).
25 Gladwin Hill, "Says Government Aided Film Reds," *New York Times*, 17 May 1947: 8.
26. Goodman, *Committee*, 214.
27. Ibid. 214.
28. Cabell Phillips, "Un-American Committee Puts on Its 'Big Show,'" *New York Times*, 26 October 1947: IV, 7.
29. Ibid.
30. Ibid.
31. Ceplair & Englund, 279–87.
32. Ceplair & Englund, 280.
33. Ceplair & Englund, 281.
34. HUAC, Public Hearings Regarding Communist Infiltration of the Motion-Picture Industry, 21 October 1947: 92.
35. Ibid. 104.
36. Ibid. 23 October 1947: 224.

37. Ibid. 27 October 1947: 294–5.
38. Bertolt Brecht, who, as an alien, did not think he could rely on the Constitutional rights of Americans, testified that he had never been member of the Communist Party and departed immediately for Switzerland.
39. Goodman, *Committee*, 234.
40. Ibid. 236.
41. Ibid. 229.
42. Ibid. 229 [Hearing, October 20, 1947: 53].
43. Ceplair & Englund, 331. Article 16 reads: "At all times commencing on the date hereof and continuing throughout the production and distribution of the Pictures, the [artist] will conduct himself with due regard to the public conventions and morals, and will not do anything which will tend to degrade him in society or bring him into public disrepute, contempt, scorn, or ridicule, or that will tend to shock, insult, or offend the community or public morals of decency or prejudice the corporation or the motion picture industry in general."
44. "Movies to Oust Ten Cited for Contempt of Congress," *New York Times*, 26 November 1947: 27.
45. Ring Lardner, Jr., "My Life on the Black List," *Saturday Evening Post* 234 (14 October 1961): 40.
46. *Safeguarding Civil Liberties*, UCLA: Oral History Project, 1974: 120.
47. Bentley, *Thirty Years*, 196. Brewer later explained: "We had a program of separating the hard-core Communist from those who were duped into going along. Once they were isolated and people knew them, then they were no problem. . . . As links showed up, the MPA would publicize them. For example, if something surfaced that proved a certain person was a Communist agent, we would simply expose it. That's all you needed to do. Once they were exposed, they couldn't work. Any man that admitted that he was a Communist during that period would've been fired. And there was no blacklist, in its true sense" (quoted in Griffin Fariello, *Red Scare: Memories of the American Inquisition, an Oral History* [New York: Norton, 1995], 115).
48. Ceplair & Englund, 387. See also John Cogley, *Report on Blacklisting*, Vol. I, *Movies* (New York: Fund for the Republic, 1956), 97, 110–11, 127.
49. Quoted in Fariello, 322–3.
50. John Cogley, *Report on Blacklisting*, Vol. II, *Radio-Television* (New York: The Fund for the Republic, 1956), 93–9.
51. Goodman, *Committee*, 404.
52. Ceplair & Englund, 295–6.
53. Screen Actors Guild Board to Gale Sondergaard, 20 March 1951, quoted in Ceplair & Englund, 367–8.
54. Ceplair & Englund, 367.
55. Goodman, *Committee*, 327–8.
56. Ceplair & Englund, 371.
57. *New York Herald Tribune*, 19 August 1955.
58. HUAC, Public Hearings on Communist Infiltration of the Motion-Picture Industry, Part 1, 21 March 1951: 107.

59. Ibid. 110.
60. Quoted in Victor Navasky, *Naming Names* (New York: Viking Penguin, 1980), 373.
61. HUAC, Public Hearings, Investigation of Communist Activities in the New York Area, Part 3, 6 May 1953: 1347.
62. Ibid. 1350.
63. David Platt, *People's Daily World*, 27 March 1951; quoted in Bentley, *Thirty Years*, 299.
64. *New York Times*, 12 April 1951: 7.
65. Bentley, 486. Kazan has denied that any such thing occurred, calling Kraber's statement the "'big lie' technique of Hitler" and maintaining that "the truth was that Darryl [Zanuck] had called me into his office and explained that since I was now a controversial figure, he couldn't pay me my salary or anything like it on the last picture remaining on my contract" [*Elia Kazan: A Life*. New York: Knopf, 1988, 469–70].
66. Samuel Sillen, *Daily Worker*, 17 April 1952; quoted in Hoover, *Masters*, 183.
67. Goodman, *Committee*, 402.

Chapter 2: The Social Drama

1. Victor Turner, *The Anthropology of Performance* (New York: PAJ, 1987), 33.
2. Victor Turner, *Schism and Continuity in African Life* (Manchester: Manchester UP, 1957), 93.
3. Ibid.
4. Victor Turner, "Liminality and the Performative Genres," in *Rite, Drama, Festival, Spectacle: Rehearsals Toward a Theory of Cultural Performance*, ed. John J. MacAloon (Philadelphia: ISHI, 1984), 24–5.
5. The discussion of the drama from which this and subsequent quotations are drawn appears in Turner's *Anthropology of Performance*, 34–5.
6. Walter Goodman, *The Committee: The Extraordinary Career of the House Committee on Un-American Activities* (New York: Farrar, Straus, and Giroux, 1968), 5.
7. J. Edgar Hoover, *Masters of Deceit: The Story of Communism in America and How to Fight It* (New York: Holt, 1958), vi.
8. Ibid. 72.
9. Larry Ceplair & Steven Englund, *The Inquisition in Hollywood: Politics in the Film Community 1930–1960* (New York: Anchor/Doubleday, 1980), 99–100.
10. Ibid. 98.
11. Anti-Communists actually used this language. In his interrogation of Abe Burrows, John S. Wood tried to assay the extent of Burrows' guilt for being friendly with Communists, while having no political or ideological interest in the Party:

   Mr. Burrows: I didn't say I was by association. But I say they thought me one, and I was assumed to be one, and I am not denying they had a right to.
   Mr. Wood: You mean to say that, to a full extent you conducted yourself and participated in all of the Communist activities at that time with a reservation in your own heart?

Mr Burrows: Yes, sir. That is very well put. [HUAC, Public Hearings, Communist Infiltration of Hollywood Motion-Picture Industry, Part 10, 12 November 1952: 4501.]

12. Hoover, *Masters*, 89.
13. HUAC, Public Hearings, Communist Infiltration of the Hollywood Motion-Picture Industry, Part 3, 22 May 1951: 536.
14. Ibid. Part 2, 25 April 1951: 412.
15. Hoover, *Masters*, 5.
16. Ibid. 5.
17. Ceplair & Englund, 202.
18. Ceplair & Englund, 203.
19. Quoted in Eric Bentley, *Thirty Years of Treason: Excerpts from Hearings before the House Committee on Un-American Activities, 1938–1968* (New York: Viking, 1971), 39.
20. Hoover, *Masters*, 4.
21. Ibid. 84.
22. Ibid. 89.
23. HUAC, Executive Hearing, Communist Infiltration of the Hollywood Motion-Picture Industry, 21 March 1951, Executive Session.
24. HUAC, Public Hearings, Subversive Involvement in Disruption of the Democratic Party National Convention, 5 December 1968: 2809.
25. Sir James George Frazer, *The Golden Bough* (1922; rpt. New York: Macmillan, 1963), 666.
26. Ibid.
27. Goodman, *Committee*, 236–7.
28. René Girard, *The Scapegoat*, trans. Yvonne Freccero (Baltimore: Johns Hopkins UP: 1986), 15.
29. Committee on Un-American Activities, U. S. House of Representatives, *100 Things You Should Know About Communism in the U. S. A.* House Document No. 136, 82nd Congress, 1st Session, *House Documents*, Vol. 7, 3 January–20 October, 1951: 6.
30. HUAC, *100 Things You Should Know About Communism and Education*. Ibid. 47.
31. *100 Things You Should Know About Communism in the U. S. A.*, 13, 20.
32. *100 Things You Should Know About Communism and Education*, 55.
33. *100 Things You Should Know About Communism in the U. S. A.*, 16.
34. Girard, *Scapegoat*, 14–15.
35. *Congressional Record*, 19 February 1946; quoted in Goodman, *Committee*, 182.
36. Hoover, *Masters*, 26.
37. Ibid. vi.
38. Richard M. Nixon, "Plea for an Anti-Communist Faith," *Saturday Review of Literature*, 24 May 1952: 12.
39. Hoover, *Masters*, 319.
40. Ibid. 55, 45, 35.
41. *100 Things You Should Know About Communism and Religion*, 35.
42. HUAC, Public Hearings, Investigation of Communism in the Metropolitan Music School, 11 April 1957: 783.

43. Richard Schechner, "Victor Turner's Last Adventure," in Turner, *The Anthropology of Performance* (New York: PAJ, 1987), 10.
44. Turner, *Anthropology*, 70.
45. Bentley, *Thirty Years*, 947.
46. Girard, *Scapegoat*, 169.
47. Turner, *Anthropology*, 150.
48. HUAC, Public Hearings, Regarding Communist Infiltration of the Motion-Picture Industry, 29 October 1947: 453.
49. HUAC, Public Hearings, Communist Methods of Infiltration (Education), 26 February 1953: 113.
50. HUAC, Public Hearings, Investigation of Communist Activities in the New York City Area, Part 3, 6 May 1953: 1344.
51. Ibid. 1354–6.
52. Girard, *Scapegoat*, 12.
53. Ibid. 12.
54. HUAC, Public Hearings on HR 4422 and HR 4581, Proposed Legislation to Curb or Control the Communist Party of the United States, 10 February 1948; quoted in Bentley, *Thirty Years*, 259.
55. Girard, *Scapegoat*, 40.
56. Ibid. 39.
57. Girard, *Scapegoat*, 8.
58. Hoover, *Masters*, 83.
59. Ibid. 77–8.
60. Ceplair & Englund, 243.
61. Hoover, *Masters*, 303.
62. Girard, *Scapegoat*, 36.
63. Roy Brewer, I. E. Chadwick, Art Arthur, Ronald Reagan, Jack Dales, and Alexander Kempner, "You Can Be Free Men Again!" *Hollywood Reporter*, 6 June 1952; rpt. Bentley, *Thirty Years*, 405.
64. Hearings, 10 February 1948; quoted in Bentley, *Thirty Years*, 256.
65. Girard, *Scapegoat*, 35.
66. Hoover, *Masters*, 103.
67. HUAC, Public Hearings Regarding Hanns Eisler, 24 September 1947: 60.
68. HUAC, Public Hearings, Communist Infiltration of the Hollywood Motion-Picture Industry, Part 7, 28 February 1952: 2364.
69. "Garfield, Ferrer 'Investigate' Selves as Prelude to April 20 Red Hearings," *Variety*, 11 April 1951; rpt. Bentley, *Thirty Years*, 296.
70. Girard, *Scapegoat*, 43.
71. Hearings, 19 February 1948, quoted in Bentley, *Thirty Years*, 277.
72. Girard, *Scapegoat*, 105.
73. Quoted in Stephen J. Whitfield, *The Culture of the Cold War* (Baltimore: Johns Hopkins UP, 1991), 81.
74. Girard, *Scapegoat*, 86.
75. HUAC, Public Hearings, Regarding Communist Infiltration of the Motion-Picture Industry, 29 October 1947: 401.
76. Goodman, *Committee*, 325.
77. Ibid. 325.

78. HUAC, Public Hearings, Regarding Communist Infiltration of the Motion Picture Industry, 27 October 1947: 293–5.
79. Hearings, 29 October 1947: 442.
80. For a full discussion of the waiver doctrine, see Victor Navasky, *Naming Names* (New York: Viking Penguin, 1981), 34.
81. John Sanford has explained how he developed the "diminished Fifth" strategy for his wife, screenwriter Marguerite Roberts: "I said, 'This is what you're going to do. When they ask you the question, 'Are you now or have you ever been a Communist?' your answer will be 'I am not a Communist.' They won't let you stop there. They'll say, 'Were you ever?' Then you take the Fifth Amendment. But you are not a Communist. . . . You're telling the studio that you're not a Communist." (quoted in Griffin Fariello, *Red Scare: Memories of the American Inquisition, An Oral History* (New York: Norton, 1995), 290.
82. HUAC, Public Hearings, Communist Infiltration of the Hollywood Motion-Picture Industry, Part 7, 30 April 1952: 2417.
83. Quoted in Walter Goodman, "How Not to Produce a Film," *New Republic* 127 (26 December 1955): 13.
84. Quoted in Fariello, 258.
85. Quoted in Goodman, *Committee*, 435.
86. HUAC, Public Hearings, Communist Infiltration of the Hollywood Motion-Picture Industry, Part 1, 21 March 1951: 83.
87. Goodman, *Committee*, 316.
88. Navasky, *Naming Names*, 28–29.
89. "Loyal Actors Call for Film Industry Purge of all Subversives," *Los Angeles Evening Herald & Express*, 23 March 1951; rpt. Bentley, *Thirty Years*, 299.
90. "The Truth About the 'Blacklist,'" quoted in Bentley, *Thirty Years*, 202.
91. "Reds Talk or Face Jailing, Says Dies," *New York Times*, 27 March 1940: 13.
92. Goodman, *Committee*, 315.
93. Ceplair & Englund 371–2.
94. HUAC, Public Hearings, Regarding Communist Infiltration of the Motion-Picture Industry, 30 October 1947: 515.
95. Ibid. 518–19.
96. HUAC, Public Hearings, Communist Infiltration of the Hollywood Motion-Picture Industry, Part 1, 21 March 1951: 95.
97. HUAC, Public Hearings, Communist Methods of Infiltration (Education), 25 February 1953: 43.
98. HUAC, Public Hearings, Communist Infiltration of the Hollywood Motion-Picture Industry, 21 March 1951: 93–4.
99. Lillian Hellman to John S. Wood, 19 May 1952, recorded in HUAC, Public Hearings, Communist Infiltration of the Hollywood Motion-Picture Industry, Part 8, 21 May 1952: 3545–6.
100. John S. Wood to Lillian Hellman, recorded in Hearings, Ibid., 3546.
101. Lillian Hellman to John S. Wood.
102. HUAC, Public Hearings, Investigation of the Unauthorized Use of U. S. Passports, Part 4, 21 June 1956: 4685–8.
103. HUAC, Public Hearings, Investigation of Communist Activities in the Los Angeles Area, Part 6, 2 June 1953: 2356.

104. HUAC, Public Hearings, Communist Infiltration of the Hollywood Motion-Picture Industry, Part 1, 21 March 1951: 107.
105. Larry Parks to Harold Velde, 15 July 1953, quoted in Bentley, *Thirty Years*, 346.
106. "The Night Ed Murrow Struck Back," *Esquire* 100 (December 1983): 467.
107. "Praise Pours in on Murrow Show," *New York Times,* 11 March 1954: 19.
108. Goodman, *Committee*, 463.
109. Bentley, *Thirty Years*, 951.
110. Passport Hearings, 21 June 1956.
111. HUAC, Public Hearings on Bills to Make Punishable Assistance to Enemies of the U. S. in Times of Undeclared War, Part 1, 19 August 1966: 1204.
112. HUAC, Public Hearings, Subversive Involvement in Disruption of the 1968 Democratic Party Convention, 2 December 1968: 2498.
113. *Watkins v. U.S.* (354 U.S. 178). See Goodman, *Committee*, 378, 379.
114. *Barenblatt v. U.S.* (360 U.S. 109). See Victor Rabinowitz, *Unrepentant Leftist: A Lawyer's Memoir* (Champaign: U of Illinois P, 1996).
115. Goodman, *Committee*, 503–4.
116. Ibid. 480.

Chapter 3: Dramatizing Directly

1. Dorothy B. Jones, "Communism and the Movies," in John Cogley, *Report on Blacklisting*, Vol. I, *Movies* (New York: Fund for the Republic, 1956), 215.
2. Jones, 231.
3. Karel Reisz, "Hollywood's Anti-Red Boomerang: Apple Pie, Love, and Endurance versus The Commies," *Sight and Sound* 22 (January–March 1953): 135.
4. Reisz, 132–5.
5. Nora Sayre, *Running Time: Films of the Cold War* (New York: Dial, 1982), 80.
6. Sayre, 82–3.
7. Victor Navasky, *Naming Names* (New York: Viking Penguin, 1981), 42 n.
8. Quoted in Randy Roberts and James S. Olson, *John Wayne: American* (New York: Free Press, 1995), 377.
9. Roberts and Olson, 378.
10. "Big Jim McLain," *Time,* 29 September 1952: 93.
11. Bosley Crowther, "Big Jim McLain," *New York Times*, 18 September 1952: 35.
12. Otis L. Guernsey, "Big Jim McLain," *New York Herald-Tribune*, 15 September 1952.
13. "Brog.," "Big Jim McLain," *Variety*, 27 August 1952: 6.
14. William Whitebait, *The New Statesman and Nation* 44 (1 November 1952): 509.
15. *Thirty Pieces of Silver* (New York: Blue Heron Press, 1954), 5.
16. In his memoir *Being Red*, Fast explains how he learned from his 1,100–page FBI file how important this agency considered the play. He says that the FBI had become aware of the play – which was published in book form in England – from a European 'informant,' as they put it, and they asked for a copy

of the play. Even though it was then running in three European theaters, their informants could find neither a copy nor an abstract. The FBI, as their record in my file states, then handed the problem over to the Central Intelligence Agency. After several weeks, this brilliant organization . . . sent their memo to the FBI, admitting that they were unsuccessful in obtaining a copy of the Howard Fast play. It had meanwhile been copyrighted and published in the United States, but neither of these organizations . . . thought of going to the Library of Congress, where the play could be had simply for the asking. (*Being Red* [Boston: Houghton Mifflin, 1990], 158–9)

17. "The Missing Communist" (1956; rpt. *What Is Theatre?* New York: Atheneum, 1968), 313.

18. HUAC, Public Hearings, Investigation of Unauthorized Use of U. S. Passports, Part 4, 21 June 1956: 4683. Subsequent quotations are from the same hearing.

19. A mimeographed copy of *You're Next*, subtitled *A Political Playlet*, resides in the John Gassner Collection, Harry Ransom Humanities Research Center, University of Texas at Austin. The script is undated, but bears the notation "produced by Stage for Action, 130 W. 42nd St., New York, NY." My thanks to Curator Melissa Miller for bringing the script to my attention. Page references appear in the text.

20. Arthur Miller, *Timebends* (New York; Grove, 1987), 229.

21. Ibid. 230.

22. Ira A. Levine, *Left-Wing Dramatic Theory in the American Theatre* (Ann Arbor: UMI, 1985), 84.

23. Ibid. 124.

24. Eric Bentley, ed. *Thirty Years of Treason: Excerpts from Hearings before the House Committee on Un-American Activities, 1938–1968.* (New York: Viking, 1971), xxviii. Of course one witness, Paul Robeson did have the temerity to question his interrogators about their names and where they lived, and Bentley features that testimony in *Are You Now*.

25. Eric Bentley, *Rallying Cries: Three Plays* (Evanston, Ill.: Northwestern University Press, 1977), 3.

26. Ibid. 4.

27. Ibid. 3.

28. Gwyn Sullivan, "'50s Politics Through a Needle's Eye," New York *News World*, 22 October 1978: 2B.

29. Victor Navasky, *Naming Names* (New York: Viking, 1980), 314–29. See also Harold Garfinkel, "Conditions of Successful Degradation Ceremonies," *American Journal of Sociology* 61 (January 1956): 420–24.

30. "Are You Now or Have You Ever Been," *Yale Alumni Magazine* (January 1973): 26.

31. "Bentley on Blacklisting," *New York Times*, 29 January 1979: C12.

32. "Yale Rep to Premiere New Documentary Drama," clippings file, Billy Rose Theatre Collection, New York Public Library for the Performing Arts.

33. John Beaufort, "Are You Now . . . " *Christian Science Monitor*, 5 December 1973: B10.

34. Jules Chametzky, "From HUAC to Watergate," *Performance* 7 (Fall 1973): 23.

35. Ibid. 23.
36. Victoria Radin, "Are You Now or Have You Ever Been," London *Observer,* 12 June 1977: 26.
37. "Pit.," "Are You Now or Have You Ever Been," *Variety,* 2 November 1977: 84.
38. Ted Whitehead, "Red Devils," *Spectator,* 5 November 1977: 27.
39. Chametzky, 21.
40. Sullivan, 2B.
41. "Pit.," 84.
42. Susan Corbett, "Are You Now Or Have You Ever Been," *The Stage & Television Today* 23 (June 1977): 11.
43. John Peter, "Theatre" *The Sunday Times* (London), 4 September 1977.
44. Stephen J. Whitfield, *The Culture of the Cold War* (Baltimore: Johns Hopkins U P, 1991), 119–20
45. Ernest Kinoy, quoted in Jeff Kisseloff, *The Box: An Oral History of Television, 1920–1961* (New York: Viking, 1995), 428. According to producer Robert Markell, when the CBS executives first saw the script for "Blacklist," they said, "'It has to be about the movies. It can't be about television, because there's no blacklist in television" (Kisseloff, 429).
46. Walter Goodman, "How Not to Produce a Film," *The New Republic* 127, (26 December 1955): 13.
47. Ibid. 13.
48. Ernest Kinoy, "Blacklist," in *Electronic Drama: Television Plays of the Sixties,* ed. Richard Avedon and David Manning White (Boston: Beacon, 1971), 107. Videotape at Museum of Television and Radio, New York.
49. The published script reads: "It's a heresy hunt . . . a lynching for unpopular political opinions. Who gave Judson Kyle the right to be prosecutor and judge and jury and executioner" (112).
50. The published script reads: "No climax. No rescue. No neat satisfying ending. We do the best we can with the next case" (134).
51. The published script reads: "People are afraid . . . afraid of Communists . . . Socialists . . . anybody – They're not sure who" (134).
52. "Still With Us," *The Commonweal* 79 (31 January 1964): 495.
53. "A Report on Senator Joseph R. McCarthy," *See It Now,* CBS Television, 9 March 1954. Rpt. ed. Edward Bliss, Jr., *In Search of Light: The Broadcasts of Edward R. Murrow 1938–1961.* (New York: Knopf, 1967), 247–8.
54. Whitfield, 169.
55. Quoted in Navasky, *Naming Names,* 387.
56. "'The Front' – Production Information," Billy Rose Theatre Collection, New York Public Library for the Performing Arts, Lincoln Center.
57. Quoted in Frank Segers, "Ritt Muses on Columbia's Sell for 'The Front,' Comedy on Blacklist, Not Funny Theme," *Variety,* 29 October 1975: 3.
58. Quoted in Thomas Meehan, "Woody Allen in a Comedy About Blacklisting? Don't Laugh," *New York Times,* 7 December 1975: sec. 2, 17.
59. Meehan, D17.
60. Cogley, Vol. 2, *Radio – Television,* 64.
61. Ibid., 64–5.

62. Walter Bernstein, *Inside Out: A Memoir of the Blacklist* (New York: Knopf, 1996), 203–37; Abraham Polonsky, "The Effects of the 'Blacklist' on a Writer," *New York Times* Oral History Collection, Part I, No. 16: 156–66. See also, Larry Ceplair& Steven Englund, *The Inquisition in Hollywood* (Garden City, N.Y.: Anchor/Doubleday, 1980), 404.

63. Robert Asahina, "Faking It," *New Leader* 58 (25 October 1975): 23.

64. Quoted in Cogley, Vol. 2, 55.

65. "The Front," *Cineaste* 7.4 (Winter 1976–77): 44.

66. Asahina 24.

67. Ibid. 24.

68. Andrew Sarris. *Politics and Cinema* (New York: Columbia U P, 1978), 49.

69. Geoff Brown, *Sight and Sound* 46 (Winter 1976–77): 58

70. Biskind, "The Front," 44.

71. Robert Hatch, "Films," *The Nation*, 16 October 1976: 379.

72. David Denby, "The Usual Suspects," *New York* 24 (1 April 1991): 59.

73. Norman Panama and Melvin Frank, *Dictionary of Literary Biography*, Vol. 26, *Screenwriters* (Detroit: Gale, 1984), 244.

74. Victor Navasky, "Has 'Guilty by Suspicion' Missed the Point?" *New York Times*, 31 March 1991: sec. 2, 16.

75. Ibid. 16.

76. Denby, 58.

77. Katharine Salter, "*Guilty by Suspicion*: An Indictment," *American Cinematographer* (March 1991): 26.

78. "'Guilty by Suspicion' – Production Information," 6. Billy Rose Theatre Collection, New York Public Library for the Performing Arts, Lincoln Center.

79. Denby, 58.

80. Victor Navasky, "Expert Witness," *Premiere* (December 1991): 134.

81. Ibid. 134.

82. Lewis Archibald, "A Liberal Mind: It Says All the Right Things, But Never Gets Mad About Them," *Downtown*, 20 March 1991: 23A.

Chapter 4: Witch Hunt

1. Marion L. Starkey, *The Devil in Massachusetts* (New York: Knopf, 1949), 282.

2. McAlister Coleman, "The Witches of Salem," *The Nation* 169 (3 September 1949): 232.

3. Ibid. 233.

4. James R. Newman, "'A Blind and Most Bloody Rage,'" *New Republic* 121 (24 October 1949): 17–19.

5. See Arthur Miller, *Timebends: A Life* (New York: Grove, 1987) 315–16, and Brenda Murphy, *Miller: Death of a Salesman* (Cambridge: Cambridge UP, 1995), 136–38.

6. Arthur Miller, *Timebends*, 330.

7. Kazan has given his version of the events in *Elia Kazan: A Life* (New York: Knopf, 1988), 449–50, 460–61.

8. C. W. E. Bigsby, *A Critical Introduction to Twentieth-Century American Drama*, Vol. 2 (Cambridge: Cambridge UP, 1984): 197.

9. Miller sketched Kazan's behavior in this situation overtly in the character Mickey in *After the Fall* (1964). James J. Martine articulates the complexity of Miller's emotions at this point very effectively in *The Crucible: Politics, Property, and Pretense* (New York: Twayne, 1993), 61–2.

10. Bigsby, *Introduction*, 197.

11. Miller detailed his reading in an unpublished letter to Stephen Green, M.D., 11 August 1973, which is in the Harry Ransom Humanities Research Center, University of Texas at Austin.

12. Charles W. Upham, *Salem Witchcraft: With an Account of Salem Village and A History of Opinions on Witchcraft and Kindred Subjects* (1896; rpt. New York: Ungar, 1959) Vol. I, 402–3.

13. Quoted in David Levin, *What Happened in Salem?* 2nd. Ed. (New York: Harcourt Brace, 1960) 59.

14. "Arthur Miller's *The Crucible*: Background and Sources," *Modern Drama* 20 (1977): 283.

15. Arthur Miller, *The Crucible: Text and Criticism*, ed. Gerald Weales (New York: Viking, 1971), 150.

16. Arthur Miller, *The Crucible* (New York: Viking, 1953), 118. Subsequent references appear in the text.

17. *Arthur Miller and Company*, ed. Christopher Bigsby (London: Methuen, 1990), 80–1.

18. Quoted in Saul Pett, "Play Needs Message, Miller Says," *Providence Journal*, 15 February 1953.

19. See, for example, *Collected Plays*, 47, and Henry Hewes, "Broadway Postscript: Arthur Miller and How He Went to the Devil," *The Saturday Review* (31 January 1953): 24–6.

20. Quoted in Henry Brandon, "The State of the Theater," *Harper's* 221 (November 1960); rpt. *Conversations with Arthur Miller*, ed. Matthew C. Roudané (Jackson: UP of Mississippi, 1987) 61.

21. *Theatre at the Crossroads* (New York: Holt, Rinehart, and Winston, 1960), 275–6.

22. L. S., "'The Crucible,'" *The Nation* (7 February 1953): 131.

23. Eric Bentley, "Miller's Innocence," *New Republic* (16 February 1953): 22.

24. "New Plays in Manhattan," *Time* (2 February 1953): 48.

25. "'The Crucible,'" *New York Times*, 1 February 1953: sec. 2, 1.

26. Miller supported his statement in *Timebends* with the observation that the best minds of the time, here and in Europe, inside and outside the churches, would have been indignant to be told there were no witches when the Bible on three different occasions warns against dealing with them. Addison, Dr. Johnson, King James, and the entire British church hierarchy shared their view of Blackstone, the voice of English jurisprudence himself, who declared, "To deny the possibility, nay the actual existence of witchcraft and sorcery, is at once flatly to contradict the revealed Word of God, in various passages both of the Old and New Testament; and the thing itself is a truth to which every nation in the world hath in its turn borne testimony, either by examples seemingly well attested, or by prohibitory laws, which at least suppose the possibility of commerce with evil spirits." (339–40)

27. See Bentley, "Miller's Innocence," 23 and David Levin, "Salem Witchcraft in Recent Fiction and Drama," *New England Quarterly* 28 (December 1955): 541.
28. *Arthur Miller's Collected Plays* (New York: Viking, 1957): 42–3.
29. Phillip Gelb, "Morality and Modern Drama," *Educational Theatre Journal* 10 (1958): 190–202.
30. Hewes, 21.
31. Robert Warshow, "The Liberal Conscience in 'The Crucible,'" in *The Scene Before You*, ed. Chandler Brossard (New York: Rinehart, 1955), 200. A. P. Foulkes offers an interesting analysis of Warshow in his "Demystifying the Witch Hunt (Arthur Miller)," *Literature and Propaganda* (London and New York: Methuen, 1983): 95–7.
32. Warshow, 191.
33. Ibid. 198.
34. *Collected Plays*, 40.
35. On the fronts, see Walter Bernstein, *Inside Out: A Memoir of the Blacklist* (New York: Knopf, 1996) 212–20. Larry Ceplair has written a good general overview of the show in "You Are There," *Emmy* 4.1 (January/February 1982): 43–7.
36. As a matter of record, Mather cautioned against too great a reliance on spectral evidence, and he thought the Salem trials went too far in this respect.
37. L. F., "'The Witchfinders,'" *New York Times*, 11 May 1956: 22.
38. Louis O. Coxe, *The Witchfinders: A Play in Three Acts*. Unpublished typescript, in the private collection of Helen Coxe Cheney.
39. L.F., "'The Witchfinders.'"

Chapter 5: Inquisition

1. *Joan of Arc: The Image of Female Heroism* (New York: Alfred A. Knopf, 1981), 7.
2. For a full explanation of the name, see Warner, 199.
3. *Joan of Arc* (1841), trans. Albert Guérard (Ann Arbor: U of Michigan P, 1957).
4. Vita Sackville-West, *Saint Joan of Arc* (1936; rpt. New York: Doubleday, 1991), 314.
5. Michelet, 120–1.
6. Sackville-West, 324.
7. Warner, 269.
8. See Sackvillle-West, n. 4, and *The Trial of Jeanne D'Arc*, trans. W. P. Barrett (New York: Gotham House, 1932); and Milton Waldman, *Joan of Arc* (Boston; Little, Brown, 1935).
9. Quoted in *Playing Joan: Actresses on the Challenge of Shaw's Saint Joan*, ed. Holly Hill (New York: Theatre Communications Group, 1987), 44.
10. Ibid. 44.
11. Lawrence Langner, "'Saint Joan' – A Play for Today," *New York Times*, 30 September 1951: sec. 2, 1.

12. Ibid.

13. "Maid of Orleans," *New York Times,* 14 October 1951: sec. 2, 1.

14. "Drama," *The Nation* 173 (27 October 1951): 361.

15. "A Fiery Particle," *Time* 66 (28 November 1955): 82.

16. Jean Anouilh, *The Lark,* trans. Christopher Fry (London: Methuen, 1955). The Fry translation is used here because it is a nearly word-for-word translation of the original, while the Hellman play is a looser adaptation.

17. Ibid. 58.

18. Ibid. 58.

19. Euphemia Van Rensselaer Wyatt, *"The Lark," Catholic World* 128 (January 1956): 308.

20. Ibid. 308.

21. Richard Moody, *Lillian Hellman: Playwright* (New York: Pegasus, 1972), 247. See also Henry W. Knepler, *"The Lark,* Translation vs. Adaptation: A Case History," *Modern Drama* 1 (May 1958): 15–28 and Carl Rollyson, *Lillian Hellman: Her Legend and Her Legacy* (New York: St. Martin's, 1988) 354–9.

22. Murray Schumach, "Shaping a New Joan: Miss Hellman Discusses Adapting *The Lark,*" *New York Times,* 13 November 1955, sec. 2, 3.

23. Ibid. 3.

24. Jean Anouilh, *The Lark,* adapted by Lillian Hellman (New York: Dramatists Play Service, 1957), 46. Subsequent page references refer to this text. In the original, the line reads, "Mais pour ce qui est de ce que j'ai fait, je ne m'en dédirai jamais" (Jean Anouilh, *L'Alouette* [Paris: La Table Rond, 1953], 106).

25. Lillian Hellman to John S. Wood, 19 May 1952, recorded in HUAC, Public Hearings, Communist Infiltration of the Hollywood Motion-Picture Industry, Part 8, 21 May 1952: 3546.

26. Eric Bentley, *"The Lark," New Republic* 127 (5 December 1955): 21.

27. *Lillian Hellman: The Collected Plays* (Boston: Little, Brown, 1971), 658.

28. Maxwell Anderson to Donald Ogden Stewart, 11 March 1941, *Dramatist in America: Letters of Maxwell Anderson, 1912–1958,* ed. Laurence G. Avery (Chapel Hill: U of North Carolina P, 1977), 110.

29. Maxwell Anderson to Elmer Rice, 13 February 1952, in *Dramatist in America,* 256.

30. Ibid.

31. Maxwell Anderson, Letter to the Editor, *Atlantic Monthly,* 30 August 1948, in *Dramatist in America,* 224.

32. Maxwell Anderson, "Looking Backward: Playwright Tells Why He Wrote *Joan* and How He Signed His Star," *New York Times,* 1 December 1946, sec. 2, 3.

33. Ibid.

34. Maxwell Anderson, *Joan of Lorraine,* rev. ed. (New York: Dramatists Play Service, 1947), 20. Subsequent page numbers refer to this text.

35. Maxwell Anderson, *Off Broadway: Essays About the Theatre* (New York: William Sloane, 1947), 76.

36. Anderson, *Off-Broadway,* 77.

37. "Pickets Mar Bow of Bergman Play," *New York Times,* 30 October 1946: 29.

38. Quoted in Russell Rhodes, "Director Catches Up on History Studying Life of Joan of Arc," *New York Herald Tribune*, 21 November 1948.

39. Maxwell Anderson to John Mason Brown, 18 May 1949, in *Dramatist in America*, 231. Ingrid Bergman described to her biographer the strategy she used to bring Anderson around to her view of Joan, in both the play and the film, explaining:

   > Maxwell Anderson's Joan was sweet and shy and very feminine, but in his theatrical terms he used her to help illustrate his own arguments about faith and modern problems, and I didn't think that came into our story at all. What we tried to do in the movie was the real Joan, from the documents and the trial, the girl who went out onto the battlefield and cried when she saw the terrible horror of medieval battle. I've always thought that the real character of Joan is revealed by her own words, the words she spoke at her trial. (Ingrid Bergman and Alan Burgess, Ingrid Bergman: My Story [New York: Delacorte, 1972], 178)

40. Leo Mishkin, "Joan of Arc Heavy with Sheer Color and Pageantry," New York *Morning Telegraph*, 12 November 1948: 2.

41. Maxwell Anderson and Andrew Solt, *Joan of Arc: Text and Pictures from the Screen Play* (New York: Sloane, 1948), 80. Subsequent page numbers refer to this text.

42. Donald Kirkley, "'Joan of Arc' On Screen," *Baltimore Sun*, 26 January 1949: 12.

43. Kate Cameron, "Ingrid Bergman an Inspired Saint Joan," New York *Daily News*, 12 November 1948: 74.

44. John McCarten, "Joan of Arc," *New Yorker* (13 November 1948): 130.

45. This and subsequent quotations are from "CBS Is There: The Execution of Joan of Arc," broadcast on CBS Radio, 29 February 1948. Audiotape at Museum of Television and Radio, New York.

46. This and subsequent quotations are from "You Are There: The Execution of Joan of Arc," CBS Television, broadcast 29 March 1957. Videotape at Museum of Radio and Television, New York.

47. *Galileo: Heretic*, 1983; trans. Raymond Rosenthal (Princeton: Princeton UP, 1987), 258.

48. Quoted in Jerome J. Langford, *Galileo, Science and the Church*, 3rd ed. (Ann Arbor: U of Michigan P, 1992), 146.

49. Redondi, 259.

50. Langford, 150.

51. Redond,i 260.

52. Langford, 152.

53. Ibid. 154.

54. Quoted in the *Hartford Courant*, 1 November 1992: 2.

55. Bertolt Brecht *Journals*, ed. John Willett, trans. Hugh Rorrison (New York: Routledge, 1993), 359.

56. Quoted in Ronald Hayman, *Brecht: A Biography* (New York: Oxford UP, 1983), 217.

57. Quoted in Brecht: *Plays, Poetry and Prose* , Vol. 5, Part I: *Life of Galileo*, ed. John Willett and Ralph Manheim, trans. John Willett (London: Methuen, 1980), 125. Subsequent page numbers refer to this text.

58. *Journals*, 308.

59. Gerhard Szczesny, *The Case against Bertolt Brecht*, trans. Alexander Gode (New York: Ungar, 1969), 17.

60. James K. Lyon, *Bertolt Brecht in America* (Princeton: Princeton UP, 1980), 319.

61. HUAC, Public Hearings, Regarding the Communist Infiltration of the Motion-Picture Industry, 30 October 1947: 502.

62. *Journals*, 372.

63. Quoted in Lyon, 335.

64. Bertolt Brecht to Hanns Eisler (November 1947), *Letters*, , ed. John Willett, trans. Ralph Mannheim (New York: Routledge, 1990), 441.

65. Charles Higham, *Charles Laughton: An Intimate Biography* (Garden City, N.Y.: Doubleday, 1976), 141.

66. Richard Watts, "Charles Laughton Stars in Brecht's 'Galileo,'" New York *Post*, 8 December 1947.

67. Irwin Shaw, "Theatre: The Earth Stands Still," *New Republic* 119 (29 December 1947): 36.

68. *Variety*, 22 December 1947, clippings file, Billy Rose Theatre Collection, New York Public Library for the Performing Arts.

69. Thomas R. Dash, *Women's Wear Daily*, 22 December 1947, clippings file, Billy Rose Theatre Collection, New York Public Library for the Performing Arts.

70. Barrie Stavis, *Lamp at Midnight* (South Brunswick, N.J.: A. S. Barnes, 1966), 52.

71. Lee Newton, "New Stages Production of Stavis' 'Lamp at Midnight,'" *Daily Worker*, 25 December 1947: 13.

72. Joseph T. Shipley, "'Lamp at Midnight,'" *The New Leader*, 22 December 1947, clippings file, Billy Rose Theatre Collection, New York Public Library for the Performing Arts.

73. Euphemia van Renssalaer Wyatt, "Lamp at Midnight," *The Catholic World* 120 (January 1948) : 456.

74. *Hallmark Hall of Fame: Lamp at Midnight*, NBC Television, 27 April 1966. Videotape at Museum of Television and Radio, New York.

75. Quoted in Abraham Polonsky, You Are There *Teleplays: The Critical Edition* (Northridge, Calif.: Center for Telecommunication Studies), 72.

76. Polonsky 72–3.

77. "The Crisis of Galileo," in Abraham Polonsky, You Are There *Teleplays*, 84. Broadcast on CBS Television, 19 April 1953. Videotape at Museum of Television and Radio, New York.

78. Eric Bentley, *The Brecht Commentaries* (New York: Grove, 1987), 183.

79. Eric Bentley, *The Recantation of Galileo Galilei*, in *Rallying Cries: 3 Plays by Eric Bentley* (Evanston, Ill.: Northwestern UP, 1977), 110.

Chapter 6: Informers

1. For Miller's account of his waterfront experience, see Arthur Miller, *Timebends: A Life* (New York: Grove, 1987), 146–56; for Elia Kazan's ver-

sion, see Michel Ciment, *Kazan on Kazan* (New York: Viking, 1974), 102–03.

2. *Elia Kazan: A Life* (New York: Knopf, 1988), 401.

3. Malcolm Johnson had described the incident on which this scene, and the similar one in *On the Waterfront*, is based. It took place during the depression of the thirties, when 500 men were lined up on a New York pier hoping for work. "A ship was in, the first in weeks. A new hiring boss took one look at the gaunt, desperate faces of those 500 men and lost his nerve. With a gesture of resignation he tossed the 100 checks into the air, turned, and walked away. Five hundred men fought like animals for a hundred brass checks and a half day's work" (*Crime on the Labor Front* [New York: McGraw-Hill, 1950], 138–9).

4. This discussion is based on the copy of "The Hook" at the Harry Ransom Humanities Research Center, University of Texas at Austin. Albert Wertheim has recently published the only substantial critical discussion of the screenplay, based on a copy at the Lilly Library, Indiana University, in his article, "*A View from the Bridge*" in *The Cambridge Companion to Arthur Miller*, ed. Christopher Bigsby (Cambridge: Cambridge UP, 1997), 101–8.

5. Roy Brewer has corroborated Kazan's version of the story:

> One day I had a call from the labor relations director that Cohn wanted to see me. I walked into his office and there was Kazan and Miller. I was supposed to tell them how I wanted the script changed. Well, I realized this was a pretty big order and one for which I was unprepared. They asked me what I objected to in the script. . . . I got an inspiration. I said, "Well, maybe if we had the representatives of the *People's Worker* come down here" – that was a contraction of the *People's World* and the *Daily Worker* – "and offer their services to help lick these gangsters, and this fellow would tell him, 'Get off the waterfront! You're worse that the gangsters!'" (Quoted in Griffin Fariello, *Red Scare: Memories of the American Inquisition, An Oral History* [New York: Norton, 1995], 121–2)

6. *Timebends: A Life*, 305.

7. The story of the film projects is told in detail by Kenneth Hey in "Ambivalence as a Theme in *On the Waterfront* (1954): An Interdisciplinary Approach to Film Study," *American Quarterly* 31.5 (Winter 1979): 673–7.

8. Thomas H. Pauly, *An American Odyssey: Elia Kazan and American Culture* (Philadelphia: Temple UP, 1983), 187.

9. Budd Schulberg, *On the Waterfront* (Carbondale, Ill.: Southern Illinois UP, 1980), 132.

10. Hey, 677.

11. "I can see your point and though I don't agree I'm not going to contest it. . . . The fact is, I'm not in the least religious" (Michel Ciment, *Kazan on Kazan* [New York: Viking, 1974], 112). For the Christ symbolism, see Peter Biskind, "The Politics of Power in *On the Waterfront*," *Film Quarterly* 29 (Fall 1975): 25–38; and Hey, 679–81 and 689–90.

12. Pauly, 213.

13. Pauly, 213–14.

14. Quoted in Stuart Byron and Martin L. Rubin, "Elia Kazan Interview," *Movie* 19 (Winter 1971–2): 8.

15. Victor Navasky, *Naming Names* (New York: Viking, 1980), 210.
16. Ibid. 210.
17. *The Culture of the Cold War* (Baltimore: Johns Hopkins UP, 1991), 113.
18. Arthur Miller, *A View from the Bridge: Two One-Act Plays* (New York: Viking, 1955), 95–6. Subsequent page numbers refer to this text. The original one-act version is used here in preference to the two-act version as revised for the London production because of its greater immediacy to Miller's original intention and work on the play.
19. Eric Bentley, "Theatre," *The New Republic* 127 (19 December 1955): 21. Subsequent page numbers refer to this text.
20. Quoted in Navasky, 199. Navasky, who also printed the story without corroboration, follows it with the remark, "Apocryphal? Perhaps." He makes no mention of Miller's denial of the story.
21. "A Letter from Arthur Miller," *New York Post*, clippings file, John Gassner Collection, Hobitzelle Theatre Arts Library, University of Texas at Austin.
22. Byron and Rubin, 7.
23. Nora Sayre, *Running Time: Films of the Cold War* (New York: Dial, 1982), 155.
24. Ibid. 169.
25. Arthur Miller, "What Makes Plays Endure?" *New York Times*, 15 August 1965; rpt. *The Theater Essays of Arthur Miller*, ed. Robert A. Martin and Steven R. Centola. Rev. Ed. (New York: Da Capo, 1996), 260–1.
26. "Arthur Miller," *The American Theater Today*, ed. Alan S. Downer (New York: Basic Books, 1967), 94.
27. C. W. E. Bigsby, "The Fall and After," *Modern Drama* 10 (1967): 126.
28. See Arthur Miller, *After the Fall: A Play in Two Acts* (New York: Viking, 1964), and Arthur Miller, *After the Fall: A Play in Two Acts: Final Stage Version* (New York: Viking, 1964). The prompt-book belonging to production stage manager Robert Downing, which is in the Harry Ransom Humanities Research Center, University of Texas at Austin, shows that the dialogue used in the Lincoln Center production is that which is printed in the Final Stage Version.
29. Quoted in Nancy and Richard Meyer, "'After the Fall': A View from the Director's Notebook," *Theatre: Annual of the Repertory Theatre of Lincoln Center*, ed. Barry Hyams (New York: Hill and Wang, 1965), 57.
30. "After the Fall of a Dream," *Show* 4.8 (September 1964): 45.
31. *After the Fall, Final Stage Version*, 26.
32. Meyer and Meyer, 43.

Chapter 7: Forensics

1. Quoted in Harry Gilroy, "Anti-Communist Novel Dramatized," *New York Times*, 7 January 1951: sec. 2, 1.
2. "At the Theatre," *New York Times*, 15 January 1951: 13.
3. "From Lorca Down," *The New Republic* 124 (5 February 1951): 23.
4. HUAC, Public Hearings, Communist Infiltration of the Hollywood Motion-Picture Industry, Part 8, 30 April 1952: 2417.
5. Richard Moody, *Lillian Hellman: Playwright* (New York: Pegasus, 1972) 233–4. See also William Wright, *Lillian Hellman: The Image, the Woman*

(New York: Simon and Schuster, 1986) 244–54 and Carl Rollyson, *Lillian Hellman: Her Legend and Her Legacy* (New York: St. Martin's, 1988), 317–30.

6. *Lillian Hellman: The Collected Plays* (Boston: Little, Brown, 1971), 442.

7. Lillian Hellman to John S. Wood, 19 May 1952, recorded in HUAC, Public Hearings, Communist Infiltration of the Hollywood Motion-Picture Industry, Part 8, 21 May 1952: 3545–6.

8. Margaret Marshall, "Drama," *The Nation* 169 (12 November 1949): 478.

9. Harold Clurman, "Theatre: Robles, Hellman, Blitzstein," *New Republic* 121 (5 December 1949): 22.

10. Ibid.

11. *Conversations with Arthur Miller*, ed. Matthew Roudané (Jackson: UP of Mississippi, 1987), 144–5.

12. Ibid. 80.

13. *Arthur Miller's Collected Plays*, Vol. II (New York: Viking, 1981), 280.

14. Roudané, 338–9.

15. Lawrence Lowenthal, "Arthur Miller's *Incident at Vichy*: A Sartrean Interpretation," *Modern Drama* 18 (1975): 29.

16. Jean-Paul Sartre, "Forgers of Myth," *Playwrights on Playwriting*, ed. Toby Cole (New York: Hill and Wang, 1961), 122.

17. Roudané 80. Miller explained the play's implications at greater length and with his customary lucidity in an unpublished introduction dated 17 December 1964, a copy of which is in the Miller Collection, Harry Ransom Humanities Research Center, University of Texas at Austin.

18. *The Caine Mutiny: A Novel of World War II* (Garden City, N.Y.: Doubleday, 1951), 447.

19. *The Culture of the Cold War* (Baltimore: Johns Hopkins UP, 1991), 61.

20. *The Caine Mutiny Court-Martial* (Garden City, N.Y.: Doubleday, 1954), 67.

21. Charles Higham, *Charles Laughton: An Intimate Biography* (Garden City, N.Y.: Doubleday, 1976), 185.

22. Seymour Peck, "Play from the Log of the 'Caine,'" *New York Times*, 17 January 1954: sec. 2, 1.

23. Richard Watts, Jr., "Dramatic Problem of Navy Justice," *New York Post*, 21 January 1954; *New York Theatre Critics Reviews*, ed. Rachel W. Coffin 15 (1954), 383.

24. "'Caine Mutiny,'" *New York Times*, 31 January 1954: sec. 2, 1.

25. Harold Clurman, "Theater," *The Nation* 178 (13 February 1954): 138–9.

26. "The Mutiny That's Raising Cain," *The Nation* 178 (27 March 1954): 260–1.

27. "Captain Bligh's Revenge," *New Republic* 126 (15 February 1954): 21.

28. "The Stage," *The Commonweal* (26 February 1954): 523.

29. Hanson W. Baldwin, "The 'Caine Mutiny' Issue," *The New York Times Magazine*, 21 March 1954: 12–13.

30. Tynan, *"The Caine Mutiny Court-Martial,"* (1956); rpt. *Curtains* (New York: Atheneum, 1961), 272–3.

31. "Theatre," *America* 90 (13 February 1954): 516.

32. "The Wouk Mutiny," *Time* 66 (5 September 1955): 48.

33. "The Age of Wouk," *The Nation* 181 (5 November 1955): 399.

34. Humphrey Bogart, "The Way I See Queeg," *The American Weekly* (27 June 1954): 9.
35. Martin Hill, "The Legendary Wake of the Caine Mutiny," *New York Times,* 11 October 1953: sec. 2, 5.
36. Saul Levitt, *The Andersonville Trial* (New York: Dramatists Play Service, 1960) 12.
37. "Verdict: Suspenseful Hit," New York *Journal American,* 30 December 1959; rpt. *New York Theatre Critics Reviews,* ed. Rachel W. Coffin 20 (1959): 182.
38. "An Electronic Globe," *Saturday Review* (13 June 1970): 40.
39. "Tragedy Unrealized," *Christian Century* 77 (3 February 1960): 137.
40. *Billy Budd* (New York: Hill and Wang, 1962) 35.
41. HUAC, Public Hearings, Communist Infiltration of the Hollywood Motion-Picture Industry, Part 3, 23 May 1951: 624.

Conclusion: Further Fields

1. Harry Schein, "The Olympian Cowboy," *American Scholar* 24.3 (Summer 1955): 316. See also Philip French, *Westerns* (London: Secker and Warburg, 1977). In a rather extraordinary denial of the film-makers' politics, Brian Neve reads *High Noon* as an endorsement of the conservatives' "standing up to communism" (*Film and Politics in America: A Social Tradition* [London: Routledge, 1992]), 185. For a discussion of this line of interpretation, see Phillip Drummond, *High Noon* (London: BFI, 1997), 72–3.
2. "Carl Foreman," interview by Joe Medjuck, *Take One,* (January–February, 1972); quoted in Maurice Yacowar, "Cyrano de H.U.A.C.," *Journal of Popular Film* 5.1 (1976): 71. See also, Carl Foreman, "On the Wayne," *Punch* (14 August 1974): 240–2 and Carl Foreman, "High Noon Revisited," *Punch* (5 April 1972): 448–50.
3. Sayre, *Running Time: Films of the Cold War* (New York: Dial Press, 1982), 176.
4. "A Western Legend," *New York Times,* 3 August 1952: sec. 2, 1.
5. Mark Twain,"The Man That Corrupted Hadleyburg," in *The Complete Short Stories of Mark Twain,* ed. Charles Neider (Garden City, N.Y.: Doubleday, 1957) 349–50.
6. Carl Foreman, *High Noon,* in *Three Major Screenplays,* eds. Malvin Wald and Michael Werner (New York: Globe, 1972), 147.
7. *Seeing is Believing: How America Taught Us to Stop Worrying and Love the Fifties* (New York: Pantheon, 1983), 47.
8. Clippings file, Billy Rose Theatre Collection, New York Public Library for the Performing Arts.
9. Philip T. Hartung, "The Screen," *The Commonweal* 52 (18 August 1950): 460.
10. *Seeing,* 21.
11. "From the Nightmare Factory: HUAC and the Politics of Noir," *Sight and Sound* 55 (Autumn 1986): 266. Kemp argues that *film noir* "pictures share a set of implicit, perhaps even inadvertent attitudes to society which readily lend themselves to interpretations as left-wing" (268). I would argue that fear, paranoia, and fatalism are, rather, the antithesis of the post-war leftist

ideology, at least as it was articulated by its spokespeople, and that a film like *Panic in the Streets* proceeds from a deep suspicion of the leftist ideal-ization of "the people."

12. *Elia Kazan: A Life* (New York: Knopf, 1988), 377.

13. "Everyone's a Movie Star in New Orleans," New York *Herald Tribune,* 9 July 1950, sec. 5, 1.

14. *Seeing,* 31.

A Note on Archives and Library Collections

Several library collections have been indispensable to this study. A list of the most important includes the following:

Billy Rose Theatre Collection, New York Public Library for the Performing Arts. Includes unpublished scripts and screenplays, photographs, press books, reviews and clippings files, as well as other research materials. Undated newspaper clippings in the list of "Works Cited" below are from the clippings files in this collection.

Museum of Television and Radio, New York.
Includes video- and audiotapes of broadcasts, as well as a large database of information on media productions.

Harry Ransom Humanities Research Center, University of Texas at Austin.
Includes large collections of scripts, letters, clippings, and other materials related to specific playwrights such as Arthur Miller, Maxwell Anderson, and Lillian Hellman, as well as letters and other items related to productions.

Lilly Library, Indiana University.
Includes screenplays, press books, and other material related to film productions.

Homer Babbidge Library and Special Collections, Thomas R. Dodd Research Center, University of Connecticut Libraries.

I am greatly indebted to the staff of my home institution's research library, as well as its research collections.

Works Cited

Primary and Secondary Sources

Anderson, Maxwell. *Joan of Lorraine*. Rev. ed. New York: Dramatists Play Service, 1947.
    "Looking Backward: Playwright Tells Why He Wrote *Joan* and How He Signed His Star." *New York Times*, 1 December 1946: sec. 2, 3.
    Off Broadway: Essays About the Theatre. New York: William Sloane, 1947.
Anderson, Maxwell and Andrew Solt. *Joan of Arc: Text and Pictures From the Screen Play*. New York: Sloane, 1948.
Anouilh, Jean. *L'Alouette*. Paris: La Table Rond, 1953.
    The Lark. Adapted by Lillian Hellman. New York: Random House, 1956; New York: Dramatists Play Service, 1957.
    The Lark. Trans. Christopher Fry. London: Methuen, 1955.
Archibald, Lewis. "A Liberal Mind: It Says All the Right Things, But Never Gets Mad About Them." *Downtown* (20 March 1991): 22A–23A.
Asahina, Robert. "Faking It." *New Leader* 58 (25 October 1975): 23–4.
Atkinson, Brooks. "At the Theatre." *New York Times*, 15 January 1951: 13.
    "'Caine Mutiny.'" *New York Times*, 31 January 1954: sec. 2, 1.
    "'The Crucible.'" *New York Times*, 1 February 1953: sec. 2, 1.
    "Maid of Orleans." *New York Times*, 14 October 1951: sec. 2, 1.
Avery, Laurence G. Ed. *Dramatist in America: Letters of Maxwell Anderson, 1912–1958*. Chapel Hill: University of North Carolina Press, 1977.
Baldwin, Hanson W. "The 'Caine Mutiny' Issue." *New York Times Magazine*, 21 March 1954: 12–13, 37, 39, 42.
Barrett, W. P. *The Trial of Jeanne D'Arc*. New York: Gotham House, 1932.
Beaufort, John. "Are You Now . . ." *Christian Science Monitor*, 5 December 1973: sec. B, 10.
Bentley, Eric. *The Brecht Commentaries*. New York: Grove, 1987.
    "Cpt. Bligh's Revenge." *New Republic* 126 (15 February 1954): 21.
    "*The Lark*." *New Republic* 127 (5 December 1955): 21.
    "Miller's Innocence." *New Republic* 125 (16 February 1953): 22–3.
    "The Missing Communist" (1956; rpt. in *What Is Theatre?* New York: Atheneum, 1968, 309–15).
    Rallying Cries: 3 Plays by Eric Bentley. Evanston, Ill.: Northwestern University Press, 1977.
    "Theatre." *New Republic* 127 (19 December 1955): 21.

The Theatre of Commitment. New York: Athenaeum, 1967.

ed. *Thirty Years of Treason: Excerpts From Hearings Before the House Committee on Un-American Activities, 1938–1969.* New York: Viking, 1971.

Bergman, Ingrid, and Alan Burgess. *Ingrid Bergman: My Story.* New York: Delacorte, 1972.

Bernstein, Walter. *Inside Out: A Memoir of the Blacklist.* New York: Knopf, 1996.

"Big Jim McLain." *Time* 63 (29 September 1952): 93.

Bigsby, C. W. E. *Confrontation and Commitment: A Study of Contemporary American Drama, 1959–1966.* Columbia: University of Missouri Press, 1968.

A Critical Introduction to Twentieth-Century American Drama. Vol. 2. Cambridge and New York: Cambridge University Press, 1984.

"The Fall and After–Arthur Miller's Confession." *Modern Drama* 10 (1967): 124–36.

ed. *Arthur Miller and Company.* London: Methuen, 1990.

The Cambridge Companion to Arthur Miller. Cambridge: Cambridge University Press, 1997.

Biskind, Peter. "The Front." *Cineaste* 7 (Winter 1976–7): 44–5.

"The Politics of Power in *On the Waterfront.*" *Film Quarterly* 29 (Fall 1975): 25–38.

Seeing is Believing: How America Taught Us to Stop Worrying and Love the Fifties. New York: Pantheon, 1983.

Bogart, Humphrey. "The Way I See Queeg." *The American Weekly* (27 June 1954): 9.

Bosworth, Patricia. "Daughter of a Blacklist That Killed a Father." *New York Times,* 27 Sept. 1992: sec. 2, 1.

"Memories of HUAC." *The Nation* 245 (24 Oct. 1987): 436–7.

Brecht, Bertolt. *Journals.* Ed. John Willett. Trans. Hugh Rorrison. New York: Routledge, 1993.

Letters 1913–1956. Trans. Ralph Manheim. Ed. John Willett. London: Methuen, 1990.

Plays, Poetry, and Prose. Vol. 5, Part I: *Life of Galileo.* Eds. John Willett and Ralph Manheim. Trans. John Willett. London: Methuen, 1980.

Brewer, Roy, I. E. Chadwick, Art Arthur, Ronald Reagan, Jack Dales, and Alexander Kempner. "You Can Be Free Men Again!" *Hollywood Reporter* 6 June 1952; rpt. in Bentley, *Thirty Years of Treason,* 405–6.

"Brog." "Big Jim McLain." *Variety,* 27 August 1952: 6.

Brown, Geoff. "The Front." *Sight and Sound* 46 (Winter 1976–7): 58.

Byron, Stuart, and Martin L. Rubin. "Elia Kazan Interview." *Movie* 19 (Winter 1971–2): 1–13.

Cameron, Kate. "Ingrid Bergman an Inspired Saint Joan." New York *Daily News,* 12 November 1948: 74.

Caute, David. *The Great Fear: The Anti-Communist Purge Under Truman and Eisenhower.* New York: Simon & Schuster, 1978.

Ceplair, Larry. "You Are There," *Emmy* 4.1 (January–February 1982): 43–7.

Ceplair, Larry, and Steven Englund. *The Inquisition in Hollywood: Politics in the Film Community 1930–1960.* Garden City, N. Y.: Anchor/Doubleday, 1980.

Chambers, Whittaker. *Witness.* New York: Random House, 1952.

Chametzky, Jules. "From HUAC to Watergate." *Performance* 7 (Fall 1973): 21–8.

Ciment, Michel. *Kazan on Kazan*. New York: Viking, 1974.

Clemens, Samuel L. (Mark Twain). "The Man That Corrupted Hadleyburg" in *The Complete Short Stories of Mark Twain*, Ed. Charles Neider, 349–90. Garden City, N.Y.: Doubleday, 1957.

Clurman, Harold. "From Lorca Down." *New Republic* 124 (5 February 1951): 22–3.

"The Mutiny That's Raising Cain." *The Nation* 178 (27 March 1954): 260–1.

"Theater." *The Nation* 178 (13 February 1954): 138–9.

"Theatre: Robles, Hellman, Blitzstein." *New Republic*. 121 (5 December 1949): 21–2.

Cogley, John. *Report on Blacklisting*. 2 vols. New York: Fund for the Republic, 1956.

Coleman, McAlister. "The Witches of Salem." *The Nation* 169 (3 September 1949): 232.

Corbett, Susan. "Are You Now or Have you Ever Been." *The Stage & Television Today* 23 (June 1977): 11.

Coxe, Louis O. *The Witchfinders: A Play in Three Acts*. Unpublished typescript, in the private collection of Helen Coxe Cheney.

Coxe, Louis O., and Robert Chapman. *Billy Budd*. New York: Hill and Wang, 1962.

Crowther, Bosley. "Big Jim McLain." *New York Times*, 18 September 1952: 35.

"A Western Legend," *New York Times*, 3 August 1952: sec. 2, 1.

Dash, Thomas R. "Lamp at Midnight." *Women's Wear Daily*, 22 December 1947.

Denby, David. "The Usual Suspects." *New York*. 24 (1 April 1991): 58–60.

Dmytryk, Edward. *Odd Man Out: A Memoir of the Hollywood Ten*. Carbondale: Southern Illinois University Press, 1996.

"Drama Review." *Champion Labor Monthly* 3.10 (September 1938): 33–4.

Driver, Tom F. "Tragedy Unrealized." *Christian Century* 77 (3 February 1960): 136–7.

Drummond, Phillip. *High Noon*. London: BFI, 1997.

English, Richard. "We Almost Lost Hawaii to the Reds." *Saturday Evening Post* 224 (2 February 1952) 17–19, 50, 54.

"What Makes a Hollywood Communist?" *Saturday Evening Post* (30 August 1952): 16–17, 41, 44.

"Everyone's a Movie Star in New Orleans," New York *Herald Tribune*, 9 July 1950: sec. 5, 1.

Fariello, Griffin. *Red Scare: Memories of the American Inquisition, an Oral History*. New York: Norton, 1995.

Fast, Howard. *Being Red*. Boston: Houghton Mifflin, 1990.

Thirty Pieces of Silver. New York: Blue Heron Press, 1954.

"Fiery Particle, A." *Time* 66 (28 November 1955): 76–8, 81–2, 83.

Flanagan, Hallie. *Arena: The Story of the Federal Theatre* (1940; rpt. New York: Limelight, 1969.)

Foreman, Carl. *High Noon*. In *Three Major Screenplays*. Ed. Malvin Wald and Michael Werner, 155–258. New York: Globe, 1972.

"High Noon Revisited." *Punch* (5 April 1972): 448–50.

"On the Wayne." *Punch* (14 August 1974): 240–2.

Foulkes, A. P. *Literature and Propaganda*. London and New York: Methuen, 1983.

Frazer, Sir James George. *The Golden Bough*. (1922; rpt. New York: Macmillan, 1963.)

French, Philip. *Westerns*. London: Secker and Warburg, 1977.

Friedman, Lester D. "A Very Narrow Path: The Politics of Edward Dmytryk." *Film and Literature Quarterly* 12 (1984): 214–24.

"The Front–Production Information." Billy Rose Theatre Collection, New York Public Library for the Performing Arts.

"Garfield, Ferrer 'Investigate' Selves as Prelude to April 20 Red Hearings." *Variety*, 11 April 1951; rpt. Bentley, *Thirty Years of Treason*, 295–6.

Garfinkel, Harold. "Conditions of Successful Degradation Ceremonies." *American Journal of Sociology* 61 (January 1956): 420–4.

Gassner, John. *Theatre at the Crossroads*. New York: Holt, Rinehart, and Winston, 1960.

Geismar, Maxwell. "The Age of Wouk." *The Nation*. 181 (5 November 1955): 399–400.

Gelb, Phillip. "Morality and Modern Drama." *Educational Theatre Journal* 10 (1958): 190–202.

Gilroy, Harry. "Anti-Communist Novel Dramatized." *New York Times*, 7 January 1951: sec. 2, 1.

Girard, René. *The Scapegoat*. Trans. Yvonne Freccero. Baltimore: Johns Hopkins University Press, 1986.

  Violence and the Sacred. Trans. Patrick Gregory. Baltimore: Johns Hopkins University Press, 1972.

Goodman, Walter. *The Committee: The Extraordinary Career of the House Committee on Un-American Activities*. New York: Farrar, Straus, and Giroux, 1968.

  "How Not to Produce a Film." *New Republic* 127 (26 December 1955): 12–13.

Goyen, William. "After the Fall of a Dream: What Went Wrong at Lincoln Center." *Show* 4.8 (September 1964): 44–8, 86–9.

Guernsey, Otis L. "Big Jim McLain." *New York Herald-Tribune*, 15 September 1952.

Halberstam, David. *The Fifties*. New York: Villard, 1993.

Hartung, Philip T. "The Screen." *Commonweal* 52 (18 August 1950): 460–1.

  "The Screen." *Commonweal* 56 (15 July 1952): 390.

Hatch, Robert. "Films." *The Nation* 202 (16 October 1976): 378–9.

Hayes, Richard. "The Stage: *The Caine Mutiny Court Martial*." *Commonweal* 58 (26 February 1954): 523–4.

Hayman, Ronald. *Brecht: A Biography*. New York: Oxford University Press, 1983.

Hellman, Lillian. *Lillian Hellman: The Collected Plays*. Boston: Little, Brown, 1971.

Hewes, Henry. "Broadway Postscript: Arthur Miller and How He Went to the Devil." *Saturday Review* (31 January 1953): 24–6.

Hey, Kenneth. "Ambivalence as a Theme in *On the Waterfront* (1954): An Interdisciplinary Approach to Film Study." *American Quarterly* 31.5 (Winter 1979): 666–96.

Higham, Charles. *Charles Laughton: An Intimate Biography*. Garden City, N.Y.: Doubleday, 1976.

Hill, Gladwyn. "Says Government Aided Film Reds." *New York Times*, 17 May 1947: 8.

Hill, Holly, ed. *Playing Joan: Actresses on the Challenge of Shaw's Saint Joan*. New York: Theatre Communications Group, 1987.

Hill, Martin. "The Legendary Wake of the Caine Mutiny." *New York Times*, 11 October 1953: sec. 2, 5.

Hoover, J. Edgar. *Masters of Deceit: The Story of Communism in America and How to Fight It.* New York: Holt, 1958.

A Study of Communism. New York: Holt, Rinehart, and Winston, 1962.

Johnson, Malcolm. *Crime on the Labor Front.* New York: McGraw-Hill, 1950.

Jones, Dorothy B. "Communism and the Movies." In John Cogley, *Report on Blacklisting.* Vol. 1, *Movies.* New York: Fund for the Republic, 1956.

Kanfer, Stefan. *A Journal of the Plague Years.* New York: Atheneum, 1973.

Kazan, Elia. *Elia Kazan: A Life.* New York: Knopf, 1988.

Kemp, Philip. "From the Nightmare Factory: HUAC and the Politics of Noir." *Sight and Sound* 55 (Autumn 1986): 266–70.

Kinoy, Ernest. "Blacklist." In *Electronic Drama: Television Plays of the Sixties.* Ed. Richard Avedon and David Manning White. Boston: Beacon, 1971, 92–135.

Kirkley, Donald. "'Joan of Arc' on Screen." *Baltimore Sun*, 26 January 1949: 12.

Kisseloff, Jeff. *The Box: An Oral History of Television, 1920–1961.* New York: Viking, 1995.

Knepler, Henry W. "*The Lark*, Translation vs. Adaptation: A Case History." *Modern Drama* 1 (May 1958): 15–28.

Krutch, Joseph Wood. *American Drama Since 1918.* New York: Braziller, 1957.

"Drama." *The Nation* 173 (27 October 1952): 360–1.

L. F. "'The Witchfinders.'" *New York Times*, 11 May 1956: 22.

L. S. "'The Crucible.'" *The Nation* 179 (7 February 1953): 131–2.

Lamb, Chris. "Herblock Talks about Life as a Cartoonist." *Editor and Publisher* 124 (29 June 1991): 32–4.

"Lamp at Midnight." *Variety*, 22 December 1947. Clippings File, Billy Rose Theatre Collection, New York Public Library for the Performing Arts.

Langford, Jerome J. *Galileo, Science, and the Church.* 3rd. Ed. Ann Arbor: University of Michigan Press, 1992.

Langner, Lawrence. "'Saint Joan' –A Play for Today." *New York Times*, 30 September 1951: sec. 2, 1.

Lardner, Ring, Jr. "My Life on the Black List." *Saturday Evening Post* 234 (14 October 1961): 38–40.

Laurence, William L. "Truman Charges Smears and Gossip." *New York Times*, 14 Sept. 1948: sec. 1, 24.

Lawrence, W. H. "Truman Assails Committee on Un-American Activities." *New York Times*, 23 Sept. 1948: sec. 1, 26.

Levin, David. "Salem Witchcraft in Recent Fiction and Drama." *New England Quarterly* 28 (December 1955): 537–46.

What Happened in Salem? 2nd Ed. New York: Harcourt Brace, 1960.

Levine, Ira. *Left-Wing Dramatic Theory in the American Theatre.* Ann Arbor, Mich.: UMI, 1985.

Levitt, Saul. *The Andersonville Trial.* New York: Dramatists Play Service, 1960.

Lewis, Anthony. "A Red-Party Form Linked to Miller." *New York Times*, 25 Aug. 1957: 20.

Lewis, Theophilus. "Theatre." *America* 90 (13 February 1954): 516.

"Links Movie Chiefs to 'Big Plot' on U. S." *New York Times,* 1 July 1945: 20.

Lowenthal, Lawrence D. "Arthur Miller's *Incident at Vichy:* A Sartrean Interpretation." *Modern Drama* 18 (1975): 29–41.

"Loyal Actors Call for Film Industry Purge of All Subversives." *Los Angeles Evening Herald & Express,* 23 March 1951; rpt. in Bentley, *Thirty Years of Treason,* 299–300.

Lyon, James K. *Bertolt Brecht in America.* Princeton: Princeton University Press, 1980.

Marshall, Margaret. "Drama." *The Nation* 169 (12 November 1949): 478.

Martin, Robert. "Arthur Miller's *The Crucible:* Background and Sources," *Modern Drama* 20 (1977): 279–92.

Martine, James J. *The Crucible: Politics, Property, and Pretense.* New York: Twayne, 1993.

McCarten, John. "Joan of Arc," *New Yorker* (13 November 1948): 130.

McClain, John. "Verdict: Suspenseful Hit." New York *Journal American,* 30 December 1959; rpt. *New York Theatre Critics Reviews.* Ed. Rachel W. Coffin 20 (1959): 182.

Meehan, Thomas. "Woody Allen in a Comedy About Blacklisting? Don't Laugh." *New York Times,* 7 December 1975: sec. 2, 1, 17.

Meyer, Nancy and Richard. "'After the Fall': A View from the Director's Notebook." *Theatre: Annual of the Repertory Theatre of Lincoln Center.* Ed. Barry Hyams. New York: Hill and Wang, 1965.

Michelet, Jules. *Joan of Arc. (Jeanne d'Arc,* 1841) Trans. Albert Guérard. Ann Arbor: University of Michigan Press, 1957.

"Midsection: Notes on the Blacklist." *Film Comment* 23 (November/December 1987): 37–59.

Miller, Arthur. *After the Fall: A Play in Two Acts.* New York: Viking, 1964.

——. *After the Fall: A Play in Two Acts: Final Stage Version.* New York: Viking, 1964.

——. *Arthur Miller's Collected Plays.* New York: Viking, 1957.

——. *Arthur Miller's Collected Plays.* 2 vols. New York: Viking, 1981.

——. *The Crucible.* New York: Viking, 1953.

——. *The Crucible: Text and Criticism.* Ed. Gerald Weales. New York: Viking, 1971.

——. "The Night Ed Murrow Struck Back." *Esquire* 100 (December 1983): 460–62, 465, 467–68.

——. *Timebends: A Life.* New York: Grove, 1987.

——. *A View From the Bridge: Two One-Act Plays.* New York: Viking, 1955.

——. "What Makes Plays Endure?" *New York Times* 15 August 1965; rpt. *The Theater Essays of Arthur Miller.* Ed. Robert A. Martin and Steven R. Centola. New York: Da Capo, 1996, 258–63.

——. *You're Next: A Political Playlet.* Mimeo. In Harry Ransom Humanities Research Center, University of Texas at Austin.

Mishkin, Leo. "Joan of Arc Heavy with Sheer Color and Pageantry." New York *Morning Telegraph,* 12 November 1948: 2.

Mitgang, Herbert. *Dangerous Dossiers: Exposing the Secret War Against America's Greatest Authors.* New York: Donald I. Fine, 1988.

Moody, Richard. *Lillian Hellman: Playwright.* New York: Pegasus, 1972.

Morris, William. *The American Heritage Dictionary of the English Language.* New College Edition. Boston: Houghton Mifflin, 1978.

"Movies to Oust Ten Cited for Contempt of Congress." *New York Times*, 26 November 1947: 27.

Murphy, Brenda. *Miller: Death of a Salesman*. Cambridge: Cambridge University Press, 1995.

Murrow, Edward R. "A Report on Senator Joseph R. McCarthy." *See It Now*. In *In Search of Light: The Broadcasts of Edward R. Murrow 1938–1961*. Ed. Edward Bliss, Jr., 247–8. New York: Knopf, 1967.

Navasky, Victor. "Expert Witness: 'Guilty by Suspicion.'" *Premiere* (December 1991): 134.

——. "Has 'Guilty by Suspicion'" Missed the Point?" *New York Times*, 31 March 1991: sec. 2, 9, 16.

——. *Naming Names*. New York: Viking, 1980.

Neve, Brian. *Film and Politics in America: A Social Tradition*. London: Routledge, 1992.

"New Plays in Manhattan." *Time* (2 February 1953): 48.

Newman, James R. "'A Blind and Most Bloody Rage.'" *New Republic* 121 (24 October 1949): 17–19.

Newton, Lee. "New Stages Production of Stavis' 'Lamp at Midnight.'" *Daily Worker*, 25 December 1947: 13.

Nixon, Richard M. "Plea for an Anti-Communist Faith." *Saturday Review of Literature* 35 (24 May 1952): 12–13.

O'Reilly, Kenneth. "The F.B.I. – HUAC's Big Brother." *The Nation* 230 (19 January 1980): 42– 5.

Panama, Norman, and Melvin Frank. *Dictionary of Literary Biography*. Vol 26. *Screenwriters*. Ed. Stephen O. Lesser and Randall Clark. Detroit: Gale, 1984.

Pauly, Thomas H. *An American Odyssey: Elia Kazan and American Culture*. Philadelphia: Temple University Press, 1983.

Peck, Seymour. "Play from the Log of the 'Caine.'" *New York Times*, 17 January 1954: sec. 2, 1.

Péguy, Charles. *The Mystery of the Charity of Joan of Arc*. Trans. Julian Green. London: Hollis and Carter, 1950.

Peter, John. "Theatre." *The Sunday Times* (London), 4 September 1977: 39.

Pett, Saul. "Play Needs Message, Miller Says." *Providence Journal* 15 February 1953. Clippings File, Billy Rose Theatre Collection, New York Public Library for the Performing Arts.

"Pickets Mar Bow of Bergman Play: Leaflets Against Racial Bias Distributed at Capital Debut." *The New York Times* 30 Oct. 1946: 29.

"Pinks Plan to Stalinize Studios." *Variety*, 16 September 1933: 1, 3.

"Pit." "Are You Now or Have You Ever Been." *Variety*. 2 November 1977: 84.

Polonsky, Abraham. "The Effects of the 'Blacklist' on a Writer." *New York Times* Oral History Collection, Part I, No. 16.

Polonsky, Abraham ("Jeremy Daniel"). "The Crisis of Galileo." In *You Are There Teleplays: The Critical Edition*. Ed. John Schultheiss and Max Schaubert. Rev. ed. Northridge, Calif.: CTS, 1997, 68–100. Broadcast on CBS Television, 19 April 1953. Videotape at Museum of Television and Radio, New York.

"Praise Pours in on Murrow Show." *New York Times*, 11 March 1954: 19.

Rabinowitz, Victor. *Unrepentant Leftist: A Lawyer's Memoir*. Champaign: University of Illinois Press, 1996.

Radin, Victoria. "Are You Now or Have You Ever Been . . . ," London *Observer*, 12 June 1977: 26.

Redondi, Pietro. *Galileo: Heretic*. Trans. Raymond Rosenthal. Princeton: Princeton University Press, 1987.

Reisz, Karel. "Hollywood's Anti-Red Boomerang: Apple Pie, Love, and Endurance versus The Commies." *Sight and Sound* 22 (January–March 1953): 132–7, 148.

Rhodes, Russell. "Director Catches Up on History Studying Life of Joan of Arc." *New York Herald Tribune*, 21 November 1948. Clippings File, Billy Rose Theatre Collection, New York Public Library for the Performing Arts.

Roberts, Randy, and James S. Olson. *John Wayne: American*. New York: Free Press, 1995.

Rollyson, Carl. *Lillian Hellman: Her Legend and Her Legacy*. New York: St. Martin's, 1988.

Rosswurm, Steven. "FBI Files on the House Committee on Un-American Activities." *Journal of American History* 74 (1988): 1405–6.

Roudané, Matthew, C. ed. *Conversations with Arthur Miller*. Jackson: University Press of Mississippi, 1987.

Sackville-West, Vita. *Saint Joan of Arc*. (1936; rpt. New York: Doubleday, 1991).

Safeguarding Civil Liberties. Los Angeles: UCLA Oral History Project, 1974.

Salter, Katharine. "*Guilty by Suspicion:* An Indictment." *American Cinematographer* (March 1991): 26–33.

Sarris, Andrew. *Politics and Cinema*. New York: Columbia University Press, 1978.

Sartre, Jean-Paul. "Forgers of Myth." *Playwrights on Playwriting*. Ed. Toby Cole. New York: Hill and Wang, 1961.

Sayre, Nora. *Running Time: Films of the Cold War*. New York: Dial, 1982.

Scharine, Richard G. *From Class to Caste in American Drama: Politcal and Social Themes Since the 1930s*. Westport, Conn: Greenwood, 1991.

Schechner, Richard. *Between Theater & Anthropology*. Philadelphia: University of Pennsylvania Press, 1985.

Schein, Harry. "The Olympian Cowboy," *American Scholar* 24.3 (Summer 1955): 309–20.

Schulberg, Budd. *On the Waterfront*. Carbondale, Ill.: Southern Illinois University Press, 1980.

Schumach, Murray. "Shaping a New Joan: Miss Hellman Discusses Adapting *The Lark*." *New York Times*, 13 November 1955: sec. 2, 3.

Sczczesny, Gerhard. *The Case Against Bertolt Brecht*. Trans. Alexander Gode. New York: Ungar, 1969.

Segers, Frank. "Ritt Muses on Columbia's Sell for 'The Front,' Comedy on Blacklist, Not Funny Theme." *Variety*, 29 October 1975: 3.

Shaw, Irwin. "Theatre: The Earth Stands Still." *New Republic* 119 (29 December 1947): 36.

Shayon, Robert Lewis. "An Electronic Globe." *Saturday Review* (13 June 1970): 40.

Shipley, Joseph T. "Lamp at Midnight." *The New Leader*. 30 (22 December 1947).

Starkey, Marion L. *The Devil in Massachusetts*. New York: Knopf, 1949.

Stavis, Barrie. *Lamp at Midnight*. South Brunswick, N.J.: A. S. Barnes, 1966.

"Still With Us." *Commonweal* 79 (31 January 1964): 495.

Stone, I. F. *The Haunted Fifties*. London: Merlin, 1963.

Sullivan, Gwyn. "50s Politics Through a Needle's Eye." New York *News World*, 22 October 1978: 2B.

Talese, Gay. "Truman Day Here: Talk, Walk, Talk." *New York Times*, 30 Apr. 1959: 17.

Trumbo, Dalton. *The Time of the Toad: A Study of Inquisition in America and Two Related Pamphlets*. New York: Perennial Library, 1972.

Turner, Victor. *The Anthropology of Performance*. New York: PAJ, 1987.

"Liminality and the Performative Genres." In *Rite, Drama, Festival, Spectacle: Rehearsals Toward a Theory of Cultural Performance*. Ed. John J. MacAloon. Philadelphia: ISHI, 1984.

Schism and Continuity in an African Society: A Study of Ndembu Village Life. Manchester: Manchester University Press, 1957.

Turner, Victor and Edith. "Performing Ethnography." *The Drama Review* 26 (1982): 33–50.

Tynan, Kenneth. "*The Caine Mutiny Court-Martial*" (1956; rpt. *Curtains*, 272–3. New York: Atheneum, 1961).

Upham, Charles W. *Salem Witchcraft: With an Account of Salem Village and a History of Opinions on Witchcraft and Kindred Subjects*. 2 Vols. (1896; rpt. New York: Ungar, 1959).

Vaughn, Robert. *Only Victims: A Study of Show Business Blacklisting*. New York: Putnam, 1972.

Waldman, Milton. *Joan of Arc*. Boston: Little, Brown, 1935.

Warner, Marina. *Joan of Arc: The Image of Female Heroism*. New York: Knopf, 1981.

Warshow, Robert. "The Liberal Conscience in 'The Crucible': Arthur Miller and his Audience." *Commentary* (March 1953): 265–71. Rpt. *The Scene Before You*. 191–203. Ed. Chandler Brossard. New York: Rinehart, 1955.

Watts, Richard, Jr. "Charles Laughton Stars in Brecht's 'Galileo.'" New York *Post*, 8 December 1947. Clippings File, Billy Rose Theatre Collection, New York Public Library for the Performing Arts.

"Dramatic Problems of Navy Justice." *New York Post*, 21 January 1954; *New York Theatre Critics Reviews*. Ed. Rachel W. Coffin 15 (1954): 383.

Weales, Gerald. "Arthur Miller." In *The American Theater Today*. Ed. Alan S. Downer. New York: Basic Books, 1967, 85–98.

"Arthur Miller and the 1950s." *Michigan Quarterly Review* 37.4 (Fall 1998): 635–51.

Wertheim, Albert. "The McCarthy Era and the American Theatre." *Theatre Journal* 34.2 (1982): 211–22.

"*A View from the Bridge*." In *The Cambridge Companion to Arthur Miller*. Ed. Christopher Bigsby. Cambridge: Cambridge University Press, 1997, 101–14.

Wexley, John. *The Judgment of Julius and Ethel Rosenberg*. New York: Cameron & Kahn, 1955.

Whitebait, William. "Big Jim McLain." *The New Statesman and Nation* 44 (1 November 1952): 509.

Whitehead, Ted. "Red Devils." *Spectator* (5 November 1977): 27.

Whitfield, Stephen J. *The Culture of the Cold War.* Baltimore: Johns Hopkins University Press, 1991.

Wouk, Herman. *The Caine Mutiny: A Novel of World War II.* Garden City, N.Y.: Doubleday, 1951.

"The Wouk Mutiny." *Time* 66 (5 September 1955): 48–50, 52.

The Caine Mutiny Court-Martial. Garden City, N.Y.: Doubleday, 1954.

Wright, William. *Lillian Hellman: The Image, the Woman.* New York: Simon and Schuster, 1986.

Wyatt, Euphemia Van Rensselaer. "Lamp at Midnight." *The Catholic World* 120 (January 1948): 456.

"*The Lark.*" *Catholic World* 128 (January 1956): 308–9.

Yacowar, Maurice. "Cyrano de H.U.A.C." *Journal of Popular Film* 5.1 (1976): 68–75.

Government Documents

United States Congress. House of Representatives. Committee on Un-American Activities.

Documents

82nd Congress: House Documents, Vol. 7, 3 January–20 October 1951.

No. 136. *100 Things You Should Know About Communism in the U. S. A.; 100 Things You Should Know About Communism and Religion; 100 Things You Should Know About Communism and Education; 100 Things You Should Know About Communism and Labor; 100 Things You Should Know About Communism and Government; Spotlight on Spies.*

No. 137. *Guide to Subversive Organizations and Publications.*

Hearings

Special Committee, 1938–1944.

Public Hearings, Vol. 4. 19, 22, 23, and 28 November; 1 and 5–9 December 1938. (Federal Theatre Project)

Standing Committee, 1945–1967.

80th Congress: Hearings Regarding Hanns Eisler, 24–26 September 1947; Hearings Regarding Communist Infiltration of the Motion-Picture Industry, 20–24 and 27–30 October 1947 (Hollywood Ten Hearings); Hearings on H. R. 4422 and H. R. 4581, Proposed Legislation to Curb or Control the Communist Party of the United States, 5, 6, 9–11, 19 and 20 February 1948 (Arthur Garfield Hays).

81st Congress: Hearings Regarding Communist Infiltration of Labor Unions, Part 1, 9–11 August 1949, Part 2, 5–6 December 1949; Testimony of Edward G. Robinson, 27 October and 21 December 1950.

82nd Congress: Hearings Regarding Communist Infiltration of Hollywood Motion-Picture Industry, Part 1, 8 and 21 March and 10–13 April 1951 (Larry

Parks); Part 2, 17 and 23–25 April and 16–18 May 1951 (Edward Dmytryk); Part 3, 22–25 May and 25–26 June 1951 (José Ferrer, Budd Schulberg); Part 4, 17–19 September 1951; Part 5, 20, 21, 24, and 25 September 1951 (Carl Foreman); Part 6, 10 May and 10–12 September 1951; Part 7, 24 and 28 January, 5 February, 20 March, and 10 and 30 April 1952 (Elia Kazan, Michael Blankfort); Part 8, 19–21 May 1952 (Lillian Hellman); Part 9, 19 August and 29 September 1952; Part 10, 12 and 13 November 1952 (Abe Burrows).

83rd Congress: Hearings Regarding Communist Methods of Infiltration (Education), 25–27 February 1953 (Granville Hicks); Investigation of Communist Activities in the New York City Area, Part 1, 4 May 1953; Part 2, 5 May 1953; Part 3, 6 May 1953 (Lionel Stander); Investigation of Communist Activities in the Los Angeles Area Part 4, 2 June 1953 (Lee J. Cobb); Communist Methods of Infiltration (Entertainment), Part 1, 13 January 1954; Part 2, 14 December 1954.

84th Congress: Hearings Regarding Investigation of Communist Activities, New York Area, Parts 6–8 (Entertainment), 15–18 August and 14 October 1955 (Tony Kraber, Zero Mostel); Investigation of the Unauthorized Use of U. S. Passports (Parts 1–4), 23–25 May and 12–14 and 21 June 1956 (Arthur Miller, Paul Robeson); Investigation of So-Called Blacklisting in Entertainment Industry (Report of the Fund for the Republic, Inc.), Parts 1–3, 10–13, 17, and 18 July 1956 (John Cogley).

85th Congress: Hearings Regarding the Investigation of Communism in the Metropolitan Music School, Inc., and Related Fields, Part 2, 7 and 8 February and 11 and 12 April 1957 (Earl Robinson); Investigation of the Unauthorized Use of U. S. Passports, Part 5, 26 July 1957; Communism in the New York Area (Entertainment), 18 and 19 June 1958, 8 May 1958, 1 April 1957 (Joseph Papp).

89th Congress: Hearings on Bills to Make Punishable Assistance to Enemies of the U. S. in Time of Undeclared War, Part 1, 16–19 August 1966, Part 2, 19, 22 and 23 August 1966 (Steven Cherkross).

90th Congress: Hearings on Subversive Involvement in Disruption of 1968 Democratic Party National Convention, 2–4 December 1968 (Tom Hayden, David Dellinger).

Screen Credits

Big Jim McLain (1952), pr. Robert Fellows; dir. Edward Ludwig; w. James Edward Grant and Richard English.

The Caine Mutiny (1954), pr. Stanley Kramer; dir. Edward Dmytryk; w. Stanley Roberts.

The Front (1976), pr. Martin Ritt and Charles H. Joffe; dir. Martin Ritt; w. Walter Bernstein.

Guilty By Suspicion (1991), pr. Arnon Milchan; dir./w. Irwin Winkler.

High Noon (1952), pr. Stanley Kramer; dir. Fred Zinnemann; w. Carl Foreman.

Joan of Arc (1948), pr. Walter Wanger; dir. Victor Fleming; w. Maxwell Anderson and Andrew Solt.

On the Waterfront (1954), pr. Sam Spiegel; dir. Elia Kazan; w. Budd Schulberg.

Panic in the Streets (1950), pr. Sol Siegel; dir. Elia Kazan; w. Richard Murphy.
Saint Joan (1957), pr./dir. Otto Preminger; w. Graham Green.
The Witches of Salem (1957), pr. Raymond Borderie; dir. Raymond Rouleau; w. Jean-Paul Sartre.

Television and Radio Credits

The Caine Mutiny Court-Martial. CBS Television. 19 November 1955. Videotape at Museum of Television and Radio, New York. W. Herman Wouk.
"Fear on Trial." CBS Television. 1975. Videotape at Museum of Television and Radio, New York. W. David W. Rintels.
The Defenders
  "Blacklist." CBS Television. 18 January 1964. Videotape at Museum of Television and Radio, New York. W. Ernest Kinoy.
Hallmark Hall of Fame
  "Lamp at Midnight." NBC Television. 27 April 1966. Videotape at Museum of Television and Radio, New York. W. Barrie Stavis.
  "The Lark." NBC Television. 10 February 1957. Videotape at Museum of Television and Radio, New York. W. Jean Anouilh/ Lillian Hellman.
See It Now
  "A Report on Senator Joseph R. McCarthy." CBS Television. 9 March 1954. Video tape in Museum of Television and Radio, New York.
  "Reply By Senator McCarthy." CBS Television. 6 April 1954. Videotape in Museum of Television and Radio, New York.
You Are There
  "The Boston Tea Party." CBS Television. 15 February 1953. Videotape at Museum of Television and Radio, New York. W. Arnold Schulman.
  "The Crisis of Galileo." CBS Television. 19 April 1953. Video tape at Museum of Television and Radio, New York. W. "Jeremy Daniel" (Abraham Polonsky).
  "The Death of Joan of Arc." CBS Radio. 29 August 1948. Audiotape at Museum of Television and Radio, New York. W. Max Ehrlich.
  "The Death of Socrates." CBS Television. 3 May 1953. Video tape at Museum of Television and Radio, New York. W. "Kate Nickerson" (Arnold Manoff).
  "The Execution of Joan of Arc." CBS Television. 1 March 1953. Videotape at Museum of Television and Radio, New York. W. "Jeremy Daniel" (Abraham Polonsky).
  "The First Salem Witch Trial." CBS Television. 29 March 1953. Videotape at Museum of Television and Radio, New York. W. "Kate Nickerson" (Arnold Manoff).

Index